English G 21

D5

Grundausgabe
für differenzierende
Schulformen

Vokabel Trainer
Cornelsen

Vokabeltrainer-App

Verfügbar für: iOS, Android und Windows Phone

Cornelsen

English G 21 • Band D 5 • Grundausgabe

Im Auftrag des Verlages herausgegeben von
Prof. Hellmut Schwarz, Mannheim
Wolfgang Biederstädt, Köln

Erarbeitet von
Susan Abbey, Nenagh, Irland
Claire Lamsdale, Llangybi, Wales
Barbara Derkow Disselbeck, Köln
Laurence Harger, Wellington, Neuseeland
Allen J. Woppert, Berlin

unter Mitarbeit von
Wolfgang Biederstädt, Köln
Joachim Blombach, Herford
David Christie, Banbury, England
Helmut Dengler, Limbach
Martina Schroeder, Stedtlingen
Jennifer Seidl, München
Udo Wagner, Voerde
Herbert Willms, Herford
sowie Uwe Chormann, Einselthum

in Zusammenarbeit mit der Englischredaktion
Dr. Christiane Kallenbach (Projektleitung);
Dr. Eva Grabowski (verantwortliche Redakteurin);
Susanne Bennetreu (Bildredaktion); Stefanie Bayer;
Britta Bensmann; Dr. Philip Devlin; Cornelia Frisse;
Bonnie S. Glänzer; Renata Jakovac; Anne Linder;
Michaela Schmidt; Nathalie Schwering; Kathrin
Spiegelberg; Uwe Tröger; Klaus G. Unger; Bastian
Wiesemann *sowie* Olivia Gruver

Beratende Mitwirkung
Walter Droste, Spenge; Birgit Heinemann, Neu
Wulmstorf; Bernd Jost, Salzbergen; Heike Jurenz,
Neukirch/Lausitz; Heike Meisner, Bad Klosterlausnitz;
Gabriele Rotter, Wiesbaden;
Karl Starkebaum, Diekholzen

Illustrationen
Silke Bachmann, Hamburg; Roland Beier, Berlin;
Carlos Borrell, Berlin; Dylan Gibson, Pitlochry;
Christian Görke, Berlin; Graham-Cameron Illustration,
UK: Eoin Coveney; Alfred Schüssler, Frankfurt/Main

Für die freundliche Unterstützung bei der Foto-Story
Unit 4 „Berlin: City survival kit" danken wir GLS
Sprachenzentrum Berlin; „Kauf Dich Glücklich", Berlin;
„Berliner Imbiss", Leipziger Strasse, Berlin.

Layoutkonzept
Aksinia Raphael; Korinna Wilkes

Technische Umsetzung
Aksinia Raphael; Korinna Wilkes;
Stephan Hilleckenbach; Rainer Bachmaier

Umschlaggestaltung
Klein & Halm Grafikdesign, Berlin

www.cornelsen.de
www.EnglishG.de

1. Auflage, 6. Druck 2019

Alle Drucke dieser Auflage sind inhaltlich unverändert
und können im Unterricht nebeneinander verwendet
werden.

Druck und Bindung: Livonia Print, Riga

ISBN 978-3-06-031324-2 – broschiert
ISBN 978-3-06-031375-4 – gebunden

PEFC
PEFC/12-31-006

PEFC zertifiziert
Dieses Produkt stammt aus nachhaltig bewirtschafteten Wäldern und kontrollierten Quellen.
www.pefc.de

Dein Englischbuch enthält folgende Teile:

Units 1 2 3 4	die vier Kapitel des Buches
Getting ready for a test	Hier kannst du dich gezielt auf einen Test vorbereiten.
EXTRA: Text File	viele interessante Texte zum Lesen (passend zu den Units)
Skills File (SF)	Beschreibung wichtiger Lern- und Arbeitstechniken
Grammar File (GF)	Zusammenfassung der Grammatik der Units; Übersichten über die Zeitformen (*present, past, future*)
Vocabulary	Wörterverzeichnis zum Lernen der neuen Wörter jeder Unit
Dictionary	alphabetisches englisch-deutsches Wörterverzeichnis

Die Units bestehen aus diesen Teilen:

Lead-in	Einstieg in das neue Thema
Part A, B, C, D	neuer Lernstoff mit vielen Aktivitäten
Practice	Übungen
How am I doing?	Hier kannst du dein Wissen und Können überprüfen.

In den Units findest du diese Überschriften und Symbole:

Exploring language	Hier lernst du anhand von Beispielen, neue sprachliche Strukturen zu verstehen und richtig anzuwenden.
STUDY SKILLS	Einführung in Lern- und Arbeitstechniken
Dossier	Schöne und wichtige Arbeiten kannst du in einer Mappe sammeln.
SPEAKING COURSE	Sprechkurs in vier Kapiteln
EVERYDAY ENGLISH	Übungen zum Bewältigen wichtiger Alltagssituationen
ENGLISH FOR JOBS	Übungen zur Vorbereitung auf typische berufliche Situationen
MEDIATION	Hier vermittelst du zwischen zwei Sprachen.
VIEWING	Aufgaben zu Filmausschnitten
Now you	Hier sprichst und schreibst du über dich selbst.
REVISION	Übungen zur Wiederholung
WORDS	Übungen zu Wortfeldern und Wortverbindungen
Extra	zusätzliche Aktivitäten und Übungen
	Partnerarbeit / Gruppenarbeit
	nur auf CD / auf CD und im Schülerbuch
	Filmausschnitte auf DVD
	Textaufgaben
	leichtere Übungen / schwierigere Übungen
	parallele Übungen auf zwei Niveaus
more help	Hier findest du zusätzliche Hilfen für das Lösen einer Aufgabe.

Inhalt

Australia	The world of work	Teen world	Exploring cities

Australia

1 Around Australia

Look at the photos. Some of them have already got captions. Match the captions below to the other photos.

- **1** Surfing on the East Coast
- **2** A spider
- **3** The Big Banana
- **4** The Flying Doctor
- **5** An Australian road sign
- **6** Kangaroos

2 A road trip

a) *In the holidays Danny and his dad go on a trip round Australia. Listen and follow the road trip on the map. Where do they go?* ▸ *SF Listening (p. 134)*

They start in ... Then they go to ...

b) *Listen again and look at the photos. Danny took seven of them. Which ones?*

c) *These sentences are from Danny's e-mails to his mum. Use ten of the words in the box to complete the sentences.*

busy • camping • cook • east • people • plane • rain • snake • soon • stars • straight • south • surf • trouble

- The traffic on the (1) coast was very (2). We drove past the place where I learned to (3).
- In the outback there aren't so many (4). We saw a small (5) next to the road. It was the Flying Doctor. Somebody was in (6).
- Last night we went bush (7) and slept under the (8). That was great!!! Dad made a fire and we used it to (9) our meals and keep warm.
- Now we're on the road to Perth, it's long and (10).

G

H Road trains at a roadhouse

I

J A monster dumper truck

K A barbecue at Gran's house

E

F

D

C

3 Extra Living in Australia

a) *Would you like to live in Australia? Why (not)? What would be new and exciting? Make notes.* more help ▸ *D p. 89*

b) *Make appointments with three students. Discuss your ideas about living in Australia.*

▸ **Text File 1** *(pp. 104–105)* • *WB 1 (p. 2)*

A Mum in Melbourne

B Sydney Harbour

AUSTRALIA – YESTERDAY AND TODAY

1 READING Group puzzle (part 1)

Divide the class into groups. Each group should study one of the following sections (A, B, C, or D). Discuss the questions in your group. Everybody should write down the answers.

A Facts about Australia

Population	21.2 million
Capital	Canberra (348,000)
Largest cities	Sydney (4.3 million)
	Melbourne (3.8 million)
	Brisbane (1.8 million)

a) *Look at the map on the front inside cover and find out:*
- What are the names of the different parts of Australia? (states and territories)
- Where is the capital city? (in the east/south, on the coast, near ...?)
- In which states are the three largest cities?

Extra *On a sketch map of Australia fill in all the states and large cities.*

Melbourne Harbour

b) **Extra** *Use the scale on the map on the front inside cover and find out:*
- The distance around the coast of Australia is (more/less) than 20,000 km.
- From east to west it's about ... km.
- From north to south it's about ... km.

B Things are different Down Under

On the right you can see a map of the world. On this map Europe is in the middle and Australia is down at the bottom. That's why people sometimes call Australia 'Down Under'.

Because Australia is in the southern half of the world some things are different there. For example, the seasons are different. When it is winter in Europe, it is summer in Australia.

Also the stars look different there. The five stars on the right of the Australian flag represent the Southern Cross. That is a group of stars that you can see in Australia, but not in Europe.

The British flag is at the top of the Australian flag. This shows Australia's link with Britain. The big star at the bottom represents the Australian states and territories.

\> 1 *Why is Australia sometimes called Down Under?*
2 *In Australia is July in the winter or in the summer?*
3 *What do the different parts of the Australian flag represent?*

C A short Australian timeline

44,000 BC
The Aborigines are already in Australia at this time.

1770
There are between 500,000 and one million Aborigines at this time. But many are killed by Europeans or die of illnesses that Europeans have brought to Australia.

1901
By this time, only 150,000 Aborigines are left.

Early 1600s
The first European ships arrive.

1770
Captain James Cook takes Australia for Britain.

1788–1868
The British send prisoners to Australia.

1901
Australia becomes independent.

1 The timeline shows that the first people in Australia were the ...
2 The first Europeans found Australia ... years later.
3 Between 1788 and 1868 many of the British people who went to Australia were ...
4 The arrival of the white people was a (good/bad) thing for the Aborigines because ...

D Amazing Aussie animals

The kangaroo and the koala are examples of special Australian animals that aren't found in other parts of the world. Other examples are the platypus and the emu. Australia is also famous for its poisonous snakes and spiders. The most poisonous spider in the world is the Australian funnel web spider. But nobody has died of a spider bite in Australia since 1955.

Over the years people have brought animals from other parts of the world to Australia. A new example is the cane toad. These toads kill many Australian animals but no animal kills them. So now they are a big problem in some parts of the country.

1 Which of the animals in the photos is new to Australia? Why is it a problem?
2 Which of these animals is dangerous for people?

2 Group puzzle (part 2)

a) *Make new groups (A1, B1, C1, D1; A2, B2, ...). Tell your new group what you found out about Australia. Take notes on the other information.*
▸ *SF Taking notes (p. 135)* • **Text File 2** *(pp. 106–107)* • *WB 2 (p. 3)*

b) *Go back to your first group (A, B, C, D) and compare your information. Did you all understand the same things? If not, read the texts to check your information.*

P1 //O Facts and figures ► D p. 90

a) *Complete the sentences about chart* **1**.

> 300 million people • population • smaller • smallest • the UK

The first chart shows the ______ in four countries: Australia, the UK, the USA and Germany.
The USA has the biggest population – ______.
The populations of the other countries are much ______.
The population of Germany and ______ are nearly the same.
Australia has the ______ population.

b) *Look at chart* **2**. *Match the sentence halves.*

– The second chart compares ...	...than Australia and the USA.
– The USA is ...	...the size of the same four countries.
– Australia is ...	...nearly the same size.
– Germany and the UK are ...	...the biggest country.
– They are much smaller ...	...nearly as big as the USA.

c) *What do the two charts together tell us about Australia?*
The charts tell us that ... is very big, but the ... is very small. So it must be quite crowded/empty there.

d) **Extra** *Write about chart* **3**.
The chart shows the different ...
There are ... groups: ...
The largest group is the ... They're about ... per cent of the population.
The other groups are much ...
Asians represent about ... per cent of the population.
The Aborigines, the first people in Australia, are only ... per cent of the population today.

Remember

In German you write 2,5.
*In English you write 2.5 and you say 'two **point** five'.*

STUDY SKILLS **Talking about charts**

When you are talking about a chart, first say what it shows. (Tip: The title can help you.) Then give some details.

Use phrases like:
This chart shows/compares ...
... is/has the biggest/smallest/...
... is (much) bigger/smaller than ...
... and ... are nearly the same ...

► *SF Talking about charts (p. 133)*

1 Population in millions

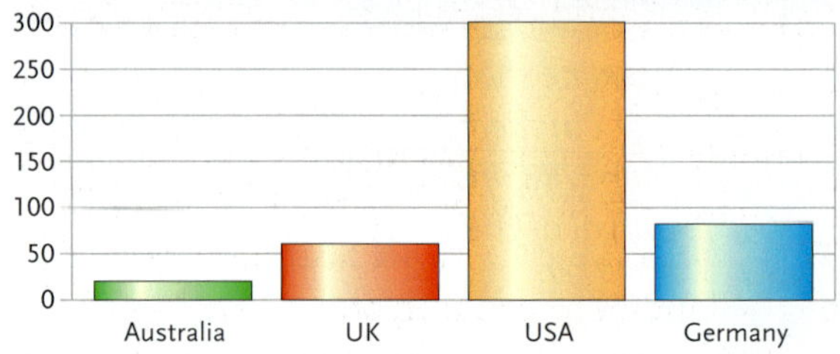

2 Land area in million sq km

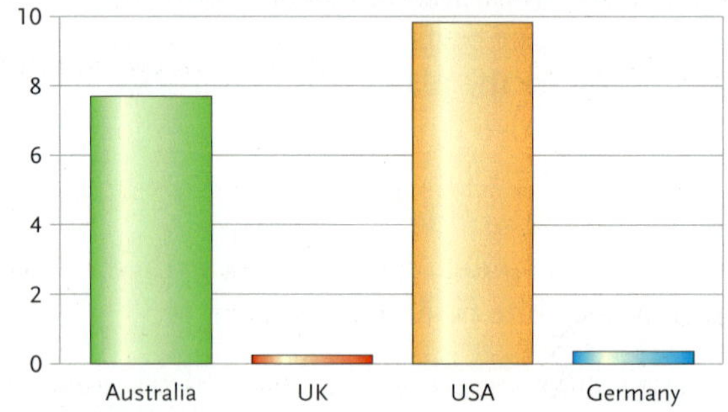

3 Ethnic groups in Australia

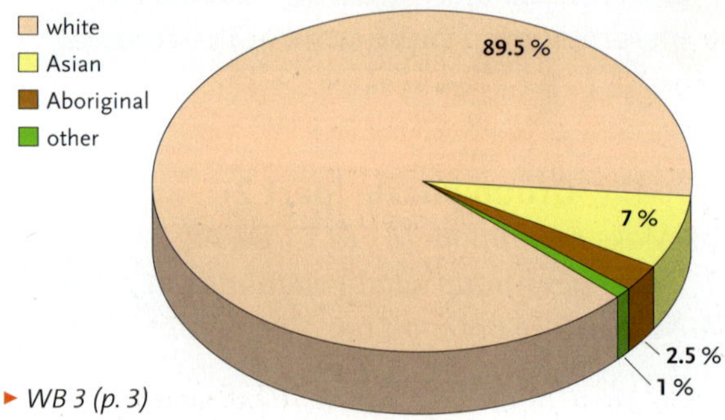

► *WB 3 (p. 3)*

P2 //O REVISION Australian animals (Tenses: simple present) ▸ D p. 89

Healesville Sanctuary near Melbourne is a great place to find out about Australian animals

a) *Choose the correct **simple present** forms.*
There (is/are) 43 different kinds of kangaroos. You (find/finds) them all over Australia. They (eats/eat) grass and leaves. They (doesn't need/don't need) much water. When it's hot they often (sits/sit) under trees and (doesn't move/don't move) all day. The biggest kangaroo (is/are) the Red Kangaroo. It (jumps/jump) two metres and (moves/move) at about 20–25 km/h.

When a kangaroo baby is born, it (lives/live) in its mother's pouch, a kind of bag, for ten months. Babies (is fed/are fed) by their mother until they (is/are) 18 months old. Kangaroos (doesn't live/don't live) long, just 4–6 years.

b) *Complete the text with the correct form of the verbs in brackets.*
You only ... (find) koalas in some parts of Australia. The koala ... (look) like a bear, but it ... (be) a bear. Koalas ... (sleep) at night. That's when they ... (move) around. They only ... (eat) the leaves of one kind of tree (eucalyptus tree). They ... (need) water because there ... (be) so much water in the leaves.

When a baby koala is born, it ... (move) into its mother's pouch for the next six months. Then it ... (ride) on its mother until it ... (be) about a year old. Koalas usually ... (live) for 10–12 years.

c) *What new facts did you find out about Australian animals?*

▸ GF 3: Talking about the present (p. 153)

P3 //O REVISION A trip to Australia (Tenses: simple past) ▸ D p. 91

Lea, from Germany, met Ben on the last day of her trip to Australia. Complete the dialogue.

arrived • climb • flew • go • saw • see • stayed • swam • walked • was (2x) • went • were

Great Barrier Reef

Ben So Lea, when did you arrive in Australia?
Lea I *arrived* in Melbourne six weeks ago.
Ben How long did you stay in Melbourne?
Lea I ... about three days.
Ben Did you like the city?
Lea Yes, it ... really great.
Ben Where did you go after that?
Lea I ... to Brisbane.
Ben Did you go by bus or did you fly?
Lea I ...
Ben Did you learn to surf in Brisbane?
Lea Oh no, I didn't ... surfing. I ... too scared.
Ben Did you see any Australian animals?
Lea I didn't ... any koalas, but I ... lots of kangaroos. They ... amazing. And I ... at the Great Barrier Reef.
Ben Did you visit Uluru?
Lea Yes, of course, and I ... around it. I didn't ... it, but some other tourists did.

▸ GF 4: Talking about the past (pp. 154–155) • WB 4–6 (pp. 4–5)

TEENAGERS IN AUSTRALIA

1 Our lives: an online project

Hi, my name's Tara. I go to Bay View High School in Darwin. I'm working on this project with Todd. We want to tell you about our lives. We'd like to hear from students in other countries and learn about their lives.

(1) Darwin is a great place to live. It's at the 'top end' of Australia. The climate is tropical. So it's warm all year. We have two seasons: 'the Dry' (April to November) and 'the Wet'. The Wet is a great season. We get amazing tropical storms and lots of rain.

(2) Todd is my classmate and cousin. His family lives in the outback. He stays with my family during the week and goes to school with me. At weekends Todd goes back to his family's farm. It's a two-hour drive from Darwin.

(3) Our school is near the coast and we do a lot of outdoor education. One of our school subjects is scuba diving! How cool is that! (Of course we do normal subjects – like English and Maths – too.)

(4) Our school day starts at 8 am and ends at 2.30 pm. Our summer holidays are in December and January. There's lots to do at weekends here. I like swimming in the waterfalls in the National Parks near here. There's just one thing. You have to be careful. There might be crocodiles!

(5) The sun is very strong in Australia. We spend a lot of time outdoors, so we have to be careful. We protect ourselves from the sun with clothes, sunglasses, hats and sunscreen.

(6) Before he came to Bay View High School, Todd did School of the Air. With School of the Air, kids learn at home with the TV, radio and internet. Todd says that it was cool, but he likes being in the city too.

A

B

C

D

E

F

> *Choose a photo (A–F) for each section of the text (1–6). Then choose one sentence from the section as a caption for each photo.*

2 Now you

a) *What facts did you learn about teenage life in Australia from the online project?*

b) *What aspects of your life do you think the Australian students would find interesting?*

► *SF Reading course (pp. 136–137)*

c) **Extra** *What questions would you like to ask these students about their lives?*
Think: *Write at least two questions.*
Pair: *Compare with a partner.*
Share: *Discuss with another pair.*
List your top three questions.

3 Mad about sport

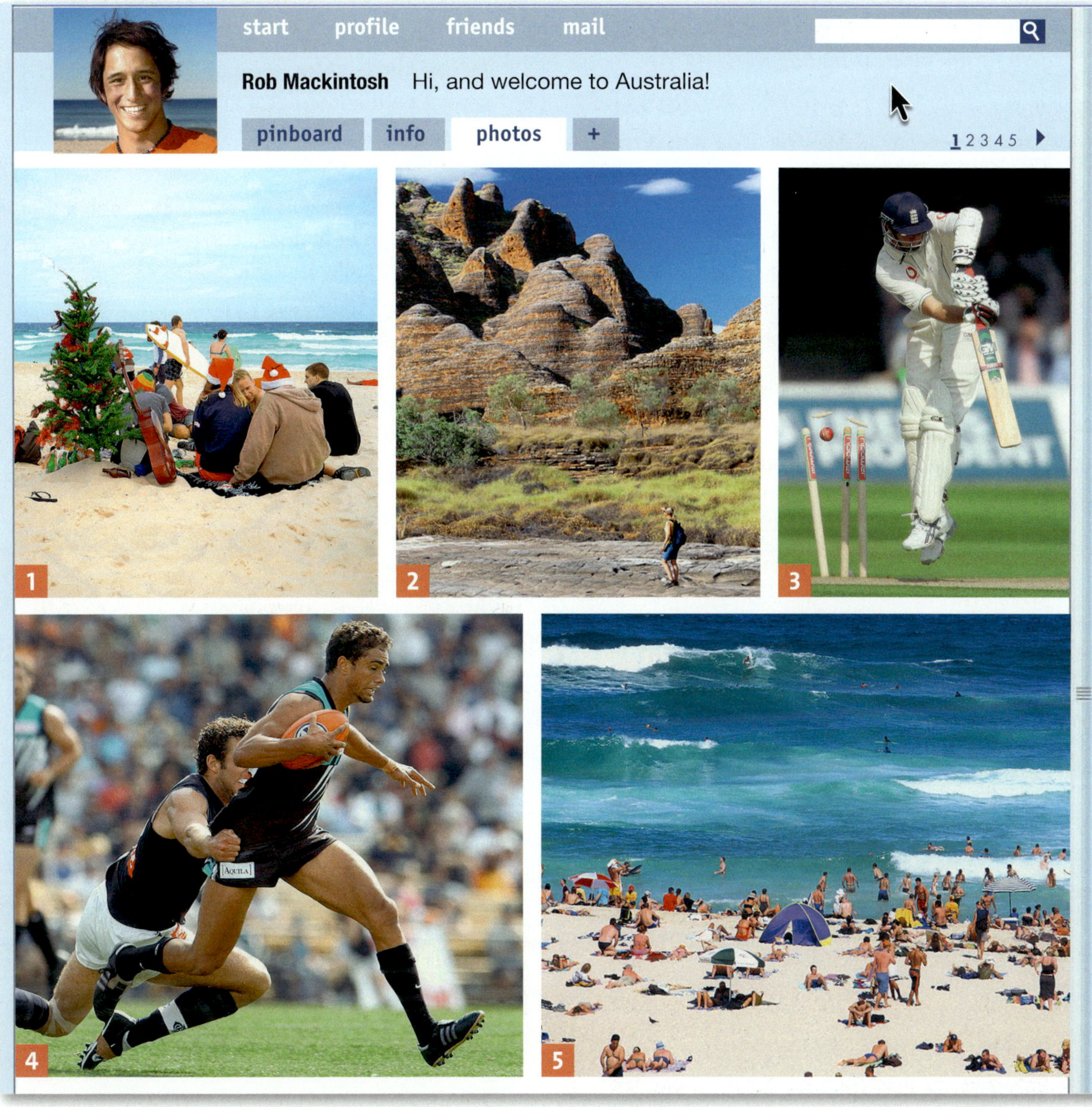

a) *Look at the photos and name the sports.*

Australian Rules football • cricket • hiking • surfing • swimming

b) *Read the sentences below. Then listen to Rob. What sport is it?*

1 It's Rob's favourite sport.
2 Rob thinks it's a really exciting game.
3 It's a mix of football and rugby.
4 If you do it, you can see animals.
5 Everybody in Australia does it.

c) *Talk about the role of sport in your life.*

- Are you as mad about sport as Rob? Or do you like other activities better? (Which ones?)
- Do you do sport for fun/ to keep fit/…?
- Are you a couch potato?

- I do … every … in winter/ summer.
- I often go …/ play …
- I sometimes watch … on TV.

d) **Extra** *Write a short text **Sport and me** for your DOSSIER.*

► *SF Writing course (pp. 142–143)*

EVERYDAY ENGLISH

P1 WRITING Our lives (Writing an e-mail)

a) *Read p. 12 again. Find two things in Tara's text that you found interesting or surprising.*

b) *What can you tell Tara and Todd? Make notes.*
- What can you say about the area where you live?
- What about the seasons?
- Where is your school?
- What are the most interesting subjects?
- What's your school day like?
- When are your summer holidays?

c) *Find sentences in Tara's text on p. 12 that might help you to write about your life.*

d) *Write an e-mail to Tara or Todd like the one on the right.*

► *SF Writing informal letters (p. 146)*

Hi Tara

This is ... from Germany. I found your e-mail project on the internet. I think it's very interesting to learn about your life in Australia.

I was really surprised to read that .../about ...
I think it's great that you can .../have ...
You're very lucky that you can ...

You say that you'd like to hear about teenagers in other parts of the world. Well, I go to ... school in ...
... is a great place to live. My life in Germany is (a bit/very) different. For example ...

Please write back soon.
Best wishes
...

P2 MEDIATION At the police station

You meet a German tourist at Bondi Beach in Sydney. Someone has stolen his surfboard. He wants to report the theft at the police station.

a) *This is the German boy's story. How can you say these things in English?*

Das Brett war weg, als er zurückkam.

Er hat ein Eis gekauft.

Sie haben nichts gesehen.

Es ist vor 20 Minuten passiert.

Es passierte nahe der *Lifeguard Station*.

Sein Surfbrett wurde gestohlen.

Er hat die Nachbarn am Strand gefragt.

b) *Look at the first part of the dialogue. What could you say?*

Tourist Danke, dass du mitgekommen bist. Ich bin so aufgeregt. Ich kriege kein Wort Englisch raus. – Da, die Polizistin scheint frei zu sein.
Officer What can I do for you?
Tourist Also wir ... also mein ... Sag du ihr, dass mein Surfbrett gestohlen wurde.
You ...
Officer I see. Well, when and where did it happen?
You ...
Tourist Vor 20 Minuten. Drüben am Strand, in der Nähe der *Lifeguard Station*.
You ...
Officer Are there any witnesses?
Tourist Was meint sie?
You Vermutlich will sie wissen, ob es Zeugen gibt. – Excuse me, what does *witness* mean?
Officer Someone who saw something. Did anybody see the thief? Did anyone see anything?

c) *Listen to the whole conversation. Help the boy.*

► *SF Mediation (p. 147)* • *WB 7–8 (pp. 5–6)*

P3 SPEAKING What about surfing? (Having a conversation)

► SF p. 140

a) Complete the dialogue. Use phrases from the box. Then listen and check.

My name's • idea • meet • time • fantastic • Hi • surf • surfboard • welcome • place

Anna Hello!
Rob Hi! Great waves today!
Anna Yes, they look ________.
Rob They're perfect for surfing.
Anna I'm Anna, by the way.
Rob Hey Anna, how are you doing? ________ Rob.
Anna Good to ________ you, Rob.
Rob So, is this your first ________ at Bondi Beach?
Anna Yes, it is. What an amazing ________!
Rob Can you ________?
Anna No, but I'd like to learn. Do you know where I can rent a ________ for the day?
Rob Sure. You can rent them at the surf school over there.
Anna That's a great ________. Thanks.
Rob You're ________. Have fun.
Anna Good bye.
Rob See you later.

b) Find phrases for the different parts of the conversation.

1 *Sich begrüßen, z. B.* **Hello, ...**
2 *Sich vorstellen, z. B. ...*
3 *Small Talk machen, das heißt, Fragen stellen und sie freundlich beantworten, z. B. ...*
4 *Sich bedanken, z. B. ...*
5 *Das Gespräch beenden und sich verabschieden, z. B. ...*

c) Act out the conversation above with a partner.

d) You meet someone at a café in Sydney. Have a conversation.

Partner A	Partner B
Begrüße B freundlich!	Erwidere die Begrüßung. Stell dich vor.
Stell dich vor.	Mach Small Talk, z. B. frag, ob er/sie zum ersten Mal in Sydney ist.
Antworte, z. B. sag, wie du die Stadt findest. Stell eine Frage, z. B. frag, ob er/sie weiß, wo man ein Fahrrad mieten kann.	Antworte, z. B. sag, dass es ein Fahrradgeschäft in der Nähe gibt.
Bedanke dich.	Sag, nichts zu danken. Wünsche viel Spaß und verabschiede dich.
Verabschiede dich.	

► WB 9 (p. 6)

THE ABORIGINAL PEOPLE OF AUSTRALIA

1 A tour of Uluru

Sunrise Tours to Uluru

Welcome to our home

Walk around Uluru with us.
See through our eyes.
Listen to our stories.
Learn about our culture.

Our ancestors have lived around Uluru (Ayers Rock) for many thousands of years. This is an important place for us.

Walk with us

Learn about Aboriginal art and …

… Aboriginal music and dance

Our grandparents tell us the traditional stories. Their grandparents told them the same stories. These stories tell us how the land started, how the people and animals came here, where to find food and what we should and shouldn't do.

We believe that the land, plants and animals are as important as people. That's why we respect the land and everything that lives on it.

Look for and eat bush food

Meet our local Anangu guides

Details

Our Anangu guides speak their traditional languages.
Then their words are translated into English for you.
The tour starts one hour before sunrise (for the exact time look at the notice board in your hotel the day before the tour).
Starting point: The Aboriginal Cultural Centre
Return: 10.00 am (summer) or 11.00 am (winter)
Duration: 4.5–5 hours
Price: Adult: $ 80*
Children: $ 40*
(*price includes breakfast in a restaurant)
Address:
Uluru-Kata Tjuta National Park, Yulara, Northern Territory 0872, Australia
Telephone +61 (8) 895…
Website: ww…

1. How do Aboriginal people learn about their culture?
2. What do Aboriginal people believe is more important: people, animals, plants, the land?
3. What are the local Aboriginal people called?
4. Where does the tour start?
5. Do you need to have breakfast before you leave your hotel?
6. **Extra** *What is the cost of the tour in Euros?*

Tip: *Check the exchange rate on the internet.*

2 Talking to a tour group

a) *Look at the postcards. Which one would you send from Uluru (Ayers Rock)?*

b) *Listen to the tour guides. Would you still choose the same card? Why (not)?*

c) *Listen again. Complete the sentences correctly.*

1. (Deb/Tommy) is the guide who speaks to the tour group in the local language.
2. Sunrise Tours (gives jobs/tells stories) to local people.
3. The tour group went to the rock in the (evening/morning).
4. At sunrise and at sunset the rock changes (place/colour).
5. The local people say to tourists: (You're not allowed to climb the rock! / Please respect our culture!)
6. The German guest climbed Uluru. Later he (was/wasn't) sorry.

► *SF Listening (p. 134)*

3 The 'stolen generations'

From 1910 to 1970 the Australian government took thousands of Aboriginal children away from their families. They were called the 'stolen generations'.

The Guardian **11th February 2008**

Children were stolen – Now a nation says sorry

Barbara McMahon in Alice Springs

Zita Wallace was stolen from her Aboriginal family when she was seven years old. Wallace told us that she still remembered that day. She was taken to a home for orphans. She said that she would never forget the first night in the home. 'It was awful. I put my head under my blanket and cried.'

Wallace was one of the 'stolen generations'. At least 100,000 mixed-race children were taken from their families by the Australian government. The idea was to make the children more like white people. They weren't allowed to see their families or to speak their own languages. Zita Wallace didn't see her mother again for nearly 50 years.

This racist policy didn't end until 1970. But Aboriginal people still have problems. 'A lot of our people got into drugs and alcohol,' said Wallace.

Wallace is happy that the Australian Government is ready to say sorry now. 'They are saying that it was wrong. That's very important for us.'

Wallace said that she didn't want money from the government. 'But I can't wait to hear that word: sorry.'

Zita Wallace with her mother's sister Aggie

1. *How old was Zita when she was stolen?*
2. *Why did the government take the children?*
3. *How old was Zita when she saw her mother again?*
4. *Why is Zita happy in 2008?*

► *SF Reading course (pp. 136–137)* • **Text File 3** *(pp. 108–109)*

P1 VIEWING Rabbit-proof fence

Rabbit-proof fence is a film about three Aboriginal girls. The girls are stolen, but they escape and walk 1,900 km to get back home.

a) *Watch the scene on the DVD.*
As you watch, think about how it makes you feel.

nervous • scared • sad • happy • ⁺relaxed • quiet

– At the beginning everything is ...
– I felt ... when the policeman tried to catch the children.
– At the end I felt ...

b) *Watch the scene again. This time listen carefully to the soundtrack. What do you hear at these points in the scene? How do you feel? Choose one green sentence and one red sentence for each photo.*

1

2

3

At this point in the scene ...

The music gets faster and you hear a drum.	The music is sad and soft. People start to cry.	Suddenly there's a noise.
You feel how helpless they are.	You know that something bad is going to happen.	You feel the panic.

P2 Extra WRITING A film review

a) *Complete this review with words from the box.*

ending • interesting • main • director • true story • about • stars • takes place

Rabbit-proof fence is a ... The ... is Phillip Noyce and the ... are Everlyn Sampi, Tianna Sansbury, and Laura Monaghan. They are very young, but they're fantastic!

The film ... in Australia in 1931. It's ... three Aboriginal girls who are taken away from their mothers. The ... characters are Molly, Daisy and Gracie.

The film is sometimes a bit slow. But I liked it because it was ... . I learned a lot about Aboriginal people. I liked the soundtrack too. The ... is happy in one way. But it's also very sad. It's a great film! Everyone should see it.

b) *Write a short review of a film that you've seen recently. Use some of these words and phrases.*

The title of the film is ...
It's a comedy/science fiction film/action film/love story/...
It's about ...
The director is ...
The stars are ...
It takes place in ...
The main characters are ...
The film is exciting/interesting/slow/...
The special effects are great/boring/...
The soundtrack is fantastic/terrible/...
The ending is (a bit/very) happy/sad.
People who like action/comedies/fantasy/... should see this film.

▸ WB 10–11 (p. 7)

P3 Exploring language | Indirect speech

a) *Die Autorin des Artikels auf S. 17 berichtet, was Zita Wallace gesagt hat. Vergleiche Zitas eigene Worte und das, was im Zeitungsartikel stand.*

'I still remember that day.'	Wallace told us that she still remembered that day.
'I'll never forget the first night in the home.'	She said that she would never forget the first night in the home.
'I don't want money from the government.'	Wallace said that she didn't want money from the government.

b) *Wie ändern sich die Verben in diesen Sätzen?*

simple present > simple past
will > …

▸ GF 1: Indirect speech I (p. 151)

P4 //O On the way home from school (Indirect speech: simple present) ▸ D p. 91

Dougie is telling his friends a story.
Complete the text. Use words from the red box.

came • could • didn't know • didn't play • had • knew • needed • was

I was on my way home from school when a tourist stopped me. He said that he (1) some help. He told me that he (2) a digeridoo and that he (3) a lot about it.

I said that I (4) the didgeridoo. But I told him that I (5) someone who (5) help him. I think that he was surprised when I said that the name of this person (6) Max and that he (7) from Germany!

P5 Tourists at Uluru (Indirect speech: simple present and will-future)

Report what the tourists said.

1 The woman told the reporter that lots of tourists … She added that she …

2 The man said that … He thought that it …

3 The boy said that … He hoped that he …

4 The girl thought that … She said that …

▸ WB 12–14 (pp. 8–9)

In the outback

adapted from the novel *A prayer for Blue Delaney* by Kirsty Murray

STUDY SKILLS **Reading stories**

When you read a story, you don't have to understand every word. The important thing is to understand what is happening. So don't look up every new word in the dictionary!
If you really can't follow the story because you don't understand a word, first try to guess the meaning of the word. If that doesn't work, use a dictionary.
Stop now and then, and think about what you have just read. Summarize it in your head. Then go on reading.

► *SF Reading stories (p. 138)* • *SF Working out the meaning of words (p. 136)*

In the 1950s the population of Australia was very small. The government wanted more people, so orphans were sent from the UK to children's homes in Australia.
In this story, Colm is one of these orphans. He is sent to a home, but he doesn't like it. He runs away. He meets an old man, Bill, and his dog Rusty. Bill says that Colm can come with him and Rusty in his old car. He calls the car Tin Annie. He is going to repair the Dog Fence.

They drove through the Victoria Desert towards the Dog Fence. There was nothing to see, just rock and sand and the long, long fence.

Emu

'What if we have problems with the car?' asked Colm.

'Don't you worry about that. Tin Annie is half camel half jeep. She'll be fine.'

'But what if we would lose our way?'

Bill smiled. 'We'll follow the fence, mate. It's three thousand miles long. We can't lose it.'

They stopped where an emu had crashed into the fence.

'Emus can go 30 miles an hour. They don't see the fence till they've hit it,' said Bill.

Colm waited while Bill repaired the fence. Later they stopped to fill in a hole that a wombat had made. Colm fell asleep. When he woke up, he was really hot. There were flies everywhere. He took a long drink of water. The water was as warm as tea, but it was good.

Wombat

The days went on, long and boring. Colm's neck hurt from always turning his head one way to watch the fence. After a few days Colm started to fill the wombat holes while Bill repaired the other holes in the fence. They ate tinned beef and tinned vegetables until Colm felt he couldn't eat them any more. And the nearest town was hundreds of miles away.

One morning, Rusty wasn't there when they woke up.

'Where is that damn dog?' said Bill. He put two fingers in his mouth and whistled.

'Bill,' called Colm. 'Bill, here, I've found her! But something's wrong! Hurry!'

Rusty was under a bush. She was shaking.

'What is it?' asked Colm.

'I think she's eaten dingo bait. Poison. It might be better to put her down.'

Bill took Rusty over to the car and put her on her blanket. He picked up a knife that he used to kill rabbits.

'No! What are you doing!' Colm grabbed Bill's arm. 'We have to save her.'

'For chrissake, get out of my way,' said Bill. Quickly, he made cuts on the side of Rusty's ears. Blood came out.

'Now go and get some water,' Bill told Colm. When Colm came back, Bill threw salt into the water. He took Rusty in his arms. 'I'll keep her mouth open. You give her the water.'

The salt water made Rusty throw up. She threw up again and again. When she had finished, Bill put her on her old blanket under a bush. Colm sat next to her.

'Here, you need a break,' said Bill. 'Go and sit in the car. I'll call you if I need you.'

'What are you going to do? You can't shoot her, Bill. You can't.'

'I'm hoping it won't come to that.'

Colm walked back to the car. He tried not to cry.

The morning grew hotter. Colm fell asleep. When he woke, he prayed.

He was still praying when he heard the sound of Rusty's bark. He ran across to her.

'I prayed for her,' said Colm. 'Maybe it helped.'

'Maybe it did,' said Bill. 'Between your prayers and my hard work, she'll be OK.'

After some more adventures Bill finds work and a place to stay with an old friend at Tara Downs cattle station.

'C'mon. I've got a job to do,' said Bill. 'Can't sit around talking all day. A wild boar is making trouble just south a bit.'

They drove off. Rusty put her head out of the open window. The fine red sand flew up around the sides of the car.

Boar

'This is the place. We'll follow it on foot from here. You stay with me.'

Colm followed Bill through the bushes. A terrible smell was in the air. The smell grew stronger. Rusty led them to a dead steer. A cloud of flies flew up in the air.

'He was here not that long ago,' said Bill.

They climbed up a hill and scanned the countryside. Nothing.

'Damn, he heard us.'

Bill turned to walk back to the steer. There was a noise in the bushes. It was the black boar.

Colm jumped behind a rock as the boar hit the old man. Bill shouted. Rusty sank her teeth into the boar's leg, but it turned and cut her with its tusks. Rusty yelped and fell.

Colm jumped out from behind the rock. He had to do something.

'Run, Colm,' shouted Bill. 'Get help!'

Colm ran down the path. He was nearly at the car when he heard a terrible scream. He stopped and turned. What if Bill was killed before he could get help? What should he do?

Suddenly he knew that there was only one answer and there was no time to lose.

Colm ran back. He picked up a stick on the way and he hit the boar with it. But it was no good. Colm threw the stick down and grabbed Bill's gun. He was shaking. He knew that if he hit the animal in the back, it would only make it wild. He let out a scream, a long loud scream.

The boar turned round. For a moment it looked at him. Then it ran towards him. Colm shot it.

The kickback from the gun made Colm fall backwards. He fell on the ground next to Rusty.

'Colm, my mate,' said Bill. Then he lay back in the red sand and passed out.

Bill's leg was bleeding badly. Colm ran back to the car and grabbed an old shirt to put on the wound. He had to get help. He had to drive Tin Annie. Colm took a deep breath and turned the key. Tin Annie started. He didn't know how to drive backwards so he drove forward, carefully. He stopped near Bill.

It took some time but in the end Colm put Bill into the car. Then he picked up Rusty. He could hear the dog's heart and it gave him hope.

Colm drove fast along the track. Every time they hit a stone Bill groaned, but at least that meant he was still alive.

Then Tin Annie stopped. Colm tried to start the car again and again, but it didn't work. He would have to go on foot and leave Bill and Rusty in the car.

The house was at least a mile away and his head hurt, but he ran fast.

'It's Bill. An accident. There was a boar.'

Then Colm sank down on his knees. People came from all sides. An engine started up and strong arms helped Colm to his feet.

'Bill needs me,' said Colm.

'It's all right. They're getting the Flying Doctor out here. It's too far to drive to the hospital in Katherine. We don't know if the old man will make it.'

'He will make it,' said Colm. 'He can't die.'

Working with the text

1 The story

Choose the correct answers.

1 Bill, Colm and Rusty are in the outback ...
- A because they're on a camping trip.
- B because Bill has to repair the Dog Fence.
- C because they want to see wild animals.

2 One day something is wrong with Rusty ...
- A and they have to shoot her.
- B and they can't help her.
- C but they save her.

3 Colm shoots the black boar ...
- A because it hurt Bill and his dog badly.
- B because it hurt the dog.
- C because it made a big hole in the fence.

4 Colm has to run to the nearest house ...
- A because the car doesn't work any more.
- B because there isn't enough petrol in the car.
- C because he can't drive the old car.

5 Colm got help for Bill ...
- A by phoning the Flying Doctor Service.
- B by asking the people in the house.
- C by running fast to the next Flying Doctor station.

2 The end of the story

a) *How do you think the story goes on? Choose one of the endings (A or B), or think of your own.*

b) *Write your ending.*

more help ► D p. 92

c) *In groups of 4 or 5, read out your stories.*

► WB 15 (p. 9)

How am I doing?

► SF Check yourself (p. 129)

a) *Find or choose the correct answers.*

Facts about Australia

1 Name three important Australian cities.
2 Name three typical Australian animals.
3 Name two things Australians do to protect themselves from the sun.
4 Name three sports Australians like to do.
5 When it's winter in Germany, it's ... in Australia.
A spring B summer C autumn D winter
6 What other word do Australians use to talk about the bush?
A hinterland B desert C outback D Dreamland
7 The largest ethnic group in Australia are ...
A the Asians.
B the African Australians.
C the Aborigines. D the Whites.
8 Aborigines of the 'stolen generations' ...
A were thieves.
B were taken away by Whites.
C lived before 1600.
D built the Dog Fence.

Grammar

9 What did they say? Put these sentences in indirect speech.
a) Kim: 'I'll have a great time Down Under.'
b) Jess: 'I just love kangaroos.'
c) Tom: 'Frank wants to visit Uluru.'
d) Lara: 'I can come back.'

Words

10 In a chart you can ... the size of different countries.
A complete B control C compare D copy
11 When a room is full of people then it's ...
A empty. B crowded. C poisonous. D cloudy.
12 When you visit a city you can often ... a bike for the day.
A buy B ride C offer D rent
13 If you get up early in the morning on a wonderful day you can watch the ...
A sunset. B sunscreen. C sunrise. D sunglasses.

Talking about charts

14 The chart on the right ... where the Australian population lives: in cities, near or ... from cities. The ... group (69%) lives in cities. The ... biggest group lives near cities and the ... group lives far from cities. So ...% of the population don't live in cities.

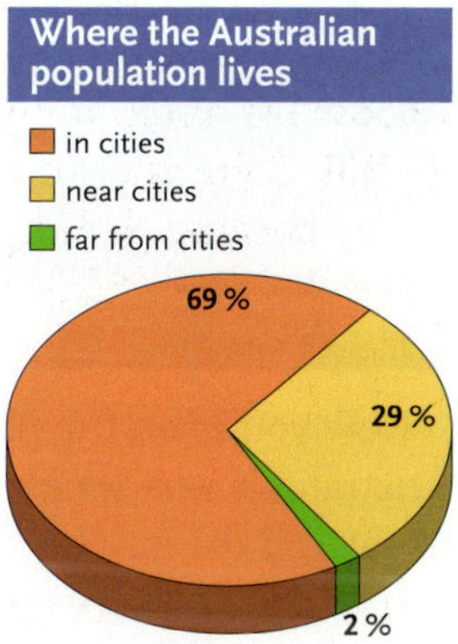

b) *Check your answers on p. 204 and add up your points.*

c) *If you had 23 or more points, well done!*
Where did you make mistakes? The chart below will tell you what you can do to improve your English.

No.	Areas	Find out more	Exercises
1– 8	Australian facts	Unit 1 (pp. 6–13, 17)	WB 1–2 (pp. 2–3)
9	Indirect speech I	GF 1 (p. 151)	P 3–5 (p. 19), WB 12–13 (p. 8)
10–13	Words	Vocabulary (pp. 159–162)	WB 11 (p. 7), 14 (p. 9)
14	Talking about charts	Part A (p. 10), SF (p. 133)	P 1 (p. 10), WB 3 (p. 3)

► **Skills check 1** *WB (pp. 10–14)*

1 WORDS Travelling on holiday

Fill in the right word. Use the words from the box.

breakfast • (to) change • city centre • departure gate • key card • (to) land • meal • ticket • suitcases • taxi

You're flying to Australia for your dream holiday! At the airport, you first (1) *check in*. Then you go to the (2). For your flight it's gate D21.

Now you're on the plane. The flight to Australia is very long and on the way you need to eat and drink. The flight attendant offers you a hot (3). There are lots of nice things on the menu today.

Your first stop is Singapore Airport. There you have to (4) planes. After eight more hours you (5) in Australia. Of course, you hope that your (6) arrive too! If not, you'll have to go to the lost luggage office.

So how do you travel from the airport into the (7)? Well, the quickest and easiest way is to take a (8), but it's expensive: it costs about 50 Australian dollars. Of course it's cheaper to take a train. A single (9) to the city only costs 15 Australian dollars.

Now – tired but happy – you're at your hotel. The receptionist gives you the (10) to your room and tells you about the hotel – for example, the times when you can have (11) in the mornings.

2 WORDS At the beach

a) *Australia has fantastic beaches. Here are some things that you can do at the beach. Which activities do you do on the beach? Which do you do in the sea? Make two lists.*

swimming • reading a magazine • surfing • playing beach volleyball or baseball • windsurfing • water skiing • scuba diving • relaxing in the sun • relaxing and listening to music • building sandcastles • canoeing • ...

On the beach	*In the sea*
reading a magazine	...

b) *Compare your lists with a partner. Then tell your partner which activities you think are the most fun and say why.*

3 Australia's dangerous animals (Simple past)

Read about Australia's dangerous animals. Then complete the text. Use the ***simple past****.*

Australia has a lot of dangerous and poisonous animals. There are snakes, spiders and sometimes sharks. The most dangerous animals of all are crocodiles. Two or three people die every year in Australia in crocodile attacks.

Crocodiles can kill you! If you think there may be crocodiles in the water, you shouldn't swim there!

There's a crocodile in our tent!

In January 2005, two young Australian (1) *went* (go) camping near the Pentecost River in the north of Australia.

At 2 o'clock in the morning, they (2) ... (be) asleep. Suddenly a crocodile (3) ... (come) into their tent. They (4) ... (run) to their car and (5) ... (climb) onto it. They (6) ... (not/know) where the crocodile was but they (7) ... (not/want) to come down. It (8) ... (be) safest to stay on their car.

The next day, at about 10 o'clock in the morning, two policemen (9) ... (find) the young people. They (10) ... (save) their lives.

Smile please!

In 2008, a tourist in Queensland was stupid – but lucky. He (11) ... (be) in a boat on a river when a crocodile (12) ... (swim) slowly towards the boat.

The man's friend (13) ... (be) on land. 'Put your hand in the water and play with the crocodile!', he (14) ... (shout). 'I'm going to take a photo.' Seconds later, the crocodile (15) ... (try) to bite the man's hand. 'It was a scary moment!', he (16) ... (say) later.

▸ *GF 4: Talking about the past (p. 154)*

4 WRITING One day last year ...

a) *Below is a very short story! Can you make it more interesting? Write the story again.*

Jake was on his bike in the mountains. He fell off and broke his leg. He called for help with his mobile phone. Some people saved him. He went to hospital. He met Ann, a nurse. They fell in love. They got married.

b) *Compare your story with a partner's.*

When?	one day last year, last September, first, then, next, after that, in the end, ...
Who?	the man/woman/person/people who ...
How?	quickly, slowly, suddenly, ... (really) amazing/awful/... (feel) happy/sad/excited/...
Linking words	because, but, so (that), when, while, ...

▸ *SF Writing course (pp. 142–143)*

1 LISTENING Travelling to Australia

You are travelling to Australia with your family. You are going to hear five announcements or short conversations on your journey.
- *Look at the questions below for 30 seconds.*
- *You will hear all the recordings **twice**.*
- *Now listen and write down the correct answer – A, B or C.*

1 You fly first from Germany to Heathrow Airport in London. There, you hear this announcement.
'Flight Qantas 201 to Sydney is now boarding at ...'

A GATE 7 B GATE 17C C GATE 4

2 You are on the plane from London to Sydney. It is time for a hot meal. The flight attendant says you can choose ...

A

B

C

3 You have just arrived at Sydney airport. But one of your suitcases is missing! The man tells you to go to the lost luggage office. It is ...

A just over there
B on the first floor
C next to the passport office

4 You take a taxi from the airport into the city. The taxi journey costs...

A AU$ 50 B AU$ 52.50 C AU$ 55.50

5 Now you are at your hotel. The receptionist says that breakfast tomorrow is from ...

A 06:00–10:00 B 06:30–09:30 C 07:00–10:30

2 LISTENING Shark attack!

You are going to hear a radio news programme from Australia. It is about a young Australian called Jon Kerry. Jon was attacked by a great white shark. The programme is in two parts.

- *Look at the questions below for 30 seconds.*
- *You will hear the two parts of the programme **twice**.*
- *Now listen and do the tasks.*

a) *Listen to the first part of the programme and choose the correct answer – A, B, C.*

1 The shark attacked Jon while he was ...
- A swimming.
- B surfing.
- C diving.

2 The shark bit into Jon's ...
- A arm.
- B foot.
- C leg.

3 After the attack, the shark ...
- A swam off.
- B stayed near Jon.
- C attacked a second person.

4 While Jon was swimming back to the beach, he was really ...
- A happy.
- B scared.
- C excited.

5 Jon's ... saved his life – they tied a rope[1] around his leg.
- A friends
- B mum and dad
- C brothers

b) *Listen to the second part of the programme and write down 'T' (true) or 'F' (false)*

1 Jon has only one leg now.
2 Sharks don't normally attack people.
3 Many more Australians die in road accidents than from shark attacks.
4 If you think there may be sharks in the sea, it is safest to swim alone.
5 You shouldn't swim in the early morning or in the evening.

[1] (to) tie a rope [rəʊp] *Seil binden*

3 LISTENING What are they talking about?

You are going to hear five short conversations.

- *Look at the eight pictures below for 30 seconds.*
- *You will hear all the conversations* **twice**.
- *Now listen. Choose one picture for each conversation. There are three pictures that you don't need. Write down A, B, C, ...*

A

B

C

D

E

F

G

H

4 WRITING A scary moment!

Finish this story in your own words. Write 70–100 words.

It was a Saturday afternoon in September. I was bored, so I decided to ...

- *What did you decide to do?*
- *Where were you?*
- *Were there other people with you?*
- *What happened next?*
- *And then?*
- *How did you feel?*
- *What happened in the end?*

Remember

- *Use the simple past* (I went, I saw, it was ...).
- *When you have finished, check your story for mistakes.*

How am I doing?

Check your answers to tasks 1–3 (Listening tasks) on p. 204.

About the test

Bei diesem ersten Test konntest du Aufgaben ausprobieren, die dir in einer zukünftigen Abschlussprüfung begegnen könnten. Wenn du Probleme bei einzelnen Testaufgaben hattest, ist das noch kein Grund zur Beunruhigung. Du hast noch viel Zeit zum Üben. Denk dran: Übung macht den Meister!

Listening

Aufgabe 1 bis 3 waren Tests zur Überprüfung deiner Fertigkeit im Hörverstehen. Die folgenden drei Fragen helfen dir herauszufinden, wie du damit zurechtgekommen bist. Lies die Fragen durch und entscheide, was für dich zutrifft.

1 Wie leicht oder schwer war die Aufgabe?

	leicht	ging so	ziemlich schwer	sehr schwer
Task 1				
Task 2				
Task 3				

► *SF Listening (p. 134)*

2 Was war bei den Aufgaben schwer?

a) Die Personen sprachen zu schnell.
b) Die Akzente waren schwer zu verstehen.
c) Es gab sehr viele Informationen im Text. Ich konnte nicht die richtigen Antworten herausfinden.
d) Die Zeit war zu kurz, ich konnte nicht alle Aufgaben beenden.
e) Es gab Wörter und Wendungen, die ich einfach nicht verstanden habe.
f) Es gab so viele Dinge, die ich nicht verstanden haben, so dass ich Panik bekommen habe.

3 Wie hast du die Aufgaben gelöst?

a) Zuerst habe ich die Aufgaben aufmerksam gelesen, damit ich genau wusste, was ich heraushören sollte.
b) Ich habe mir die Aufgaben erst nur kurz angesehen und sie dann später gründlich beim Hören gelesen.
c) Ich habe beim ersten Hören so viele Antworten wie möglich notiert. Beim zweiten Hören habe ich alles überprüft und die fehlenden Antworten ergänzt.

► *SF How to do well in a test (pp. 148–149)*

Writing

Aufgabe 4 (***A scary moment!***) war eine Schreibaufgabe. Arbeite mit einem Partner/einer Partnerin. Tauscht eure Texte aus und lest sie euch durch.
Kopiert den Beurteilungsbogen *(assessment sheet)* und füllt ihn aus. Denkt daran: es geht darum, deinem Partner/deiner Partnerin eine Rückmeldung zu geben die ihm/ihr hilft, bessere Texte zu schreiben.

Assessment sheet	☹		😐		☺	
Name ...	1	2	3	4	5	Comments
Hat dein Partner/deine Partnerin ...						
1 ... grammatische Fehler gemacht (bei den Zeitformen, bei der Pluralbildung usw.)?						
2 ... abwechslungsreichen Wortschatz benutzt?						
3 ... längere Sätze geschrieben und sie mit **linking words** (*because, and, but, so, ...*) verbunden?						
4 ... einen Text geschrieben, der klar und einfach zu verstehen ist?						

► *SF Writing course (pp. 142–143)*

top jobs

Welcome to the top jobs website.

- Are you leaving school soon?
- Do you need ideas for jobs?
- Are you thinking about an apprenticeship?
- Do you want to learn something new?

Then this is the website for you!

It's just the first step!

Your first job is important but it's just the first step. Today some people change their jobs many times.
You can learn important skills in every job – even in Saturday jobs or if you work as a volunteer. It's all good experience.

Luke, a mechanic in a garage

Leena, an office worker

Greg, a care assistant in an old people's home

Billy, a roofer for a building company

Zahid, a vet's assistant in an animal clinic

Sarah, a painter

Jess, a forklift driver for an international company

Rachel, a hairdresser on a ship

Ella, a shop assistant in a sports shop

1 Top jobs

a) *Make notes about your favourite job from the website. Write at least three things.*

- It looks interesting/(a bit) dangerous/ difficult/exciting/...
- You work with animals/old people/...
- You work in a team/outside/...
- You meet people/repair things/carry heavy things/look after people/serve customers/...
- You have to be artistic/calm/fit/strong/ polite/organized/hard-working/sporty/...
- You (don't) have to work shifts/weekends/...
- I (don't) think the pay is good.

b) *Talk to a partner.*

Partner A: What's your favourite job?

Partner B: A care assistant.

Partner A: Really? Why do you like that job?

Partner B: You work ... You look after ... You have to be ... I think it looks ...

Partner A: I like that job too. / I don't like that job.

Partner B: Well, what's *your* favourite job?

2 What's the job really like?

a) *Listen. You will hear three of the people from the website.*

- *Which of the people do you hear?*
- *Which of them likes their job?*

b) *Listen again. Take notes.*
Write down two good things that each person says about his or her job.

▸ SF Listening (p. 134)

3 Extra Now you

Talk about your plans for the future.

I'm leaving school soon/in a year/...
I'd like a job as a ...
I'd like to work in/for a ...
I'd like to do an apprenticeship in ...

▸ GF 5: Talking about the future (p. 156) • WB 1 (p. 15)

PERSONALITY QUIZ

What's the right job for you?

Are you still looking for your dream job? Try our fun quiz.

1 You want to print your homework, but your dad says the printer isn't working. You say:

- A 'Stupid printer! I hate it!'
- B 'Don't worry, Dad. It's not important.'
- C 'I can see the problem. I can repair it.'
- D 'It's OK, I'll print my homework at school.'

2 Your parents ask you to do jobs at home.

- A You disappear!
- B You say OK. It's normal that everyone in the family helps.
- C You try to think of better ways to do the job.
- D You do the job really quickly so that you can do more interesting things.

3 You're happy when …

- A you're with a big group of friends.
- B other people are happy.
- C you solve a difficult problem.
- D you finish everything on your to-do list.

4 How would your teachers describe you?

- A 'Always late!'
- B 'A dreamer.'
- C 'A techie.'
- D 'An organized and reliable student.'

5 Which is your dream holiday?

6 If you were a fruit, what would you be?

- A A banana.
- B A soft summer fruit, like a strawberry.
- C A tomato. (Did you know they're a fruit, not a vegetable?)
- D I'm not a fruit! I hate silly questions like this!

Count how many As, Bs, Cs and Ds you have.

► WB 2 (p. 15)

THE RESULTS

Mostly A

Your personal qualities:

- **You're an energetic and confident person.**

You love an adventure. You're artistic and you like making things. You hate rules! You want life to be fun and exciting.

Your perfect job: an actor, a singer, a dancer, a waiter, a model, a film star, a DJ, a hairdresser, a sports coach

Mostly B

Your personal qualities:

- **You're a calm, polite, friendly, helpful person.**

You're good at talking to people. You like working in a team.

Your perfect job: a care assistant, a vet's assistant, an artist, a reporter, a photographer, a writer

Mostly C

Your personal qualities:

- **You're a hard-working person.**

You're interested in everything – plants, animals, technology. You want to understand how things work. You're always on the internet.

Your perfect job: a private detective, a truck driver, a shop assistant in a computer shop, a zoo worker, an assistant in a garden centre

Mostly D

Your personal qualities:

- **You're a reliable, organized person.**

You have a lot of fun with your friends, but you're serious about your work. You like clear instructions and you think rules are important.

Your perfect job: a builder, a roofer, a forklift driver, an office worker, a gardener, a sportsman or sportswoman, a soldier, a cook

1 The quiz

a) *Do the quiz and read your results.*

b) *What do you think of your results? Talk to your partner.*

2 Personal qualities

a) Think: *Find personal qualities on this page that match these jobs. Make lists.*

a teacher • a firefighter

b) Pair: *With a partner agree on the three most important personal qualities for each job.*

c) Share: *Form a group with another pair. Compare your lists.*

d) **Extra** *List some personal qualities that are needed for your favourite job.*

P1 ◯ WORDS Jobs

a) *Collect as many job words as you can. Look at p. 33 for ideas.*

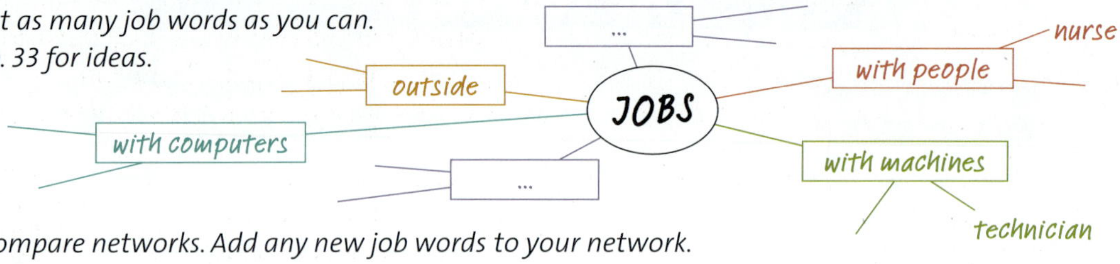

b) *Compare networks. Add any new job words to your network.*

P 2 WORDS Job profiles

a) *Read the job profile below. Match it to one of the jobs in the photos.*

> In this job you have to be very calm. An important part of the job is checking equipment so you must be very careful. You have to like working in a team too. This is a great job because it's exciting and you can save people's lives. This isn't a good job for people who don't like blood. Working shifts might be a problem for some people too.

1 care assistant

b) **Extra** ● *Write a job profile. Choose an interesting job. Find out about:*

- what you have to do in the job
- the personal qualities that you need
- what's good/difficult about the job.

more help ▸ D p. 93

2 vet's assistant

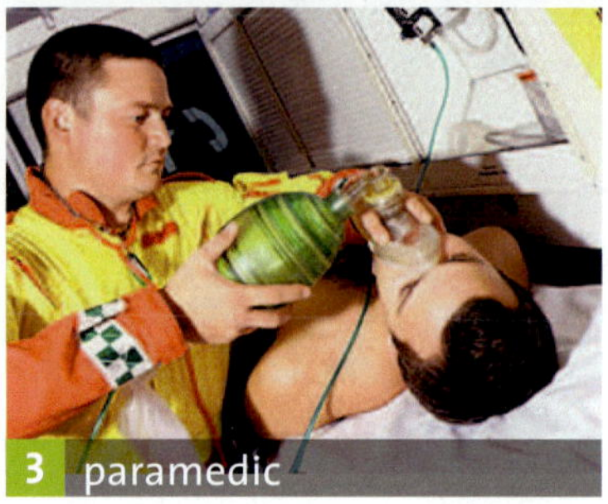
3 paramedic

P 3 WORDS Your profile

a) *Make a chart for yourself like this.*

Personal qualities	Interests	Possible jobs
– good at talking to people – confident – ...	– interested in computers – like designing things – sport – ...	– ...

more help ▸ D p. 94

b) *Use your chart to write a short text. You can put your profile in your DOSSIER.*

> Personal qualities:
> I'm a confident person, but I can be shy when I meet new people. I like working in a group, but I can work alone too. I ...
> Interests:
> I have a lot of interests. I enjoy sport, for example ...
> I'm also interested in ...
> Possible jobs:
> I'm not sure what job I want to do. Maybe I'll be a ...
> This might be a good job for me because ...

▸ WB 3 (p. 16)

P4 MEDIATION Summer jobs in Britain

a) *Look at these job ads. Choose one job that you would like to do.*

b) *Tell your partner, in German, about the ad. Say:*
– what you have to do in the job
– what personal qualities you need.

PARKVILLE HOTEL

Are you looking for a summer job?

Are you a friendly, hard-working person? We have a job for you in the kitchen of our busy hotel restaurant. You will prepare vegetables etc. Apply with CV to Parkville Hotel, Parkville Place, Cambridge, CB1 1VP

Can you ride?
Do you love horses?

Prize-winning riding centre is looking for friendly and organized people to work in July and August. You must like working with animals and children. If you are interested, please send a CV to:
Long's Riding Centre, Cambridge CB24 499

BJ'S BURGERS

BJ'S BURGERS RESTAURANT

Summer work for helpful, reliable people. You must be good at working in a team. You will serve customers and clean the restaurant. Interested? Then download an application form.

Spend your summer in the park!

Gino's ice cream

We're looking for friendly, reliable sales assistants to sell ice creams, snacks and cold drinks in the park. Jobs for 6 people. Must work weekends. Send your CV to: ginoice@hotmail.com

► *SF Mediation (p. 147)*

P5 WRITING Filling in a form

a) *Fill in a copy of the form for yourself.*

b) *Check your partner's form. Use this checklist:*
– Did your partner fill in the correct information?
– Did your partner use a black pen?
– Did your partner write clearly?
– Are there any spelling mistakes?

► *WB 4–5 (pp. 16–17)*

Job application form for BJ'S BURGERS

Personal details (Please write clearly and use a black pen.)

First name(s): Jade Louise   Surname: Hunter
Address: 3 Oakwood Close, Cambridge CB1 7LY
Tel no (home): 01223 456238   Tel no (mobile): 07938 575593
Email address: jlhunter@mvmail.com

Your work experience

Company	From	To	What did you do?
Sugar'n' Spice Café	July 2008	Sept 2008	Prepared food, served customers, and cleaned the kitchen in a busy café

Your education

School	From	To	Subjects
Cambridge High School	2005	to date	GCSEs in Maths, English, French, Art, Design and Technology

More about you: Look at these pairs of statements. Which statement describes you best? For each pair of statements, choose A or B. Example:

	A		B	
	I like working in a team.	X	I like working on my own.	
1	I work carefully.	X	I work quickly.	
2	I do what I am asked to do.		I volunteer for work.	X
3	I work best on my own.		I work best with others.	X
4	I think the customer is always right.	X	I think the customer is often wrong.	

APPLYING FOR A JOB

1 A CV

Jamie wants to apply for this job.

The Coffee Pot

Waiter/waitress for busy café (weekends). Work in a friendly team. Apply with CV to: The Coffee Pot, High Street, Hertford SG14 3SY

Look at his CV. Which of these things are on it?

address • age • date of birth • nationality • postcode • sex • surname • telephone number

▸ *SF A CV (p. 145)*

Jamie Williams
12 Bluebell Court, Old Hall Green, Hertfordshire SG11 1DS
Telephone: 01920 462233 | Email: jwilliams29@aol.com

Personal statement	I am a hard-working, reliable student. I enjoy school, but I would like to get more work experience too. I like working in a team.
Education	
since 2005	The Chauncy School, Ware (secondary school)
1998–2005	Little Hadham School (primary school)
Qualifications	
Studying for GCSEs in:	English, Maths, Music, Science, French, History, Art
Other skills	First-aid certificate, computer skills I can drive a moped
Work experience	Two weeks in a hotel, babysitting job at weekends
Hobbies and interests	Member of Ware Youth Club, I play table tennis and basketball in after-school clubs
References	Mrs K Smith, Manager, Hertford House Hotel ksmith@herthousehotel.co.uk

12 Bluebell Court
Old Hall Green
Hertfordshire SG11 1DS

The Coffee Pot
High St
Hertford SG14 3SY

30 November 2010

Dear Sir or Madam

I am writing about your advertisement in the Weekly Gazette for a job as a waiter in your café. I would like to apply for the job. I enclose my CV.

As you can see from my CV, I did work experience in a hotel. I worked in the kitchen and at the reception. I also served customers in the restaurant which I enjoyed very much.

I look forward to hearing from you.
Yours faithfully

Jamie Williams

Jamie Williams

2 A letter of application

True or false?

1. Jamie saw the advert in a café.
2. He doesn't send his CV.
3. He has worked as a waiter before.

STUDY SKILLS **Formal letters**

In a formal letter like this
– *write 'I am' (not 'I'm')*
– *write 'advertisement' (not 'advert').*

Start and end a formal letter like this:
– Dear Sir or Madam
→ Yours faithfully
– Dear Mrs Smith
→ Yours sincerely

▸ *SF Writing formal letters (p. 146)*

P1 STUDY SKILLS Looking at CVs

a) *Look at the job advert and make notes:*

1 What do you have to do in the job?
2 What kind of person are they looking for?

1 You have to help on ... and in ...
2 You have to be ..., ..., speak ... and like ...

Meadows Home Farm We are looking for people to join our team and help us this summer on the farm and in our farm shop. If **you're energetic and fit, speak good English and like the countryside**, send a CV & letter of application to Jane Hall, Home Farm Shop, Harston, Cambridge CB22 4BE or jh@homefarm.co.uk

b) *Partner B: Go to p. 86.*
Partner A: Tell your partner about this person.

The name of this person is ...
She is from ...
has got these qualifications: ...
did some work experience in ...
is interested in ...

Then listen to your partner. He/She will tell you about another person. Take notes.

c) *Look back at your notes from a). Who should get the job? Why?*

I think ... should get the job because ...
– he/she has studied English for ... years
– he/she did work experience in a ...
– he/she's interested in ...

CURRICULUM VITAE

Lisa Dickhaus
Rosenstrasse 12, 42857 Remscheid, Germany
Telephone: + 49 202 334 84
Email: lidickhaus@email-rs.de

Education
2005–2010 Sophie Scholl-Gesamtschule (secondary school), Remscheid, Germany
2001–2005 Eisernstein Primary School, Remscheid, Germany

Qualifications
Studying for *Hauptschulabschluss* (similar to GCSEs)
Languages: I've studied English for 7 years

Work experience
Work experience in a zoo shop (3 weeks)

Hobbies and interests
My hobbies are cycling and badminton. I am very interested in animals and the countryside.

References
Mrs Schwede (manager of zoo shop),
Zoo Wuppertal, Hubertusallee 30,
42117 Wuppertal, Germany

P2 //O STUDY SKILLS Writing a letter of application ► D p. 92

Rewrite this letter. Replace the underlined parts with words and phrases from the box.

apply for • I am • I enclose • I can speak it quite well • I have • I look forward to hearing from you • I am writing about • Ms Hall • served customers • Yours sincerely

► **Text File 4** *(pp. 110–112)* • *WB 6–7 (p. 18)*

Dear Jane

My mum saw your advertisement in the Cambridge News. I would like to have the job. Here is my CV. I'm 17 years old and I leave school at the end of June.

I've studied English for six years and I'm not bad at it. This year I worked in a zoo for three weeks. I worked in the office and sold things in the zoo shop.

Write back soon.
Love

Lisa Dickhaus

Lisa Dickhaus

A REALITY TV SHOW

1 What's on today?

Saturday

6.30 pm

THE BUSINESS

The BUSINESS is a reality show for teenagers. This week the big boss is Rita McQueen from the fashion company RMQ. The candidates are two teenagers, Lucy and Mani. They have to do an interview with Rita and show her how good they are. The prize is two weeks' work experience as Rita's assistant. But first the two teens get some tips from coach Simon Gubbins.

'Big boss' Rita McQueen. Who will she choose?

Which reality TV shows do you watch? Is there one like this on German TV?

2 Top tips for interviews

a) *Read Simon's top tips for interviews. Which three tips do you think are the most important?*

b) *Agree on three top tips with a partner.*

- My three top tips are ...
- It's very important to smile/not to talk ...
- I think it's more important to wear .../ not to talk too much/...
- OK, let's take ...

Relax! Before an interview listen to music or do yoga.

Don't talk too quickly.

Dress suitably. Don't wear bright colours or too much make-up.

Listen carefully to the questions!

Smile in the interview!

Do some research about the company.

Prepare answers to interview questions like 'Tell me about yourself', 'What are your strengths?', 'What are your weaknesses?'

Don't talk too much. But don't give one-word answers!

c) **Extra** *Choose one of the interview questions. Prepare an answer for yourself.*

3 VIEWING The interviews

a) *Watch the interviews. Give points to Mani and Lucy on copies of the chart below.*

b) *Count the points. Who is your winner? Who is the winner in the class?*

c) *Watch the results. Who is Rita's winner? What do you think of Rita's decision?*

I (don't) agree with Rita. I think ... was (much/a bit) better than ...
... was more relaxed/dressed more suitably/ listened more carefully/talked better/was better prepared. For example he/she ...

Assessment sheet	☹		😐		☺
The candidate	**1**	**2**	**3**	**4**	**5**
1 was relaxed and friendly				✓	
2 dressed suitably					
3 listened carefully					
4 talked well (not too much/too little)					
5 was well prepared					

P1 SPEAKING How would you describe yourself? (Taking part in a job interview) ► SF p. 140

a) *Read this job interview for a weekend job in a shop. Choose the best answers – A or B.*

(1) *Interviewer* Hello, I'm Jack Bond. I'm the manager.
You A Hi. B Hello, nice to meet you.

(2) *Interviewer* Did you have a good trip here?
You A It was fine, thanks. B No, but I'm here now.

(3) *Interviewer* Thanks for your application. My first question is: Why do you want to work for us?
You A Well, my mum saw your advert and she told me that I should apply.
B Well, I think I'd be good at this kind of work.

(4) *Interviewer* How would you describe yourself?
You A I'm hard-working and reliable. I'm also interested in new technology.
B I have a lot of friends and I'm interested in computer games and music.

(5) *Interviewer* Have you got any experience?
You A Well, we did work experience at school – I worked in a hotel – but it was really boring.
B Yes. I did three weeks' work experience in a hotel. I really enjoyed it.

(6) *Interviewer* What are your weaknesses?
You A I'm not great at Maths. Or English.
B My marks in Maths weren't great last year, but my marks are better this year.

(7) *Interviewer* Now, do you have any questions about the job?
You A Yes. What are the hours of work? B Yes. How long are the breaks?

(8) *Interviewer* You have to work from 8.30 to 3 o'clock and you get two 20-minute breaks. OK? Well, thanks for coming. Good bye.
You A Good bye and thank you very much. B See you later.

b) *Practise the interview with a partner.*

c) *You're going to take part in an interview. Partner A is the candidate. Partner B will ask the questions (go to p. 86). Partner C will assess the candidate (go to p. 88).*

Partner A: Read the role card on the right and prepare yourself for the interview.

d) *At the end of the interview, swap roles.*

► WB 8 (p. 19)

ROLE CARD Partner A:

You're going to an interview for this job:

A **local football club** is looking for **friendly, reliable students** to work at the stadium shop shop on Saturday afternoons. You will sell drinks, snacks etc. **Apply now!**

1 Be ready to tell the interviewer about:
- Your personal qualities:
  I'm a ... person.
  I like .../I'm good at ...
- Your interests:
  In my free time I .../At weekends I ...
- Why you're interested in the job:
  I love football/I live near the stadium/...

2 Prepare some questions:
Can you tell me ... (about the pay/the hours, what I have to do, ...)?

P2 //O REVISION Talking to a teacher (Indirect speech)

▸ D p. 94

Steve had an interview. Complete the text. Use the verbs in the box.

could • did • had • liked • wanted • was • were

Steve told his teacher that he *was* a confident person. He said that he (2) work in a team. He added that he (3) lots of ideas. He also said that he (4) working with children and that he sometimes (5) babysitting. He told the teacher that he (6) to be a child care assistant. He also said that his favourite subjects (7) Art and Maths.

(1) I'm a confident person.

(2) I can work in a team.

(3) I have lots of ideas.

(4) I like working with children.

(5) I sometimes do babysitting.

(6) I want to be a care assistant.

(7) My favourite subjects are Art and Maths.

▸ GF 1: Indirect speech I (p. 151)

P3 Extra Did you see THE BUSINESS last night? (More on indirect speech)

a) *Read the 'TV Talk' about The Business. What did Mani, Simon and Rita really say? Choose A or B.*

Max1234 (2 days ago) Did you see The
(1) Business last night? I loved it when Mani told Rita that he was the best. Did you see Rita's face?!?! What was your favourite 'Mani moment'?

Flipper (2 days ago) The best part was
(2) when they were in the shop. Simon told Mani to buy a tie. I laughed so much when I saw the tie that Mani bought!

AliceW (1 day ago) Yeah! That tie was
(3) crazy! The coach told them not to be shy – not a problem for Mani!

(4) **EJ** (1 day ago) Rita asked Mani if he had any weaknesses. And he said no!
(5) And then Mani asked Rita when he could start!! He's amazing!

1
A I'm the best.
B He was the best.

2
A Mani, buy a tie.
B Mani bought a tie.

3
A Don't be shy.
B You should be shy.

4
A Do you have any weaknesses?
B Did you have any weaknesses?

5
A When could he start?
B When can I start?

▸ Extra GF 2: Indirect speech II (p. 152)

b) *What did Simon really say?*

1 Simon told Mani to listen. → A 'Mani, listen.' B 'Mani listened.'
2 Simon asked Lucy to talk more. → A 'Lucy, please talk more.' B 'I want to talk more.'
3 Simon told Mani not to talk too much. → A 'Mani, you don't talk too much.' B 'Mani, don't talk too much.'

c) *What did they really ask?*

1 Rita asked Mani what his interests were. → A 'What were Mani's interests?' B 'Mani, what are your interests?'
2 The presenter asked Lucy if she was nervous? → A 'Lucy, are you nervous?' B 'Was Lucy nervous?'

▸ WB 9–10 (p. 20)

P4 LISTENING Calling about an interview

a) Listen to the phone call. Complete the message.

For:	Mr White
From :	... ...
Message:	He wanted to check his ... time
	– ... tomorrow ...
	His phone no. is 07786 ...

b) Listen to the next call. Complete Jemma's notes.

Interview time: ... tomorrow
Place: Bond Street ...
big ... building
Ask for ... at the ... desk

► SF Listening (p. 134)

P5 ENGLISH FOR JOBS Important phrases

a) Match the phrases to the pictures A–D.

- Are you ready to order, sir/madam?
- Hold the line, please. I'll check.
- How much do you want to change?
- Can you come at 12.45 today?
- The exchange rate is ... to the pound.
- What's your size?
- How do you want your money?
- Can I help you?
- Try this size.
- Would you like anything else?
- What would you like to drink?
- What's the problem?

A

B

C

D

b) Listen to the four dialogues on the CD. Were you right?

c) What different ways do the people start the conversation with a customer?

d) Choose one of the four situations and work out a dialogue. One of you works in Germany in a bank, in a shop, ... – the other is a tourist who doesn't speak German. Then present it to your group or class.

In a bank
You want to change some Australian dollars to euros in a bank. (Exchange rate: 1 AUS dollar = 50 cents)

In a shop
You want to buy a T-shirt in a department store.

In a café or restaurant
You want to order two pieces of apple cake and two hot chocolates in a café.

At the dentist's
You've got a toothache. You phone a dentist to make an appointment.

more help ► D p. 95

► Text File 5 (p. 113) • WB 11–13 (pp. 21–22)

HOME NEWS MUSIC SPORT SCIENCE BUSINESS

BUSINESS

How to be a teenage millionaire

September 2007

Before you read the article, look at the pictures. Then talk about this question with a partner:

Ashley Qualls is a rich American teenager. How do you think she got her money?

She has a Saturday job. • Her parents are rich. • She has an internet company. • ...

Ashley Qualls from Detroit is only 17, but she's already a successful businesswoman with her own company. Ashley's idea was very simple. Her website, whateverlife.com, offers free designs. Teenagers can use them for their websites.

Ashley (her friends call her "AshBo") loves playing with colours and designs on her computer. She started to design websites when she was about nine years old. In 2004, when she was 13, her mother gave her $8. With that money she bought the address whateverlife.com. She didn't want to start a business. She just wanted to show her web designs to her friends.

People liked Ashley's designs and soon her website became very popular. First she had

100 visitors. Then 5,000. Now her website has over 3,000 designs and gets over seven million visitors a month. Big advertising companies started to get interested. In September 2005 Ashley received her first cheque for $2,700. The business now brings in about $70,000 a month. Ashley's designs are still free. All the money comes from the advertisements on the website.

Ashley enjoyed school and she was a good student. But when Ashley's business got bigger, it was difficult to go to school and run a company. In January 2006, six months before her 16th birthday, she left school. "Everybody was shocked," she says. She still studies at home, but she now has more time for her business.

Some people say Ashley was just lucky. But she also has a lot of ambition and she works very hard. She has to be tough too. She has to be the 'big boss'. Her mother works for her as a manager. She also pays some of her friends to work for her after school and at weekends.

It's not easy to be someone's boss and their friend. Last year one of Ashley's friends was working for her, but Ashley thought she wasn't working hard enough! They're still friends, but things were difficult at that time. Now Ashley has strict rules. Everybody has to do at least 25 designs a week. "It's just business," Ashley says.

Ashley misses the normal life of a teenager. And she even misses school! She sometimes goes back to her old school just for the day. Her friends will finish high school soon. "They're all excited and it's sad that I won't be a part of that," she says.

And what comes next? She wants to study design, and she's thinking of going to design school in New York, which she says is her "dream city".

Ashley with some of her friends

Working with the text

1 Quick facts

Copy the list and fill in the missing information about Ashley Qualls.

Name:	*Kind of business:*
Her friends call her:	*People who work for her:*
Age:	*First cheque:*
Hometown:	*Number of visitors per month:*
Age she left school:	*Future plans:*

2 The story

a) //O *Match the sentence halves about Ashley.* ► *D p. 96*

1 Ashley Qualls is only 17 years old, but she's already got ...
2 Teenagers can download Ashley's designs ...
3 Ashley began to design websites when she was ...
4 She started the website to show her designs ...
5 Ashley earns money from ...
6 Ashley is a teenager so she knows ...
7 Ashley's relationship with some of her friends is special because she's ...

a from her website.
b to her friends.
c what teenagers like.
d advertising companies.
e nine years old.
g their boss too.
f her own company.

b) *Are these sentences true or false? Find places in the text to support your answer.*

1 Ashley's web designs cost a lot of money.
This is false. It says in line xx that...
2 Ashley left school when she was 15.
3 Ashley never liked school.
4 Ashley is her mother's boss.
5 Ashley is going to leave school with her friends.
6 Maybe Ashley will study in New York.

c) *Would you like Ashley's life? Tell a partner what you think.*
I'd like to... / But I wouldn't want to ...

study at home • earn lots of money • pay my friends to work for me • be the boss • work so hard • have no time to relax • ...

3 Extra The designs

a) O *What do you think of the designs on p. 42 and on this page?*
I like all/some of them.
I like the one with (the bike/the hearts/...)
I don't like them at all. I don't like the colours/the motifs/...

b) *What kind of designs would you like for your website? Think about colours, motifs, ...*
– I like designs with (flowers/cars/bikes/...)
– My favourite colours are ...
– I'd like space in the design for (my own pictures/my friends' comments/jokes/...)

c) *Design a layout or a logo for Ashley's website*

d) ● *Apply for a job at whateverlife.com. Write your CV and letter of application. If you have a design, enclose it with your application.*
You can put your application in your DOSSIER.

► *SF A CV / SF Writing formal letters (pp. 145–146)* • *WB 14 (p. 22)*

How am I doing?

► SF Check yourself (p. 129)

a) *Find or choose the correct answers.*

Describing personal qualities

1 Use an adjective from the box for the underlined words.

artistic • calm • energetic • reliable • polite

a) She's not excited or nervous.
b) She's a person who does what she promises.
c) They're always nice to everyone.
d) I'm good at painting and drawing.
e) He's someone who never seems to be tired.

2 Complete the sentences with the two adjectives that are best for a hotel job.

a) I'd say that I'm a ... and ... person.
A calm B heavy C helpful
b) In this job you have to be ... and ...
A impolite B hard-working C reliable
c) He's successful because he's ... and ...
A organized B suitable C confident

CVs

3 Match the following words or sentences to one of the CV headings (A or B).

a) 2001–2005 Moerike Primary School, Köngen
A Qualifications B Education
b) I'm an energetic and reliable person.
A Personal statement B References
c) Four weeks in a café
A Other skills B Work experience

Letters of application

4 Start a letter of application with **Dear Sir or Madam** when ...
A you know B you don't know the name of the person you're writing to.

5 Say where you found out about the job ...
A at the beginning of the letter.
B at the end of the letter.

6 When you're writing, use ...
A short verb forms (I'm, I don't, etc.).
B long verb forms (I am, I do not, etc.).

7 Always enclose your ...
A CV. B photo and one of your family.

8 When you know the name of the person that you're writing to, end the letter with ...
A Yours faithfully ...
B Yours sincerely ...

Words

9 What's the English word for ...?
a) Mechaniker/in
b) Pfleger/in (in einem Altenheim)
c) Bauarbeiter/in
d) Tierarzthelfer/in
e) Gärtner/in

10 Michael had to fill in a form, what did he write down? Match the words from the box to the following words.

date of birth • first name • surname • place of birth

a) Michael
b) Müller
c) 10 October 1990
d) Hamburg

b) *Check your answers on p. 205 and add up your points.*

c) *If you had 20 or more points, well done!*
Where did you make mistakes? The chart below will tell you what you can do to improve your English.

No.	Areas	Find out more	Exercises
1– 2	Personal qualities	Unit 2 (pp. 30–33)	P 1–3 (p. 34), WB 3 (p. 16)
3– 8	CV, letter of application	Part B (p. 36), SF (p. 145–146)	P 1–2 (p. 37), WB 5–7 (pp. 17–18)
9–10	Words	Vocabulary (pp. 163–165)	P 1–2 (p. 34), WB 1 (p. 15), 13 (p. 22)

► Selbsteinschätzung 1–2 WB (p. 23) • **Skills check 2** WB (pp. 24–28)

Pick of the day

OUR LIVES 2.00 pm **W3FM** Radio

Radio MONDAY

In this new series, teenagers from all over the world answer questions about their lives. This week we hear from Keira and Lina.

Keira (left), 15,
lives in Kent, England

Lina, 17,
is from Ife, Nigeria

Tell us about your family life.
I'm an only child. I get on OK with my parents. They're quite relaxed.

What are your hobbies?
I love shopping. At the moment I'm mad about boots. I've got blue boots, black boots ... My favourite boots are white. They look great! – No really, it's true. They look really cool!

What do you like most in your life and what would you change?
My friends are very important to me. Keisha and Emma are my two best friends. If I have a problem – like with a boy – I talk to my friends. I text them all the time. I'm sending Emma a text now while I'm talking to you!
What would I change? I'd like more pocket money! I never have enough money.

Tell us about school.
School? It's a bit boring. What else can I say?

What's your ideal job?
I don't know. Mum says I should get a job where I have to talk on the phone a lot!

Tell us about your family life.
I have four sisters and two brothers. My father is a mechanic. My mother is a businesswoman. She sells bags at the market.

What are your hobbies?
I like reading and listening to music, but I don't get much time for hobbies. After school I help Mum at the market, then I go home to study.

What do you like most in your life and what would you change?
I love my school. I've got lots of friends there. There aren't enough books for every student at our school. It would be nice to have more books and computers.

Tell us more about school.
On school days I get up at 5 am. It takes me an hour to walk to school. School starts at 7.45 and ends at 2 pm but I do extra classes after school until 5 pm.

What's your ideal job?
I'd like to be a teacher.

Next week
we hear from two more teenagers, Drew and Adnan.

Drew, 17,
from Eugene, Oregon in the US

Adnan, 17,
was born in Bosnia, but now lives in Cardiff, Wales

1 Keira and Lina

a) *Match the sentences to Keira and Lina. Who could say these sentences?*

1 I have a big family.
2 My friends are important to me.
3 I spend a lot of time shopping.
4 I don't like school very much.
5 I don't know what I want to do when I leave school.

b) *Choose Keira or Lina and take notes like this:*

	Keira	
Family	parents relaxed	
Hobbies	shopping, friends	
Problems	...	
School		
Job plans		

c) *Introduce Keira or Lina to your partner.*

2 Drew and Adnan

a) *Listen to Drew and Adnan. Which pictures (1–5) go with which teenager?* ▸ SF Listening (p. 134)

b) *Work in a group. Give each member of the group a heading from the chart in* **1** *(Family, Hobbies, ...). Listen again and take notes on your heading for Drew and Adnan. At the end put your notes together.*

3 Now you

a) *Which of the four teenagers did you find the most interesting? Say why.*

b) **Extra** *Write to one of the teenagers. Before you start, make notes about yourself: family, hobbies, problems, school, job plans.*
Use a chart or a mind map. Then write an e-mail or a letter. ▸ SF Writing informal letters (p. 146)

You can put your text in your DOSSIER.

more help ▸ D p. 96 ▸ WB 1 (p. 29)

MOBILE TEENS

1

Can you live without your mobile phone?

by Lily Brown

> *What do you use your mobile for? Before you read make a list.*

MY MOBILE is my best friend! I use it to communicate with all my mates, to find out what's happening and to organize my life. With it, I feel safe and I don't get bored. Without it, I'm lost!

So, can I live without my mobile phone? New research has shown that 13 million people in Britain are addicted to their mobile phones. Am I one of them? To find out, I gave up my mobile for a day.

LATE FOR SCHOOL
Arrghhh! My mobile is also my alarm clock. I wake up half an hour AFTER the bus leaves. Not a good start.

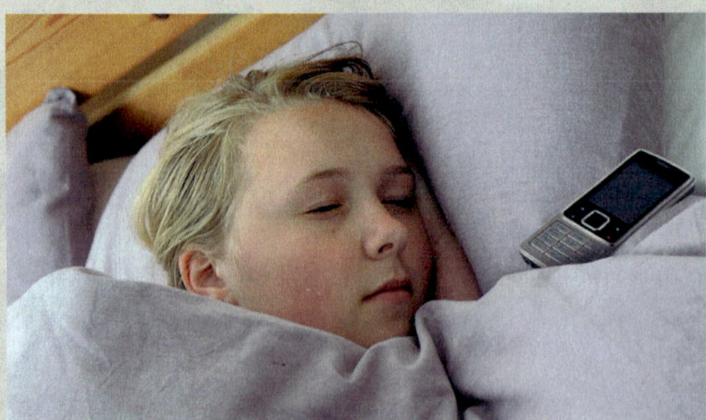

I CAN'T COMMUNICATE
I run out of the house. My friend always waits for me at the bus stop. I'll just call to tell her I'll be ... oh no, I can't.

> *What does the writer use her mobile for? Make a list. Does she use it for the same things?*

I FORGOT!
Today is my big sister's birthday. As usual I forgot to send her a card. I'll text her and ... no phone! Sorry big sis!

WAITING FOR MY BOYFRIEND
I wait for my boyfriend to meet me outside the school. Where is he? After nearly half an hour he doesn't arrive. I give up and go home. It's SO annoying when you don't know what's happening!

BACK HOME
I'm back at home and feeling bored. The phone rings. 'Where are you?' It's my boyfriend. He's at the shopping centre with some of our mates. He sent me a text this afternoon. But of course I didn't get it. I'm not happy. Not happy at all.

So, am I addicted to my mobile? I think I am! I can't live without it, not even for one day!

Are you addicted to your mobile?

	yes	no
1 Is it OK to send a text message and talk to somebody at the same time?		
2 Is it OK to talk on a mobile in a café or restaurant?		
3 Is it OK to write or read a text message at a wedding or a funeral?		
4 Is it OK to film someone secretly with your mobile?		
5 Do you feel safer if you have your mobile with you when you are out late?		
6 Do you feel unhappy if your mobile phone doesn't ring all day?		
7 Have you ever read or written a text message in a lesson at school?		
8 Have you ever made or received calls that you don't want your parents to know about?		
9 Have you ever asked someone out by text message?		
10 Have you ever dumped your girlfriend/boyfriend by text message?		

Have you answered **YES** to all these questions? Then perhaps you are addicted!

2 Now you

a) *Answer the questions in the questionnaire.*

b) *Compare your answers in a group.*

- I answered ... to question 1/2/...
  What did you answer?
- I had the same answer as you.
  I had a different answer.
- I think it's OK to ... because ...
  I don't think it's OK to ... because ...
- I feel .../I don't feel ...
- I have sometimes/often/never
  made or received ...
  read or written ...

c) *How many times did you answer YES? Do you think you're addicted to your mobile phone?*

d) *What about the other people in your group? Put together the results of your group (or your class). Then present the results to your class.*

- Most/... % of the students in our group are ...
- Most/... % of the students have .../think ..

"YES JASON, YOU MAY GO TO THE LAVATORY, BUT NEXT TIME JUST RAISE YOUR HAND."

lavatory = toilet

▸ WB 2 (p. 29)

EVERYDAY ENGLISH

P1 SPEAKING Say what you think

a) *Read this letter to the editor about the article* ***Can you live without your mobile phone?*** *on p. 48. Do you agree with the writer or not?*

33 Garden St
Bristol
BS1 6NJ

Bristol Evening Post
Bristol BF99 7HD

25 March 2011

Dear Sir or Madam

I read your article 'Can you live without your mobile?' in yesterday's paper.

I think we all use mobiles too much. When you sit in the train or bus, nobody chats to each other. Everybody is texting or talking on their mobile.
I get very annoyed when I am sitting next to someone on the bus and I have to listen to their conversation.

I think mobiles should be banned from buses, trains and all public places!

Yours faithfully

Jonathan Whitbred
Jonathan Whitbred

b) *Prepare to say what you think of the letter. You can use the phrases below. Make notes.*

- I agree with the writer of the letter completely.
- I don't agree with the writer at all.
- I think it's a good/stupid/unrealistic idea to ban mobiles from public places because ...
- I think people should ...
- In my opinion it's (not) true that ...
- I think the writer is right/wrong/funny/old-fashioned/unfair/unrealistic/...
- I can/can't understand why the writer gets annoyed when ...

c) *Sit in a double circle. Tell two or three different partners what you think about the letter. React to your partner's opinions.*

P2 WRITING A letter to the editor

Read the article ***Can you live without your mobile phone?*** *on p. 48 again. Write a letter to the editor of the newspaper. In your letter:*
– Say what you think of the article (interesting/boring/...). Give reasons.
– Describe what you and your friends use your phones for.
– Do you think it's possible to be addicted to your phone? Give your opinion.

► *SF Writing formal letters (p. 146) • SF Correcting your text (p. 143) • WB 3–4 (p. 30)*

Tip

This is a formal letter. Follow the rules for formal letter writing. The letter in 1 can help you
– to structure a formal letter
– to start and end a formal letter.
Look for other useful phrases in the letter above and don't forget your name and address, or the paper won't print your letter!

more help ► *D p. 97*

P3 //O WORDS You and your mobile ▸ D p. 97

Complete the dialogue. Choose the best answer from the brackets.

A: Hey, that (alarm/ringtone) sounds great. Where did you get it?
B: I (called/downloaded) it from this cool website.
A: Have you got the website address?
B: No, not here. It's at home.
A: (Text/Call) me the address when you get home. Anyway, so who is the (text message/letter) from?
B: It's from Chloe. Oh, no, she's waiting at the wrong place.
A: Well, (check your mailbox/call) her and tell her to come here.
B: I can't. There's no money on my phone.
A: Oh right. Let's see if I've (saved her number/missed a call) in my (calendar/contacts). – Yes, here it is. I'll (call/download) her. – Oh, wait, it says here that I've (missed a call/taken a picture). I'll just (check the time/ check my mailbox) to see who it was.
B: Who was it?
A: My mum. I'll (call her back/check the time) later. OK, so I'll just tell Chloe to meet us here, OK?
B: Right.

P4 ENGLISH FOR JOBS Useful phrases

a) O *Customer or shop assistant: Who says what?*

- That's a really nice mobile.
- My mobile doesn't work.
- I'll take one.
- Do you speak English?
- There's your receipt.
- Can I pay by credit card?
- You could buy a new SIM card.
- How do you want to pay – cash or credit card?
- Can you enter your PIN, please?
- I'll take these headphones, please.
- There's your change.

b) *Listen to the dialogue in a mobile phone shop. Were you right?*

c) *Partner B: Go to p. 87. Partner A: Read this role card.*

Then act out the dialogue in a mobile phone shop with your partner.

▸ *WB 5–6 (pp. 30–31)*

ROLE CARD Partner A:

You work as a shop assistant in a mobile phone shop.
You have phones that cost € 20, € 30, and € 40.
Talk to the customer.
– Find out what he/she wants.
– When the customer is ready, ask how he/she wants to pay.
– Give him/her the receipt and say goodbye.

TEENS IN TROUBLE

1

Bad boy?

By Jeremy Armstrong

When SHANE Preston from Darlington (in the North-East of England) was 14, he was a bored troublemaker.

He broke all the rules. He vandalized his local area. He broke windows and kicked footballs against his neighbours' cars. He rode motorbikes on the pavement, he caused trouble at school and he got into fights.

Banned

Things got so bad that Shane was given an ASBO (an antisocial behaviour order) by the court. He was banned from some areas of his town, he was not allowed to leave home between 9 pm and 7 am and posters with his name and photo were put up in his area.

> **'When he saw posters with his photo in town, it was really bad.'**
> **Mum, Paula**

His Mum says: 'It was difficult for him. When he saw posters with his photo in town, it was really bad.'

Three years later

Shane (17) is reliable and hard-working. He has nearly finished his apprenticeship as a builder. He works as a volunteer and has helped to build a children's play area. 'I've grown up,' Shane says. 'I stay out of trouble now.'

1. *What did Shane do wrong? Write a list.*
2. *What was he not allowed to do? (two things)*
3. *How has he changed?*
4. *Do you think banning someone from some areas is a good idea?*

2 Bad girl?

It's Thursday morning and Fabio is running into school because he's a bit late. He sees a group of younger students from his school still at the bus stop.

Fabio is surprised. Why are the kids still outside? Lessons have already started. He watches them.

What do you think is going on here?

3

Steve and Kofi are year-9 students. They often write graffiti near the school. Today Steve's cousin Michelle is with them.

4

Michelle hesitates. She has never been in trouble before, but she also doesn't want to lose Steve and Kofi as friends. She doesn't know what to do.

5

Michelle is very nervous and feels under pressure from Kofi and Steve. She begins to write ...

6

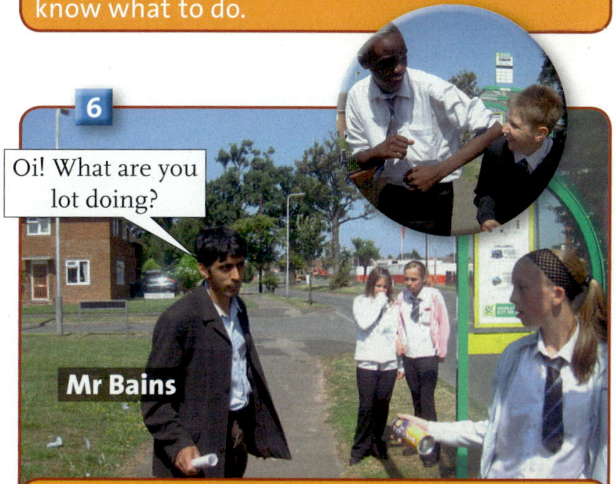

Suddenly they all hear a shout. Steve and Kofi run into the school when they see a teacher, Mr Bains. Michelle is too shocked to move.

7

Mr Bains knows that Michelle is a good student. He can't understand why she did it. He wants to know who she was with.

8

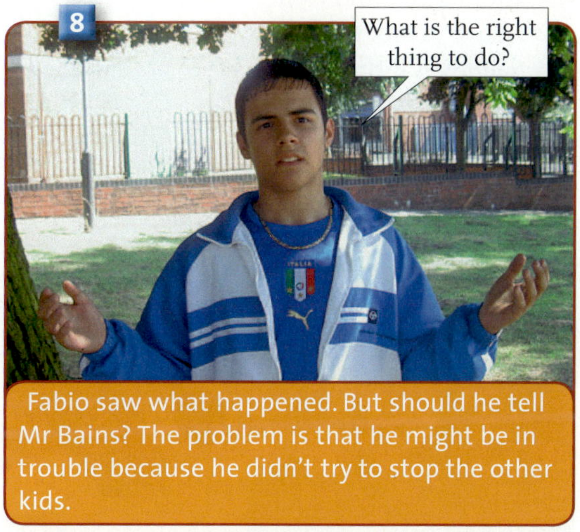

Fabio saw what happened. But should he tell Mr Bains? The problem is that he might be in trouble because he didn't try to stop the other kids.

\> 1 *Why do you think Michelle did it?*

2 *Do you think Fabio will tell Mr Bains?*

▸ *WB 7 (p. 31)*

P1 SPEAKING What do you think? (Having a discussion)

► SF p. 141

a) *Remember Fabio from the photo story on pp. 52–53? Listen to his discussion with two friends and answer these questions:*

1. What do Fabio's friends think he should do?
2. What does Fabio decide to do in the end?

b) *Listen again, then choose the correct phrases from the box for these situations.*

1. Fabio says this to his friends at the beginning.
2. Fabio says this when his friends start to speak but he still has something to say.
3. Helen says this when she's thinking about what Fabio has said.
4. Helen says this when she wants to hear David's opinion.
5. David says this when he thinks Helen is right.
6. Fabio says this at the end.

A I know, you're both right.
B Wait a minute. Let me finish!
C What do you think?
D I see what you mean. But I still think ...
E I agree. You should ...
F I want to hear what you have to say.

c) *Prepare to take part in a discussion. Choose one of the role cards. Work with other people who have the same card. Think about what you could say. Use phrases from the box in b).*

ROLE CARD:
Michelle
- I have to meet Mr Bains at lunch break. He wants to know the names of the two boys. I really don't want to say anything about Steve and Kofi.
- I have to talk to my friends. I'll find out what they think. Then I'll decide what I have to do.

ROLE CARD:
Alex, one of Michelle's friends
- I don't think Michelle should tell Mr Bains about the boys. I know Steve and Kofi. They'll be angry if she does.
- Mr Bains will be OK. Michelle has never been in trouble before.

ROLE CARD:
Jordan, one of Michelle's friends
- I think Michelle should tell Mr Bains exactly what happened.
- I don't like Steve and Kofi. I think they are troublemakers. Michelle shouldn't worry about her cousin Steve.

more help ► D p. 98

d) *When you're ready, do the role play.*

e) **Extra** *Assess your part in the discussion. Give yourself points out of 5.*

Assessment sheet	☹ 1	2	😐 3	4	☺ 5
I talked enough in the discussion.					
I finished what I wanted to say.					
I listened to my partner carefully.					
I used some discussion phrases.					
The other people understood me.					

► WB 8 (p. 32)

P2 //O WORDS Teenage trouble

▸ D p. 99

Choose the right answer. Then read the correct sentence out loud.

1 If you **vandalize** something ...
  A you break it.✓
  B you steal it.
2 If you **stay out of trouble** ...
  A you break the rules.
  B you follow the rules. ✓
3 If you **get into fights** ...
  A you attack people. ✓
  B you watch other people fighting.
4 If you are **a troublemaker** ...
  A you stay out of trouble.
  B you cause trouble. ✓
5 If you **hang around** ...
  A you stand in the street and do nothing.✓
  B you bully people.

▸ **Text File 6** *(pp. 114–116)*

P3 VIEWING High school boot camp

High school boot camp is a film about the Eagle Academy in Florida. Teenagers in trouble go there for six months. They don't have to go there. They choose to go. Why? Because they want to change their lives, learn discipline and respect, get fit, and get better grades at school.

a) *Boot camp or summer camp? Match the statements below. Discuss with your partner.*
1 You can decide what you want to do.
2 You must get up very early.
3 The adults shout at you.
4 The adults are very easy-going.
5 You must follow the rules.
6 The adults talk and joke with you.
7 You can wear what you want.
8 The adults are very strict.
9 You have to wear a uniform.
10 You can get up late.

b) *Watch **part 1** of the DVD (the first day at the camp). Say what you think about the boot camp.*
– I think the camp is ...
– I think the boys/the adults are ...

afraid • awful • funny • loud • mad • nervous • quiet • scared • scary • shocked • +shocking • stupid • unfriendly • ...

c) *Watch **part 1** again. Take notes on what happens. Compare your notes in a group.*
The boys have to shout 'Sir yes Sir' / 'Ma'am yes Ma'am'.
They have to run everywhere. The adults ...

d) **Extra** *Choose one thing from your notes in c) and say why you think this happens at the boot camp.*
– I think the boys have to stand like soldiers so that they can learn ...
– I can't understand why they have to ...

e) *Watch **part 2** of the DVD. It's the boys' last day. Do they feel good or bad about their time at the boot camp? Give as many of their reasons as you can.*

f) **Extra** *Are boot camps a good idea for young people? Say what you think.*
– You learn discipline.
– You forget everything after you leave.
– Discipline doesn't change a person.
– You have to learn to follow the rules.
– People should think, not just follow rules.
– You get really fit.

▸ *WB 9 (p. 33)*

Teens getting involved

1

Don't just sit there – do something!

Volunteer news for young people

Volunteering is a great way to:
- Meet new people
- Be part of a team
- Learn new skills
- Get work experience
- Get free training and qualifications
- Help other people

"I've had a fantastic time and learned a lot about myself."
"Working as a volunteer can help you to find out if a job is suitable for you and it looks good on your CV."
"I've done lots of new things! I never thought that I could do them."
"I met lots of amazing people and many of them are my best friends now."
"It's really great to help other people."

Volunteer Profiles

Fashion show:

■ AMY, 17

We are often told that young people are lazy, but Amy says that's not fair. "Young people have great ideas, but sometimes they don't know what to do with them," she says. This summer Amy had nothing to do, so she organized a fashion show with her friends. The money was sent to a centre for homeless young people.

Making friends:

■ TARA, 18

"So many old people are on their own. Gwen is a 94-year-old lady who loves to play scrabble. I was asked to spend an hour every week playing scrabble with her. I am surprised how important this hour has become for me. And Gwen has become such a good friend."

Football coach:

■ ROBERT, 16

Robert trains the under 10s football team. "I started helping because I love football. At first it was just an hour every week but now it's a big part of my life. I enjoy it as much as the kids. I want to get a job in a sports centre, so it's good work experience."

Helping hand:

■ ROSHAN, 15

Roshan is in a group of volunteers called 'Helping Hand'. The picture shows the group in a community centre. "By the end of just one day the place looked so different," says Roshan. "All the rooms were cleaned and the walls were painted. Everyone had fun and made lots of new friends."

> 1 *How do these young people help other people?*
2 *What does volunteering give them?*
3 *What kind of volunteering can young people do in your town/area?*

P1 WRITING What do you think?

a) Collect ideas on the topic

You have to write a short text on this topic: First brainstorm your ideas alone. The article on p. 56 can help you. Make some notes.

Then work with other students. Listen to their ideas. Add to your notes if you can.

What kind of volunteer work would you like to do and why?

b) Plan and structure your writing

Remember

A good text should have three main parts:

1 **Beginning:**
Start with general sentences about your topic. Complete this sentence or think of your own beginning.

There are lots of projects and clubs that young people can join if they want to volunteer. I'm interested in ... so I'd really like to ...

2 **Middle:**
Write more about your topic. Here you have to say what you want to do and why. Describe the type of work you would like to do. Explain why you would like to volunteer. Use your notes from a).

I'd like to organize ... / spend time with ... / train ... / work in a group that ... / ...

I think this would be a great way to ...
Working as a ... would help me to ...
I want to work as a ... so this would be good work experience.
I already do volunteer work and it's fun / I meet ... / ...

3 **End:**
Finally sum up your thoughts or draw conclusions.

To sum up, I think volunteering would be good / interesting / ... But the problem is that there aren't many ... near me.
I'd like to volunteer, but I'm not sure if I'd have time / ...

► *SF Using paragraphs (p. 142) • Brainstorming (p. 139)*

P2 MEDIATION Volunteer work in Germany

You're looking at a website about the FSJ (Freiwilliges Soziales Jahr). An American exchange student wants to know more about it

- Explain what kind of things you can do.
- Give some examples of where you can do it.
- Say why it is a good thing to do.

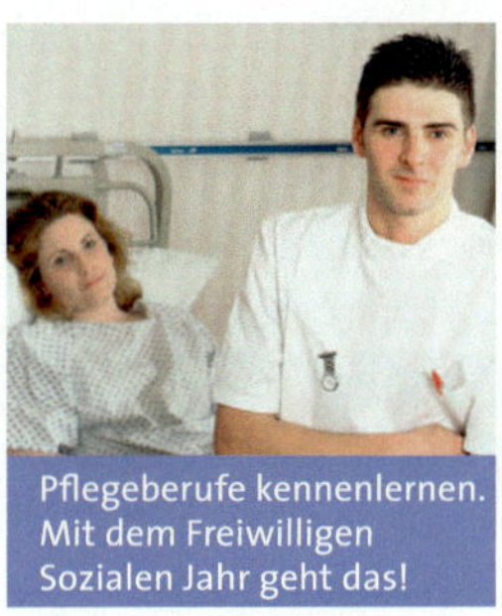
Pflegeberufe kennenlernen. Mit dem Freiwilligen Sozialen Jahr geht das!

Freiwilliges Soziales Jahr – eine Erfahrung fürs Leben

Das Freiwillige Soziale Jahr (FSJ) bietet Jugendlichen die Chance, etwas für sich und andere Menschen zu tun. Hier kann man Erfahrungen für den späteren Beruf sammeln oder sich ausprobieren und weiterentwickeln.

Wer kann das FSJ machen?
Man muss die Schulpflicht erfüllt haben, über 16 und unter 27 Jahre alt sein.

Wie lange dauert das FSJ?
In der Regel 12 Monate, mindestens jedoch 6 Monate. Es ist möglich, das FSJ in Blöcken und im In- und Ausland zu absolvieren.

In welchen Einrichtungen kann man das FSJ machen?
In Krankenhäusern, Alten- und Pflegeheimen, Einrichtungen für behinderte Menschen, Kindertagesstätten, Jugendzentren.

Was macht man in diesen Einrichtungen?
Es geht um die Unterstützung der dort tätigen Fachkräfte bei der Betreuung und Pflege der Menschen in der Einsatzstelle (Behinderte, Kranke, Senioren oder Kinder).

► *SF Mediation (p. 147) • SF Paraphrasing (p. 139) • WB 10–13 (pp. 34–35)*

The caller by Robert D. San Souci (adapted)

Look at the pictures. What kind of story do you think this is?

▸ *SF Working out the meaning of words (p. 136)*

adventure story • comedy • love story • scary story

It was hot at Aunt Margaret's funeral. Lindsay was uncomfortable in her black dress. She was angry because she wanted to be with her best friend, Missy, getting ready for a party.

Lindsay's father's cellphone rang. Everyone looked. He went red and turned it off.

After the funeral, some people came to Lindsay's house. Lindsay had to nod and look sad as they talked about how nice her aunt had been.

"But she could get angry," said Lindsay's father, laughing. "She could be terrible if she thought someone was rude or unkind."

When the people left, Lindsay ran to her room to change her clothes for the party. She took out Aunt Margaret's gold ring with real diamonds. She had always loved it, and Aunt Margaret had promised it to her before she died. Her mother had told her that she should wear the ring only at special times. Well, going to Missy's party was special!

Her cellphone rang.

A tired, old voice said, "Lindsay, darling, this is Aunt Margaret."

"Right! Nice try, Missy – see you in a few minutes." She put her ring in her pocket so her parents wouldn't see and ran down the stairs.

"Where's Dad? He wanted to drive me to Missy's."

"He's looking for his phone in the car," her mother said. "It fell out of his pocket."

Lindsay and her father looked for his phone but they couldn't find it.

At Missy's party, all the girls were jealous of the ring on Lindsay's finger. She forgot about the phone joke.

Her cellphone rang.

She heard the same tired, old voice saying, "Lindsay, this is Aunt Margaret. I must talk to you."

OK, so it wasn't her friends. She whispered to her friends, "It's my horrible brothers. They want me to think it's my aunt's ghost ... Is it *really* you, Aunt Margaret?" asked Lindsay. She tried to sound scared.

"Yes. I just wanted to hear your voice again. You were my favorite niece. You loved me best."

Lindsay looked at the ring as she talked.

"Well, it was really your ring that I loved. I hated going to see you in that old people's home. I only came because I wanted your ring. Goodbye, Aunt Margaret!" Lindsay ended the call.

She checked the phone. Her brothers were calling from her father's cellphone. They must have found it in the car.

Lindsay was spending the night at Missy's.

After the party, the two girls went upstairs. Missy's parents were visiting neighbors – they would be back soon.

Lindsay's phone rang.

"Lindsay, I am very disappointed in you." The same voice. "I'm coming to get the ring back."

Lindsay ended the call. It had come from her father's cellphone. She called the number but there was no answer. She called home. Her mother answered.

"Mom," she said, "Darren and David are so stupid. They're calling me on Dad's phone."

"That's not possible," said her mother. "They're watching TV. And your father is sure he dropped his phone at the funeral this afternoon. Maybe someone ..."

There was a loud noise. The phone died and the lights in the house went out.

"This is cool," said Missy. "We can tell ghost stories."

"I don't want to," said Lindsay. She wanted to go home.

There was a knock downstairs at the front door. *Thump. Thump. Thump.*

Missy got up to see who was at the door.

"Don't!" cried Lindsay. "Please, don't go."

"Don't be stupid," said Missy. "Stay here if you're so scared. What a baby!" She left.

Lindsay closed the bedroom door and locked it.

Her cellphone rang.

"Lindsay, I've come for my ring, you unhappy child. I'm at the bottom of the stairs right now. Let's play that game that we played when you were a little girl. You loved it, didn't you – you loved being scared."

"Missy? This isn't funny."

But Missy's phone was on the bed.

"One step, two – I'm coming for you," said the voice on the phone.

Thump, thump on the stairs.

"Three steps, four – better lock the door. Five steps, six – say your prayers quick."

Lindsay hung up and called home.

"Seven steps, eight – not long to wait," said her mother's voice.

She hung up and dialed 911.

"Nine steps, ten – we're near the end," said a man's voice.

She threw the phone onto the bed.

"Eleven, twelve, and one step more – too late for you, I'm at the door!" It was Aunt Margaret's angry voice.

Someone knocked loudly. *Thump! Thump! Thump!*

"Go away! Leave me alone! I didn't mean what I said!" Lindsay started to cry.

"Ha ha!" cried Missy through the door. "You're crying! This is better than telling ghost stories! I'm going to tell everyone that you cried. You think you're so cool with that stupid ring. But you're not!"

Lindsay opened the door. "I never want to talk to you again!" she shouted.

But it wasn't Missy with Lindsay's father's phone in a muddy hand as the lights came on.

Working with the text

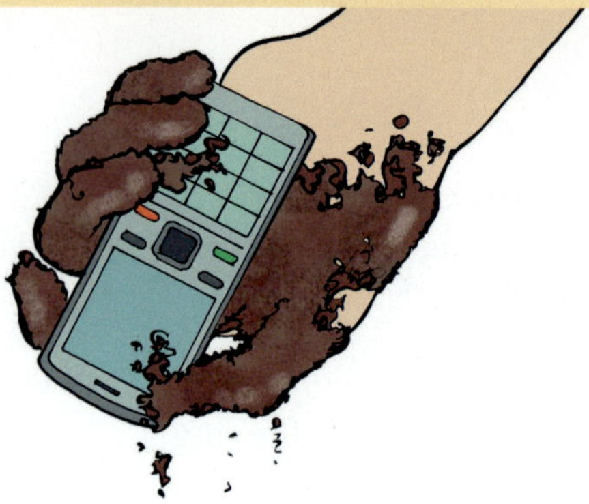

1 Who is it?

Who do you think is 'the caller' with the muddy hand at the end of the story?

2 //O The story ▸ D p. 99

Choose the correct answers.

1 A girl named Lindsay has got a diamond ring from (her aunt/her dad/her friend).
2 She gets some calls from someone who says it's (her brothers/her aunt/her mum).
3 At first Lindsay thinks it's (her aunt/her friend/her brothers).
4 When Lindsay is at Missy's house, there's a knock at the front door. Lindsay asks Missy (to go and open the door/to lock the door/not to go to the door).
5 Lindsay thinks that (her dad/her aunt/her mum) has come to get her.

3 More on the story

Choose the right answers.

1 Lindsay was uncomfortable ...
A because she was at a funeral.
B because her dress was black.
C because it was hot.

2 The people said that Aunt Margaret was ...
A unkind.
B nice.
C sad.

3 Lindsay's father said that Aunt Margaret could get angry ...
A when he laughed at her.
B when he rang her.
C when people were unkind.

4 Lindsay was in a hurry to go to Missy's house because she wanted to ...
A look for her father's cellphone.
B show her friends her ring.
C talk to her friends.

5 The other girls were jealous of Lindsay's ring and Lindsay was very ...
A happy.
B sad.
C disappointed.

6 After the party ...
A all the girls stayed at Missy's house.
B Missy and Lindsay were at home alone.
C Lindsay went home.

7 Lindsay told her mother that her brothers ...
A were calling her.
B weren't calling her.
C were watching TV.

8 When the lights went out Missy was ...
A scared.
B excited.
C unhappy.

9 When Lindsay said 'I never want to see you again', she thought she was talking to ...
A Missy.
B her aunt.
C her father.

4 Extra Beyond the story

What scary films have you watched recently? Do you like scary stories or scary films? Give reasons for your answer.

I love/don't like scary films. Last week/ Friday/... I saw ...
I like comedies/romantic films/action films/... better.
I (don't) like being scared.
I like/hate it when something scary happens.

▸ **Text File 7** *(pp. 117–120)* • *WB 14 (p. 36)*

How am I doing?

a) *Find or choose the correct answers.*

Teen world

1 You may be addicted to your mobile phone if you ...
- A call your friends once a day.
- B use it to take some photos.
- C can't live a day without it.
- D can give up your phone for a day.

2 UK teenagers can get ASBOs for ...
- A good school work.
- B bad school work.
- C success at sport.
- D antisocial behaviour.

3 If you get an ASBO you ...
- A aren't allowed to go to school.
- B can be banned from some areas of your town.
- C must do volunteer work.
- D must join a youth club.

4 Volunteering is a great way to ...
- A get better marks at school.
- B help your parents at home.
- C spend your money.
- D help other people.

Words and phrases

5 How do you want to pay? ... or credit card?
A Money B Pounds C Cash D Receipt

6 I'll just save your phone number in my ...
A mailbox. B contacts. C text. D ringtone.

7 For the underlined words put in one of these words or phrases: communicate, dial, dump someone, enter.
a) call 911 b) end a relationship
c) talk with someone d) put in your PIN

8 Complete the sentences with these words: ask (someone) out, carefully, knock, set.
- a) Don't forget to ... your alarm clock.
- b) If you really like her, you should ... her ...
- c) Listen ..., this is really important.
- d) ... on the door before you enter the room.

9 Complete the sentences with these words or phrases: at all, at a time, completely, as usual.
- a) Well, he's my friend, but yesterday I didn't like his behaviour ...
- b) He was late for school ...
- c) You're right, I agree with you ...
- d) Sorry, but I can only listen to one ...

10 Complete the sentences with these words: decide, only child, secret, wedding.
- a) I have no sisters or brothers. I'm an ...
- b) My sister got married yesterday. It really was a very nice ...
- c) Don't tell Tim what I just told you. It's a ...
- d) I can't ... what to do. Should I go to the cinema with Pia or should I stay at home?

Speaking

11 Write down one expression:
You're having a discussion with your friends. What can you say if you ...
- a) agree with an opinion?
- b) disagree with an opinion?
- c) want to ask for his/her opinion?
- d) haven't finished and you want to say something more about this topic?

b) *Check your answers on p. 206 and add up your points.*

c) *If you had 21 or more points, well done!*
Where did you make mistakes? The chart below will tell you what you can do to improve your English.

No.	Areas	Find out more	Exercises
1– 4	Teen world	Unit 3 (pp. 48–49, 52–53, 56)	P 2 (p. 55),WB 1 (p. 29), 7 (p. 31)
5–10	Words and phrases	Vocabulary (pp. 166–169)	P 3–4 (p. 51), WB 2 (p. 29), 5 (p. 30), 9 (p. 33), 11 (p. 34), 13 (p. 35)
11	Speaking	SF (p. 141)	P 1 (p. 54), WB 3 (p. 30), 8 (p. 32)

1 WORDS Talking about movies

a) *Look at this picture of a film set. Match the words to the letters in the picture.*
– an actor
– an actress
– a (film) director
– a camera
– a director's assistant

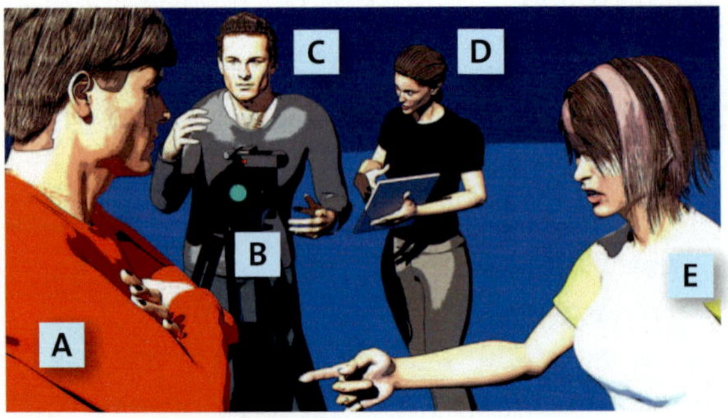

b) *Finish the sentences about movies on the right with the words and phrases in the box.*

(to) film • film company • popular • Oscars • role • star • stars

1 The movie was ...
Millions of people went to see it.
2 The most famous actor in the movie was Brad Pitt. He was the ... of the movie.
3 Film ... like Brad Pitt are very rich.
4 The film won nine ..., one for Best Actor and one for Best Film Music.
5 Paramount is a big ... in Hollywood. Others are Sony Pictures, MGM and Walt Disney.
6 Where did they ... the movie *The Lord of the Rings*? – It was filmed in New Zealand, I think.
7 Who played the ... of Harry Potter in the Harry Potter films? – Oh, that was the British actor, Daniel Radcliffe.

2 SPEAKING Talking about magazines

There are hundreds of different kinds of magazines. Some you can read every week, some come out once a month. Some are cheap, some are very expensive.

a) *Look at these two magazines. What could you find in them? Think about articles, stories, interviews, photos, ...*

b) *Work in a group of 3 or 4 students. What other kinds of magazines can you think of? (computer magazines/magazines for girls/ magazines about ...) Brainstorm your ideas and write a list.* ▸ SF Brainstorming (p. 139)

Now find out about the magazines that the students in your group read and why they read them:
– You like ... magazines. Why?
– Why are you interested in ...?
– What's special about ...?

c) *Tell the class about the magazines that you read in your group and why.*
In our group we read ...
We read ...
because we like/are interested in ...
because the magazine is interesting/has lots of good photos and posters, ...

3 MEDIATION Kennedy Space Center

Du besuchst im Sommer mit deiner Familie die USA und möchtest ihnen kurz auf Deutsch etwas über das Kennedy Space Center erzählen.
Deine Eltern möchten wissen:

– was man dort machen kann
– wie die Öffnungszeiten sind
– was es kostet.

▸ *SF Mediation (p. 147)*

4 SPEAKING Talking about a picture

a) *Finish the sentences about this picture.*

WHO/WHAT?
In this picture I can see ...
WHERE?
He's ...

WHAT IS HE/ARE THEY DOING?
He's sitting in the grass and he's ...

OTHER THINGS?
I can also see ...
In the background, there's ...
In the foreground on the right there's ...

OPINION?
I think he's feeling ...
I like the picture because ...

b) *Find a photo in your book that you like. Describe it to a partner.*

▸ *SF Describing pictures (p. 128)*

5 SPEAKING Having a conversation

Use the phrases below to have a conversation with a partner. You can talk about films, magazines, what you did last weekend, the town where you live ...

Saying hello	Hello. Hi. My name's ... (What's your name?)
Likes and dislikes	I like ... (What about you? And you?)
Showing interest	Really? Oh, that's interesting! Great! Fantastic! Wow!
Agreeing / disagreeing	Yes, me too. That's right! / Oh, I don't. / Sorry, I don't agree. / ...
Asking more questions	So when did you ...? Why ...? How long ...? Where ...?
Finishing the chat	Nice talking to you. See you again/later. Bye!

▸ *SF Having a conversation (p. 140)*

1 READING Magazines

These American high school students all like different magazines.
But which student reads which magazine?

a) *Read about the students A – E and the magazines 1 – 6.*

b) *Match the students and the magazines. (Be careful! There are five students but six magazines!)*

c) *Write down your answers like this: Student A – Magazine …*

Student A : Conrad

Conrad loves sports. He plays in two teams in his high school and he always watches games on TV with his dad.

Student B : Brittany

Brittany loves clothes. She often makes her clothes herself. One day, she would like to be a clothes designer.

Student C : Jeanette

Jeannette has an online blog. She knows all about websites, software and hardware. Her friends always ask her when they have a 'technical' problem.

Student D : John Paul

John Paul likes football but he likes computer games best. He plays online with his friends every weekend.

Student E : Ricki

Ricki plays the guitar in a band in his neighbourhood. He doesn't have much money, but when he can he goes to concerts.

MAGAZINES

1 **MUSIC 4U** America's best music magazine. Articles, interviews, posters – and a free music DVD every month! If you're into rock, metal, rap or whatever, you MUST read this!

2 **FASHION TODAY** All the latest news from the world of fashion. Don't miss this month's special report on the Berlin Fashion Week!

3 **WHERE TO GO?** Are you looking for your dream holiday? We have the answer! Photos and articles from around the world. Plus this week – win a FREE trip to Europe.

4 **COMPUTER MONTHLY** The magazine for computer experts everywhere. This month – we test the latest laptops for you. Plus! FREE CD-ROM.

5 **GO! GO! GO!** Want to read all the latest news about baseball, football, ice hockey or soccer? Want to know about the players? Then there is only one magazine for you – GO! GO! GO! And this month – you have a chance to win fabulous FREE tickets for one of up to 20 games around the States. Buy GO! GO! GO! today.

6 **X-GAMES** Welcome to our world of video and computer games. Articles. Reports on all the latest games. This month: an interview with one of the world's top games programmers.

2 MEDIATION A visit to London

Im Juli besuchst du mit deiner Familie für eine Woche London. Du hast diese Broschüre über Londoner Sehenswürdigkeiten gefunden und möchtest mit deiner Familie darüber sprechen.

Mach dir Notizen auf Deutsch und beantworte für jede Sehenswürdigkeit folgende Fragen:
- Was für eine Sehenswürdigkeit ist das und was kann man dort sehen und tun?
- Wann ist die Sehenswürdigkeit geöffnet?
- Was kostet der Eintritt?

Things to see and do in London

The Tower of London is England's most famous castle. It is 900 years old. See the Queen's crown, the dungeons … and much more! Go on a tour of the castle and listen to the Beefeaters, the colourful guides at the Tower!

Opening times Sunday / Monday: 10:00 – 17:30
Tuesday – Saturday: 9:00 – 17:30
Prices Adult: £17.00
Child (5-15): £9.50 (Under 5 FREE)

The London Eye
is the world's biggest wheel. It is on the River Thames, just opposite the Houses of Parliament. It is 135 metres high. From the wheel you can see all of London!

Opening times Every day 10:00 am – 9:00 pm
Prices Adult: £17.00
Child (5-15): £8.50 (Under 5 FREE)

Come and meet all the world's most famous people at **Madame Tussaud's** Waxworks – Madonna, Brad, Angelina, Barack Obama … and many more! Stand next to your favourite star and have your picture taken to show at home.

Opening times Every day 9:30 am – 5:30 pm
Prices Adult: £22.50
Child (5-15) £18.50 (Under 5 FREE)

London Zoo is the perfect day out for all the family with giraffes, monkeys, zebras, gorillas … and much more! London Zoo is one of the oldest in the world. A nice way to get there is by canal boat from Camden Market.

Opening times The zoo is open every day of the year except Christmas Day.
Summer: 10:00 – 18:00
Prices Adult: £18.50
Child (3-15) £15.00 (Under 3 FREE)
Family (2 adults + 2 children): £53.70

3 READING Dev Patel

This text is from an online British movie magazine. Read the article first all through at least once, then do the tasks on the opposite page.

Meet Dev Patel, teenage movie star

Dev Patel is the star of the hit movie *Slumdog Millionaire*. In the movie, Dev is Jamal, a 17-year-old Indian boy from Mumbai, India's biggest city. He is very poor and lives in the slums of Mumbai (he's a 'slumdog') but he wins the gameshow on Indian TV called *Who wants to be a millionaire*? He becomes rich and finds the girl he loves. But Dev doesn't come from India. He lives in England. So how did he get the role of Jamal?

Dev Patel was born near London in 1993. His parents are Indians. They both came to England from India when they were about twenty. They met and got married.

Dev went to a typical English secondary school. His first hobby was martial arts – karate then tae-kwon-do. He was excellent at both and even took part in the Youth Olympics. But then Dev was in a play at his school. He really loved it and wanted to become an actor.

Dev's mum thought this was a great idea. She wanted to help him. When Dev was 14, his mum found a small advertisement in a newspaper. A TV company wanted people for a TV series called *Skins*. It was about a group of teenage friends. Dev wrote to the TV company – and got a part in the show. It was his first role as an actor.

He was in the show for three years. It was very popular on TV in Britain. A person who often watched the show was Caitlin Boyle. Her dad is a famous British film director, Danny Boyle. In 2008 Mr Boyle wanted an actor for a part in a new movie. The movie was *Slumdog Millionaire*. He couldn't find the right actor in India. Then Caitlin told her dad about Dev. Mr Boyle watched the TV show, saw Dev, and … a couple of weeks later, Dev got the part of Jamal.

Slumdog Millionaire was filmed in Mumbai and Dev was there for five months. It was like a dream. He was on a film set. With him were a world-famous director, some of the best known film stars in India, real kids from the slums of Mumbai, and the beautiful young actress who is his girlfriend in the movie. Dev found it all very hard but very exciting.

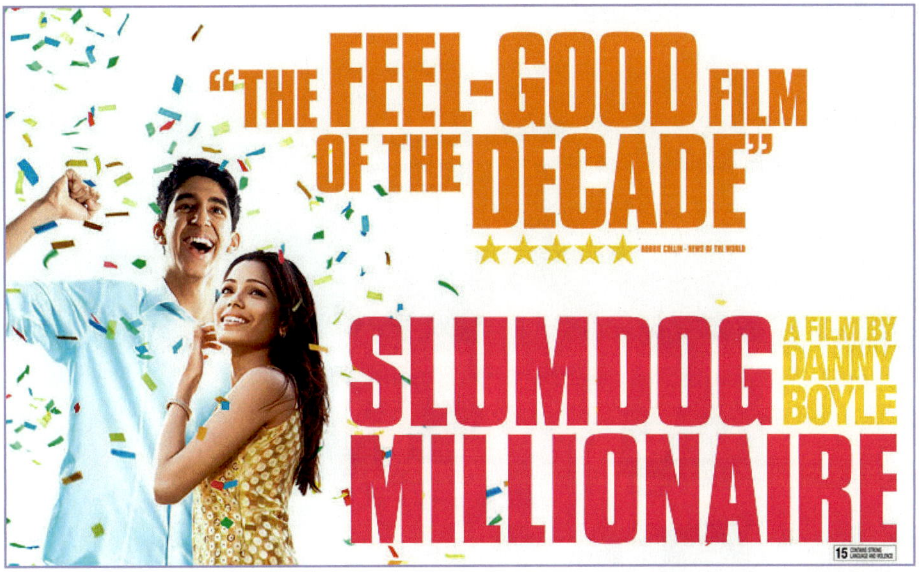

Questions on the text

a) *True or false? Write down 'T' or 'F'.*

1 The film *Slumdog Millionaire* is about an Indian boy called Jamal.

2 Jamal lives in Mumbai, a small town in India.

3 Jamal is very poor but he becomes rich.

4 Dev Patel plays the role of Jamal in the movie.

5 Dev Patel has Indian parents and he was born in India.

6 Dev hated being in the movie – it was very hard.

b) *Choose the correct answer – A, B, C or D.*

1 What did Dev Patel like most at school?
- A Karate.
- B Taek-won-do.
- C Being in a play.
- D Going to the Youth Olympics.

2 How did Dev Patel get the role in the TV series *Skins*?
- A His mum was in the show.
- B His teenage friends helped him.
- C The TV company wrote to Dev Patel.
- D Dev answered an advertisement in a newspaper.

3 Dev Patel got the part of Jamal in the movie because ...
- A a famous British film director's daughter saw him in the TV series *Skins*.
- B Dev was a famous actor in India.
- C Dev's dad was a famous film director.
- D a famous British film director watched the TV series *Skins* for three years and so he knew Dev.

4 Why was Dev Patel in Mumbai for five months?
- A He wanted to find a girlfriend.
- B *Slumdog Millionaire* was filmed there.
- C He lived in the slums there.
- D He dreamed about the city.

4 SPEAKING Talking about a picture

Partner A

Describe to your partner what you can see in this photo. (Partner B: just listen). Speak for about one minute.

– Where are the people?
– What are they doing?
– Describe their feelings.
– Would you like to be one of the people in the photo? Why (not)?

Partner B

Now you. Describe this picture to your partner. (Partner A: just listen). Speak for about one minute.

– Where are the people?
– What are they doing?
– What other things can you see in the picture?
– What do you think? Do you like the town where these people live? Why (not)?

5 SPEAKING Hi!

You meet somebody on holiday and you want to find out about her/him.

a) *First, copy and fill in the chart below for YOU.*

Birthday	
Favourite subject(s) at school	
Favourite music	
Hobbies	

b) *Now talk to your partner. Find out the information for her/him.*

Begin like this:

Hi! My name's ... What's your name?

How am I doing?

Check your answers to tasks 1 and 3 on p. 207.

About the test

Auch beim zweiten Test konntest du Aufgaben ausprobieren, die dir in einer zukünftigen Abschlussprüfung begegnen könnten. Diesmal ging es um solche, die dein Können beim Lesen, bei der Sprachmittlung und beim Sprechen testen sollten. Wenn du Probleme beim Lösen einzelner Testaufgaben hattest, ist das noch kein Grund zur Beunruhigung oder Panik. Denk dran: Übung macht den Meister!

Reading

Aufgabe 1 und 3 waren Tests zur Überprüfung deiner Fertigkeiten im Lesen. Die folgenden drei Fragen helfen dir herauszufinden, wie du damit zurechtgekommen bist. Lies die Fragen durch und entscheide, was für dich zutrifft.

1 Wie leicht oder schwer war die Aufgabe?

	leicht	ging so	ziemlich schwer	sehr schwer
Task 1				
Task 3				

▸ *SF Reading course (pp. 136–137)* • *SF How to do well in a test (pp. 148–149)*

2 Was war bei den Aufgaben schwer?

a) Die Texte waren lang und kompliziert.
b) Es gab Wörter und Wendungen, die ich nicht verstehen konnte.
c) Der Text enthielt viele Informationen. Ich konnte einfach nicht die richtigen Anworten im Text finden.
d) Die Aufgaben waren anders, als die, die wir im Unterricht gemacht haben.

3 Wie hast du die Aufgaben gelöst?

a) Ich habe zuerst die Aufgaben sorgfältig gelesen, damit ich wusste, wonach ich im Text suchen sollte.
b) Zuerst versuchte ich, die Hauptgedanken des Texts zu finden. Das half mir, Wörter zu verstehen, bei denen ich mir unsicher war, was sie bedeuten.
c) War ich mir bei einer Aufgabe unsicher, habe ich sie zunächst ausgelassen und bin später darauf zurückgekommen.
d) Ich habe den Text überflogen, als ich spezifische Informationen suchte.
e) Ich habe am Ende alle Antworten erneut überprüft, um zu sehen, dass ich keine unnötigen Fehler gemacht habe.

Speaking

1 **Task 4: Talking about a picture**

Copy and fill in the assessment sheet below about your partner's description in the fourth task.

Assessment sheet	☹		😐		☺	
Name ...	1	2	3	4	5	Comments
Hat dein Partner/deine Partnerin ...						
1 ... laut und deutlich genug gesprochen?						
2 ... genügend zu sagen gehabt?						
3 ... alle Fragen beantwortet?						
4 ... abwechslungsreichen Wortschatz benutzt?						
5 ... seine/ihre Gedanken verständlich zum Ausdruck gebracht?						

2 **Task 5: Hi!**

Look at the checklist on the right and talk about how well you did in the fifth task, the dialogue about your hobbies and interests.

▸ *SF Speaking course (pp. 140–141)*

a) Wir haben einander zugehört.
b) Wir haben ausführliche Antworten gegeben.
c) Wir haben Interesse an den Aussagen des anderen gezeigt.
d) Unser Gespräch verlief flüssig.

Unit 4 Exploring cities

mumbai

A A traffic jam in Mumbai

B Juhu beach in Mumbai

C The Gateway of India in Mumbai

City fact file

Country: India • **Continent:** Asia

Other names: Bombay, City of Dreams

Population: 13.9 million • **Size:** about 440 sq km

Languages: Marathi is the official language, but you can also hear many other languages like Hindi, Gujarati and English. All of them are official languages in India.

What's good? Going to the beach, sightseeing, exciting street markets, delicious food

What's bad? Traffic, very crowded, pollution, the big contrast between rich and poor people

Other facts: A third of the population live in slums in poor quality homes and many live on the street. It is home to Bollywood – India's film industry.

1 Comparing cities

Look at the photos and the fact files.

– How are the cities different? Find three things.

– How are they similar? Find two things.

... is bigger/more crowded than ...

In both cities you can see/hear ...

2 City visits

a) *Listen to Karen, Rohan and Amy talk about the cities that they visited. Take notes on a chart.*

	Karen	Rohan	Amy
– where they are from	...	...	...
– what city they travelled to	...		
– how long they stayed			
– why they went there			
– what they liked about the city			

► SF Taking notes (p. 135)

D Johannesburg city centre

E Children in a township in Joburg

Johannesburg

F A shopping street in Johannesburg

City fact file

Country: South Africa • **Continent:** Africa

Other names: Joburg, Jozi

Population: 3.9 million • **Size:** over 1,600 sq km

Languages: Most people speak Afrikaans, Zulu, Sesotho or English. All of them are official languages in South Africa.

What's good? Shopping in the malls, perfect weather, exciting art and music scenes, international sports events

What's bad? Crime, AIDS, unemployment, the big contrast between rich and poor people

Other facts: 20 % of the people live in poor areas called townships with no electricity or water. The suburb of Sandton is called the richest square kilometre in Africa.

b) *Listen again. What aspects of city life does each person talk about?*

	Karen	Rohan	Amy
– public transport	✗	✓	...
– crowded streets	...		
– pollution			
– sightseeing			
– crime			
– the contrast between rich and poor			
– speaking English			

▸ SF Listening (p. 134) • WB 1 (p. 37)

3 Now you

a) *Name some other big cities. Which city would you like to visit? Why?*

b) **Extra** *Write a city fact file for Berlin or another city. Put it in your DOSSIER.*

MUMBAI

1

The real Mumbai?

Hi! I'm going to Mumbai next month (I'm from the US). What's it like? I would like to know about the 'real' Mumbai (not the tourist Mumbai). What's good and what's bad?

Hi! I live in Mumbai and I will try to answer your questions.
I came to Mumbai from a small village in India when I was seven. My parents wanted to find a better life. They knew that in the city there are good schools, modern hospitals and more jobs.
When I first came here I hated it. It was so different from my village. I hated the dirt and the pollution. I hated the crowded streets, buses and trains. The contrast between rich and poor people made me sad. There are so many poor and homeless people in Mumbai. I think most people feel like I did when they first arrive. They are shocked. Mumbai is a crazy, crowded, fast, noisy, dirty place.
Now I'm older, I see different things. I love the friendly people – they are really positive and helpful. And I love the energy of the city. Life here is never boring – every day there is something new and exciting. For example, I love going to Juhu Beach with my friends. It's full of people and it's great fun!
To see some of my photos of Mumbai click here.

> 1 *Why did Deepa's family move to Mumbai?*
> 2 *How did she feel about Mumbai at first? And now?*

I think Deepa's story is typical of the 'real' Mumbai.
Every day more people come here from India's villages. They hope that they will find work and a better life. There are lots of rich people here, but a lot of very poor people too. I read that six million people live on less than 1 US dollar a day. Many people live in slums or sleep on the streets.

I ❤ MUMBAI!!! It's the best city in the world!
It has great public transport (OK, the trains and buses are crowded in the rush hour, but at other times they're great). You can shop in big modern shopping malls or colourful street markets. You can hang out where all the rich and famous people go – you might even see a Bollywood film star!

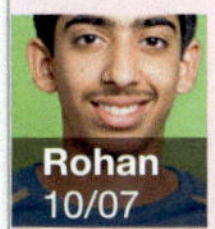

Hi Balu! I've just been to Mumbai – it's an amazing place! Here are some tips:
1. Be prepared for a big culture shock when you first arrive!
2. Do a tour of the city with a local tour guide.
3. Eat at Swati Snacks. (Like most tourists, I was nervous about Indian food because I didn't want to get sick, but this place is very clean and the food is delicious.)

> 1 *Read the four answers to Balu's questions. Pick out the good and bad things about Mumbai and write them down in two lists.*
> 2 *Would you like to visit Mumbai?* (I would/wouldn't like to visit Mumbai because ...)

2 VIEWING Transport in Mumbai

a) *This film shows the main types of transport in Mumbai? What do you think they are? Write a list. Then watch and check your answers.*

b) *Watch again. Which is true – A, B or C?*

1 Buses and trains are ...
- A for local people only.
- B cheap but very crowded.
- C hard to find.

2 Black and yellow taxis ...
- A are more comfortable than the blue taxis.
- B cost less than the blue taxis.
- C are bigger than the blue taxis.

3 Drivers of the blue taxis ...
- A sometimes speak English.
- B always speak English.
- C never speak English.

4 Auto-rickshaws are a good idea ...
- A when you are in the suburbs.
- B when you want to go to the airport.
- C when you are in a traffic jam.

5 When you are walking in Mumbai, it can be difficult to ...
- A follow local people.
- B understand local people.
- C cross the street.

Auto-rickshaws in Mumbai

c) **Extra** *What types of transport are there in your area? Which do you use and why?*
- In my town/city/area there are ...
- I never/sometimes/often/always go by ...
- I never use ...
- ... is/are cheap/expensive/comfortable/...

d) **Extra** *Watch another film about Mumbai. What's similar to a big city in Germany? What's different? Find examples.*

▸ **Text File 8** *(pp. 121–122)*

P1 WORDS City words

a) //O ▸ D p. 99

Look at the texts on pp. 72–73 again. Collect city words in a copy of this chart.

Buildings and places	Transport	People	Problems
sch _ _ _ s *schools*	bu _ es	tou _ _ _ _ s	di _ _
hos _ _ _ _ _ s	tra _ _ s	fil _ st _ _ s	poll _ _ _ _ _
sho _ _ _ _ _ _ ma _ _ s	ru _ _ ho _ _		sl _ _ s
str _ _ _ mar _ _ _ _ s	pub _ _ _ tran _ _ _ _ _		

b) O *Compare your charts and add more words. Here are some ideas:*

business people • bus stops • cafés • cars • city centre • crime • department stores • libraries • museums • office workers • railway stations • restaurants • shop assistants • sights • skyscrapers • squares • taxis • theatres • traffic • traffic jams • …

c) *Choose at least ten words from your chart and match them with adjectives from the box below, e.g.*

clean • colourful • crowded • dirty • exciting • expensive • famous • fast • friendly • great • homeless • huge • modern • noisy • rich • tall • too much/many

too much traffic, exciting museums, crowded buses, …

d) *Write five sentences about big cities using the words that you have collected.*

- *Big cities are …*
- *There are lots of / There is a lot of …*
- *There aren't any …*
- *You see lots of …*
- *You can / can't meet / visit / go to …*

P2 SPEAKING A big city – a good or a bad place to live?

a) *First divide the class into group A and group B. Then form smaller groups of three or four students. Make a placemat.*

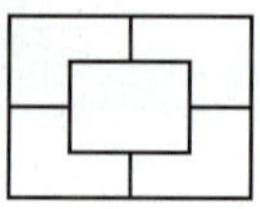

b) *Group A:*
Each student should think of reasons why a big city is a good place to live. Write down your ideas in the placemat.
Group B:
Each student should think of reasons why a big city is a bad place to live. Write down your ideas in the placemat.

more help ▸ D p. 100

c) *In your small group agree on the three best reasons why a big city is a good or bad place to live.*

– I think big cities are good/bad because …
  … they are crowded/exciting/dirty/…
  … there are lots of shopping malls/…
  … you can go sightseeing/…
– I think so too. / I (don't) agree.
– What about …?
– That's a good point.
– Let's choose …
– Who's for/against …?

d) *Report your ideas to the class.*

▸ WB 2–3 (p. 38)

P3 SPEAKING I'm not feeling well

It's not nice to get ill when you're travelling. But if it happens, you sometimes need to see a doctor.

a) *Check that you know these words.*

a cold • +the flu • a headache • +a pain in my arm/knee/... • a sore throat • a stomach ache • a temperature • +a virus

feel cold/hot/ill/weak ... • be sick • my head/stomach/... hurts

+cream • +medicine • +pills • +prescription

b) *Complete this dialogue with words from the boxes in a). Then check with your partner.*

Doctor So what seems to be the problem?
Patient I feel ..., Doctor.
Doctor Does anything ... ?
Patient Yes, I have a pain in my ... and I ...
Doctor Mmm, when did it start?
Patient Last night. And I've been ... too.
Doctor I'm sure you've got a ... – I don't think it's serious. Take this ... You'll feel better soon.
Patient Thank you.

c) *Partner B: You are the patient. Go to p. 87. Partner A: You are the doctor. Find out what the patient's problem is. Then swap roles.*

ROLE CARD Doctor

Ask questions like these:
- So what seems to be the problem?
- Does anything hurt? Where does it hurt?
- What happened?
- When did it start?

Give your patient advice like this:
- I (don't) think it's serious.
- Take this prescription.
- The pills/... should help you soon.
- You have to go to hospital.

P4 MEDIATION Sore throat lozenges

You have a sore throat. You don't think it's serious. But you want to get some lozenges.

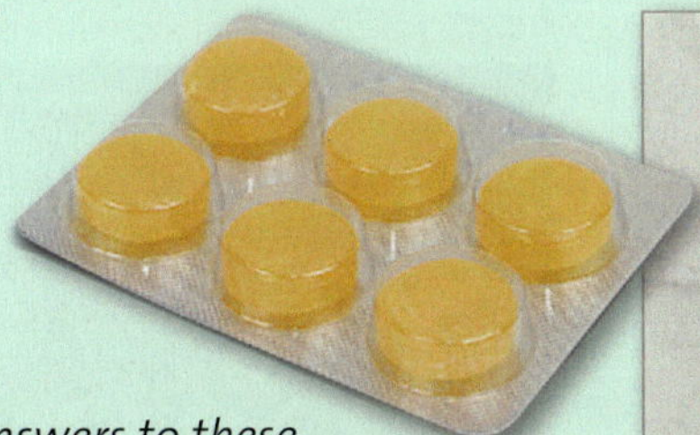

Scan the text for the answers to these questions.
Then check with your partner.
- Wogegen ist das Medikament?
- Wie muss man es einnehmen?
- Wann sollte man das Medikament nicht nehmen?
- Wann sollte man einen Arzt aufsuchen?

Drug facts

Uses: In case of minor irritation, pain, sore throat and sore mouth.

Directions: One every two hours.

Warnings: Do not use this product if you have allergies.
Do not take this product for more than 7 days.
If you get a severe sore throat or sore mouth together with a high temperature, a headache or vomiting, stop taking the lozenges and see a doctor.

► SF Mediation (p. 147) • WB 4–5 (p. 39)

JOHANNESBURG

1 A young person's guide to Johannesburg

Aaron works as a tour guide for South Africa Tourism. He lives in Johannesburg.

OK, let's be honest! Johannesburg is not perfect. You have probably heard stories about crime, pollution and AIDS in the city. And it's true that these are problems in Johannesburg. But there is another side to the city – a side that you don't always hear about in the news. Johannesburg is starting to change and today it is one of the most exciting cities in Africa. Here is my list of the top five things to do.

1 Try the amazing nightlife:

In Joburg we know how to party and have fun.

2 Go shopping:

If you love shopping, you'll love Joburg! We have some great malls and you will probably find that the prices here are much better than at home.

3 Look for wild animals:

Johannesburg is the perfect place to start a tour of the world famous Kruger National Park.

4 Find out about the history of Johannesburg:

Visit the Apartheid Museum in Soweto. From 1948 until the early 1990s we had a system called 'apartheid'. The white racist government said that white people and black people must live and work in different areas. Black people were 70% of the population, but they had no rights.

5 Take a Soweto tour:

A Soweto tour shows you another side of Johannesburg. In the apartheid time, black people had to live in special areas that were called townships. They are still where some of the poorest people live today. Soweto (**So**uth **We**stern **To**wnship) is probably the most famous township. Local guides will show you the culture and how people live here.

\> 1 *Some people don't think Johannesburg is a good place for a holiday? Why?*
2 *Do you think that Aaron's list of things to do sounds interesting? Why (not)?*

► *WB 6 (p. 40)*

2 In the township: Karen's blog

Karen, from Ireland, went to Johannesburg as a volunteer. She wrote this blog while she was there.

▪ **Sunday** Arrived in Joburg today. It's a big, big city. Saw some amazing modern buildings and huge shopping malls from the bus. Some people here have a lot of money! Our hotel is in a rich area called Sandton. You see lots of people (black and white) out in restaurants and going to nightclubs etc. We start work tomorrow. Feeling a bit nervous! I've read lots of stories on the internet about problems in Johannesburg (crime, AIDS, pollution etc). The hotel and all the houses near here have guards with big dogs because of the problems with crime.

▪ **Monday** We went to the township today. What a contrast to the area where our hotel is! The people in the township are mainly black and they're poor. The houses are very small and are made of bits of wood, metal, anything the people can find. They usually don't have water or electricity. I was shocked.

▪ **Tuesday** It was very hot today. I painted all day. There are always kids around when we're working. They don't speak much English but they're very funny. I really love the way they're always laughing and joking.

▪ **Thursday** Talked to a teacher from the township. She talked a bit about the old days under apartheid. She told me that townships were the only places where black people were allowed to live when she was young. Her hero is Nelson Mandela, South Africa's first black president. He was elected in 1994. She also told me that some of the kids in the group that hang around with me probably have AIDS. It's so sad.

▪ **Friday** Our two weeks are over. I'll be back in Ireland in three days time. This has been an unforgettable experience. We've built more than 200 houses. I'm proud of our work, but so much more is needed. I'll never forget the people. Especially the kids. They gave me more than I gave them.

\> 1 *Why was Karen in Johannesburg? Where did she stay? Where did she work? How were the two parts of the city different?*

2 *Do you think Karen had a good time? Why (not)? Find phrases in the blog where Karen describes her feelings.*

3 Extra Finding out more

a) *Work in a group. Half the group should work on text 1 on p. 76, the others should work on text 2 on p. 77. Scan your text for information about:* basic facts about Johannesburg, the townships, apartheid. *Take notes.*

more help ▸ *D p. 100*

b) *Compare notes with people who read the same text.*

c) *Now share your information with the people in your group who read the other text.*

▸ **Text File 9** *(pp. 123–125)* • *WB 7 (p. 40)*

P1 Test yourself

Look again at the texts on pp. 76–77. Then do these tasks.

a) *True, false or not in the text?*

Aaron's text (p. 76)

1 Aaron thinks that Johannesburg is interesting for young people.
2 A township is where rich people live.
3 The Apartheid Museum opened in 2001.

Karen's text (p. 77)

1 Karen stayed in a poor area of Johannesburg.
2 Karen wants to go back to Johannesburg soon.
3 Karen stayed in Johannesburg for two weeks.

b) *Finish the sentences. Use information from Aaron's text (p. 76).*

1 You can hear bad things about Johannesburg. Two examples are ... and ...
2 At the Apartheid Museum you can learn about ...
3 Johannesburg is a good place for people who want to see wild animals, because ...

c) ● *Answer the questions. Use information from Karen's text (p. 77).*

1 What were the first things that Karen noticed when she arrived in Johannesburg? List two things.
2 What did Karen notice about the houses in the township? List two things.

d) *List at least three words or phrases for:*

– different types of buildings in a city
– problems in a city
– things to do in a city

e) *Do you think you would like to go to Johannesburg? Why (not)? Write at least three sentences.*

f) **Extra** *Write a short e-mail to Karen about her blog.*

– Tell her who you are and where you're writing from.
– Say what you think of her trip to Johannesburg.
– Ask her one question about her trip.

P2 WORDS Word building (Adjectives)

a) *The adjectives on the left are new, but you know words like them. Complete the chart for* juicy, jobless *and* unforgettable.

Adjective	Word building	German
bloody	blood + y	blutig
juicy	...	
cloudless	cloud + less (-less means 'without')	
jobless	...	
unforgivable	un + forgive + able (un- means 'not', able means 'you can do this')	
unforgettable	...	

b) *Complete the sentences with adjectives from a).*

1 Forgetting your birthday was an ... mistake.
2 After the factory closed, the number of ... people in the town went up.
3 During apartheid there were ... fights between black Africans and the white police.
4 These oranges are really sweet and ...
5 Seeing elephants in the Kruger National Park was an ... experience.
6 In the summer there is usually a ... sky over Johannesburg.

▸ WB 8 (p. 41)

P3 SPEAKING Describing photos

a) *Look carefully at the photos and listen to the description. Which photo is it – A or B?*

b) *With your partner describe the other picture.*
- This is a photo of …
- I can see … in the foreground/…
- The people are …
- They're wearing …
- I think they are going to …
- The view on each side of the bridge is very different.
- On the left of the bridge there are … I think they are … They look …
- In the background on the right I can see …

c) **Extra** *Find a picture in this unit and prepare to describe it to a partner.*
more help ▸ D p. 101

d) **Extra** *Your partner should listen to the description. Can he/she find the picture in this unit?*

A

B

▸ SF Describing pictures (p. 128)

P4 WRITING Photos of home

These photos were taken by people who live in the townships of Johannesburg.

a) *Choose one of the photos. Describe it. What does it tell you about life in the townships?*

A

B

C

b) **Extra** *Find or take some photos of your home town or area.*
Then describe one of the photos. Explain what it tells other people about where you live.

▸ WB 9 (p. 41)

Berlin: City survival kit

When you go to a foreign city for the first time, things are not always as you expect them to be – as these young visitors to Berlin discovered …

1 *The foreign visitors find some things different in Germany. Find at least three examples in the text.*

2 *Find phrases that might be useful if you visit another country.*

P1 Conversation in a hostel

How to play

Throw the dice. When you land on a square, try to do the task in English.
- *If your answer is OK, you can stay on that space.*
- *If your answer is wrong, you must go back to where you came from.*
- *If you speak German, you must go back two spaces.*

START Es gibt einige Gäste in der Jugendherberge, die nur Englisch sprechen.

1. Erzähle ihnen, dass du ein Bett in einem Schlafsaal hast, weil es billiger ist.
2. Free.
3. Frag, woher sie kommen und wie lange sie schon in Deutschland sind.
4. Frag, ob sie Deutschland mögen und was ihnen am besten gefällt.
5. Frag, wie viele Sprachen sie sprechen.
6. Sag, dass du Englisch kannst. Du lernst es in der Schule.
7. Sag ihnen, wie alt du bist. Frage, wie alt sie sind.
8. Miss a turn.
9. Frag, wie sie hierher gereist sind.
10. Sag, wie viele Geschwister du hast und wie sie heißen.
11. Erzähle, was du gern in deiner Freizeit machst. (Nenne drei Dinge.)
12. Sag zwei Dinge, die Touristen in deiner Heimatstadt machen können.
13. Move back two spaces.
14. Lebst du lieber in der Stadt oder auf dem Land? (Nenne drei Gründe.)
15. Sag, dass bei euch der Supermarkt sonntags geschlossen ist.
16. Frag einen Gast, wie man seinen Namen buchstabiert.
17. Buchstabier deinen Vor- und Nachnamen.
18. Sag, was deine Lieblingsstadt ist und warum. (Nenne zwei Gründe.)
19. Move on two spaces.
20. Sag, dass die Post heute bis 17 Uhr geöffnet hat.
21. Sag, wie der öffentliche Nahverkehr in deiner Stadt ist.
22. Miss a turn.
23. Frag, ob sie für heute Abend Pläne haben.
24. Frag, ob sie essen gehen möchten.
25. Sag, wo man gut essen kann.
26. Schlag vor, was sie in Deutschland essen sollen.
27. Move back two spaces.
28. Schlag vor, dass ihr gemeinsam etwas unternehmen könntet.
29. **FINISH**

P2 ENGLISH FOR JOBS At reception

Hotel receptionists all over the world have to be very polite. They have to manage lots of situations with very different guests.

a) *Listen to three dialogues. What are they about? Take notes.*
Then report: In dialogue 1/2/... the guest ...

wants to book a room • +wants to check in • is waiting for a message • doesn't want breakfast in the restaurant • +wants a wake-up call • doesn't want to use the lift • finds out that the hotel is full on Friday

b) *Now listen to the dialogues again. Which of these phrases are used by receptionists?*

Would you please fill in this form? | I'm afraid we're nearly fully booked. | Can I have my key, please? | Of course, sir/madam. | Can I have a wake-up call, please? | What can I do for you? | Have a pleasant stay. | Is there a message for me? | You're welcome. | ... your name and address, please. | I'm very sorry. | We'll take it.

c) *Choose one of the situations below and prepare a dialogue. Present it to your group or class.*

A
- A new guest has arrived.
- He/She has to fill in the form before he/she gets the key for room 253.

B
- A guest is asking for a single room with a bathroom.
- He/She needs an internet connection in the room too.

C
- A guest comes back in the evening and asks for his/her key.
- He/She would like to have something to eat.

more help ▸ D p. 102

P3 LISTENING Can I leave a message, please?

You will hear three telephone messages. Copy the notes below. Then listen and complete the messages.

Telephone message
For: *Lilly Good, Room ...*
From: ...
Message:
Please phone ...
... worry,
it's ... news!

Telephone message
For: *Ben Smith*
From: ...
Message: *Meet at the Brandenburg Gate tomorrow at ... – NOT ...*
Please ... if it's OK.
Mobile phone number: ...

Telephone message
For: *..., Room ...*
From: ...
Message:
She'll be at ...
near ...
this evening at ...

▸ WB 10–11 (p. 42)

P 4 SPEAKING A talk about Berlin (Giving a presentation)

► SF p. 141

a) *You are going to listen to a talk on Berlin. As you listen, complete the sentences below. The phrases in the box can help you.*

+basic • chart • +divide • +Finally • First • have a look • look at • questions • sections • +slide • sum up • topic

1 The ... of my talk today is 'Berlin: an amazing city'.
2 I'm going to ... this talk into four ...
3 ..., I'll give you some general facts about the city of Berlin.
4 Next I'll ... the history of Berlin.
5 ..., I'll present some interesting Berlin sights.
6 Now please ... at the population of Berlin.
7 On the next ... you'll see a ... of the different groups of people who live in the city.
8 Those were the ... facts. Next I'd like to talk about the history of Berlin.
9 To ... my talk, we have seen that Berlin is a very exciting place to visit.
10 Are there any ... or comments on anything I've said?

b) *Match the sentences in a) to these steps:*
1 Introduce your topic.
2 Give an outline of your talk.
3 Make clear when you are starting a new section of your talk.
4 Explain visual materials as you use them.
5 Summarize your main points and make it clear that you've finished.
6 Invite questions and/or discussion.

c) *Work in a group of three or four. Collect information for your own talk. You can talk about Berlin or another city. Use the internet, brochures, encyclopedias, history books, etc.*
Possible topics are: a tour of the city, sport in the city, three reasons to visit the city, ...

► SF Research (p. 131)

Tip

If you want to talk about Berlin, you might want to use these English phrases. Do you know what they are?

the Brandenburg Gate • the fall of the Wall • the reunification of Germany

Collect other useful phrases that you find in your research.

d) *In your group agree on the main topics for your talk. Divide your talk into clear parts. Decide how you would like to present your information (poster, transparencies, computer + projector, ...).*

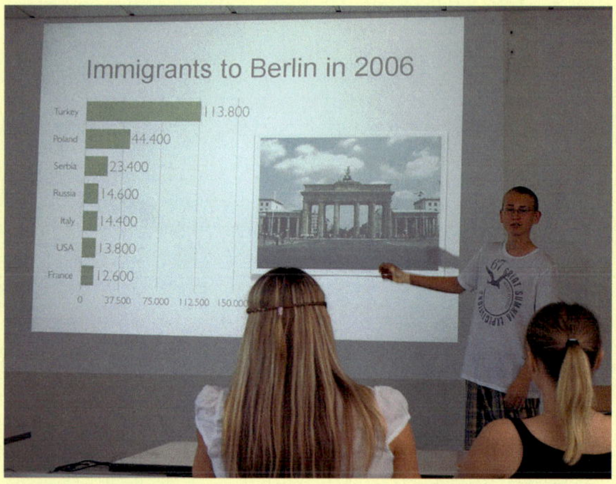

STUDY SKILLS Using visual materials

Visual materials are maps, timelines, posters, transparencies, charts etc.
They make your presentation more interesting and easier to understand. They will also help you while you are talking.

When you talk about the pictures, charts etc. use phrases like these:
– In this photo/chart you can see ...
– The next picture/slide shows ...
– On the left there's a ...
– As you can see in this chart ...
– In the background ...

> *What could the student in the picture above say?*

► SF Using visual materials (p. 132) • WB 12–15 (pp. 43–44) • **Text File 10** (p. 126)

How am I doing?

a) *Find or choose the correct answers.*

City facts

1 Write down the name of the country.
   a) Mumbai is a big city in ...
   b) Johannesburg is a big city in ...

2 Mumbai's famous film industry is called ...
   A Indywood. B Jollywood.
   C Bollywood.

3 What's not a typical problem in Johannesburg?
   A crime B earthquakes
   C AIDS D unemployment

4 Most of the poor people in Johannesburg live in ...
   A Sandton. B the city centre.
   C townships.

Giving a presentation

5 What is the best order for these steps in a presentation?
   A Sum up your main points.
   B Introduce your topic.
   C Invite questions and comments.
   D Give an outline of your talk.

Words

6 Find words that mean nearly the same:
   a) summarize: s _ _ _ p
   b) in the end: f _ _ _ _ _ y
   c) difference: c _ _ _ _ _ _ t
   d) general (facts): b _ _ _ c

7 Find the opposite.
   a) single room – ...
   b) city centre – ...
   c) check in – ...
   d) take a message – ...

8 Complete the sentences with these words or phrases: **dormitory**, **fully booked**, **queue**.
   a) Pia and Linn can't have a room in the hotel because it is ...
   b) Not far away is a hostel where they can stay but only in a ...
   c) There are lots of people waiting outside the museum so Mia and Zoe have to ...

9 Write down three reasons why you might need to see a doctor.

10 Complete the sentences with these words or phrases: **Never mind**, **rush hour**, **traffic jam**, **typical**.
   a) Buses and trains are always full in the ...
   b) Today there was a big ... because of an accident on one of the main streets.
   c) 'That's ...,' my friend said. 'Something always happens when I'm in a hurry.'
   d) I said, '... – Look, there's our teacher. He's late for school too.'

11 Find the adjective.
   a) There are no clouds – the sky is ...
   b) I will never forget the trip to the Kruger National Park. It was an ... adventure.
   c) A cake that is made with lots of cream is very ...

b) *Check your answers on p. 207 and add up your points.*

c) *If you had 22 or more points, well done! Where did you make mistakes? The chart below will tell you what you can do to improve your English.*

No.	Areas	Find out more	Exercises
1– 4	City facts	Lead-in, Parts A–B (pp. 70–77)	
5	Giving a presentation	SF (p. 141)	P 4 (p. 84), WB 14–15 (p. 44)
6–11	Words	Vocabulary (pp. 170–173)	P 1 (p. 74), P3 (p. 75), P 2 (p. 78), WB 2 (p. 38), 8 (p. 41), 12 (p. 43)

► *Selbsteinschätzung 3–4 WB (p. 45)*

Unit 2 **Part B**

P1 STUDY SKILLS Looking at CVs

► *Unit 2, Part B (p. 37)*

b) *Listen to your partner. He/She will tell you about a someone who wants the job. Take notes.*

Then tell your partner about this person.

The name of this person is ...
He ...
– is from ...
– has got these qualifications: ...
– did some work experience in ...
– is interested in ...

Cem Demir
Kantstrasse 65, 24943 Flensburg, Germany
Telephone: 0049 122 39 09 090
E-mail: Cem.demir@flensmail.de

Personal statement
I am a hard-working person. I can work as part of a team, or on my own. I like working with machines.

Education
2009 to date Eckener-Schule-Flensburg (technical college)
2004–2009 Niebüll Hauptschule, Flensburg (secondary school)
2000–2004 Eickum Primary School

Qualifications
2009 *Hauptschulabschluss* (similar to GCSEs)

Other skills
I can drive a car.
Languages: English (5 years), Danish (3 years))

Work experience
Four weeks in a garage

Hobbies and interests
I play football for the school team.
I help on my uncle's farm every Saturday.

References
Mr Meier (manager of garage), Auto Centrum, 24941 Flensburg, Germany

Unit 2 **Part C**

SPEAKING COURSE Part 2

P1 SPEAKING How would you describe yourself? (Taking part in a job interview)

c) Partner B*: You have to interview partner A for a job. Read the role card to prepare for the interview.*

► *Unit 2, Part C (p. 39)*

Partner B: Role card

You're going to interview a candidate for this job ►

- Welcome the candidate. Be friendly!
- Ask the candidate
  - about his/her personal qualities
    *(What kind of person are you? **or:** Tell me about yourself.)*
  - about his/her interests
    *(What are your interests? **or:** Tell me about your hobbies.)*
  - why they're interested in the job
    *(Why are you interested in the job? **or:** Why do you want to work for us?)*
- At the end ask the candidate if he/she has any questions.
  *(Any questions? **or:** Have you got any questions?)*

A **local football club** is looking for **friendly, reliable students** to work at the stadium shop on Saturday afternoons. You will sell drinks etc.
Apply now!

HORNBY F.C.

- Answers the questions.

  Use this information:
  - Workers have to sell soft drinks, ice cream and snacks, clean the shop, work for about 5 hours.
  - Pay: £5.52 per hour
  - Workers can watch the matches!
- Thank the candidate and say goodbye.

Unit 3 **Part A**

P4 ENGLISH FOR JOBS Useful phrases ▸ Unit 3, Part A (p. 51)

c) *Read this role card. Then act out the dialogue in a mobile phone shop with your partner. Here are the sentences and questions from p. 51 again. You might need some of them for your role.*

Partner B:

ROLE CARD

You're in a mobile phone shop and you want to buy something. Talk to the shop assistant.

- You're interested in a cheap mobile phone.
- You don't want to pay more than €25.
- You want to pay with a credit card.

That's a really nice mobile.

My mobile doesn't work.

You could buy a new SIM card.

I'll take one.

How do you want to pay – cash or credit card?

I'll take these headphones, please.

There's your change.

Can you enter your PIN, please?

There's your receipt.

Do you speak English?

Can I pay by credit card?

Unit 4 **Part A**

P3 SPEAKING I'm not feeling well ▸ Unit 4, Part A (p. 75)

c) *Partner B: You are the patient. Partner A is the doctor. Decide what your problem is and tell the doctor how you feel. Answer the doctor's questions. Then swap roles.*

Role card: Patient

Tell the doctor how you feel and what happened:
- I feel sick/tired/hot/...
- I have a cold/the flu/a temperature/a headache/ a sore throat/a pain in my stomach/...
- My arm/leg/knee/... hurts.
- Maybe I have a virus.
- It started two days ago/last week/...
- I fell off my bike. / I fell in the shower. / I hurt my leg when I was playing football. / ...

You can also ask questions like these:
- Do you think it's serious?
- What else can I do?

Unit 2 **Part C**

P1 SPEAKING How would you describe yourself? (Taking part in a job interview)

▸ *Unit 2, Part C (p. 39)*

c) ***Partner C****: Partner B will interview partner A for this job. You have to watch the interview and assess the candidate. Read the advert. Then copy the assessment sheet and prepare for the interview.*

A **local football club** is looking for **friendly, reliable students** to work at the stadium shop on Saturday afternoons.
You will sell drinks etc.
Apply now!

HORNBY F.C.

ASSESSMENT SHEET

Name of candidate ....

The candidate:	Points
1 was relaxed and friendly	...
2 listened carefully	
3 talked well (not too much / too little)	
4 was well prepared	

Points
1 poor
2 below average
3 average
4 good
5 very good

When the interview is finished, tell the candidate how he/she did in the interview.

– You were (very) relaxed. / You weren't relaxed.
  I gave you five/four/two/... points for that.
– You listened / You didn't listen carefully.
  I gave you two/one/... points for that.
– You talked / You didn't talk well.
  I gave you ... points for that.
– You were/weren't well prepared.
  I gave you ... points for that.
– You have all together ... points.

Unit 1 Lead-in

3 Extra Living in Australia

a) more help ▸ *Unit 1, Lead-in (p. 7)*
Would you like to live in Australia? Why (not)? What would be new and exciting? Make notes.
Here are some useful words and phrases.

– I'd like/I wouldn't like to live there because …
– I think the coast/countryside looks …
– There is/are … there.
– They've got/haven't got …
– You can …
– The weather's …
– I'm afraid of …

a long way from Germany • amazing • awesome • barbecues • beautiful • beaches • exciting • fantastic • go camping • go swimming • go to the sea • have great holidays • hot • interesting • snakes • spiders • sunny • wild animals • …

Unit 1 Part A

P 2 //● REVISION Australian animals (Tenses: simple present) ▸ *Unit 1, Part A (p. 11)*

Healesville Sanctuary near Melbourne is a great place to find out about Australian animals

a) *Complete the text with the correct form of the verbs in brackets.*

There … (be) 43 different kinds of kangaroos. You (find) them all over Australia. They … (eat) grass and leaves. They … (need) much water. When it's hot they often … (sit) under trees and … (move) all day. The biggest kangaroo … (be) the Red Kangaroo. It … (jump) two metres and … (move) at about 20–25 km/h.

When a kangaroo baby is born, it … (live) in its mother's pouch, a kind of bag, for ten months. Babies … (be fed) by their mother until they … (be) 18 months old. Kangaroos … (live) long, just 4–6 years.

b) *Use the key words below to write a text about koalas.*

- only find koalas – some parts of Australia
- the koala – look like bear – but – not a bear
- not sleep at night
- that's when – move around
- only eat leaves – one kind of tree (eucalyptus tree)
- not need water – because – so much water in the leaves
- when baby born – move into mother's pouch – for next six months
- then ride – on mother – until – one year old
- usually live – 10–12 years

c) *What new facts did you find out about Australian animals?* ▸ *GF 3: Talking about the present (p. 153)*

Unit 1 Part A

P1 //● Facts and figures ► Unit 1, Part A (p. 10)

a) *Complete the sentences about chart* **1**.
The first chart shows the ... in four countries: Australia, the UK, the USA and Germany.
The USA has the biggest population – 300 ... people.
The populations of the other countries are much ...
The population of Germany and ... are nearly the same.
Australia has the ... population.

b) *Write sentences about chart* **2** *in the same way.*
The second chart compares the ... of the same four countries.
... is the biggest country.
... is nearly as big as the USA.
... and ... are nearly the same size. They are much smaller than ...

c) *What do the two charts together tell us about Australia?*
The charts tell us ...
So ... (crowded/empty) ...

d) **Extra** *Write about chart* **3**.
– Say what the chart shows.
– Give details.

Remember

In German you write 2,5.
In English you write 2.5 and you say 'two **point** five'.

STUDY SKILLS Talking about charts

When you are talking about a chart, first say what it shows. (Tip: The title can help you.) Then give some details.

Use phrases like:
This chart shows/compares ...
... is/has the biggest/smallest/...
... is (much) bigger/smaller than ...
... and ... are nearly the same ...

► SF Talking about charts (p. 133)

1 Population in millions

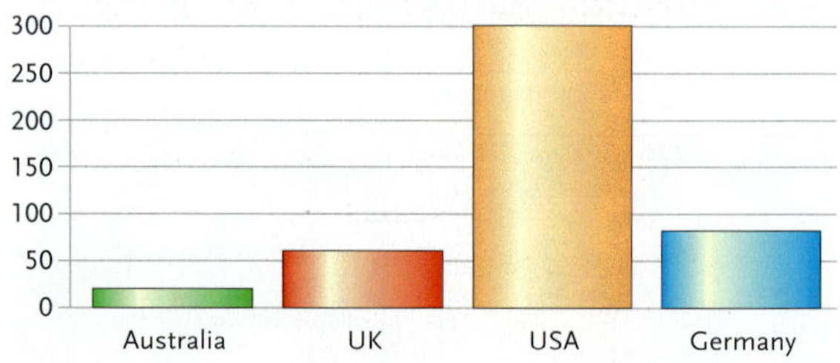

2 Land area in million sq km

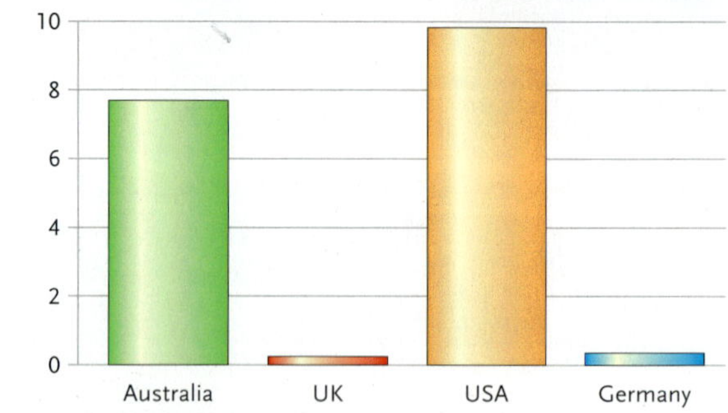

3 Ethnic groups in Australia

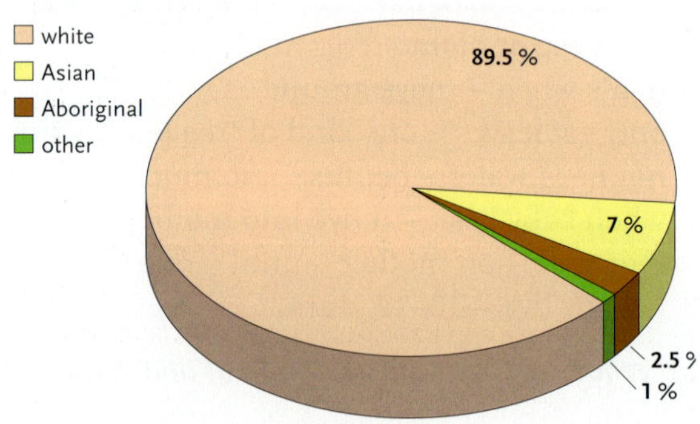

Unit 1 **Part A**

P3 //● REVISION A trip to Australia (Tenses: simple present) ► *Unit 1, Part A (p. 11)*

Lea, from Germany, met Ben on the last day of her trip to Australia. Complete the dialogue.

Ben So Lea, when did you arrive in Australia?
Lea I *arrived* (arrive) in Melbourne six weeks ago.
Ben How long did you stay in Melbourne?
Lea I ... (stay) about three days.
Ben Did you like the city?
Lea Yes, it ... (be) really great.
Ben Where did you go after that?
Lea I ... (go) to Brisbanc.
Ben Did you go by bus or did you fly?
Lea I ... (fly).
Ben Did you learn to surf in Brisbane?
Lea Oh no, I ... (go) surfing. I ... (be) too scared.
Ben Did you see any Australian animals?
Lea I ... (see) any koalas, but I ... (see) lots of kangaroos. They ... (be) amazing. And I ... (swim) at the Great Barrier Reef.

Great Barrier Reef

Ben Did you visit Uluru?
Lea Yes, of course, and I ... (walk) around it. I ... (climb) it, but some other tourists did.

► *GF 4: Talking about the past (p. 154)*

Unit 1 **Part C**

P4 //● On the way home from school (Indirect speech: simple present) ► *Unit 1, Part C (p. 19)*

Dougie is telling his friends a story. Complete the text.

I was on my way home from school when a tourist stopped me. He said that he (1) some help. He told me that he (2) a digeridoo and that he (3) a lot about it.

I said that I (4) the didgeridoo. But I told him that I (5) someone who (5) help him. I think that he was surprised when I said that the name of this person (6) Max and that he (7) from Germany!

Unit 1 **Part D**

In the outback Working with the text

2 The end of the story ► Unit 1, Part D (p. 22)

b) more help *Write your own ending with the help of the key words below.*

- the next day – two policemen – come
- Colm – opens door – ask the boy – for name
- tell him – has to come with them – take him – children's home
- Colm – says: 'can't go with you – have to stay with – Rusty'
- 'help Bill – when back from hospital'
- the two policemen – leave Colm there/take him to ...
- ...

- three weeks later – in the outback – with Bill and Rusty
- this time – Colm – drives – car
- Bill – problems with his legs – watches Colm
- Colm – repairs – fence – does good job
- Bill – happy with Colm's work
- Colm – stay with Bill – as long as – wants to stay
- ...

Unit 2 **Part B**

P2 //● STUDY SKILLS Writing a letter of application ► Unit 2, Part B (p. 37)

Rewrite this letter. Replace the underlined parts.
Use words and phrases from the box.
(You don't need them all.)

application • apply for • I am • I earned money • I enclose • my experience • I can speak it quite well • I have • I look forward to hearing from you • I am writing about • I will • Ms Hall • qualifications • served customers • Yours sincerely

► *SF Writing formal letters (p. 146)*

Dear Jane

My mum saw your advertisement in the Cambridge News. I would like to have the job. Here is my CV. I'm 17 years old and I leave school at the end of June.

I've studied English for six years and I'm not bad at it. This year I worked in a zoo for three weeks. I worked in the office and sold things in the zoo shop.

Write soon
Love

Lisa Dickhaus
Lisa Dickhaus

Unit 2 **Part A**

P 2 WORDS Job profiles

▸ Unit 2, Part A (p. 34)

b) **Extra** ● more help

You want to write a job profile. The steps below might be helpful:

Step 1

Choose a job.

Step 2

What do you have to do in the job? Make notes.

In this job you have to ...

drive a lorry/... • repair • sell • look after • give instructions • check equipment • work with computers/ machines/animals • talk to people • serve customers • carry heavy things • ...

Step 3

What personal qualities do you need? Collect useful phrases:

You have to be ...

artistic • calm • careful • energetic • organized • polite • sporty • strong • ...

You have to like ...

working in a team • working outside • ...

Step 4

What's good about the job?

This is a great job because ...

– it's exciting/interesting/...
– you can save people's lives
– you can earn good money
– ...

Step 5

What's difficult about the job?

Working shifts/Driving a lorry/... | ... might be a problem for some people.

This isn't a good job for people who ... | don't like blood/don't like kids/...

Step 6

Write your job profile. Add pictures if you want to. You can put it in your DOSSIER.

Unit 2 Part A

P3 WORDS Your profile ▸ Unit 2, Part A (p. 34)

a) more help *Make a chart for yourself like this.*

Write down at least two words that describe you:
confident, shy, sporty, fit, energetic, artistic, calm, polite, helpful, reliable, organized, serious, hard-working, strong, friendly, ...

Personal qualities	Interests	Possible jobs
– good at talking to people – confident, – ...	– interested in computers – like designing things – sport – ...	– ...

Write down at least two jobs that you might be interested in:
painter, shop assistant, ...

Write down at least two phrases that describe what you are good at:
I'm good at ...
- talking to people
- helping/looking after people
- working in a team/in a group/alone/...
- working with children/old people/...
- working with machines/computers/...
- solving problems
- ...

Write down at least two phrases about what you are interested in:
I'm interested in ...
cars, sport, films, travel, computers, making things,
repairing things, designing things,
cooking, doing people's hair, ...

Unit 2 Part C

P2 //● REVISION Talking to a teacher (Indirect speech) ▸ Unit 2, Part C (p. 40)

*Steve had an interview. Complete the text. Use the **simple past**.*

Steve told his teacher that he *was* a confident person. He said that he (2) work in a team. He added that he (3) lots of ideas. He also said that he (4) working with children and that he sometimes (5) babysitting. He told the teacher that he (6) to be a child care assistant. He also said that his favourite subjects (7) Art and Maths.

Unit 2 **Part C**

P5 ENGLISH FOR JOBS Important job phrases

d) more help ▸ *Unit 2, Part C (p. 41)*
With a partner choose one of the four situations and work out a dialogue. Then present it to your group or class.

In a bank

A: Was kann ich für Sie tun?
B: Sorry, I don't speak German. Do you ...?
A: Yes, of course. What can I do for you?
B: I'd like to change dollars into ... euros, please.
A: No problem. How much do you want to change?
B: ..., please.
A: No problem. The exchange rate is ... euros to the dollar.
B: OK. Here you are – ... dollars.
A: ... dollars – that's ... euros. Here you are.
B: Thank you very much.
A: Thank you. Goodbye.

In a shop

A: Kann ich helfen?
B: Er, I don't speak ..., sorry.
A: I ... – Are you OK?
B: Well, no. Can I try one of these ...?
A: No problem. What's your size?
B: ...
A: Try these.
B: Where can I try them on?
A: Over there.
B: Thank you very much.
A: You're welcome.

In a café or restaurant

A: Wissen Sie schon, was Sie möchten?
B: Oh, can you speak ...?
A: Yes. Are you ready to order?
B: We'd like ... please.
A: And what would you like to drink?
B: ... please.
A: Anything else?
B: No, thanks.
A: OK. Thank you.

At the dentist's

A: Praxis Dr. ...
B: Sorry, do you speak ...?
A: A little bit. Hello. How can I help you?
B: Good morning I'm a visitor from England. Can I see the ...?
A: What's the problem?
B: I've got a really ...
A: OK. Hold the line, please. I'll check.
B: Thank you.
A: Hello. Can you come at ... today?
B: ...That's fine.
A: What's your name?
B: ...
A: OK, see you at ...
B: Thanks very much. Goodbye.

Unit 2 **Part D** **Working with the text**

How to be a teenage millionaire

2 The story ► *Unit 2, Part D (p. 44)*

a) // ● *Match the sentence halves about Ashley. Choose from a–h.*

1 Ashley Qualls is only 17 years old, but she's already got …
2 Teenagers can download Ashley's designs …
3 Ashley began to design websites when she was …
4 She started the website to show her designs …
5 Ashley earns money from …
6 Ashley is a teenager so she knows …
7 Ashley's relationship with some of her friends is special because she's …

a from her website.
b 13 years old.
c to her friends.
d what teenagers like.
e advertising companies.
f nine years old.
g her mother.
h their boss too.
i her own company.

Unit 3 **Lead-in**

3 Extra Now you

b) more help ► *Unit 3 (p. 47)*

Write to one of the teenagers. Before you start, make notes about yourself:
family, hobbies, problems, school, job plans.
Use a chart like the one in 1a) on p. 47:

Family	small, one…, parents…
Hobbies	…
…	

or a mind map:

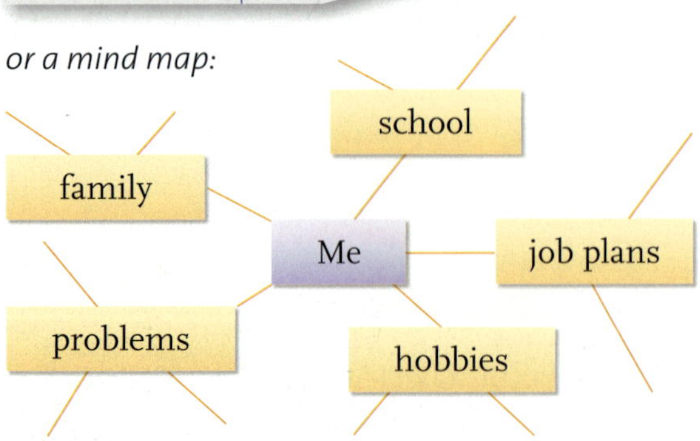

Then write an e-mail or a letter. Here are some ideas for what you could write:

Hi …

This is … from Germany. I found out about you because I read about you in a radio magazine / because you were on the radio. It was interesting to read / hear about your life in …

My life is (a bit / very) different to yours. / My life is quite like yours.
For example, I have a big / small family.
My mother / father works as a …
My parents are OK / very strict/ relaxed/ …

I have lots of hobbies. / I don't have much time for hobbies. I love playing …

My problem is that I have / don't have …

At the moment school is OK / terrible / great.
My friends / My teachers / …

In the future I want to ….

I would love to hear from you if you have time.

Best wishes
…

Unit 3 **Part A**

P2 more help WRITING A letter to the editor

▸ Unit 3, Part A (p. 50)

a) *Write a letter to the editor of the newspaper. This is a formal letter and you have to follow the rules of formal letter writing. Look at the letter on p. 50 or in the Skills File for help with where to put your address. Note down useful phrases.*

▸ *SF Writing formal letters (p. 146)*

b) *Read the article* ***Can you live without your mobile phone?*** *(p. 48) again. Then write your letter.*

- *Write a correct beginning and ending for your formal letter.*
  - Dear Sir or Madam
  - I am writing in reply to ...
- *First say what you think of the article (interesting/boring/funny/ ...).*
  - I think the article is ...
  - When I read the article I laughed / I thought of my friend and me / ...
- *Next describe what you and your friends use your phones for.*
  - I use my phone for lots of things. For example, I use it to
    - communicate with friends
    - organize my life
    - ...
  - I need my phone to ...
  - My friends sometimes ...
- *Finally answer the question: Do you think you are addicted to your phone? Say why (not).*
  - I (don't) think I am addicted to my phone because
    - I always / never ...
    - when I don't have my phone I feel ...
- Yours faithfully

▸ *SF Correcting your text (p. 143)*

Unit 3 **Part B**

P3 //● WORDS You and your mobile

▸ Unit 3, Part A (p. 51)

Complete the dialogue with the phrases in the box.

> call (3x) • check my mailbox • +contacts • downloaded • +missed a call • ringtone • +saved her number • text • text message

A Hey, that ... sounds great. Where did you get it?
B I ... it from this cool website.
A Have you got the website address?
B No, not here. It's at home.
A ... me the address when you get home. Anyway, so who is the ... from?
B It's from Chloe. Oh, no, she's waiting at the wrong place.
A Well, ... her and tell her to come here.
B I can't. There's no money on my phone.
A Oh right. Let's see if I've ... in my ... – Yes, here it is. I'll ... her. – Oh, wait, it says here that I've ... – I'll just ... to see who it was.
B Who was it?
A My mum. I'll ... her back later. OK, so I'll just tell Chloe to meet us here, OK?
B Right.

Unit 3 Part B

P1 SPEAKING What do you think (Having a discussion) ▸ Unit 3, Part B (p. 54)

c) more help *You have to prepare to take part in a discussion. Here are some phrases that you could use.*

ROLE CARD:
Michelle
You have to talk to your friends, Jordan and Alex. Find out what they think.
Then decide what to do.

- Hey guys, I've got a problem.
- I have to meet Mr Bains at lunch break.
- Should I tell Mr Bains about Steve and Kofi?
- I want to hear what you have to say.
- What do you think, Jordan/Alex?
- I think Alex/Jordan is right.
- I think I should/shouldn't tell Mr Bains.
- Thanks for talking about it.

ROLE CARD:
Alex, one of Michelle's friends
You don't think Michelle should tell Mr Bains about the boys. Say why.
Jordan doesn't agree with you. Be ready to disagree.

- You shouldn't tell Mr Bains.
- Mr Bains will be OK because you've never been in trouble before.
- The boys will be in trouble if you tell Mr Bains.
- Steve and Kofi will be angry with you.
- I don't agree with Jordan. You should ...
- I see what you mean, but I still think ...
- Wait a minute. Let me finish!

ROLE CARD:
Jordan, one of Michelle's friends
You think Michelle should tell Mr Bains about the boys. Say why.
Alex doesn't agree with you. Be ready to disagree.

- You should tell Mr Bains what happened.
- I don't like Steve and Kofi.
- They ran away. They aren't nice.
- Don't be afraid of Steve. He's a troublemaker.
- I don't agree with Alex. You should ...
- Wait a minute. Let me finish!
- I see what you mean, but I still think ...

Unit 3 Part B

P2 //● WORDS Teenage trouble

▸ Unit 3, Part B (p. 55)

Choose the right answer. Then read the correct sentence out loud.

1 If you **vandalize** something ...
- A you break it.
- B you steal it.
- C you ban it.

2 If you **stay out of trouble** ...
- A you break the rules.
- B you get into trouble.
- C you follow the rules.

3 If you **get into fights** ...
- A you watch other people fighting.
- B you attack people.
- C you don't fight.

4 If you are **a troublemaker** ...
- A you stay out of trouble.
- B you cause trouble.
- C you are hard-working.

5 If you **hang around** ...
- A you bully people.
- B you work as a volunteer.
- C you stand in the street and do nothing.

▸ **Text File 6** *(pp. 114–116)*

Unit 3 Part D

The caller Working with the text

2 //● The story

▸ Unit 3, Part D (p. 60)

Find the correct answers.

1 A girl named Lindsay has got a diamond ring from ...
2 She gets some calls from someone who says it's ...
3 At first Lindsay thinks it's ...
4 When Lindsay is at Missy's house, there's a knock at the front door. Lindsay wants ...
5 Lindsay thinks ... has come to get her. When Lindsay opens the door she sees ...

Unit 4 Part A

P1 WORDS City words

▸ Unit 4, Part A (p. 74)

a) //● *Look at the texts on pp. 72–73 again. Collect city words in a copy of this chart.*

Buildings and places	Transport	People	Problems
schools	*buses*	*tourists*	*dirt*
...	...	...	...

Unit 4 **Part A**

P2 SPEAKING A big city – a good or a bad place to live?

b) more help ▸ *Unit 4, Part A (p. 74)*

Here are some ideas that you can use:

Group A (a big city is a good place to live):

big shopping malls • concert halls • good discos • places where people can do sports • good public transport • interesting people • lots of cinemas • lots of things for young people to do • parks for skateboarders • ...

Group B (a big city is a bad place to live):

crime • crowded trains and buses • everything is more expensive • noisy • not enough parks • pollution • too many people • too much traffic • ...

Unit 4 **Part B**

3 Extra Finding out more ▸ *Unit 4, Part A (p. 77)*

a) more help *Take notes about Johannesburg.*
You won't find answers to all the questions in your text.

Johannesburg (basic facts)	Find words in the text to describe the city. What problems does Aaron/Karen write about in the text?
Townships	What are they? What are they like? Who lives there? What famous township does Aaron/Karen write about in the text?
Apartheid	What was it? When did it start/finish? What famous person does Aaron/Karen write about in the text?

Unit 4 **Part B**

P3 SPEAKING Describing photos

▸ Unit 4, Part B (p. 79)

c) more help *You have to describe a picture from the unit to your partner. If you need some help, follow these steps.*

Step 1 *Look through all the pictures in Unit 4. Choose a picture that you find interesting.*

Step 2 *Collect as many words and phrases as you can for the people and things in your picture.*

Step 3 *Try to answer these questions. Make some notes.*

What can you see in the picture?
- This is a picture of ...
- I can see ... in the middle (in the background, on the right, on the left, etc.)
- There's a .../There are some ... behind the ...
- I think it's a ...
- Perhaps/Maybe it's a ...
- The people are wearing ...
- ...

What do you think is happening in the picture? If you're not sure, try to guess.
- The people are walking/sitting ...
- I think/Perhaps/Maybe they are going to ...
- The boy/girl/... looks tired/angry/...
- I think he/she ...
- ...

Can you say anything more about the picture?
- The picture shows what it's like in a ...
- I (don't) like the picture because ...
- When I look at the picture I feel ... because ...
- I'd like to/I wouldn't like to go to this place because ...
- ...

Step 4 *Practise saying your description.*

▸ *SF Describing pictures (p. 128)*

Unit 4 **Part C**

P 2 ENGLISH FOR JOBS At reception

c) more help ▸ *Unit 4, Part C (p. 83)*

Choose one of these dialogues. Practise it with a partner.

A A new guest has arrived. He/She has to fill in the form before he/she gets the key for room 253.

Receptionist __ Hello, how can I help you?
Guest __ My name is ... I booked a ... room (for ... nights).
Receptionist __ Just a moment. Yes, here we are. Please fill in ...
Guest __ Thank you.
Receptionist __ We just need your ... – And sign here, please.
Guest __ Where?
Receptionist __ Here at the bottom. Here's your ... – room 253.
Guest __ Thank you.
Receptionist __ You're welcome. Have a nice stay.

Wenn ihr mehr machen wollt:
Vielleicht hat der Gast mehr Fragen, z. B. wo ist das Restaurant/der Aufzug, wann ist das Frühstück, kann der Gast im Zimmer frühstücken, er/sie möchte geweckt werden, ...

B A guest is asking for a single room with a bathroom. He/She needs an internet connection in the room too.

Receptionist __ Hello, can I help you?
Guest __ Yes, I'd like a ... with ...
Receptionist __ Just a moment. Yes, here we are.
Guest __ Oh yes, I need an internet connection in the room.
Receptionist __ OK, a room with internet. – Please fill in this ... – We just need your name and address. And sign here, please.
Guest __ Where?
Receptionist __ Here at the bottom. Here's your ... – room 342.
Guest __ Thank you.
Receptionist __ You're welcome. Have a nice stay.

Wenn ihr mehr machen wollt:
Was ist, wenn das Hotel kein Zimmer mit Internetanschluss hat? Gibt es andere Möglichkeiten (Internetcafé in der Nähe, ...) oder sucht der Gast ein anderes Hotel?

C A guest comes back in the evening and asks for his/her key. He/She would like to have something to eat.

Guest __ Room number ... Can I have my ..., please.
Receptionist __ Room number ... Of course, here you are.
Guest __ There's one other thing. I'd like to ... in the hotel restaurant.
Receptionist __ I'm very sorry, sir/madam. The ... is already closed.
Guest __ Oh dear. OK. Thanks anyway.
Receptionist __ Good night sir/madam.
Guest __ ...

Wenn ihr mehr machen wollt:
Der Gast möchte ein paar Tipps, wo man in der Nähe des Hotels noch etwas essen kann.

TF 1 Australian signs

1 Signs talk

a) *Make groups of five. Each person describes one of the signs 1–5. You can use a dictionary.*

– On sign ... you can see ...
– It says that there might be ...

b) *Discuss in your group. What do you think each sign means? Where would you find the signs?*

– I think sign ... means that it's dangerous to/ you have to be careful because ...
– I think you would find this sign by the road/ by a river/in a forest/on the beach/...

2 Role play

You and your partner want to go swimming, but you see sign 3 or 4.
Partner A: You still want to swim.
Partner B: You don't want to go into the water because of the sign.
Make a dialogue like the one below.

A: Let's go swimming/surfing.
B: Are you sure? It could be dangerous/ ...
A: I think it's OK. Lots of people are ...
B: But look at the sign. It says that ... Maybe we should read a book / go for a walk / ...
A: Ok, you're right. Let's do that.

3 Funny signs

a) *What do you think the signs on the right mean?*

b) *Draw a sign of your own – it can be serious or funny.*

c) *What does your partner think your sign means?*

5

TF 2 Ecosystems[1] in Australia

1 Food chains[2]

Plants and animals need energy, which they get from food. Plants can make their own food, so they are called **producers**. Animals must get their food by eating plants or other animals, so they are called **consumers**.

a) *Is a tree a producer or a consumer? Why?*

b) *Complete the food chain in diagram A. Use the words in the box.*

insects • crocodiles • plants • frogs

Diagram A: A food chain

Producers		Consumer 1		Consumer 2		Consumer 3
...	are eaten by	...	are eaten by	...	are eaten by	...

2 Food webs

A food web is a lot of food chains put together, like these food chains from the food web below:

grass ► kangaroos ► dingos
grass ► grasshoppers ► frogs ► kookaburras

a) *Find four more food chains in the food web in diagram B and describe them.*

Diagram B: A food web

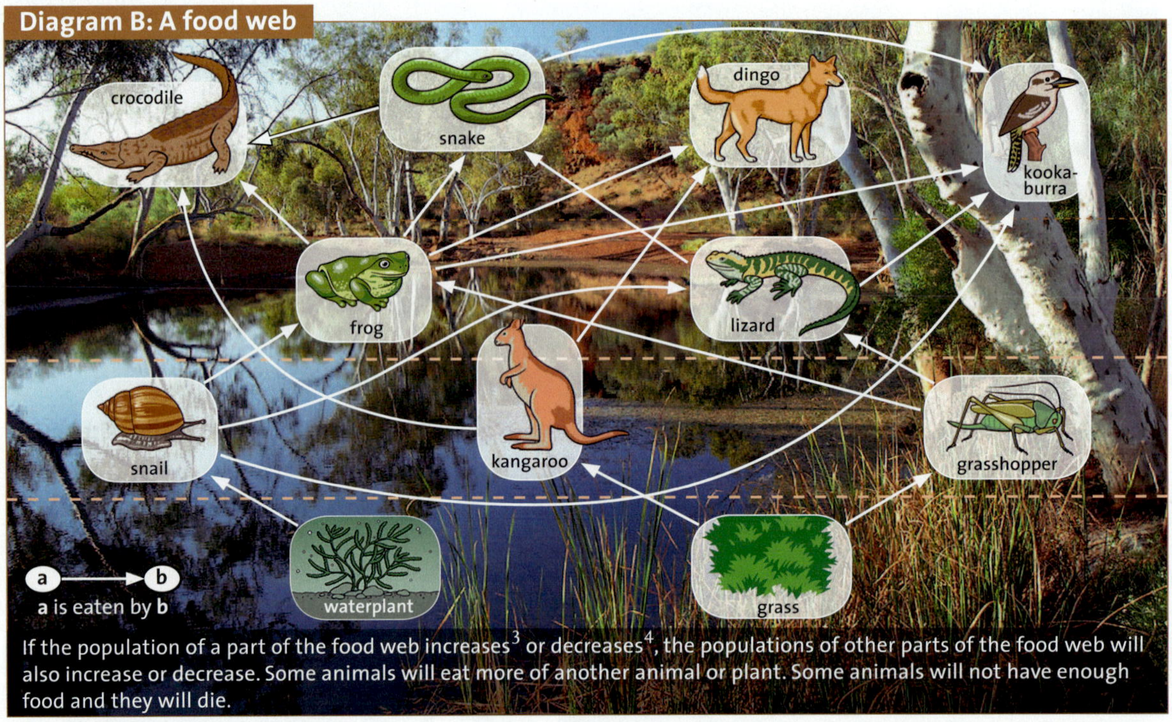

If the population of a part of the food web increases[3] or decreases[4], the populations of other parts of the food web will also increase or decrease. Some animals will eat more of another animal or plant. Some animals will not have enough food and they will die.

b) *What will happen if the population of an animal in the food web increases or decreases? Talk about what will happen to the populations of the other animals in the web.*

If the population of	snakes frogs dingos ...	increases/ decreases,	then the population of	snakes frogs dingos ...	will increase/ decrease.

If the population of kookaburras decreases, then the population of frogs will increase. If ...

[1] ecosystem ['i:kəʊsɪstəm] *Ökosystem* [2] food chain ['fu:d tʃeɪn] *Nahrungskette* [3] (to) increase [ɪn'kri:s] *zunehmen* [4] (to) decrease [dɪ'kri:s] *zurückgehen, abnehmen*

3 An ecosystem in disorder[1]

TOADZILLA!

27 March 2007

A cane toad as big as a small dog was found in Australia this week. The toad was 20 cm long – twice as big as most cane toads.

In 1935, farmers in Queensland brought 102 cane toads to Australia because they had problems with insects in their fields. They wanted the cane toads to eat the insects.

Unfortunately that was a really bad idea! Today there are about 200 million cane toads and native[2] Australian animals are in danger.

The government is now asking people to hunt cane toads and kill them. So, why is the situation so bad for the native animals of Australia?

The main reason is the fact that cane toads are poisonous. Animals (like crocodiles, snakes, lizards and birds) that try to eat the cane toad, or its eggs, die from the poison.

Another problem is that cane toads eat almost anything that moves, like native snakes, frogs, lizards and birds.

Now scientists are looking for a way to control the cane toad population in Australia ... before it's too late.

Fast facts: Cane toads

From: South America

Size: About 10 to 15 cm long.

What do they eat? Almost anything: insects, lizards, frogs and small snakes, even cat and dog food.

What are they eaten by? Snakes, lizards, crocodiles, birds (But most of them die from the toad's poison!)

Reproduction: Cane toads have about 8,000 to 35,000 eggs twice a year.

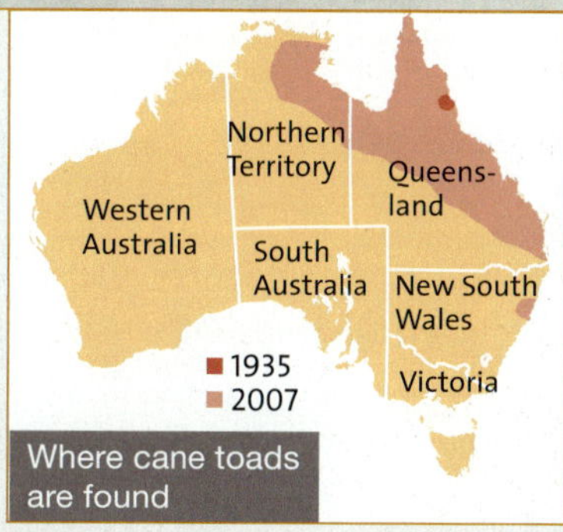

Where cane toads are found

a) *Answer the questions about the article.*

1 How did cane toads arrive in Australia?

2 Why are cane toads a problem for native animals? Give two reasons.

b) *Look at the photo, the map and the fast facts box. Describe what they show.*

Activate your English
- The photo/map/fast facts box shows/gives information about ...
- It says that ... / It shows ...
- This is a photo/map of ...
- In 1935 cane toads were found in ... In 2007 they were found in ...

c) *Look at the food web on p. 106 again. What will happen if the cane toad arrives in this place?*
- The cane toad will eat ...
- It will be eaten by ..., but they will die because ...
- If the population of cane toads increases, the population of ... will ...

4 Rabbits in Australia

The rabbit is another animal that has caused problems since it was brought to Australia. Do some research and write a fast facts box about rabbits in Australia. You can put it in your DOSSIER.

[1] in disorder [dɪsˈɔːdə] *in Unordnung; (funktions)gestört* [2] native [ˈneɪtɪv] *einheimisch*

TF 3 PROJECT: What's so special about Australia?

Divide the class into groups. Each group chooses a topic about Australia. Do the project in your group. Then present your project to the class.

Project work

1 ***Organize your group work***
Sammelt in eurer Gruppe so viele Ideen wie möglich (Brainstorming). Dann entscheidet: Welches Thema wollt ihr bearbeiten? Wer übernimmt was? Wann trefft ihr euch, um eure Ergebnisse zu besprechen?

2 ***Research and take notes***
Sammelt Informationen zu eurem Thema. Wählt die besten Quellen aus und macht euch Notizen.

3 ***Decide how to present the information***
Macht ihr ein Poster, eine Broschüre, ein Video oder eine Präsentation am Computer? Sammelt die dafür notwendigen Materialien wie Fotos, Filmausschnitte usw.

4 ***Agree on the next steps***
Wer macht was? Und bis wann?

5 ***Prepare your presentation***
Ordnet die gesammelten Informationen, Notizen und Materialien. Macht euch kurze Notizen für eure mündliche Präsentation und übt sie in eurer Gruppe ein.

► *SF Brainstorming (p. 139)* • *SF Internet research (p. 131)* • *SF Giving a presentation (p. 132)*

Will the Great Barrier Reef survive?

Here are some ideas for a topic:

Topic 1 The geography of Australia

Australia is a whole continent, so it has lots of different landscapes[1], from desert to rain forest.

- What are these places like?
- Who or what lives there? And how do they survive?
- What can you find out about the island of Tasmania?

Can you find the Daintree Rain Forest on a map?

Where's the Simpson Desert?

[1] landscape ['lændskeɪp] *Landschaft*

Topic 2 The animals of Australia

Everyone has heard of the kangaroo, and everybody loves koalas. But Australia has lots of other fascinating animals.

- Which ones can only be found in Australia?
- Which ones are dangerous?
- Are any of them in danger?
- And what's the worry about rabbits?

Why do they call it a 'Tasmanian Devil'[1]?

What's unusual about the platypus?

Why wouldn't you want to meet a 'salty'[2]?

Topic 3 The first people of Australia

- What else is there to know about the Aborigines?
- And who are the Torres Strait Islanders?
- What are their beliefs[3] and legends? Their art and music?
- And how do these groups live in modern Australia?

What are the origins of Aborigine dot[4] paintings?

Topic 4 The sports of Australia

- What sports are Aussies especially good at?
- Who are their famous sports stars?
- And what is special about Australian Rules football?

What are the rules of Aussie Rules football?

[1] devil ['devl] *Teufel* [2] salty ['sɔːlti] *salzig* [3] belief [bɪ'liːf] *Glaube, Überzeugung* [4] dot [dɒt] *Punkt*

TF 4 Diary of a teenage job hunter by Ewan Denham, 17, Swindon, Wiltshire

What would be your dream summer job? Why? How would you find a summer job?

– To find a summer job I would look in the newspaper / look on notice boards in local shops / ask friends or family / ...
– My dream summer job is a computer game tester / dog walker / football coach/ ... because I love ... / I'm good at ...

Diary of a teenage job hunter

Day 1

Yay! Summer's nearly here! It's time to start looking for my dream summer job. I've only got one rule for summer work: I will NOT work in a café. I worked in our neighbour's café once. It was OK, but I don't like serving customers. They complain all the time. (The tea's too hot, or the ice cream's too cold!) I want a different job.

Day 2

The website Jobs4u.co.uk has lots of jobs. It's a good place to start. It's easy. I choose the office work section (no cafés, no customers!) and I find seven great jobs very quickly. I write 7 applications. I quickly check the emails before I send them. No spelling mistakes – great. I expect I will get some interviews soon.

Day 3

Oops! I forgot to send my CV with the emails that I sent yesterday! I sent out another 12 emails today (with CVs this time!). The interviews should start very soon.

Day 7

No phone calls! Nix, nothing, nada! Mum says I should go next door and ask our neighbour Sandra if she's got a job for me in her café. I tell her no way. I won't work in a café this summer. I hate serving customers! I also tell her that Jobs4u has lots of new jobs today. I start looking in the general work section. I also look at giveusajob.co.uk.

Day 12

Yes! I've got an interview! At last! It's a customer service job where I'll earn £600 a week. That's really good money. I don't mind[1]

[1] I don't mind (doing) *Es macht mir nichts aus (etwas zu tun)*

serving customers for £600 a week! But my interview is in less than two hours, so I need to get ready.

Day 12, later

That was a strange interview. I still don't know much about the job. This is what happened in the interview:

Interviewer – – Hi, Ewan. I'm Carla. Did you have any problem getting here today?
Me – – No, no problems, thank you.
Interviewer – – Well we are happy to have you in our team, Ewan.
Me – – Huh. I've got the job?
Interviewer – – (laughs) If you get the job … Now, as you know, the money's good. Do you have any questions?
Me – – Um … What exactly do I have to do?
Interviewer – – You will work with in a great team and earn lots of money. Anything else?
Me – – Um, er, no, I don't think so.
Interviewer – – Well, that's great! I think you're perfect for the job.
Me – – I am?
Interviewer – – Come in tomorrow, at 9 am.

Day 13

I arrive at the office at 9 and the interviewer (Carla) is there with a small group of people.
Carla – – Hello and welcome everyone! Please sit down.
(I find a chair.)
Carla – – You are all here today because you have been chosen for a very important and exciting job.
(Sounds good)
Carla – – You are hard-working, reliable people who want to be part of a great team.
(That's me!)
Carla – – That's why you have been chosen to be part of this amazing opportunity[1].
(Great!)
Carla – – For just £200 we can show you the easy way to earn £600 a week. For this small price we will give you everything you need to start …
(Huh? I have to pay them? – Er, no thanks. I'll keep my money and look for another job. Goodbye!)

Day 14

Back to the hunt.

Day 15

Mum says why don't I try a temp agency[2]. Brilliant! I need a temporary job and temp agencies give people temporary jobs. Why didn't I think of that!

[1] opportunity [ɒpəˈtjuːnəti] *Gelegenheit* [2] temp (=temporary) agency [ˈtemp eɪdʒənsi] *Zeitarbeitsfirma*

Day 17

Today I had an interview at a temp agency. The interview went a lot better than the last one. They don't have a job for me now but they think they'll have a suitable[1] job soon. And I don't have to pay them £200 first.

Day 21

I give up. I can't do it any more. I've heard nothing from the temp agency. I don't want to waste[2] any more time looking at Jobs4u. It's time to break[3] the rules!

Day 23

I've done it! I've got a job at last. I will spend my summer working at Sandra's café. I don't know why I didn't want to work there. It's a great job and the money's OK! It's good to know that dreams can come true, isn't it?

1 Understanding the text

Are these sentences true or false?

1. In the beginning, Ewan doesn't want to work in a café.
2. On Day 2, he starts looking in the general work section.
3. He checks his CV for spelling mistakes.
4. On Day 7, Ewan tries another website.
5. At the job interview on Day 12, Ewan finds out all about the customer service job.
6. On Day 13, Ewan leaves because he doesn't want to give Carla £200.
7. Ewan gets a job with a temp agency.
8. In the end, Ewan still doesn't want to work in a café.

2 Tips for job hunters

a) *What did Ewan do right? What did he do wrong?*

b) *Write three tips for people who want a summer job.*

3 Now you

Talk about your own experience of looking for a summer or part-time job.

– What kind of job did you want?
– What did you do to find a job?
– Did you get a job? Did you like it?

[1] suitable ['suːtəbl] *geeignet, passend* [2] (to) waste [weɪst] *verschwenden* [3] (to) break (rules) [breɪk] *(Regeln) brechen*

TF 5 Songs about work

Nine to Five
by Dolly Parton

Tumble outta bed and I stumble to the
(1) kitchen/bathroom
Pour myself a cup of ambition
Yawnin', stretchin', try to come to life
Jump in the shower and the blood starts pumpin'
Out on the (2) bus/streets the traffic starts jumpin'
And folks like me on the job from nine to five

Chorus:
Workin' nine to five
What a way to make a livin'
Barely[1] gettin' by[2]
It's all takin' and no (3) receivin'/givin'
They just use your mind
And they never give you credit[3]
It's enough to drive you
(4) Crazy/Mad if you let it

Nine to five, for service and devotion
You would think that I
Would deserve[4] a fair promotion[5]
Want to move ahead
But the (5) police/boss won't seem to let me
I swear sometimes that man is out to get me
Mmmmm ...

(...)

Nine to five, yeah
They got you where they want you
There's a better (6) life/job
And you think about it, don't you?
It's a (7) rich/poor man's game
No matter what they call it
And you spend your (8) time/life
Puttin' money in his wallet

Car Wash
by Norman Jesse Whitfield

You might not ever get (1), ha (come on)
Let me tell you it's (2) digging a ditch[6] (uh)
There ain't no telling who you might meet
A (3) or maybe a common thief (yeah)

Working at the car wash, oh, oh, yeah, yeah
At the car wash, yeah, ooh, yeah, yeah
At the car wash, sing it with me now
Working at the car wash yeah, whoo, ooh

Come (4) the work gets kind of (5) (come on)
This ain't no place to be if you're planning on
(6), uh, being a star
Let me tell you it's (7) cool, cool
And the boss don't mind (8) if you're acting like a fool[7]

Working at the car wash, ohh, yeah ...

always • being a star • better than • hard • movie star • rich • sometimes • summer

1 Understanding the songs

a) *Listen to the songs. For each song, complete the gaps (1–8) with the correct words or phrases.*

b) *Listen again. Then answer these questions for each song:*

1 What sort of job do you think the woman in the song does?
2 Does she like her job? Does she like her boss?

---

[1] barely ['beəli] *kaum* [2] (to) get by *(infml) durchkommen* [3] credit *hier: Anerkennung* [4] (to) deserve [dɪ'zɜːv] *verdienen*
[5] promotion [prə'məʊʃn] *Beförderung* [6] (to) dig a ditch [dɪɡ, dɪtʃ] *einen Graben ausheben* [7] fool [fuːl] *Narr, Idiot*

TF 6 A different sort of justice[1]

1 Crime in England and Wales: some facts and figures

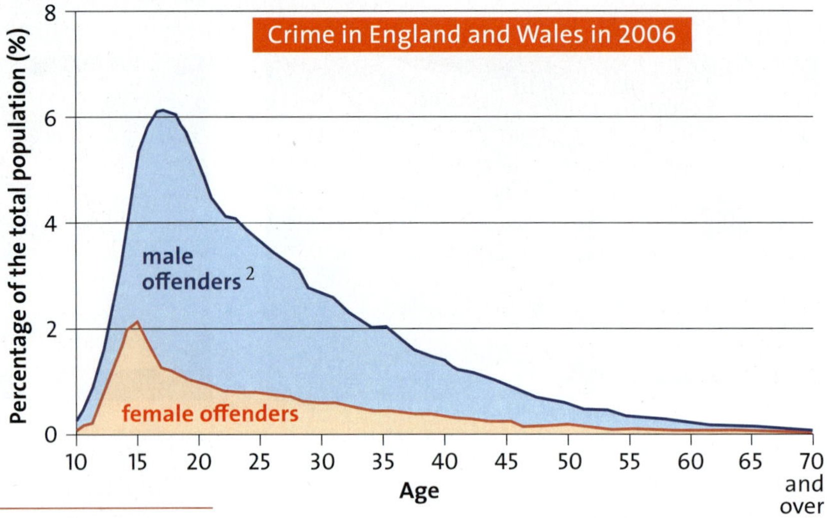

a) *Look at the chart. Complete the sentences below correctly.*

Activate your English

1. This chart gives information on the age of (offenders/victims).
2. The (red/blue) line shows males and the (red/blue) line shows females.
3. The number of female offenders (goes up/down) between the ages of 10 and 15.
4. After the age of 15 the number of female offenders (goes up/down).
5. The number of male offenders rises between the ages of (10/15) and (15/17).
6. After that the number of male offenders also (goes up/down).

b) *Are these statements true or false? Discuss with your partner.*

In England and Wales in 2006, ...

- women committed[3] fewer crimes than men.
- more teenagers committed crimes than any other age group.
- the number of 18 year-old male offenders was about twice as big as the number of 30 year-old male offenders.

2 Bus attack (Part 1)

Read this case study[4] of two young offenders in England.

One day two boys were throwing stones at the number 67 bus as it went past Gateway School. Some passengers were scared. 71 year-old Margaret Wilson was on the bus and a stone came through the window. Mrs Wilson was shocked and had a mild heart attack. The bus driver, Phil Saunders, stopped the bus and called an ambulance. Mrs Wilson was taken to hospital. Mr Saunders was shocked by what had happened. His bus company contacted the police.

[1] justice ['dʒʌstɪs] *Gerechtigkeit* [2] offender [ə'fendə] *Straftäter/in* [3] (to) commit [kə'mɪt] *(ein Verbrechen) begehen*
[4] case study ['keis stʌdi] *Fallstudie*

Sergeant Brian Yates, a police officer who worked with schools, went to Gateway School. He told the students about the attack and asked them to put a note in a box if they knew who the boys were. The notes in the box named two 15 year-old boys, Luke and Reece. After Sergeant Yates spoke to them, Luke and Reece said that they were guilty.

a) *Match the sentence halves correctly.*

1	Two boys threw stones ...	*a*	a mild heart attack.
2	A stone ...	*b*	told the students about the attack.
3	This shocked ...	*c*	an old lady.
4	She had ...	*d*	at the number 67 bus.
5	She was taken ...	*e*	if they knew who had thrown the stones.
6	A police officer ...	*f*	to hospital.
7	He asked students to write a note ...	*g*	went through the bus window.
8	Two boys, Luke and Reece, ...	*h*	were named.

b) *Why do you think the boys threw stones at the bus?*

they were bored • their friends did it • they thought it was funny • they didn't think it was dangerous • they wanted to shock people • ...

c) *What would happen to them if they were students at your school? Discuss.*

A: I think they'd have to see the head teacher. / say sorry to ... / go to court. /...
B: I agree. I think ...
C: Really? I don't agree. I think ...

3 Bus attack (Part 2)

Sergeant Yates didn't want Luke and Reece to go to court because they were so young and they had never been in trouble before. So the two boys went to a restorative justice conference[1] where they met the victims of the attack.

At the conference, Luke and Reece sat face to face with Mrs Wilson's daughter, the bus driver, people from the bus company and people from the police. Everyone talked about what had happened and agreed on what should happen next.

The conference had a very big effect on Luke and Reece.

'I'm sure Mum would be sad to see how

upset the boys are,' Mrs Wilson's daughter told the conference. 'And she'll be happy to hear that they've promised to make up for[2] what they've done.'

[1] restorative justice conference [rɪˌstɔːrətɪv ˈdʒʌstɪs ˌkɒnfərəns] *ein außergerichtliches Treffen von Täter/in, Opfer und Vermittler/in mit dem Ziel des Täter-Opfer-Ausgleichs* [2] (to) make up for sth. *etwas wieder gutmachen*

In the end, Luke and Reece agreed to go to the bus company every Saturday for six months to clean the buses. And they did. Their families reported that it had changed their behaviour. The two boys felt they had made up for what they had done and this made a big difference to them.

a) *Complete this chart to show how this case is 'different'.*

What would happen in a traditional case	What happened in this case
– The boys would go to court. – They wouldn't discuss what had happened with the victims. – A judge[1] would say what they must do. – They might go to prison for young offenders.	– *The boys went to a restorative justice conference.* – *They ...*

b) *How do you think Luke and Reece/Mrs Wilson felt ...*
– when the boys were throwing stones?
– before the conference?
– after the conference?

I think they/she felt ...

angry • disappointed • excited • glad • happy • nervous • scared • unhappy • shocked • upset • ...

4 Discussing the case

Discuss the case with your partner. The ideas in the box might help you.

A: I (don't) think the conference was a good idea in this case because ...
B: I (don't) agree because ...

– what they did was/wasn't very serious.
– they were too young/old enough to go to court.
– they hadn't been in trouble before.
– they probably will/won't get into trouble again.
– it is/isn't important to understand how the victims of a crime/the offenders feel.
– cleaning the buses for six months was/wasn't fair/too easy/a good idea.

► *SF Having a discussion (p. 141)*

SOCIAL STUDY SKILLS Case study

*Bei einer Fallstudie (**case study**) betrachtet man einen Fall zunächst **von außen**:*
– Wer ist betroffen? (Täter, Opfer, Zeugen, ...)
– Was ist genau passiert?
– Welche Lösungen und Folgen (z.B. für die Täter) gibt es?
– Was kann man aus diesem Fall lernen?
*Man kann einen Fall aber auch **von innen** betrachten:*
– Wie fühlen sich die Betroffenen?
– Wie hättest du dich verhalten?

[1] judge [dʒʌdʒ] *Richter(in)*

TF 7 **Famous** abridged and adapted from *Totally over you* by Mark Ravenhill

Before you read

How can someone become famous? Brainstorm with a partner and write down your ideas.

Someone can become famous if ... – they're a film star, a politician, ...
– they're good at sport, singing, ...

Now read the play.

CAST (all aged 14 to 16)

Girls:	**Boys:**
Kitty	Jake
Rochelle	Dan
Hannah	Tyson
Sinita	Framji
	Victor

An empty stage.
Kitty and Jake enter. Kitty is carrying a bag.

Kitty ___ Don't laugh, Jake, don't laugh at me. You mustn't laugh.

Jake ___ I won't.

Kitty ___ Even a little laugh and I'll stop.

Jake ___ I promise. Tell me. Tell me about your dream.

Kitty ___ OK. We're going to be celebrities[1]. You're going to see us everywhere. You'll see us on the front pages. You go to buy a can of coke – they'll have our faces on the side. Your screensaver, your desktop, your mobile's welcome screen – all of them will be me and Roche and H and Sin.

Pause. Then Jake laughs.

Kitty ___ Oh piss off[2], Jake. Just piss off.

Jake ___ I'm sorry, Kit. I just ... You know.

Kitty ___ What?

Jake ___ Look at us. This town, this school. It just seems such a fantasy.

Kitty ___ An ambition. That's the trouble with you, Jake. You don't want anything.

Jake ___ I want ...

Kitty ___ I don't want to see you any more.

Jake ___ What, you're ...?

Kitty ___ I'm ending this relationship. Here. Now. Goodbye.

Jake ___ No. Kit. Wait. You can't just walk away.

Kitty ___ Why not?

Jake ___ Because I love you.

Kitty ___ That's nice.

Jake ___ And you love me.

Kitty ___ Do I? Do I really, Jay? No. I don't need you any more.

Jake ___ Kitty, please.

Kitty ___ Goodbye. I'm not your girlfriend any more.

Rochelle enters.

Rochelle ___ Hi, guys.

Jake ___ What are you going to be?

Kitty ___ How do you mean?

Jake ___ What are you going to be?

Kitty ___ I told you, Jacob. Celebrities.

Jake ___ Are you going to be in a band?

Kitty ___ Maybe. I don't know.

Jake ___ Or act?

Kitty ___ Yeah. Could do.

Jake ___ Or model or present on MTV or –?

Kitty ___ Yeah, yeah, Jake...

Jake ___ Well – which one? What's going to make you famous?

Kitty ___ I don't know. I don't care. It doesn't matter.

Jake ___ You've got to have a talent.

Kitty ___ Of course, yeah.

Jake ___ And I hate to tell you this, girls, but you can't sing, you can't act, you're OK-looking, but you're not models ...

Kitty ___ We'll find a way.

Jake ___ You're dreaming, the pair of you.

Kitty ___ OK. You want to know? You want to know what's going to make us famous?

Jake ___ Yes. I want to know.

Kitty ___ OK. We're going to date[3] celebrities.

---

[1] celebrity [sə'lebrəti] *berühmte Persönlichkeit* [2] Piss off. [ˌpɪs_'ɒf] *(Vorsicht! Slang, vulgär) Hau ab!* [3] (to) date sb. [deɪt] *mit jm. (aus)gehen*

Rochelle That's right.

Jake Ha. Ha. Ha.

Jake exits[1].

Kitty Loser. We're going to show him.

Rochelle Maybe he's right, Kit. Maybe we're never going to make it.

Kitty No. You know what that horoscope said.

Rochelle I know.

Kitty 'Finish old relationships and prepare to live your dreams.' And that's exactly what we've got to do. Did you do it?

Rochelle Yeah. I did it just like you said. Only ...

Kitty I need you with me, Rochelle. We've got to stick together[2], you and me and H and Sin, we've got to be there for each other. OK?

Rochelle OK. Just ...

Kitty Yeah?

Rochelle Dan cried. When I said, 'I don't want to be your girlfriend any more,' he started to cry. And I wanted to say, 'Dan, Dan. Stop. I didn't mean it. I still love you.'

Kitty But you didn't.

Rochelle No, Kit. I didn't.

Kitty You had to do it, Roche.

Hannah enters.

Hannah Oh God. I feel like such a bitch[3]. I said, 'Tyson, this is the end.' He just said: 'Why? Why? Why?' Again and again. 'Why? Why? Why?'

Sinita enters, crying.

Sinita I hate you, Kitty. I love Framji, I do. And now. I finished with him. *(She cries.)*

Rochelle Come on, babe.

Sinita What am I going to do without him?

Kitty Do without him? Do without him? You know what you're going to do without him. Same as me without Jay, same as Roche without Dan, same as H without Ty. Be a celebrity.

Sinita And are you sure about that, Kit?

Kitty Yes of course. Totally sure. I know this is hard. But think of the reward[4]. Think of waking up in this totally fantastic house next to your totally fantastic boyfriend. Today was hard. I know that, girls. But now it's time, time to live your dreams. Are we sticking together, girls? Are we sistas?

Rochelle / *Hannah* / *Sinita* *(together)* Yeah.

Kitty Then come on. See what our horoscopes say today.

Kitty takes magazines from her bag and hands them round.

Kitty OK. Horoscope time. Oh my God. Oh my God. Look at this. 'A stranger[5] will show you the way to future happiness today.' What does that mean? Keep your eyes open for a stranger, girls.

Kitty, Rochelle, Hannah and Sinita exit. Jake and Victor enter.

Jake Victor. Will you stop following me? I want to be alone.

Victor But we said we'd go to a movie.

Jake Vic. I want to be by myself. Please.

Victor But – why?

Jake Kit finished with me.

Victor No way.

Jake Yeah. She chucked[6] me. So ...

Victor I'm sorry.

Jake And I just want to go into my room and be alone.

Dan enters.

Dan I don't believe it. I just don't believe it. Roche finished with me.

Jake She chucked you?

Dan Just sat down and said: 'I don't want to see you any more. We're finished. Over.' She wants to be a celebrity, Jay.

Jake Oh my God.

---

[1] (to) exit ['eksɪt] *hinausgehen; von der Bühne abgehen* [2] (to) stick together *(infml) zusammenhalten* [3] bitch [bɪtʃ] *(Vorsicht! Slang, abwertend) Schlampe, Miststück* [4] reward [rɪ'wɔːd] *Belohnung* [5] stranger ['streɪndʒə] *Fremde(r)* [6] (to) chuck sb. [tʃʌk] *mit jm. Schluss machen*

Tyson enters.

Tyson Bitch. Bitch. Bitch.

Jake What's that, Ty?

Tyson Hannah. What a freaking bitch. Chucked me. I've never been chucked. Never.

Jake Did she say she wanted to be ...?

Tyson A celebrity. Can you believe that? And then she chucked me. I'm so angry.

Framji enters.

Framji Guys. You'll never guess. Sin finished with me.

Jake We know. Same for all of us, Fram. Me and Kit. Dan and Roche. H and Ty. You and Sin. We've all been chucked.

Framji But – they must have planned this.

Jake That's right.

Framji I don't believe it. What a bitch.

Tyson Yeah. Total bitches. All of them.

Kitty, Rochelle, Hannah and Sinita enter.

Kitty Oh, hi. We didn't know you were here.

Jake Yeah. That's right. We're here.

Hannah We're looking for a stranger. To show the way to future happiness.

Tyson Right.

Rochelle You seen a stranger?

Dan No. Don't think so. No.

Kitty Come on, girls. They're not going to help us.

Kitty, Rochelle, Hannah and Sinita exit.

Jake We need to show them, guys.

Tyson Yeah. We need to punish[1] them.

Dan We need to hurt them.

Framji To teach them a lesson.

Jake To show them how stupid they are.

Dan But how?

Victor Maybe if I ...?

Dan What's the best way to make them suffer[2]?

Victor Can I ...? I've got an idea.

Tyson Victor. You don't know about girls.

Framji They're coming back.

Tyson Hide.

Victor Guys. I'm going to show you ... Guys.

Jack, Dan, Tyson and Framji hide.
Kitty, Rochelle, Hannah and Sinita enter.
Victor covers his face.

Victor The future. I see the future.

Rochelle Ugh. Look. A loony[3].

Sinita A loony homeless person.

Hannah Ugh. They don't wash. And they really smell.

Sinita And they get really aggressive if you don't give them money.

Rochelle Well, I'm not giving him anything.

Kitty Girls. Listen for a moment. Just listen to what he's saying.

Victor The future. The future. I see the future.

Kitty Who are you?

Hannah Kit, let's go.

Kitty No, no. We've got to talk to him.

Victor I know you. I know you. I know you. I know you.

Kitty Me?

Victor Everybody knows you.

Kitty In the future.

Victor You are famous in the future.

Kitty Oh my God. That's amazing.

Victor Your picture is everywhere in the future.

Kitty I knew it. I knew I was right.

Victor You are a line of clothes, a cola drink, a fitness video, a salad dressing, a doll, a video game, a mouse pad, a car sticker, a newspaper column, a talkshow, the most hits in a day on AOL, a remix, beauty tips, a diet plan, a chain of restaurants, a sex symbol, role-model superstar. Oh, yes, I know you. In the future I know you. In the future everybody knows you.

Kitty And Roche and H and Sin as well?

Victor And Roche and H and Sin as well.

---

1 ´(to) punish ['pʌnɪʃ] *bestrafen* 2 (to) suffer ['sʌfə] *leiden* 3 loony ['lu:i] *Irre(r), Verrückte(r)*

Rochelle Oh, my God.
Hannah Oh, my God.
Sinita Amazing.
Victor The bedrooms that you live in now will be museums – a place for all your fans to come. Coaches will stop outside your school: 'That's the place. That's where she studied.'
Rochelle That is so cool.
Sinita What will we be famous for?
Victor Do you know the band 'Awesome'?
Sinita No.
Victor Four boys. The best voices, best dance routines. Best songs. The four most famous faces of the future.
Kitty And we're ...
Victor You date them. And you're famous.
Hannah And when do we meet them? Where do we meet them?
Victor You've already met them.
Kitty We have?
Victor They are here in your school right now. 'Awesome' are among you. They are Jake and Dan and Ty and Framji.
Sinita But we just ... Oh no ...
Victor Yes?
Rochelle We just chucked them.
Victor You ...? Oh no.
Kitty Oh my God!

Kitty, Rochelle, Hannah, Sinita exit.

Working with the text

1 Understanding the play

Which headline fits the play best? Agree with a partner. Then discuss your choice with another pair.

Celebrities at local high school

Local girls dump boyfriends for their dreams

Local girls become famous

Students at local high school in successful new band

2 Understanding the details

Match the sentence halves to make a summary.

1 Kitty tells Jake that she is dumping him because ...
2 The real reason Kitty dumps Jake is that a ...
3 The other girls are upset because ...
4 But Kitty says that it is time for them ...
5 The second horoscope says that ...
6 The boys are upset because ...
7 They want to show the girls that ...
8 Victor says that ...
9 He tells the girls that ...
10 In the end, the girls are ...

a they didn't want to dump their boyfriends.
b to live their dreams.
c the boys will be famous in the future.
d the girls have dumped them.
e she doesn't need him any more.
f horoscope said she should do it.
g a stranger will show them the future.
h they were wrong to dump them.
i sorry that they dumped the boys.
j he can see the future.

3 Your reactions to the play

Talk to a partner. Say what you think of the play.

– I think it was ...
– The best bit was when ...

annoying • boring • clever • funny • interesting • realistic • sad • silly • ...

TF 8 India

1 India FAQ[1]

Is Mumbai the capital of India?
No. Mumbai is India's biggest city, but it's not the capital. The capital of India is New Delhi.

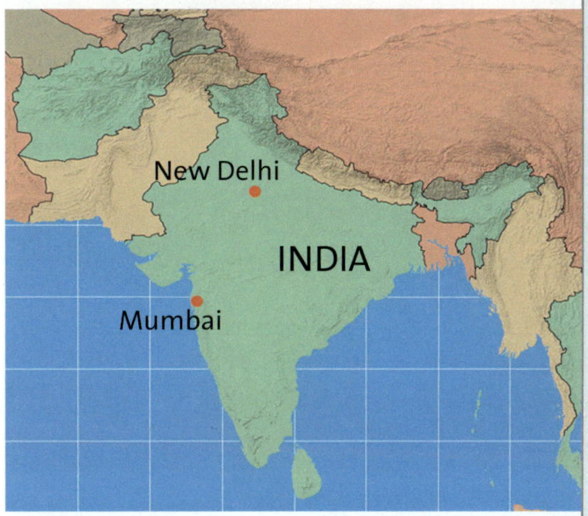

Does everyone in India speak English?
Not everyone speaks English. The main languages in India are Hindi and English, but there are over 20 other languages in India.

Why is English such an important language in India?
India was a British colony for nearly 200 years and so English became the language of government, education and business in India.
India won independence[2] from Britain in 1947, but English is still important, especially[3] in the cities. Many schools teach all school subjects in English and it is the main language spoken by office workers.
In a country with so many different languages, English is often used so that people can understand each other.

Why is Gandhi such an important person in India?
Mahatma Gandhi was born in India in 1869 and died in 1948. He spent most of his life fighting for India's independence from Britain. He won freedom[4] for his country without using violence[5]. He is known as the 'Father of India'.
Gandhi's ideas were important to Martin Luther King Jr, in the civil rights[6] movement in the US and Nelson Mandela in the fight against apartheid[7] in South Africa.

> *What do you think is the most interesting thing about India on this page?*
– I think the most surprising thing is that …
– I think it's more interesting that …

[1] FAQ (Abkürzung für 'frequently asked questions') *häufig gestellte Fragen* [2] independence [ˌɪndɪ'pendəns] *Unabhängigkeit* [3] especially [ɪ'speʃəli] *besonders, vor allem* [4] freedom ['fri:dəm] *Freiheit* [5] violence ['vaɪələns] *Gewalt* [6] civil rights [ˌsɪvl 'raɪts] *Bürgerrechte* [7] apartheid ['əpa:taɪt] *Apartheid (bis 1994 Trennung von Schwarzen und Weißen in Südafrika)*

2 BOLLYWOOD

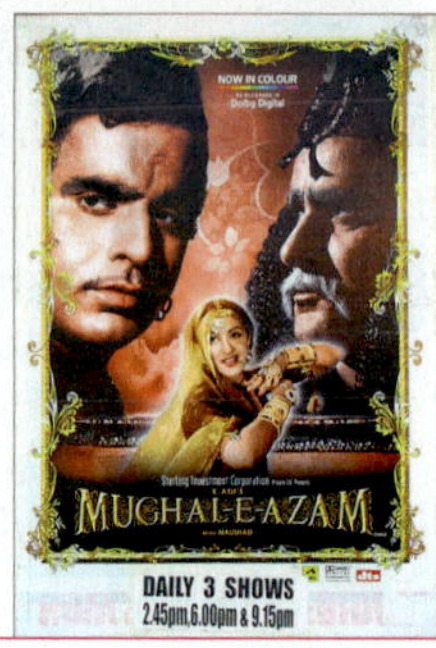

Bollywood, Bombay's Hindi language film industry, is the largest film producer in India and one of the largest in the world.

It seems that everyone in India loves a good film. Indians went to the cinema 3.9 billion times in 2007. In fact, India makes more films than Hollywood. Entertainment Weekly reported that more than 900 films are produced every year. That's more than two films every day.

Bollywood films are popular outside India too, especially in countries with a big Asian population, like Malaysia and Singapore, England, Canada, South Africa, Australia and the US.

A typical Bollywood movie is always spectacular[1] and full of colour and energy.

It always has a good-looking guy and a good-looking girl, singing and dancing, romance and drama. The poor guy always wins against the rich bad guy and there is always a happy ending.

'When people in India go to the cinema they want to forget what is happening in their real lives. They want to escape and enjoy themselves,' says Kishore Lulla, Chief Executive of Bollywood film company Eros International.

a) *Read the text and find important facts about Bollywood.*

b) *With a partner agree on the four most important facts and share them with the class.*

3 VIEWING A shop in Mumbai

a) *Are these sentences right or wrong?*

1 The film clip is about a DVD shop.
2 The owner says it is a business plus hobby.
3 All his customers are from India.

b) *Do you know any of the Bollywood stars?*

c) *How have the posters changed since the early days of Bollywood?*

The older/newer posters ...
- have actors wearing western/traditional clothes.
- are handpainted/more modern/more romantic/...

[1] spectacular [spek'tækjələ]

TF 9 South Africa

1 South Africa FAQ[1]

Is Johannesburg the capital of South Africa?
No. Johannesburg is South Africa's biggest city, but it isn't the capital. There are three capitals: Bloemfontein, Cape Town and Pretoria. Why are there three capitals? It goes back to 1910 when different areas came together to make a union[2], but they couldn't agree where the capital should be.

Which ethnic[3] groups make up South Africa's population today?
South Africa is called 'The Rainbow[4] Nation' because there are so many different groups of people. The population of about 49 million is made up of 79.2 % African, 9.2 % White, 8.9 % Coloured[5] and 2.5 % Asian

How long have there been white people in South Africa?
The ancestors of some of today's white South Africans arrived in the 17th and 18th centuries. They came from the Netherlands, France, Britain and Germany. Many more Europeans arrived after gold was discovered in the 19th century.

Do most people speak English in South Africa?
There are eleven official languages in South Africa: Zulu, Xhosa, Afrikaans, Pedi, English, Tswana, Sotho, Tsonga, Swati, Venda and Ndebele. The number of people whose first language is English is quite small (about 8 % of the population) but a lot of people speak English as a second or third language. Today, English is seen as a very important international language and in South Africa it is the language that is most often used in newspapers, on TV, radio and websites. It is also used in business and politics.

Why is Nelson Mandela such an important person in South Africa?
Nelson Mandela was born in 1918. He spent many years in prison because he fought against apartheid in South Africa. In 1994 he became the country's first black president. A lot of people thought there would be terrible hatred[6] and violence[7] in South Africa when apartheid ended. Nelson Mandela worked hard to bring together all the different groups in the country and to build peace[8] and democracy[9].

Read the South Africa FAQ on this page and the India FAQ on page 121. Are these sentences right or wrong?

1. In both countries many different languages are spoken.
2. English is a very important language in India, but it is not so important in South Africa.
3. Johannesburg and Mumbai are the capitals and the biggest cities in their countries.
4. Both Nelson Mandela and Gandhi are important people in their countries because they fought for indepedence from Britain.

---

[1] FAQ *(Abkürzung für 'frequently asked questions') häufig gestellte Fragen* [2] union ['ju:niən] *Union, Vereinigung* [3] ethnic ['eθnɪk] *ethnisch, Volks-* [4] rainbow ['reɪnbəʊ] *Regenbogen* [5] Coloured *(in Südafrika) Mensch mit schwarzen und weißen Vorfahren* [6] hatred ['heɪtrɪd] *Hass* [7] violence ['vaɪələns] *Gewalt* [8] peace [pi:s] *Frieden* [9] democracy [dɪ'mɒkrəsi] *Demokratie*

2 Nelson Mandela: A South African hero

Nelson Mandela's story began on 18th July 1918 in a village in the Eastern Cape, South Africa. In 1925 he started primary school. A school teacher gave him the name 'Nelson'.

When he was a young man, he ran away to Johannesburg to look for a job because he didn't want to marry the girl that had been chosen for him. In Johannesburg he found that black people didn't have the same rights as white people. They had to have a pass to move around in their own country.

He became a lawyer[2] and in 1952 he opened his own law office and worked for equal rights[3] for black people. He also fought against apartheid and was arrested[4] many times between 1952 and 1963.

[1] separation of the races [sepəˈreɪʃn] *Rassentrennung* [2] lawyer [ˈlɔːjə] *Rechtsanwalt* [3] equal rights [ˈiːkwəl] *Gleichberechtigung*
[4] (to) arrest [əˈrest] *verhaften*

He and others who fought against apartheid were sent to prison for life.

While he was in prison he wasn't forgotten. People all over the world remembered Mandela. They wanted him to be free and they wanted apartheid to end in South Africa. Then at last ...

Nelson Mandela became the first black president of South Africa in 1994. He stepped down[1] as president in 1999, but he didn't stop working for equal rights and for better education and health care in South Africa.

From a comic on www.worldschildrensprize.org by Magnus Bergmar and Jan-Åke Winvist

a) *Collect information from the comic and make a fact file or a timeline about Nelson Mandela.*

b) *Do some research on the internet and add three more pieces of information to your fact file or timeline.*

[1] (to) step down *zurücktreten*

TF 10 Project: An English-speaking city

Which city?

During the last five years, your English book has taken you to lots of big cities where English is the main language: Atlanta, Bristol, Johannesburg, London, Los Angeles, Mumbai, San Francisco, Sydney, Toronto. Which of these cities would you like know more about? Or is there another English-speaking city that you would like to find out about?

Sydney

Los Angeles

Toronto

London

What makes the city special?

- What is there to do and see?
- Are there any songs or poems about the city?
- Are there any special dishes to eat?
- What's the weather like?
- What kind of sports events and teams are there?
- What famous people are connected with the city?

Would you like to ...

... try some delicious food in Singapore?

... go shopping in Hong Kong?

... see the sights of Dublin?

Your city project

1 *Suche dir andere, die die gleiche Stadt gewählt haben wie du – oder arbeite allein.*
2 *Wenn ihr in einer Gruppe arbeitet, teilt die Aufgaben untereinander auf.*
3 *Überlegt, wie ihr eure Informationen interessant präsentieren könnt. In den Boxen rechts findet ihr ein paar Vorschläge.*
4 *Präsentiert euer Projekt. Ihr könnt eine Computerpräsentation machen, Poster aufhängen, Handouts verteilen, ...*
5 *Schaut euch die anderen Präsentationen an und beurteilt sie.*

Create a booklet
Put together a mix of your own writing, newspaper articles, photos, songs, maps... For each thing, explain why you chose it.

Design a quiz
Write a good mix of question types (A/B/C or D, true/false, yes/no, who/what/when/where/why, ...) and remember to write an answer key.

Plan a two-day visit to the city
How will you get from the airport to the city centre? Where will you stay? What sights will you visit? What will you eat?

► *SF Internet research; Giving a presentation; Using visual materials with a presentation (pp. 131–132)*

Skills File – Inhalt

Im **Skills File** findest du Hinweise zu Arbeits- und Lerntechniken. Was du in den Skills-Kästen der Units gelernt hast, wird hier näher erläutert.

Was du bereits aus Band 4 von English G 21 kennst, ist mit **REVISION** gekennzeichnet, z. B.
– **REVISION Describing pictures**, Seite 128
– **REVISION Giving a presentation**, Seite 132.

Viele neue Hinweise helfen dir bei der Arbeit mit Hör- und Lesetexten, beim Sprechen, beim Schreiben von eigenen Texten, bei der Sprachmittlung und beim Lernen von Methoden.

Manchmal gibt es auch Aufgaben dazu.

STUDY AND LANGUAGE SKILLS

SF REVISION Learning words

Worauf solltest du beim Lernen und Wiederholen von Vokabeln achten?

- Lerne immer 7–10 Vokabeln auf einmal.
- Lerne neue und wiederhole alte Vokabeln regelmäßig – am besten jeden Tag 5–10 Minuten.
- Lerne mit jemandem zusammen. Fragt euch gegenseitig ab.
- Schreib die neuen Wörter immer auch auf und überprüfe die Schreibweise mithilfe des *Dictionary* oder *Vocabulary*.

Wie kannst du Wörter besser behalten?

Wörter kannst du besser behalten, wenn du sie in Wortgruppen sammelst und ordnest:

- **Gegensatzpaare** sammeln, z. B. **alive ◂▸ dead**, **majority ◂▸ minority**, **forget ◂▸ remember**
- Wörter mit **gleicher Bedeutung** sammeln, z. B. **(to) train – (to) practise**
- Wörter in **Wortfamilien** sammeln, z. B. **(to) dance**, **dance**, **dancer**, **dancing lessons**; **friend**, **boyfriend**, **girlfriend**, **friendly**, **unfriendly, ...**
- Wörter in **Wortnetzen** *(networks)* sammeln und ordnen.

SF REVISION Describing pictures

Wie kann ich Bilder beschreiben?

- Um zu sagen, wo genau etwas abgebildet ist, benutze:
  at the top/bottom • in the foreground/background • in the middle • on the left/right
- Diese Präpositionen sind auch hilfreich:
  behind • between • in front of • next to • under
- Um zu beschreiben, was die Personen auf dem Bild tun, benutze das **present progressive**.
  The girl is standing next to a woman.

Wie kann ich beschreiben, was die Personen fühlen?

Oft sollst du dich in eine Person auf einem Foto hineinversetzen und beschreiben, was sie fühlt oder denkt. Schau dir das Foto genau an und nimm dir Zeit, dir die Situation vorzustellen. Beim Formulieren helfen dir *phrases* wie:
Maybe the woman/man in the photo feels ... /is thinking about ... •
I think he/she feels/wants to/...

SF REVISION Check yourself

How am I doing?

Damit du weißt, in welchen Bereichen des Englischen du noch Schwächen hast und welche du schon beherrschst, solltest du dich immer wieder selbst überprüfen. Das kannst du auf unterschiedlichen Wegen tun. Eine Reihe von Tipps kennst du vermutlich schon.
Du kannst dich auch nach jeder Unit mithilfe der *How am I doing*-Seiten selbst überprüfen, die du schon aus Band 3 kennst. Dabei gehst du wie folgt vor:

1. Du machst die einzelnen Aufgaben und überprüfst deine Ergebnisse.
2. Dann schaust du dir die Bereiche, in denen du Fehler gemacht hast, nochmal an. Halte dich dabei an die Hinweise in der Spalte *Find out more*.
3. Nun übst du gezielt diese Bereiche. Dazu schaust du in der Spalte *Exercises* nach, wo du im Englischbuch und *Workbook* Übungen dazu findest.
4. Nach einiger Zeit machst du die Aufgaben in *How am I doing?* noch einmal und vergleichst die Lösungen mit deinen Ergebnissen vom ersten Mal.

Die Arbeit mit einer persönlichen Fehlerliste

Führe eine Liste der Fehler, die du oft machst, und nutze sie beim Schreiben von Texten als persönliche Checkliste. Hefte diese Listen in deinem Englischordner ab oder lege dir dafür ein extra Heft an (z.B. in DIN-A5).
Das Heft kannst du z.B. nach folgenden Schwerpunkten unterteilen:

1. Drittel: *Words* 2. Drittel: *Grammar* 3. Drittel: *Spelling*

Dann untersuchst du deine Klassenarbeiten und andere schriftliche Arbeiten auf deine Fehlerquellen hin. Dein/e Englischlehrer/in zeigt durch Abkürzungen am Rand, was für eine Art Fehler du gemacht hast.

WORDS

Wrong	*Correct*	*REMEMBER*
He goes to school ~~with the~~ bus.	*He goes to school by bus.*	*mit dem Bus fahren – go by bus*
We've got a ~~strong~~ teacher.	*We've got a strict teacher.*	*Nicht verwechseln! streng – strict / strong – stark*
I climbed ~~on~~ a tree.	*I climbed a tree.*	*auf einen Baum klettern – climb a tree*

Tipp

- Ergänze das Heft jedes Mal, wenn du eine Klassenarbeit oder einen Text von deinem Lehrer/deiner Lehrerin zurückbekommen oder wenn du eine *How am I doing*-Seite bearbeitet hast.
- Überprüfe, ob du bestimmte Fehler immer wieder machst. Wenn ja, such dafür Übungen in deinem Englischbuch, deinem *Workbook*, deinem *e-Workbook* oder frag deinen Lehrer/deine Lehrerin nach Übungen.
- Schau dir vor jeder Klassenarbeit die Fehler an, die du oft machst.
- Mach dir mithilfe des Grammatikteils die Regeln noch einmal bewusst, die dir besonders schwerfallen.

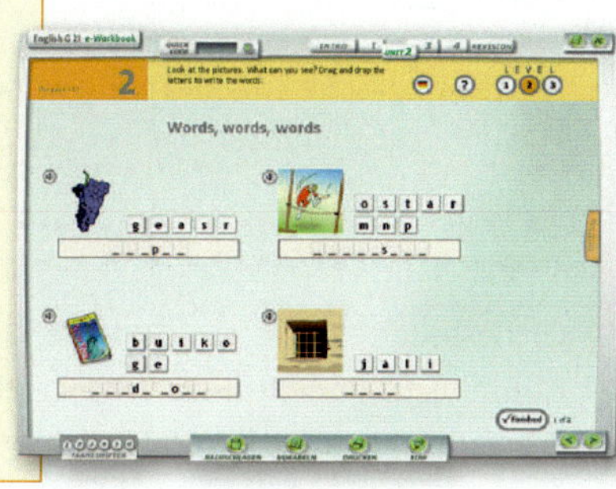

SF REVISION Using a bilingual dictionary

Wann brauche ich ein zweisprachiges Wörterbuch?

Du verstehst einen Text nicht, weil er zu viele Wörter enthält, die dir unbekannt sind, und die Worterschließungstechniken (▸ *SF Working out the meaning of words, p. 136*) helfen dir nicht weiter?
Du sollst einen Text auf Englisch schreiben, und dir fehlt das eine oder andere Wort, um deine Ideen auszudrücken? Du willst z. B. sagen, die Geschichte *In the outback* (S. 20–24) dreht sich um Bill und Colm und Bills Hund Rusty, aber du kennst das englische Wort für „drehen" nicht?
In jedem Fall hilft dir ein zweisprachiges Wörterbuch.

Wie benutze ich ein zweisprachiges Wörterbuch?

- Die **Leitwörter** oben auf der Seite helfen dir, schneller zu finden, was du suchst. Auf der linken Seite steht das erste Stichwort, auf der rechten Seite das letzte Stichwort der Doppelseite.
- Drehen ist das **Stichwort**. Alle Stichwörter sind alphabetisch geordnet: d vor e, da vor de und dre vor dri usw.
- Die **kursiv gedruckten** Hinweise helfen dir, die für deinen Text passende Bedeutung zu finden.
- Die **Ziffern** 1, 2 usw. zeigen, dass ein Stichwort mehrere ganz verschiedene Bedeutungen hat.
- **Beispielsätze** und **Redewendungen** sind dem Stichwort zugeordnet. In den Beispielsätzen und Redewendungen ersetzt eine **Tilde** (~) das Stichwort.
- Im englisch-deutschen Teil der meisten Wörterbücher findest du außerdem Hinweise auf **unregelmäßige Verbformen**, auf die **Steigerungsformen der Adjektive** und Ähnliches.
- Die **Lautschrift** gibt Auskunft darüber, wie das Wort ausgesprochen und betont wird. (→ *English sounds, p. 203*)

Dr.

Dr. (*Abk. für* ***Doktor***) Dr., Doctor
Drache dragon
Drachen *Papierdrachen* kite; *Fluggerät* hang glider

Drehbuch screenplay, script
drehen 1 *Verb mit Obj* turn; *Film* shoot*; *Zigarette* roll **2:** ***sich ~*** turn; *schnell* spin*; ***sich ~ um*** *übertragen* be* about
Drehkreuz turnstile; **Drehorgel** barrel organ ['ɔːgən]; **Drehort** location; **Drehstuhl** swivel chair; **Drehtür** revolving door
Drehung turn; *um eine Achse* rotation
Drehzahl (number of) revolutions *Pl od.* revs *Pl*
Drehzahlmesser rev counter
drei three
Drei three; *Note etwa* C; ***ich habe eine ~ geschrieben*** I got a C
dreidimensional 1 *Adj* three-dimensional **2** *Adv*: ***etwas ~ darstellen*** depict sth. three-dimensionally; **Dreieck** triangle ['traɪæŋgl]; **dreieckig** triangular [traɪ'æŋgjʊlə]

Bei kniffligen Wörtern gibt es in vielen Wörterbüchern **Info-Boxes**, in denen dir mehr Hilfen und Hinweise gegeben werden, hier z.B. für das deutsche Wort „bringen".

bringen

bring (**herbringen; mitbringen**) wird nur verwendet, wenn jemand oder etwas zum Ort des Sprechers oder Hörers gebracht wird:

Schön, dass du zu meiner Party	I'm glad you can come to my party. Can

take (**weg-, hinbringen; mitnehmen**) wird verwendet, wenn jemand oder etwas woanders hingebracht oder mitgenommen wird:

Kannst du morgen deinen Bruder zur Schule bringen?	Can you take your brother to school tomorrow?

Welche englische Entsprechung von **drehen** brauchst du in diesen Sätzen?
1. She's a good dancer, she loves to ... round and round as fast as she can.
2. Lots of Hollywood stars come to Berlin to ... their films here.

Tipp

Nimm nicht einfach die erste Übersetzung, die dir angeboten wird! Lies den Wörterbucheintrag, bis du die richtige Übersetzung gefunden hast.

REVISION Internet research

Wie kann ich das Internet zur Recherche nutzen?

Find some information about the Flying Doctor Service in Australia – so oder so ähnlich lauten Aufgaben, die dir oft als Hausaufgabe gestellt werden. Wenn du nun nach Informationen suchst, dann ist das Internet ist eine wichtige Quelle. Aber manchmal findest du dort so viele Informationen, dass du schnell den Überblick verlierst. Diese Tipps sollen dir helfen, damit du nicht im *world wide web* verloren gehst.

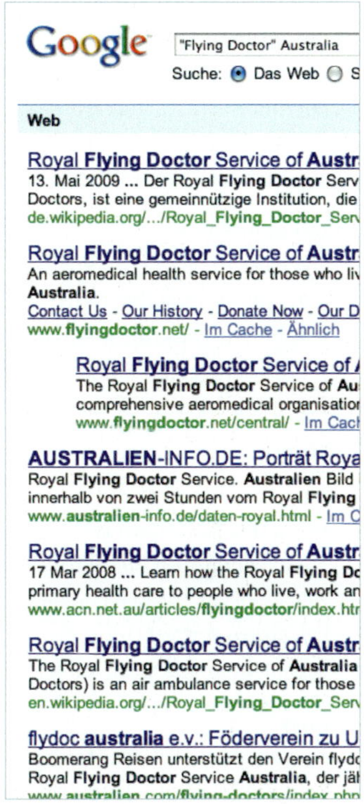

- Bevor du ins Internet gehst, mach dir eine Liste mit Schlüsselwörtern (**key words**) zu deinem Thema: *Australia, flying, doctor, ...*
- Überlege, welches Schlüsselwort oder welche Kombination von Schlüsselwörtern am besten sein könnte:
  „Flying Doctor" Australia oder **Flying+Doctor+Australia**
- Wenn du dir zunächst einen Überblick verschaffen willst, kannst du auch ein Nachschlagewerk im Internet anklicken:
  www.infoplease.com **www.en.wikipedia.org**
  Manchmal gibt es dort auch Links, die dir weiterhelfen können.
- Suchmaschinen (wie z.B. *Google, Altavista* oder *Yahoo*) helfen dir, Websites zu deinem Thema zu finden. Verwende eine Suchmaschine und gib deine Schlüsselwörter in das Suchfenster ein.
- Wenn die angezeigten Websites dir nicht helfen oder zu umfangreich sind, versuch es noch einmal, indem du deine Schlüsselwörter präzisierst.

Tipp

- Beachte: Nicht alles, was im Internet steht, ist richtig! Daher solltest du immer mehr als eine Website anschauen, um sicherzugehen, dass die Informationen stimmen.
- Suche Antworten auf die **5 Ws** (**who**, **what**, **where**, **when**, **why**).
- Bei englischen Quellen musst du nicht jedes Wort auf einer Website verstehen. Konzentrier dich auf das Wesentliche. Scanne den Text gezielt nach Informationen (**key words**), die du brauchst (▸ *Reading course S. 136*).
- Schreib die Quellen nicht wortwörtlich ab, sondern mach dir Notizen.

Wo kann ich noch Informationen finden?

Neben dem Internet gibt es natürlich weitere Quellen, wo du Informationen zu deinem Thema findest, z.B. in einem Lexikon, Atlas, Wörterbuch, Schulbuch oder auch in Zeitschriften oder Zeitungen. Auch CDs und DVDs sind mögliche Quellen. Benutze auch möglichst englische Quellen, das kann dir beim Ausformulieren deines englischen Textes helfen.

- Internet/Lexikon: alle Wissensgebiete, wichtige Personen und Ereignisse
- Atlas: geografische und politische Übersichten, Städte, Flüsse
- Wörterbücher: Rechtschreibung und Bedeutung von Wörtern
- Schulbücher: verschiedene Wissensgebiete
- Zeitungen/Zeitschriften: aktuelle Informationen zu allen Themenbereichen

SF REVISION Giving a presentation

Wie mache ich eine gute Präsentation?

Vorbereitung

- Schreib die wichtigsten Gedanken in Stichworten auf, z.B. auf nummerierte Karteikarten oder in der Mindmap.
- Übe deine Präsentation zu Hause vor einem Spiegel. Sprich laut, deutlich und langsam und mach Pausen an geeigneten Stellen.

Folien oder Poster

- Overhead-Folien oder Poster sind gut, um
  - zu zeigen, wie dein Vortrag aufgebaut ist
  - Tabellen, Diagramme usw. für alle lesbar zu präsentieren
  - die wichtigsten Punkte zusammenzufassen.
- Schreib groß und für alle gut lesbar.

Durchführung

- Bevor du beginnst, sortiere deine Vortragskarten.
- Häng das Poster auf oder leg deine Folie auf den ausgeschalteten Projektor oder bereite den Beamer vor.
- Warte, bis es ruhig ist. Schau die Zuhörer an.
- Erkläre zu Anfang, worüber du sprechen wirst. Lies nicht von deinen Karten ab, sondern sprich frei.

Schluss

- Beende deinen Präsentation mit einem abschließenden Satz.
- Frag die Zuhörenden, ob sie Fragen haben. Bedanke dich fürs Zuhören.

Ausführlichere sprachliche Hilfen für Präsentationen findest unter:
▸ *Giving a presentation – useful phrases (p. 141)*

SF Using visual materials with a presentation ▸ *Unit 4, Part C (p. 84)*

Wofür sind visuelle Materialien gut?

Deine Zuhörer/innen werden deinem Vortrag mit mehr Aufmerksamkeit folgen. Sie können sich viel mehr merken, wenn du nicht nur sprichst, sondern ihnen auch etwas zum Anschauen bietest (Visualisierungen). Das können z.B. Fotos, Cartoons, Landkarten, Zeitleisten, Diagramme, Poster oder Filmausschnitte sein.

Was muss ich bei visuellen Materialien beachten?

Vorbereitung

- Das Gerüst deines Vortrags sollte stehen, bevor du anfängst, dir darüber Gedanken zu machen, welche Visualisierungen gut passen könnten.
- Diagramme und Tabellen sind gut, um Zahlen zu verdeutlichen; Zeitleisten sind gut, um eine Entwicklung zu zeigen; Fotos und Cartoons sind gut, wenn man seinen Vortrag auflockern will.

Durchführung

- Bezieh deine visuellen Materialien in deinen Vortrag ein, um etwas zu veranschaulichen, aber lies nicht einfach von der Folie etc. ab.

SF Talking about charts

▸ *Unit 1, Part A (p. 10)*

Welche Informationen kann ich Diagrammen (charts) entnehmen?

Diagramme stellen statistische Vergleiche zwischen mindestens zwei Dingen dar. Es werden entweder absolute Zahlen oder Prozentsätze miteinander verglichen.

Welche unterschiedlichen Formen von Diagrammen gibt es?

Zwei sehr häufige Formen von Diagrammen sind die Säulendiagramme und die Kreis- oder Tortendiagramme.

- **Säulendiagramme (bar charts)** beschreiben häufig die Anzahl oder Größe von zwei oder mehr Dingen.
- **Kreis- oder Tortendiagramme (pie charts)** geben einen schnellen Überblick über die prozentuale Verteilung.

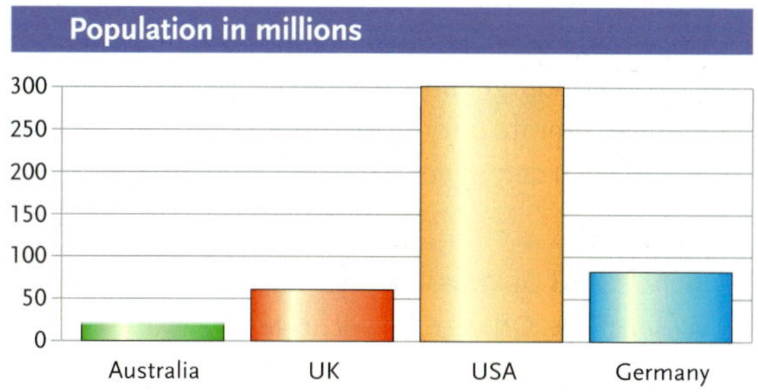

Wie kann ich beschreiben, was die Diagramme darstellen?

Um ein Diagramm zu beschreiben, solltest du folgende Fragen beantworten:

- **What is the chart about?**
  This chart is about ...
- **What does the chart compare or show?**
  The chart compares the size/number of ... •
  It shows the different ...
- **What does the chart tell you? What information does it give you?**
  ... has the largest/second largest •
  ... is (much) bigger/smaller than ... •
  ... are almost/nearly the same ... •
  The chart tells us ... • So ...

Wenn vorhanden, solltest du Aussagen über den Zeitraum der Statistik ergänzen:
The chart is about the years ...

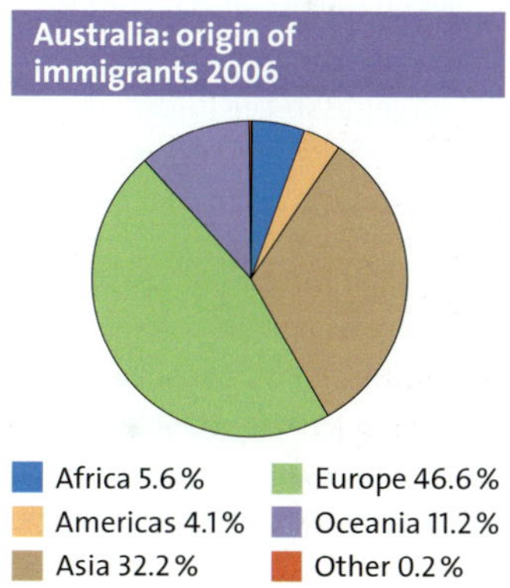

Tipp

Benutze das **simple past**, wenn du dich auf einen Zeitpunkt in der Vergangenheit beziehst: About 4 million people lived in Australia in 1900.

Benutze das **simple present** bei Aussagen über die Gegenwart (look at p. 8): Today about 21 million people live in Australia.
Benutze das *simple present* auch, wenn du deine Schlussfolgerungen wiedergibst. Millions of people came to Australia in the 20th century.

Benutze das **present perfect**, wenn du dich auf einen Zeitraum beziehst, der von der Vergangenheit bis heute reicht: Over 400,000 Asians have immigrated to Australia since 2000.

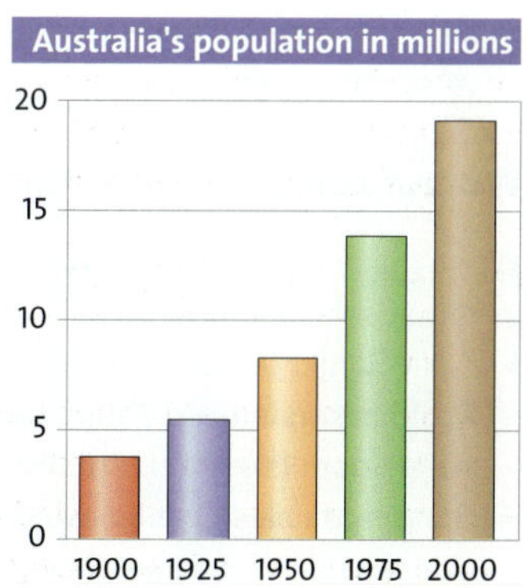

LISTENING AND READING SKILLS

SF REVISION Listening

Was muss ich allgemein beim *Listening* beachten?

Vor dem Hören:
- Überlege, worum es in dem Hörtext gehen wird. Frag dich, was du schon über das Thema weißt.
- Lies die Aufgabe gut durch, damit du weißt, worauf du achten sollst:
  - auf die Hauptgedanken oder
  - auf bestimmte Informationen, wie z.B. Namen, Uhrzeiten, Jahreszahlen.
- Bereite dich darauf vor, Notizen zu machen. Leg z.B. eine Tabelle oder Liste an.

Beim Hören:
- Keine Panik! Du musst nicht alles verstehen. Konzentriere dich auf das Wesentliche. Oft werden wichtige Informationen auch wiederholt.
- Achte auf Geräusche und unterschiedliche Stimmen. Was ein Sprecher/eine Sprecherin besonders betont, das ist wichtig!
- Wenn du gezielt nach Informationen suchst, denk an die Aufgabe und lass dich von anderen Einzelheiten nicht ablenken.
  Aufgepasst! Die Informationen, die du suchst, kommen vielleicht in einer anderen Reihenfolge vor, als du sie erwartest.
- Manche Signalwörter machen es dir leichter, den Hörtext zu verstehen:
  - Aufzählung: **and**, **another**, **too**
  - Gegensatz: **but**
  - Grund, Folge: **because, so**
  - Vergleich: **larger/older/... than**, **more**, **most**
  - Reihenfolge: **before**, **after**, **then**, **next**, **later**, **when**, **at last**
- Mach nur kurze Notizen, z.B. Anfangsbuchstaben, Symbole oder Stichworte, schreib keine ganzen Sätze.

Nach dem Hören:
- Vervollständige deine Notizen sofort.
- Konzentriere dich beim zweiten Hören auf das, was du zuerst nicht gut verstanden hast.

Worauf sollte ich bei automatischen Telefonansagen achten?

Wenn du eine telefonische Auskunft einholen willst, hörst du manchmal eine automatische Telefonansage.
- Keine Panik! Du kannst eine automatische Telefonansage mehrmals hören.
- Achte besonders auf Zahlen! Meist wirst du aufgefordert, bestimmte Tasten auf deinem Telefon zu drücken, um die gewünschte Information zu erhalten. Oft werden diese Zahlen wiederholt.
- Überlege dir vorher, welche Informationen du suchst und auf welche Schlüsselwörter du dafür achten solltest. Schreib sie auf.
- Höre dann besonders genau zu, wenn deine Schlüsselwörter genannt werden, und mach dir Notizen zu ihnen.

SPEAKING AND WRITING SKILLS

SF REVISION Paraphrasing

Worum geht es beim Paraphrasing?

Paraphrasing bedeutet, etwas mit anderen Worten zu erklären. Das ist hilfreich, wenn dir ein bestimmtes Wort nicht einfällt oder wenn dein Gegenüber dich nicht verstanden hat (siehe auch ▸ *SF Mediation, p. 147*).

Wie gehe ich beim Paraphrasing vor?

- Man kann mit einem Wort umschreiben, das dieselbe Bedeutung hat:
  to train is the same as to practise
  Oder man sagt das Gegenteil: **alive is the opposite of dead**
- Manchmal braucht man mehrere Wörter, z. B. wenn man etwas beschreibt oder erklärt. Dabei benutzt man ein allgemeines Wort (**general word**) und nennt weitere Eigenschaften: **A road train is a very long lorry.**
- Oder du umschreibst das Wort mit **... is/are like ...**
  A cabin is like a small house, it's in the country.
- Du kannst zum Umschreiben auch ein allgemeines Wort nehmen (z.B. **person**, **something**) und dieses mit einem durch **who**, **that** oder **where** eingeleiteten Satz näher erklären:
  A garage is the place where cars are checked and repaired.
  A witness is a person who has seen something and can tell the police what has happened.

SF REVISION Brainstorming

Wofür ist Brainstorming gut?

Bei vielen Aufgaben ist es nützlich, wenn du im ersten Schritt möglichst viele Ideen zum Thema sammelst. Dabei hilft dir das Brainstorming.

Wie gehe ich beim Brainstorming vor?

Schritt 1:
Schreib alle Ideen so auf, wie sie dir einfallen. Es ist zunächst völlig egal, ob sie gut sind oder nicht. Du kannst die Ideen durcheinander auf einen Zettel schreiben oder schon etwas geordnet, z.B. für jede eine neue Zeile.

Schritt 2:
Lies alle deine Ideen durch und wähle die besten aus. Dann sortiere sie und fasse sie sinnvoll zusammen. Dabei kannst du folgende **Techniken** anwenden:

1. Leg eine **Mindmap** an. Schreib das Thema in die Mitte eines Blattes Papier. Überlege, welche Oberbegriffe zu deiner Sammlung von Ideen passen. Verwende unterschiedliche Farben. Ergänze jede Idee, die zu einem Oberbegriff passt, auf einem Nebenast. Nimm dafür nur wichtige Schlüsselwörter. Du kannst statt Wörtern auch Symbole verwenden und Bilder ergänzen.
2. **The 5 Ws**: Schreib die **5** W-Fragen **Who? What? Where? When? Why?** in eine Tabelle. Die Ideen, die dir zu jeder Frage kommen, kannst du darunter schreiben.

SPEAKING COURSE – Zusammenfassung

Having a conversation ▸ *Unit 1, Part A (p. 15)*

Ein Gespräch beginnen

Ein Gespräch auf Englisch zu beginnen ist einfacher, als du vielleicht denkst. Es gibt immer mehrere Möglichkeiten:

- **wenn du jemanden begrüßen möchtest oder kennen lernst**
  Hi • Hello oder Good morning • Good evening (bei Erwachsenen) ...
  Oft kann man das Gespräch dann mit einer allgemeinen Bemerkung weiterführen: Great day today! • What a fantastic concert!
- **wenn du etwas erfragen willst** *(z.B. den Weg oder die Uhrzeit)*
  Excuse me, do you know ... • Excuse me, can you tell me ...
- **wenn du jemanden wieder triffst**
  Hi, how are you going? Hi, ..., how are things? • Hi, ... Good to see/meet you.

Ein Gespräch führen

Für den weiteren Verlauf des Gesprächs sind diese Wendungen nützlich:

- **sich vorstellen:** By the way, my name's ... • I'm ... • Nice/Good to meet you.
- **Smalltalk machen:** Have you been here before? • Is this your first ...? • Where are you from? • Do you like ...? • What about you?
- **sich bedanken:** That's great. • Thanks. / Thank you very much.
- **das Gespräch beenden/sich verabschieden:** Have fun/a nice day. • See you tomorrow/next week/later. • Bye!

Und wenn du etwas nicht verstanden hast, kannst du immer nachfragen:
Sorry, can you say that again, please? • Sorry, I didn't get that.

Tipp

- Oft hört man zur Begrüßung auch How are you? oder How do you do? Das sind einfache Begrüßungsformeln. Es wird nicht erwartet, dass man darauf eine Antwort gibt.
- Am besten sagst du einfach Fine, thanks. How about you?

Taking part in a job interview ▸ *Unit 2, Part C (p. 39)*

Sich vorbereiten

Auf ein Vorstellungsgespräch musst du dich unbedingt vorbereiten. Du solltest Fragen zu den folgenden Bereichen beantworten können:

- deine Eigenschaften (**personal qualities**), Stärken (**strengths**) und Schwächen (**weaknesses**)
- deine Interessen (**interests**) und Arbeitserfahrungen (**work experience**)
- was dich an dem Jobangebot reizt (**why you're interested in the job**).

Überleg dir auch eigene Fragen, zum Beispiel zu deinem Tätigkeitsbereich (**What would I have to do?**) oder zur Bezahlung (**What is the pay?**).

Im Vorstellungsgespräch

Im Vorstellungsgespräch ist es wichtig, dass du freundlich bist und dich als positiver und interessierter Mensch präsentierst.

- **bei der Begrüßung:** Hello, nice to meet you. • Good morning.
- **warum du dich beworben hast:** Well, I'm really interested in • I'm good at ..., so I think ...
- **wenn es um deine Joberfahrungen geht:** I really enjoyed working with ...
- **bei der Verabschiedung:** Goodbye and thank you very much.

Tipp

- Hör gut zu, wenn du etwas gefragt wirst.
- Sprich nicht zu viel, aber auch nicht zu wenig.
- Sprich nicht zu schnell.

Having a discussion ▸ *Unit 3, Part B (p. 54)*

Seine Meinung zum Ausdruck bringen und erklären

- In einer Diskussion ist es gut, wenn du möglichst klar und deutlich sagst, was du zu einer bestimmten Frage denkst: **I think ... • In my opinion ...**
- Genauso wichtig ist es, dass du Beispiele und Argumente nennst, die deine Meinung unterstützen – schließlich willst du deine Gesprächspartner von deinem Standpunkt überzeugen!
  I think ... because ... • Let me explain ... • For example ... • That's why ...

Auf andere in einer Diskussion reagieren

- Manchmal ist es notwendig nachzuhaken, weil man ein Argument nicht verstanden hat, oder darum zu bitten, jemanden ausreden zu lassen:
  Can you say that again? • Sorry, but I don't understand what you mean. • Wait a minute. Let me/him/her finish!
- Frag andere auch nach ihrer Meinung: **What do you think?**
- Wenn du die Meinung eines anderen unterstützen willst, kannst du das so zum Ausdruck bringen:
  I agree (with you/...) • That's a good point. • You're right.
- Oft widerspricht man nicht direkt, sondern leitet seine Reaktion mit **Sorry, ...** oder **I don't think** ... ein. Zeig immer Respekt für die Meinung des oder der anderen: **I don' t think you can say ... • I see what you mean, but I still think ... • Sorry, but that's not right. • Sorry, I don't agree with you • Yes, but ...**

▸ *Classroom English (pp. 214–215)*

Giving a presentation – useful phrases ▸ *Unit 4, Part C (p. 84)*

Einleitung

Nenne zu Beginn deines Vortrags dein Thema und gib einen kurzen Überblick darüber, worum es in deinem Vortrag geht:
The topic of my talk today is ... • I'm going to divide this talk into four sections. • First, I'll give you some general facts about ... • Next I'll look at ... • Finally I'll ...

Während der Präsentation

Mach deutlich, wenn du einen neuen Abschnitt in deinem Vortrag beginnst.
Now please have a look at ... • On the next side ... • Those were the basic facts. Next I'd like to talk about ...

Schluss

Am Ende deines Vortrags fass die wichtigsten Punkte zusammen. Frag deine Zuhörer, ob sie etwas nachfragen oder kommentieren möchten.
To sum up my talk I ... • Are there any questions or comments (on anything I've said)?.
Ausführlichere Hinweise zur Vorbereitung und Durchführung einer Präsentation findest du unter: ▸ *Giving a presentation (p. 132)*

REVISION WRITING COURSE – Zusammenfassung

The steps of writing

1. Brainstorming – Ideen sammeln, dann sortieren (► *SF Brainstorming, p. 139*).
2. Schreiben. Dabei achte darauf,
   - deine Sätze zu verbinden und auszubauen (*Writing better sentences*)
   - deinen Text gut zu strukturieren (*Using paragraphs*)
   - bei einem Bericht die 5 Ws abzudecken (*Writing a report*)
3. Deinen Text inhaltlich und sprachlich überprüfen (*Correcting your text*)

Writing better sentences

Linking words

Eine Geschichte klingt interessanter, wenn du die Sätze mit **linking words** miteinander verbindest. Dabei gibt es mehrere Möglichkeiten:

- **Time phrases** wie at 7o'clock, every morning, a few minutes later, then, next ...
- **Konjunktionen** wie although, because, but, so ... that, that, when, while
- **Relativpronomen** wie that und who

Adjektive und Adverbien

- Mit Adjektiven kannst du Personen, Orte oder Erlebnisse genauer und interessanter beschreiben. Vergleiche: The man looked into the room.
  ► The young man looked into the empty room.
- Mit Adverbien kannst du beschreiben, **wie** jemand etwas macht:
  The young man looked nervously into the empty room.

Using paragraphs

Structuring a text

Ein längerer Text ist besser zu verstehen, wenn er in mehrere Absätze unterteilt ist:

- eine Einleitung (**beginning**) – hier schreibst du, worum es geht
- einen Hauptteil (**middle**) – hier schreibst du mehr über dein Thema
- einen Schluss (**end**) – hier bringst du den Text zu einem interessanten Ende.

Topic sentences

Am Anfang eines Absatzes sind kurze, einleitende Sätze (**topic sentences**) gut, weil sie den Lesern sofort sagen, worum es geht, z. B.

1. Orte: My trip to ... was fantastic. / ... is famous for ... / ... is a great place.
2. Personen: ... is great/funny/interesting/clever ...
3. Aktivitäten: ... is great fun. / Lots of people ... every day.

Wie kann ich meine Absätze interessant gestalten?

- Beginne mit einem interessanten Einstiegssatz:
  You'll never guess what happened to me today! / Did I tell you that ...?
- Fang für jeden neuen Aspekt einen neuen Absatz an.
- Beende deinen Text mit einer Zusammenfassung oder etwas Persönlichem.

Writing a report – collecting and organizing ideas

Worauf kommt es bei einem Bericht an?

- Gib dem Leser **eine schnelle Orientierung**, was passiert ist.
- Beginne mit **wichtigen Informationen** und gib erst dann Detailinformationen.
- Ein Bericht gibt immer Antworten auf die **5 Ws**:
  Who? What? When? Where? Why? und manchmal auch auf **How?**
- Verwende das **simple past**.

Correcting your text

Ein Text ist noch nicht „fertig", wenn du ihn zu Ende geschrieben hast. Du solltest ihn immer mehr als einmal durchlesen:
- einmal, um zu sehen, ob er vollständig und gut verständlich ist
- noch einmal, um ihn auf Fehler zu überprüfen, z. B. **Rechtschreibfehler** ***(spelling mistakes)*** oder **Grammatikfehler** ***(grammar mistakes)***.

tomato [tə'mɑːtəʊ], *pl* **tomatoes** Tomate II

wife [waɪf], *pl* wives [waɪvz] Ehefrau II

drop (-pp-) [drɒp] fallen lassen I

forget (-tt-) [fə'get] vergessen I

Spelling mistakes

Lies deinen Text langsam, Wort für Wort, Buchstabe für Buchstabe. Wenn du unsicher bist, hilft dir ein Wörterbuch. Beachte folgende Regeln:

Tipp
- Manche Wörter haben Buchstaben, die man nicht spricht, aber schreibt, z. B. **knife**, **climb**.
- Manchmal ändert sich die Schreibweise, wenn ein Wort eine Endung erhält,
  z. B. **take** → **taking**, **terrible** → **terribly**, **lucky** → **luckily**,
  try → **tries** (**aber stay** → **stays**), **run** → **running**, **drop** → **dropped**.
- Beim Plural tritt manchmal noch ein **-e** zum **-s**, z. B. **church** → **churches**.

Grammar mistakes

Diese Tipps helfen dir, typische Fehler zu vermeiden:

Tipp
- Im **simple present** wird in der 3. Person Singular **-s** angehängt: **she knows**
- **Unregelmäßige Verben:** Manche Verben bilden die Formen des *simple past* und des Partizip Perfekt *(past participle)* unregelmäßig. Die unregelmäßigen Formen musst du lernen. Die Liste steht auf S. 212–213.
  go – went – gone; buy – bought – bought
- **Verneinung bei Vollverben:** Im *simple present* mit ***don't/doesn't***, im *simple past* mit **didn't**, z.B. **He doesn't speak French**, **he didn't learn it at school**.
- **Satzstellung**: Im Englischen gilt immer (auch im Nebensatz):
  a) subject – verb – object (SVO) **... when I saw my brother.**
  ... als ich meinen Bruder sah.
  b) Orts- vor Zeitangabe **I bought a nice book in the city yesterday.**

SF REVISION Summarizing texts

Wenn du einen Text zusammenfasst, gibst du die wichtigen Informationen oder Ereignisse in kürzerer Form wieder.

Wie gehe ich beim summarizing vor?

1. Lies den Text mindestens einmal genau durch, damit du verstehst, worum es geht. Mach dir noch keine Notizen.
2. Lies den Text erneut, Satz für Satz, durch und mach dir Notizen zu den 5 Ws:

Who? Who is the text about?
What? What happens?/What does he/she do?
Where? Where does it happen?
When? When does it happen?
Why? Why does it happen? / Why does he/she do this?

Was auf diese Fragen Antwort gibt, ist wichtig. Auslassen solltest du dagegen Beispiele, Vergleiche, Zitate, direkte Rede, ausschmückende Adjektive und andere Textteile, die der Beschreibung dienen.

3. Leg den Text nun beiseite und schreib mithilfe deiner Notizen eine Zusammenfassung des Texts in deinen eigenen Worten.

– Erklär in den ersten ein oder zwei Sätzen, worum es in dem Text geht.

• Vergleiche diese drei Anfänge einer Zusammenfassung von *In the outback* (S. 20–22). Welcher gibt am besten das Thema der Geschichte wieder?

IN THE OUTBACK is a story about Australia.

IN THE OUTBACK is a story about Bill and Colm.

IN THE OUTBACK is a story about Bill and Colm's journey along the Dog Fence.

Du kannst für deine einleitenden Sätze die folgenden phrases verwenden:
The story is about ... • **The text describes ...** • **The article shows ...** • **In the story we get to know ...**

– Im Hauptteil solltest du die wichtigen Ereignisse (z.B. einer Geschichte) oder die Hauptpunkte eines Textes (z.B. eines Zeitungsartikels) wiedergeben. Bring die Informationen in eine logische Reihenfolge.
  • Verwende dafür deine Notizen zu den **5 Ws**.
  • Schreib den Text nicht ab, sondern benutze deine eigenen Worte.

They're getting the Flying Doctor out here. It's too far to drive to the hospital in Katherine. → *They fly Bill to the hospital.*

– Schreib im **simple present**, auch wenn die Geschichte oder der Artikel in der Vergangenheit spielt. Nicht vergessen: im **simple present** wird in der 3. Person Singular **-s** angehängt: **He/She thinks.**

SF A CV ▸ *Unit 2, Part B (p. 36)*

Was ist ein CV?

„CV" bedeutet „Lebenslauf". Ein CV ist eine Zusammenfassung deiner bisherigen Ausbildung, deiner Fähigkeiten und deiner Interessen. Du brauchst einen CV, wenn du dich um eine berufliche Anstellung bewirbst. Amerikaner benutzen statt „CV" das Wort „résumé".

CURRICULUM VITAE
Oliver Schäfer

Tulpenweg 34 32051 Herford, Germany
Telephone: 00 49 5221 978036
Email: oliver.schaefer@email-hf.de

Education
2003-2009 Gutenberg-Realschule (secondary school), Herford, Germany
1999-2003 Regenbogen Grundschule (primary school), Herford, Germany

Qualifications
Studying for Fachoberschulreife (equivalent of GCSEs)
Languages: English (6 years), French (4 years)
Driving licence since 2008

Work experience
Work experience at a garage (3 weeks)

Hobbies and interests
My hobbies are cycling, doing workouts, repairing all kinds of machines. I am very interested in technical things and computers.

References
Available on request

Geburtsdatum und – ort werden in einem britischen CV **oft nicht** genannt.

Gib bei deiner Telefonnummer auch die **internationale Vorwahl** mit an.

Fettgedruckte Überschriften und eine **klare Gliederung** erleichtern das Lesen.

GCSEs gibt es nur in Großbritannien, in den USA entspricht das dem **US highschool diploma**.

An dieser Stelle kann auch eine **konkrete Person** als **Referenz** genannt werden wie im CV auf S. 38. Selbstverständlich musst du ihn oder sie vorher fragen!

Im CV auf S. 36 findest du auch die Abschnitte **Personal statement** und **Other skills** – diese Abschnitte sind möglich, aber nicht zwingend notwendig für einen CV.

Tipp

Bevor du deinen CV losschickst, geh folgende Checkliste durch:
- Habe ich weißes A4-Papier benutzt? Ist das Blatt sauber und ordentlich?
- Habe ich den CV mit einem Computer geschrieben?
- Ist die Seite klar gegliedert und gut lesbar?
- Habe ich alle zentralen Bereiche abgedeckt: meine Erfahrungen, meine Interessen, meine Fähigeiten und persönlichen Eigenschaften?
- Habe ich auch wirklich keine sprachlichen Fehler in meinem Schreiben?.

SF Writing formal and informal letters ▸ *Unit 2, p. 36*

Beim Briefeschreiben musst du unterschiedliche Regeln beachten, je nachdem ob du einen förmlichen Brief (*formal letter*) an unbekannte Personen, Behörden, Zeitschriften usw. schreibst oder einen persönlichen, informellen Brief (*informal letter*) an Freunde oder Verwandte.

Worauf kommt es bei förmlichen Briefen an? (Formal letters)

① Schreibe deine Adresse (ohne Namen) und das Datum in die rechte obere Ecke. Verwende keine typisch deutschen Buchstaben wie z.B. ß, ä, ö, oder ü.
② Die Anschrift steht links.
③ Die Anrede lautet *Dear Sir or Madam*. Wenn du den Namen des Adressaten kennst, beginne deinen Brief mit *Dear Mr/Mrs/Ms ...*
④ Verwende Langformen (*I am, I would like* statt *I'm, I'd like* etc.).
⑤ Nenne zu Beginn den Grund deines Briefes.
⑥ Bedanke dich bei Bitten und Anfragen im Voraus (*I look forward to hearing from you. Thank you.*).
⑦ Beende den Brief mit *Yours faithfully*, wenn du den Adressaten nicht kennst. Hast du den Adressaten am Anfang des Briefes mit Namen angeredet, dann schreibe *Yours sincerely*.
⑧ Unterschreibe den Brief und tippe zusätzlich deinen Namen.

Tipp

Beachte, was du zum Schreiben von Texten gelernt hast:
- Vor dem Schreiben: Ideen sammeln, dann sortieren.
- Während des Schreibens: Sätze verbinden und ausbauen; strukturieren.
- Nach dem Schreiben: Überprüfe deinen Brief inhaltlich und sprachlich. ▸ *SF Writing course, pp. 142–143*

Example for a letter of application

Schillerstr. 17
① 37067 Goettingen
Germany

② Jane Hall
Meadows Home Farm Shop
Harston
Cambridge CB22 4BE
③ Great Britain

4 May 2010

Dear Ms Hall

④
⑤ I am writing to you about the advertisement from April 21st in the Cambridge Weekly News. I would love to ④ work for you at Meadows Home Farm this summer.

I am 16 years old and I have a good level of English but would like to improve my speaking skills. I am hard-working, friendly and a fast learner. At home I look after two horses so farm work is not new to me. I have also worked in a sports shop so I have experience in serving people and working in a team. My hobbies are horse riding, playing volleyball and hiking. Please find my CV with this letter.

Thank you for your time. I look forward to hearing from you. ⑥

⑦ Yours sincerely

Tamara Wille
⑧ Tamara Wille

Was ist bei persönlichen Briefen anders? (Informal letter)

Hier sind die Regeln nicht ganz so streng. Aber beachte Folgendes:
- Schreibe deine Adresse (ohne Namen) und das Datum in die rechte obere Ecke.
- Verwende keine typisch deutschen Buchstaben wie z.B. ß, ä, ö, oder ü.
- Du benötigst keine Anschrift.
- Du kannst deinen Brief mit *Dear/Hello/Hi ...* beginnen.
- Nenne zu Beginn den Grund deines Briefes, stelle auch Fragen.
- Beende den Brief mit einem freundlichen Gruß/Ausblick/Erwartungen/...
- Schließe deinen Brief mit *Yours/Best wishes/Love/...* ab.

Alles klar? Wohin gehören die Wendungen im blauen Kasten?

	Formal letter	Informal letter
Briefanfang	Dear Mr Smith, ...	Dear Pete, ...
Briefende	...	...

Best wishes • Dear Pete • Yours faithfully • Dear Mr Smith • Yours sincerely • Lots of love • Love • Dear Sir or Madam • See you soon! • Hello Sarah • Thank you very much. • Happy birthday! I've just heard ...

MEDIATION SKILLS

SF REVISION Mediation

Wann muss ich zwischen zwei Sprachen vermitteln?

Manchmal musst du zwischen zwei Sprachen vermitteln. Das nennt man mediation.

1. Du gibst englische Informationen auf Deutsch weiter:
   Du fährst z.B. mit deiner Familie in die USA und deine Eltern oder Geschwister wollen wissen, was jemand in einem Café gesagt hat oder was an einer Informationstafel steht.
2. Du gibst deutsche Informationen auf Englisch weiter:
   Vielleicht ist bei dir zu Hause eine Austauschschülerin aus den USA oder Dänemark zu Gast, die kein Deutsch spricht und Hilfe braucht.
3. In schriftlichen Prüfungen musst du manchmal in einem englischen Text gezielt nach Informationen suchen und diese auf Deutsch wiedergeben. Oder du sollst Informationen aus einem deutschen Text auf Englisch wiedergeben.

Worauf muss ich bei *mediation* achten?

- Übersetze nicht alles wörtlich.
- Gib nur das Wesentliche weiter, lass Unwichtiges weg.
- Verwende kurze und einfache Sätze.
- Wenn du ein Wort nicht kennst, umschreibe es oder ersetze es durch ein anderes Wort.

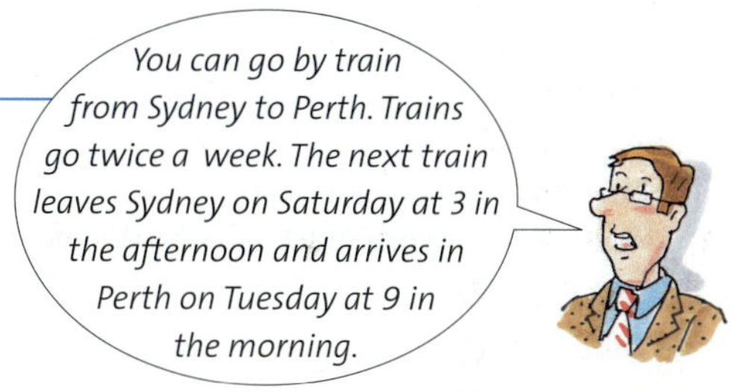

Was kann ich tun, wenn ich ein wichtiges Wort nicht kenne?

Vielleicht findest du es manchmal schwer, mündliche Aussagen oder schriftliche Textvorlagen in die andere Sprache zu übertragen, z.B. weil:
- dein Wortschatz nicht ausreicht
- dir bekannte Wörter „im Stress" nicht einfallen
- spezielle Fachbegriffe auftauchen.

Manche Wörter kannst du umschreiben,
z.B. mithilfe von Relativsätzen wie:
It's somebody/a person who ...
It's something that you use to ...
It's an animal that ...
It's a place where ...

▸ *SF Paraphrasing, p. 139*

EXAM SKILLS

SF REVISION How to do well in a test

Countdown zum Testerfolg

Ein Test ist angekündigt? Kein Grund zur Panik. Wichtig ist, dass du weißt, worauf du dich vorbereiten musst. Im Zweifelsfall frag deine Lehrerin oder deinen Lehrer. Der Countdown kann beginnen!

Eine Woche vor dem Test

1. Lies noch einmal die **Texte** der zuletzt durchgenommenen Unit (vor allem *Lead-in*, *A-Section* und *Text*, eventuell auch das *Background File*). Fasse mündlich oder schriftlich zusammen, worum es ging.

2. Wiederhole den **Wortschatz** der Unit mithilfe des *Vocabulary*, des *Wordmaster* oder des *English Coach*. Schreibe dir die Wörter und Wortverbindungen, die du immer wieder vergisst, auf ein Blatt Papier. Eine Mindmap oder ein Wortfeld helfen beim Behalten.

3. Geh noch einmal die neue **Grammatik** durch. Aufgaben zur Selbstüberprüfung und zum Üben findest du im *Practice*-Teil, auf der *How am I doing?*-Seite, im *Grammar File*, in deinem *Workbook* und im e-*Workbook*. (► *SF Check yourself, p. 129*)

Zwei oder drei Tage vor dem Test

1. Wiederhole den **Wortschatz**. Manche Wörter sitzen noch nicht? Schreibe einen kurzen Text, in dem du sie verwendest.

2. Lies die **Schülerbuch-Texte** ein weiteres Mal.

3. Erkläre einem Freund oder einer Freundin die neue **Grammatik**. Klappt nicht richtig? Dann lies nochmal im *Grammar File* nach.

Am Abend vor dem Test

1. Entspanne dich. Du kannst lesen, dich in die Badewanne legen, Musik hören, fernsehen, ...

2. Geh zur gewohnten Zeit ins Bett.

Am Morgen des Tests

1. Steh rechtzeitig auf, damit du nicht hetzen musst.

2. Lies etwas „zum Aufwärmen", aber schau nicht mehr in dein Schülerbuch.

Während des Tests

1. Denk daran: Du hast dich gut vorbereitet. Es gibt keinen Grund, nervös zu sein.

2. Konzentriere dich auf den Test, lass dich nicht ablenken.

3. Lies dir die Aufgaben genau durch. Dann löse zuerst die Aufgaben, die dir einfach scheinen. Wende dich erst danach den schwereren Aufgaben zu.

4. Aufgaben, die du bearbeitet hast, hakst du ab. So siehst du, wie du vorankommst, und behältst den Überblick.

5. Schau ab und zu auf die Uhr. Du solltest dir für den Schluss noch Zeit einplanen, um deine Antworten noch einmal durchzulesen und zu korrigieren.

Good luck!

Aufgabenstellungen verstehen

Bevor du damit anfängst, die Aufgaben zu bearbeiten, stell sicher, dass du genau weißt, was du machen sollst. Lies die Aufgabenstellung Wort für Wort langsam und gründlich und von Anfang bis Ende durch. Du kannst besonders wichtige Dinge der Aufgabenstellung unterstreichen und die Aufgabe, wenn nötig, für dich in einzelne Schritte unterteilen.

Worauf sollte ich bei Multiple-Choice-Aufgaben achten?

- Lies die Frage oder den Satz sehr genau durch.
- Bevor du dir die Lösungsangebote anschaust, deck sie mit Papier ab. Überleg dir, was die richtige Antwort sein könnte. Wenn das dann auch als eine Lösungsmöglichkeit angeboten wird, ist es meistens richtig.
- Lies immer alle vorgegebenen Lösungen, bevor du dich entscheidest.
- Achte darauf, dass du nur **eine** der Antworten ankreuzt – es sei denn, dass in der Aufgabenstellung ausdrücklich gesagt wird, dass mehrere Antworten richtig sein können.
- Mach erst alle Aufgaben so gut du kannst. Lass keine Aufgabe aus, aber geh zum Schluss zu den Fragen zurück, bei denen du unsicher bist.
- Wenn das alles nicht hilft, such nicht mehr nach der richtigen Antwort, sondern nach den falschen Antworten. Weil drei Antwortmöglichkeiten falsch sein müssen, kannst du erschließen, dass die vierte Antwort richtig ist. Hier ist ein Beispiel. Stell dir vor, du hörst folgenden Dialog.

  Boy *Wow, that was great, Dad. Thanks. Can we do it again next weekend?*

  Dad *Sure, Greg – if the weather's nice. But let's find an easier tour then – I'm a bit tired.*

Dazu wird dir die Multiple-Choice-Frage hier unten gestellt.
Greg und sein Vater müssen etwas im Freien gemacht haben, denn Gregs Dad spricht über das Wetter. Also sind die Antworten **B** und **C** falsch. Man schwimmt keine Touren, also ist **A** auch falsch. Daher muss **D** die richtige Antwort sein.

1. Greg and his dad have just
- (A) been swimming.
- (B) been to a fitness club.
- (C) seen a movie.
- (D) been on a bike ride.

Grammar File – Inhalt

Im **Grammar File** (S. 150–158) wird zusammengefasst, was du in diesem Band **über die englische Sprache** lernst.

In der **linken Spalte** stehen Beispielsätze und Übersichten.

In der **rechten Spalte** stehen Erklärungen und Hinweise.

Indirect speech (reporting verb: simple past)

Zita Wallace said **that** she still remembered that day and **that** she would never forget the first night.

◄ Wenn das **einleitende Verb im *simple past*** steht (*she said/told us/explained/answered* usw.), dann werden die Zeitformen der direkten Rede meist verändert: Sie werden um eine Zeitstufe in die Vergangenheit „zurückverschoben“ *(backshift of tenses)*.

Veränderungen der Zeitformen bei einleitendem Verb im *simple past*

	Direct speech	Indirect speech
present ► **past**	'I don't want money from the government.'	She **said** she didn't want money from the government.
	'I'm waitin– for the word "sorry".'	She sai– ... for the word "..."

► *Unit 1, Part C: P 3–5 (p. 19)*

Zu diesem **Grammar File**-Abschnitt gehören die Übungen 3 bis 5 auf S. 19 in Unit 1, Part C.

Berichte, was Ella ihrer Freundin Jill am Telef

1 'My mom is still at work.'
2 'She has to work late.
3 'Mom won't b...

Diese kleinen Aufgaben dienen der Selbstkontrolle. Schreib die Lösungen in dein Heft. Überprüfe sie dann auf Seite 158.

Additional information

The simple present (future meaning)

The next train to Bath **goes** in ten minutes.

„Additional information“-Abschnitte enthalten Grammatik, die du nicht selbst zu verwenden brauchst. Du solltest aber verstehen, was dort erklärt wird, damit du keine Schwierigkeiten mit Texten hast, in denen diese Grammatik vorkommt.

Unit 1

GF 1 Indirect speech (I) Die indirekte Rede (I)

Man kann direkt oder indirekt wiedergeben, was jemand sagt (oder gesagt hat):

Direct speech — Zita Wallace says, 'I still **remember** that day. And **I'll** never **forget** the first night.'

◄ In der **direkten Rede** wird **wörtlich** wiedergegeben, was jemand sagt. Direkte Rede steht in der Regel in Anführungszeichen (deutsch: **„...“**; englisch: **'...'**).

Indirect speech (reporting verb: simple present) — Zita Wallace says **that** she still **remembers** that day and **that** she **will** never **forget** the first night.

◄ In der **indirekten Rede** (*indirect* oder *reported speech*) wird berichtet, was jemand sagt. Die indirekte Rede wird mit Verben wie *say, tell sb., add, answer, explain, write* eingeleitet.

Indirect speech (reporting verb: simple past) — Zita Wallace said **that** she still remembered that day and **that** she would never forget the first night.

◄ Wenn das **einleitende Verb im *simple past*** steht (*she said/told us/explained/answered* usw.), dann werden die Zeitformen der direkten Rede meist verändert: Sie werden um eine Zeitstufe in die Vergangenheit „zurückverschoben“ *(backshift of tenses)*.

Veränderungen der Zeitformen bei einleitendem Verb im *simple past*

	Direct speech	Indirect speech
present ► past	'I don't want money from the government.' 'I'm waiting for the word "sorry".'	She **said** she didn't want money from the government. She **said** she was waiting for the word "sorry".
past ► past perfect	'I saw terrible things.'	She **told** us she had seen terrible things.
can* ► *could	'I can't forget those days.'	She **said** couldn't forget those days.
***will*-future ► *would* + infinitive**	'I'll never forget those days.'	She **said** she would never forget those days.
***going to*-future ► *was/were going to* + infinitive**	'The government is going to say "sorry".'	They **said** the government was going to say "sorry".
present perfect ► past perfect	'I haven't forgotten that evening.'	She **added** that she hadn't forgotten that evening.

► *Unit 1, Part C: P 3–5 (p. 19)*

Berichte, was Ella ihrer Freundin Jill am Telefon erzählt hat. Schreib die Sätze in indirekter Rede in dein Heft.

1 'My mom is still at work.' — Ella **said** her mom ...
2 'She has to work late.' — She **told** Jill that her mom ...
3 'Mom won't be home till nine.' — She **added** that her mom ...
4 'Dad will probably want a pizza.' — She also **said** her dad ...
5 'I'll call again later.' — She **told** Jill she ...

Unit 2

GF 2 Extra Indirect speech (II) Die indirekte Rede (II)

2.1 Commands and requests in indirect speech

Aufforderungen und Bitten in der indirekten Rede

Simon Mani, buy a tie.
And don't be shy.

Simon told Mani to buy a tie.
And he told him not to be shy.
Simon sagte Mani, er soll sich eine Krawatte kaufen.
Und er sagte ihm, dass er nicht schüchtern sein soll.

◄ **Aufforderungen** werden in der indirekten Rede meist mit ***tell sb. to do sth.*** (bzw. ***tell sb. not to do sth.***) wiedergegeben.

Simon Lucy, please talk more.

Simon asked Lucy to talk more.
Simon bat Lucy, mehr zu reden.

◄ Eine **Bitte** wird meist mit ***ask sb. to do sth.*** (bzw. ***ask sb. not to do sth.***) wiedergegeben.

► *Unit 2, Part C: P 3 (p. 40)*

2.2 Questions in indirect speech

Fragen in der indirekten Rede

Auch bei Fragen in der indirekten Rede werden die Zeitformen in die Vergangenheit „zurückverschoben", wenn das einleitende Verb im *simple past* steht.

Direct question (with question word) — When can I start?

Indirect question — Mani asked Rita **when** he could start.

◄ Wenn die direkte **Frage mit einem Fragewort** beginnt (*what, when, where, why, how* usw.), wird das Fragewort in der indirekten Frage beibehalten.

Direct question (yes/no question) — Do you have any weaknesses?

Indirect question — Rita asked him **if** he had any weaknesses.

◄ Handelt es sich bei der direkten Frage um eine **Frage ohne Fragewort** *(yes/no question)*, dann wird die indirekte Frage mit ***if*** („ob") eingeleitet.

► *Unit 2, Part C: P 3 (p. 40)*

Was haben sie gesagt – **A** *oder* **B***?*

1 Jack told Sophia not to forget her keys.
A 'Sophia, I forgot my keys.'
B 'Sophia, don't forget your keys.'

2 He asked Eve to take the chairs outside.
A 'Eve, please take the chairs outside.'
B 'Did you take the chairs outside, Eve?'

3 Rita asked Lucy if she was nervous.
A 'Lucy, I'm nervous.'
B 'Are you nervous, Lucy?'

4 Simon asked Mani why he was late.
A 'Why was Mani late?'
B 'Why are you late, Mani?'

GF 3 Talking about the present – Über die Gegenwart sprechen

Du möchtest ausdrücken,

– dass etwas **regelmäßig** geschieht ▸ *The simple present: GF 3.1*	→ Hanna **gets up** at 7 o'clock every morning. Hanna steht jeden Morgen um 7 Uhr auf.
– dass etwas **gerade jetzt** geschieht ▸ *The present progressive: GF 3.2*	→ It's 7 o'clock. Hanna **is getting up**. Es ist 7 Uhr. Hanna steht (gerade) auf.

3.1 The simple present

Das ***simple present*** wird verwendet,

Dave Wilson **usually** gets the bus to school.
On Mondays his mother takes him in the car.
He **never** cycles to school because it's too far.

◂ um über Handlungen und Ereignisse zu sprechen, die **wiederholt, regelmäßig, immer** oder **nie** geschehen (oft mit Zeitangaben wie *always, never, usually, sometimes, often, every week, on Mondays* usw.).

Dave and his family live in Manchester.
He plays hockey and collects models of old cars.
His dad works for a building company.

◂ um über **Dauerzustände**, **Hobbys** und **Berufe** zu sprechen.

! *He, she, it* – das „s" muss mit.

Verneinte Sätze	I don't cycle to school.	Dave doesn't walk to school.
Fragen	Do you go to school by bus? **Where** do the Wilsons live?	Does your mother take you in the car? **When** does Dave's mother take him in the car?

3.2 The present progressive

Das ***present progressive*** wird verwendet,

What's Dave doing? –
Just now he's cleaning his bike.

◂ um über Handlungen und Ereignisse zu sprechen, die **jetzt gerade im Gange** sind (oft mit Angaben wie *at the moment, now, just*).

Dave (on the phone) I can't talk right now, Jack. I'm cleaning my bike.

! Die Handlung, um die es geht, kann für einen Augenblick unterbrochen sein, z.B. durch ein Telefonat. Wichtig ist, dass sie noch nicht abgeschlossen ist.

This week Dave's grandma is staying at the Wilsons' because Dave's mum is ill.

◂ um über **vorübergehende Zustände** zu sprechen (begrenzter Zeitraum: *this week*).

Verneinte Sätze	The Wilsons aren't working.	Dave isn't watching TV.
Fragen	Are you watching TV? **What** are you doing?	Is Dave cleaning his bike? **Who** is Dave talking to?

Dave's dad works for a building company.
Look, he's working at his desk at the moment.

GF 4 Talking about the past Über die Vergangenheit sprechen

Du möchtest ausdrücken,

– dass etwas in der Vergangenheit **geschah**; das Geschehen ist **abgeschlossen** und **vorbei** ▸ *The simple past: GF 4.1*	→ Emma **left** school in 2007. Emma ging im Jahr 2007 von der Schule ab.
– dass etwas in der Vergangenheit **gerade im Gange (noch nicht abgeschlossen) war** ▸ *The past progressive: GF 4.2*	→ We **were leaving** the building when we heard the explosion. Wir waren gerade dabei, das Gebäude zu verlassen, ...
– dass etwas **vor etwas anderem** in der Vergangenheit stattgefunden hatte ▸ *The past perfect: GF 4.3*	→ Connor **had** already **left** when we arrived. Connor war schon gegangen, als wir ankamen.
– dass etwas **irgendwann** geschehen ist, oft mit **Auswirkungen auf die Gegenwart**	→ Jane **has left** her purse at home, so she can't pay for her bus ticket. Jane hat ihre Geldbörse zu Hause gelassen, ...
– dass ein Zustand **in der Vergangenheit begonnen** hat und **noch andauert** ▸ *The present perfect: GF 4.4*	→ We**'ve had** our dog for three years now – since 2007. Wir haben unseren Hund jetzt seit drei Jahren ...

4.1 The simple past

Last Friday Katie's family flew to Spain.
Letzten Freitag ist Katies Familie nach Spanien geflogen / flog Katies Familie nach Spanien.
Two years ago the Websters moved to Bath.
Vor zwei Jahren sind die Websters nach Bath gezogen.

Wenn man über Vergangenes berichtet, benutzt man überwiegend das ***simple past***. Man beschreibt damit Handlungen, Ereignisse und Zustände, die zu einer bestimmten Zeit in der Vergangenheit *(yesterday, last Friday, two years ago, in 2003, between 2005 and 2008, ...)* stattfanden.

! Im Deutschen wird in diesen Fällen oft das Perfekt verwendet, im Englischen jedoch nicht.

Verneinte Sätze	They didn't fly to France.	Katie didn't want to go at first.
Fragen	Did you go on holiday last year? **Where** did you go?	Did Katie like it? **When** did the Websters move to Bath?

4.2 The past progressive

What were you doing yesterday at 3.30? –
I was waiting for my sister at the school doors.
She was still talking to our Maths teacher.

Angela was just crossing the road when she saw her boyfriend.
Angela war gerade dabei, die Straße zu überqueren, ...

Das ***past progressive*** wird verwendet,

◂ um über Handlungen und Ereignisse zu sprechen, die zu einer bestimmten Zeit in der Vergangenheit noch im Gange, also noch nicht abgeschlossen waren.

◂ wenn man beschreiben will, was gerade vor sich ging *(she was just crossing the road)*, als etwas anderes passierte *(she saw her boyfriend)*.

Verneinte Sätze	You weren't listening.	It wasn't snowing when we left the house.
Fragen	Were you watching TV? **What** were they doing?	Was she crossing the road when it happened? **What** was she doing?

4.3 The past perfect

When Emma arrived home, her parents had already eaten.
Als Emma zu Hause eintraf, hatten ihre Eltern bereits gegessen.

Wenn man sagen will, dass etwas noch vor etwas anderem in der Vergangenheit stattgefunden hatte, dann benutzt man das ***past perfect***.

Verneinte Sätze	They hadn't gone to bed.	Emma hadn't eaten anything all day.
Fragen	Had you seen that film before? **What** had they done?	Had Emma eaten when she came home? **Where** had she been all day?

4.4 The present perfect

! Das ***present perfect*** hat mit der **Vergangenheit und mit der Gegenwart** zu tun. Es wird verwendet,

Will Smith is great. I've seen most of his films.
Luke has **already** done his Maths homework, but he has**n't** started his French **yet**.
Have you **ever** been to Paris?
– No, I haven't. But I've **always** wanted to go.

Mel has lost her mobile. Her dad is very angry.

◂ wenn man sagen will, **dass** jemand etwas getan hat oder **dass** etwas geschehen ist. Dabei ist nicht wichtig, wann es geschehen ist – ein genauer Zeitpunkt wird nicht genannt. Das *present perfect* steht oft mit Adverbien der unbestimmten Zeit wie *already, just, never, ever, not ... yet*.
Oft hat die Handlung Auswirkungen auf die Gegenwart (Mels Vater ist wütend, weil sie ihr Handy verloren hat).

We've had our new car **since April**.
Wir haben unser neues Auto seit April.

We've had our new car **for three months**.
Wir haben unser neues Auto seit drei Monaten.

◂ für **Zustände**, die in der Vergangenheit begonnen haben und jetzt noch andauern (oft mit ***since*** bzw. ***for***).

! Im Deutschen steht in diesen Fällen meist das Präsens, im Englischen muss das *present perfect* stehen.

Verneinte Sätze	I haven't been to Paris yet.	Luke hasn't done his French homework.
Fragen	Have you been to Paris? **What** have you done?	Has Mel found her mobile yet? **Which** of these films have you seen already?

GF 5 Talking about the future Über die Zukunft sprechen

Du möchtest ausdrücken,		
– dass etwas für die Zukunft **geplant** ist ▸ *The going to-future: GF 5.1*	→	I'm **going to watch** the new Bond film tonight. Ich sehe mir heute Abend den neuen Bond-Film an.
– wie etwas in der Zukunft **sein wird** (**Vorhersagen, Vermutungen**) ▸ *The will-future: GF 5.2*	→	It **will be** warm and sunny in Spain. I'm sure you'**ll like** it there. Es wird warm und sonnig sein in Spanien. Ich bin sicher, dass es dir dort gefallen wird.
– dass etwas für die Zukunft **fest verabredet** ist (es steht schon im Kalender) ▸ *The present progressive: GF 5.3*	→	We'**re having** a party on Saturday. Would you like to come? Wir geben nächsten Samstag eine Party. ...

5.1 The *going to*-future

Das **Futur mit *going to*** wird verwendet,

My boyfriend says he's going to be an engineer.
Mein Freund sagt, er will Ingenieur werden.

◂ wenn man über **Vorhaben, Pläne, Absichten** für die Zukunft sprechen will.

Look at those clouds. There's going to be a storm.
... Es wird ein Gewitter geben.

◂ um auszudrücken, dass etwas **wahrscheinlich gleich geschehen wird** – es gibt bereits deutliche **Anzeichen** dafür (*hier:* die Wolken am Himmel).

5.2 The *will*-future

Das **Futur mit *will*** wird verwendet,

It will be cold and windy, and we will get some rain in the afternoon.
I'll be 15 next October.

◂ um **Vorhersagen** über die Zukunft zu äußern. Oft geht es dabei um Dinge, die man nicht beeinflussen kann, z.B. das Wetter.

I expect Ella will be late again as usual.
Ich nehme an, Ella kommt wie üblich wieder zu spät.

◂ um eine **Vermutung** auszudrücken (oft eingeleitet mit *I think, I'm sure, I expect, maybe*).

Just a moment. I'll open the door for you.
Moment. Ich mache Ihnen die Tür auf.
I won't tell anyone what's happened. I promise.
Ich sage niemandem, was passiert ist. ...

◂ wenn man sich **spontan** – also ohne es im Voraus geplant zu haben – zu etwas **entschließt**. Oft geht es dabei um **Hilfsangebote** oder **Versprechen**.

5.3 The present progressive (future meaning)

We're driving to Scotland next Friday to visit my grandparents.
I'm meeting a friend in town tonight.

Das ***present progressive*** wird verwendet, wenn etwas **für die Zukunft fest geplant** oder **fest verabredet** ist (manchmal spricht man vom *diary future*). Durch eine Zeitangabe wie *tonight* oder aus dem Zusammenhang muss klar sein, dass es um etwas Zukünftiges geht.

Additional information

5.4 The simple present (future meaning)

The next train to Bath **goes** in ten minutes.
The next drawing class **starts** on 2 September.

Das ***simple present*** wird verwendet, wenn ein **zukünftiges Geschehen** durch einen **Fahrplan**, ein **Programm** oder Ähnliches festgelegt ist (manchmal spricht man vom *timetable future*). Verben wie *arrive, leave, go, open, close, start, stop* werden häufig so verwendet.

Grammatical terms (Grammatische Fachbegriffe)

active ['æktɪv]	Aktiv	*Beckham* ***scored*** *the final goal.*
adjective ['ædʒɪktɪv]	Adjektiv	*good, red, new, boring*
adverb ['ædvɜːb]	Adverb	*always, badly, here, really, today*
adverb of frequency ['friːkwənsi]	Häufigkeitsadverb	*always, often, never*
adverb of indefinite time [ɪnˌdefɪnət 'taɪm]	Adverb der unbestimmten Zeit	*already, ever, just, never*
adverb of manner ['mænə]	Adverb der Art und Weise	*badly, happily, quietly, well*
article ['ɑːtɪkl]	Artikel	*the, a/an*
backshift of tenses ['bækʃɪft]	Verschiebung der Zeitformen *(bei der indirekten Rede)*	*'****I'm*** *sorry.'* ► *Sam said he* ***was*** *sorry.*
command [kə'mɑːnd]	Befehl, Aufforderungssatz	*Open your books. Don't talk.*
comparison [kəm'pærɪsn]	Steigerung	*old – older – oldest*
conditional sentence [kənˌdɪʃənl 'sentəns]	Bedingungssatz	*I'd call him if I knew his number.*
conjunction [kən'dʒʌŋkʃn]	Konjunktion	*and, or, but; because, before*
countable noun ['kaʊntəbl]	zählbares Nomen	*girl – girls, pound – pounds*
definite article ['defɪnət]	bestimmter Artikel	*the*
direct speech [ˌdaɪrekt 'spiːtʃ]	direkte Rede, wörtliche Rede	***'I'm sorry.'***
gerund ['dʒerənd]	Gerundium	*I like* ***dancing****.* ***Dancing*** *is fun.*
***going to*-future**	Futur mit *going to*	***I'm going to watch*** *TV tonight.*
***if*-clause** ['ɪf klɔːz]	*if*-Satz, Nebensatz mit *if*	***If I see Jack****, I'll tell him.*
imperative [ɪm'perətɪv]	Imperativ (Befehlsform)	*Open your books. Don't talk.*
indirect speech [ˌɪndərekt 'spiːtʃ]	indirekte Rede	*Sam said* ***(that) he was sorry****.*
infinitive [ɪn'fɪnətɪv]	Infinitiv (Grundform des Verbs)	*(to) open, (to) see, (to) read*
irregular verb [ɪˌregjələ 'vɜːb]	unregelmäßiges Verb	*(to) go – went – gone*
main clause	Hauptsatz	***I like Scruffy*** *because I like dogs.*
modal ['məʊdl]	modales Hilfsverb, Modalverb	*can, could, may, must*
negative statement [ˌnegətɪv 'steɪtmənt]	verneinter Aussagesatz	*I don't like bananas.*
noun [naʊn]	Nomen, Substantiv	*Sophie, girl, brother, time*
object ['ɒbdʒɪkt]	Objekt	*My sister is writing* ***a letter****.*
passive ['pæsɪv]	Passiv	*The goal* ***was scored*** *by Beckham.*
past participle [ˌpɑːst 'pɑːtɪsɪpl]	Partizip Perfekt	*cleaned, planned, gone, taken*
past perfect [ˌpɑːst 'pɜːfɪkt]	Plusquamperfekt, Vorvergangenheit	*He cried – he* ***had hurt*** *his knee.*
past progressive [ˌpɑːst prə'gresɪv]	Verlaufsform der Vergangenheit	*At 7.30 I* ***was having*** *dinner.*
personal pronoun [ˌpɜːsənl 'prəʊnaʊn]	Personalpronomen (persönliches Fürwort)	*I, you, he, she, it, we, they; me, you, him, her, it, us, them*
plural ['plʊərəl]	Plural, Mehrzahl	
positive statement [ˌpɒzətɪv 'steɪtmənt]	bejahter Aussagesatz	*I like oranges.*
possessive determiner [pəˌzesɪv dɪ'tɜːmɪnə]	Possessivbegleiter (besitzanzeigender Begleiter)	*my, your, his, her, its, our, their*
possessive form [pəˌzesɪv fɔːm]	*s*-Genitiv	*Jo's brother; my sister's room*
possessive pronoun [pəˌzesɪv 'prəʊnaʊn]	Possessivpronomen	*mine, yours, his, hers, ours, theirs*
preposition [ˌprepə'zɪʃn]	Präposition	*after, at, in, next to, under*
present participle [ˌpreznt 'pɑːtɪsɪpl]	Partizip Präsens	*cleaning, planning, going, taking*
present perfect [ˌpreznt 'pɜːfɪkt]	*present perfect*	*We****'ve made*** *a cake for you.*
present progressive [ˌpreznt prə'gresɪv]	Verlaufsform der Gegenwart	*The Hansons* ***are having*** *lunch.*
pronoun ['prəʊnaʊn]	Pronomen, Fürwort	
quantifier ['kwɒntɪfaɪə]	Mengenangabe	*some, a lot of, many, much*
question word ['kwestʃən wɜːd]	Fragewort	*what?, when?, where?, how?*
reflexive pronoun [rɪˌfleksɪv 'prəʊnaʊn]	Reflexivpronomen	*myself, yourself, themselves*
regular verb [ˌregjələ 'vɜːb]	regelmäßiges Verb	*(to) help – helped – helped*
relative clause [ˌrelətɪv 'klɔːz]	Relativsatz	*There's the girl* ***who helped me****.*

relative pronoun [ˌrelətɪv ˈprəʊnaʊn]	Relativpronomen	*who, that, which, whose*
reported speech [rɪˌpɔːtɪd ˈspiːtʃ]	indirekte Rede	*Sam said **(that) he was sorry**.*
request [rɪˈkwest]	Bitte	*Can you help me with this?*
short answer [ˌʃɔːt‿ˈɑːnsə]	Kurzantwort	*Yes, I am. / No, I don't.*
simple past [ˌsɪmpl ˈpɑːst]	einfache Form der Vergangenheit	*Jo **wrote** two letters yesterday.*
simple present [ˌsɪmpl ˈpreznt]	einfache Form der Gegenwart	*I always **go** to school by bike.*
singular [ˈsɪŋgjələ]	Singular, Einzahl	
statement [ˈsteɪtmənt]	Aussagesatz	
subject [ˈsʌbdʒɪkt]	Subjekt	***My sister** is writing a letter.*
tense [tens]	Zeitform	
uncountable noun [ʌnˈkaʊntəbl]	nicht zählbares Nomen	*bread, milk, money, news, work*
verb [vɜːb]	Verb	*hear, open, help, go*
***will*-future**	Futur mit *will*	*I think it **will be** cold tonight.*
word order [ˈwɜːd‿ˌɔːdə]	Wortstellung	
yes/no question	Entscheidungsfrage	*Are you 13? Do you like comics?*

Lösungen der Grammar-File-Aufgaben

p.151
1 Ella said her mom was still at work.
2 She told Jill that her mom had to work late.
3 She added that her mom wouldn't be home till nine.
4 She also said her dad would probably want a pizza.
5 She told Jill she would call again later.

p.152
1 B 'Sophia, don't forget your keys.'
2 A 'Eve, please take the chairs outside.'
3 B 'Are you nervous, Lucy?'
4 B 'Why are you late, Mani?'

Diese Wörterverzeichnisse findest du in deinem Englischbuch:

- Das **Vocabulary** (Vokabelverzeichnis – S. 159–173) enthält alle neuen Wörter und Wendungen aus Band 5, die du lernen musst. Sie stehen in der Reihenfolge, in der sie in den Units vorkommen.
- Das **Dictionary** (S. 174–202) enthält den Wortschatz der Bände 1–5 in alphabetischer Reihenfolge. Dort kannst du nachschlagen, was ein Wort bedeutet, wie man es ausspricht oder wie es geschrieben wird.

So ist das Vocabulary aufgebaut:

- Hier siehst du, wo die Wörter vorkommen.
  p. 8/1 B = Seite 8, Abschnitt 1 B
  p. 11/P 2 = Seite 11, Übung 2
- Die Lautschrift zeigt dir, wie ein Wort ausgesprochen und betont wird.
- Eingerückte Wörter lernst du am besten zusammen mit dem vorausgehenden Wort, weil die beiden zusammengehören.
- Die blauen Kästen solltest du dir besonders gut ansehen.

Tipps zum Wörterlernen findest du im Skills File auf Seite 128.

Abkürzungen:

n	= *noun*	*v*	= *verb*
adj	= *adjective*	*adv*	= *adverb*
prep	= *preposition*	*conj*	= *conjunction*
pl	= *plural*	*no pl*	= *no plural*
p.	= page	pp.	= pages
sb.	= somebody	sth.	= something
jn.	= jemanden	jm.	= jemandem
AE	= *American English*	*BE*	= *British English*
infml	= *informal* (umgangssprachlich, informell)		

Symbole:

! Hier stehen Hinweise auf Besonderheiten, bei denen man leicht Fehler machen kann.

◄► ist das „Gegenteil"-Zeichen: **outdoor ◄► indoor**

~ Die **Tilde** in den Beispielsätzen steht für das neue Wort. Beispiel: **poisonous** – Be careful! That snake could be **~**.

Unit 1: Australia

p. 6/1	**spider** ['spaɪdə]	Spinne	
	barbecue ['bɑ:bɪkju:]	Grillfest, Grillparty	 a **barbecue**
	truck [trʌk], *BE auch:* **lorry** ['lɒrɪ]	Lastwagen, LKW	a **truck/lorry** 
p. 6/2	**the outback** ['aʊtbæk]	*(Australien)* das Hinterland	
	the bush [bʊʃ]	der Busch *(unkultiviertes, „wildes" Land in Australien, Afrika)*	
	bush [bʊʃ]	Busch, Strauch	

PART A Australia – yesterday and today

p.8/1 B	**that's why**	deshalb, darum	It rained all day yesterday. **That's ~** we played at home.
	season ['si:zn]	Jahreszeit	the four **~s**: spring, summer, autumn, winter
	flag [flæg]	Flagge, Fahne	the Australian **flag**
	cross [krɒs]	Kreuz	
p.9/1 C	**Aborigine** [ˌæbəˈrɪdʒəni]	*Ureinwohner/in Australiens*	noun: **Aborigine** – adjective: **Aboriginal** [ˌæbəˈrɪdʒənl]
	prisoner ['prɪznə]	Gefangene(r)	
	prison ['prɪzn]	Gefängnis	
	independent [ˌɪndɪˈpendənt]	unabhängig	Australia became ~ from Britain in 1901.
p.9/1 D	**poisonous** ['pɔɪzənəs]	giftig	Be careful! That snake could be ~.
	poison ['pɔɪzn]	Gift	
	bite [baɪt]	Biss	
	(to) **bite** [baɪt], **bit** [bɪt], **bitten** ['bɪtn]	beißen	She was **bitten** by a poisonous snake.
p.10/P 1	**figure** ['fɪɡə]	Zahl, Ziffer	The **~s** aren't 100 per cent correct. Please check them again. ! Betonung: **figure** ['fɪɡə]
	chart [tʃɑ:t]	Diagramm	
	(to) **compare** [kəmˈpeə]	vergleichen	
	nearly ['nɪəli]	fast, beinahe	= almost
	crowded ['kraʊdɪd]	überfüllt, voll	a **crowded** bus
	crowd [kraʊd]	(Menschen-)Menge, Masse; *(infml auch:)* Clique, Gruppe	
p.11/P 2	**leaf** [li:f], *pl* **leaves** [li:vz]	Blatt *(an Pflanzen)*	a **leaf** – some **leaves**
p.11/P 3	**reef** [ri:f]	Riff	

PART B Teenagers in Australia

p.12/1	**climate** ['klaɪmət]	Klima	
	tropical ['trɒpɪkl]	tropisch, Tropen-	a **tropical** island
	dry [draɪ]	trocken	**dry** ◄► **wet**

outdoor – indoor

outdoor und **indoor** stehen immer vor einem Nomen:

outdoor education	Unterricht im Freien	**indoor market**	Markthalle
outdoor temperature	Außentemperatur	**indoor toilet**	Innentoilette
outdoor swimming pool	Freibad	**indoor swimming pool**	Hallenbad

	education [ˌedʒʊ'keɪʃn]	(Aus-)Bildung; *hier:* Unterricht	
	sunscreen ['sʌnskriːn]	Sonnenschutzmittel	Before you go in the sun you should put on some **~**.
	air [eə]	Luft	
p.13/3	**couch potato** ['kaʊtʃ pəˌteɪtəʊ] *(infml)*	Stubenhocker/in; *jemand, der viel vor dem Fernseher sitzt*	

a **couch potato**

p.14/P 2	**I see.** [ˌaɪ 'siː]	Ich verstehe. / Aha. / Ach so.	Jan's English is so good because his mother is English. – Oh, **I ~**. I didn't know that.

	lifeguard ['laɪfgɑːd]	Rettungsschwimmer/in	
	lifeguard station ['laɪfgɑːd ˌsteɪʃn]	Station der Rettungs-schwimmer/innen	
	witness ['wɪtnəs]	Zeuge, Zeugin	
p.15/P 3	**conversation** [ˌkɒnvə'seɪʃn]	Unterhaltung, Gespräch	(to) **have a conversation** = ein Gespräch führen
	How are you doing?	Wie geht's? *(zur Begrüßung)*	
	(to) **rent** sth. [rent]	etwas mieten, etwas leihen	(to) **~** a flat / a car / a DVD

PART C The Aboriginal people of Australia

p.16/1	**sunrise** ['sʌnraɪz]	Sonnenaufgang	
	sunset ['sʌnset]	Sonnenuntergang	
	ancestor ['ænsestə]	Vorfahre/Vorfahrin	Grandpa says one of our **~s** was a pirate.

(to) **plant**

a **plant**

	plant [plɑːnt]	Pflanze	
	(to) **plant** [plɑːnt]	pflanzen, einpflanzen	
	(to) **respect** [rɪ'spekt]	achten, respektieren	(to) **respect** other people's rights/opinions
	respect [rɪ'spekt]	Achtung, Respekt	
	local ['ləʊkl]	Lokal-, örtlich; *hier:* einheimisch	Can you understand the ~ dialect of Stuttgart?
	traditional [trə'dɪʃənl]	traditionell	
	exact [ɪg'zækt]	genau, exakt	What's the ~ size of Australia? Do you know?
	cultural ['kʌltʃərəl]	kulturell	
	(to) **include** [ɪn'kluːd]	(mit) einschließen, enthalten *(beinhalten)*	The tour **~d** a visit to the museum.
p.17/3	**generation** [ˌdʒenə'reɪʃn]	Generation	! Betonung: **generation** [ˌdʒenə'reɪʃn]
	government ['gʌvənmənt]	Regierung	
	orphan ['ɔːfn]	Waise, Waisenkind	a child without parents
	blanket ['blæŋkɪt]	Decke *(zum Zudecken)*	

	race [reɪs]	Rasse	
	racist ['reɪsɪst]	rassistisch; Rassist/in	
p.18/P1	rabbit-**proof** ['ræbɪt pru:f]	kaninchen-sicher, kaninchen-fest	! Wörter mit **-proof**: a **weatherproof/windproof/rainproof** jacket; a **waterproof** watch; a **fireproof** door
	fence [fens]	Zaun	a **fence** 
	relaxed [rɪ'lækst]	entspannt, gelassen	All the work was done so everybody was very ~. adjective: **relaxed** – verb: (to) **relax**
	helpless ['helpləs]	hilflos	
	panic ['pænɪk]	Panik	

PART D In the outback

He's **repairing** his car.

p.20	(to) **repair** sth. [rɪ'peə]	etwas reparieren	
	desert ['dezət]	Wüste	
	hole [həʊl]	Loch	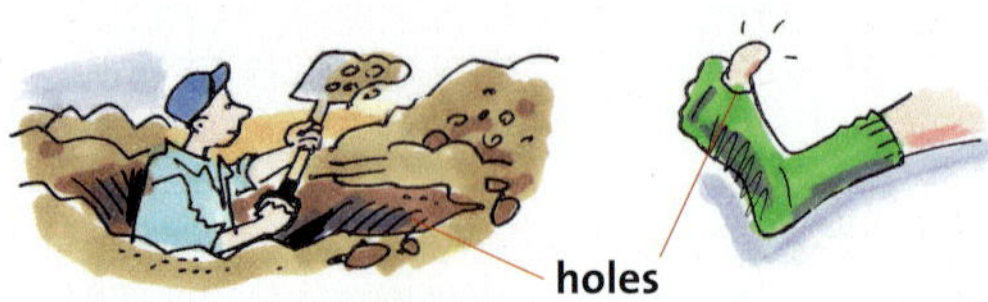
	neck [nek]	Hals, Genick	! **Hals: 1.** *(außen)* **neck** **2.** *(innen)* **throat**
p.21	(to) **shake** [ʃeɪk], **shook** [ʃʊk], **shaken** ['ʃeɪkən]	schütteln; zittern	~ the bottle before you open it. Look, he's nervous: his hands are **shaking**.
	blood [blʌd]	Blut	
	salt [sɔ:lt]	Salz	**salt** and **pepper** 
	pepper ['pepə]	Pfeffer	
	back [bæk]	Rücken	! **back**: **1.** Rücken – My **back** hurts. **2.** zurück – Let's go **back** to Sydney.
p.22	(to) **bleed** [bli:d], **bled, bled** [bled]	bluten	You're **~ing**! – Yes, I've cut my finger.
	deep [di:p]	tief	How ~ is the Atlantic Ocean?
	petrol ['petrəl]	Benzin	

Unit 2: The world of work

p.30 **apprenticeship** [ə'prentɪʃɪp]	Lehre, Ausbildung	She began her ~ as a hairdresser in 2009.
skill [skɪl]	Fähigkeit, Fertigkeit	
experience [ɪk'spɪəriəns]	Erfahrung, Erlebnis	He didn't get the job. He hasn't got enough ~. How was your trip to China? – It was a great ~.
mechanic [mə'kænɪk]	Mechaniker/in	
garage ['gærɑːʒ]	Autowerkstatt *(oft mit Tankstelle)*	
care assistant ['keər‿əˌsɪstənt]	Pfleger/in *(in einem Altenheim)*	
old people's home	Alten-, Seniorenheim	
vet's assistant [ˌvets‿ə'sɪstənt]	Tierarzthelfer/in	
office worker ['ɒfɪs wɜːkə]	Büroangestellte(r)	
roofer ['ruːfə]	Dachdecker/in	
p.31 **forklift** ['fɔːklɪft]	Gabelstapler	
p.31/1 (to) **carry** ['kæri]	tragen	! • He's **carrying** a suitcase. (Er trägt einen Koffer.) • He's **wearing** jeans and a red shirt. (Er trägt Jeans und ein rotes Hemd.)
heavy ['hevi]	schwer *(Gewicht)*	Can you help me with this box? It's very ~.
(to) **serve** [sɜːv]	bedienen *(Kunden)*	
artistic [ɑː'tɪstɪk]	künstlerisch	
calm [kɑːm]	ruhig, still	not nervous: a ~ person; quiet: a ~ sea
polite [pə'laɪt]	höflich	**polite** ◄► **impolite** [ˌɪmpə'laɪt] (= unhöflich)
organized ['ɔːgənaɪzd]	(gut) organisiert	an ~ person (= eine gut organisierte Person) ! Betonung: **organized** ['ɔːgənaɪzd] verb: (to) **organize** – adjective: **organized**
hard-working	fleißig, tüchtig	
pay [peɪ]	Bezahlung, Lohn	verb: (to) **pay** – noun: **pay** The ~ was good.

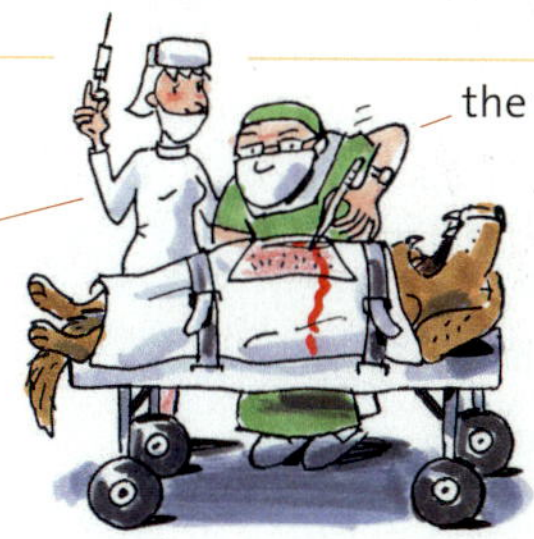

PART A Personality quiz

p.32 (to) **print** [prɪnt]	drucken	verb: (to) **print** – noun: **printer** (= Drucker)
(to) **work** [wɜːk]	funktionieren	I need your help. My printer isn't **~ing**.
(to) **ask** sb. **to do** sth.	jn. darum bitten, etwas zu tun	She **~ed** me **to** turn down the music.

ask/tell/want sb. to do sth.

She **asked** me **to help** her.	Sie bat mich, ihr zu helfen. / Sie bat mich, dass ich ihr helfe.
She **told** Daniel **to come** home early.	Sie sagte Daniel, dass er früh nach Hause kommen soll.
My sister **wants** me **to turn down** the music.	Meine Schwester möchte, dass ich die Musik leiser stelle.
! Ich möchte, **dass du mir hilfst**.	I want **you to help me.** (*Nie*: I want ~~that you help me~~.)

normal ['nɔːml]	normal, üblich	! Betonung: **normal** ['nɔːml]
(to) **solve** [sɒlv]	lösen; aufklären	(to) ~ a problem / a crime / a case

reliable [rɪ'laɪəbl]	zuverlässig, verlässlich	
p.33 **mostly** ['məʊstli]	hauptsächlich, überwiegend	Tomorrow it will be cold and ~ cloudy.
quality ['kwɒləti]	Qualität; Eigenschaft	These oranges are expensive, but very good ~. What **qualities** should a good shop assistant have?
energetic [ˌenə'dʒetɪk]	dynamisch, tatkräftig, energisch	
energy ['enədʒi]	Energie	

confident ['kɒnfɪdənt]	selbstbewusst, (selbst)sicher	
helpful ['helpfl]	hilfsbereit; hilfreich	He is a very ~ person. = Er ist sehr hilfsbereit. Your advice was ~. = Dein Rat war hilfreich.
technology [tek'nɒlədʒi]	Technologie	! Betonung: **technology** [tek'nɒlədʒi]
(to) **be serious about** sth.	etwas ernst nehmen	She **is** very ~ **about** her apprenticeship.
builder ['bɪldə]	Bauarbeiter/in	
gardener ['gɑːdnə]	Gärtner/in	
p.34/P 2 **equipment** *(no pl)* [ɪ'kwɪpmənt]	Ausrüstung; Geräte	

a **builder**

a **gardener**

p.35/P 5 **application** [ˌæplɪ'keɪʃn]	Bewerbung	**letter of application** = Bewerbungsschreiben
(to) **fill** sth. **in** [ˌfɪl_'ɪn]	etwas ausfüllen	
form [fɔːm]	Formular	
first name ['fɜːst neɪm]	Vorname	
surname ['sɜːneɪm]	Nachname	= **family name**

	work experience *(no pl)* ['wɜːk‿ɪkˌspɪəriəns]	Praktikum; Arbeits-, Praxiserfahrung(en)	**!** English: I have done **work experience** in a zoo. German: ... **ein Praktikum** in einem Zoo ...
	to date	bis heute	He sent the letter a week ago but I haven't received it **to ~**.

PART B Applying for a job

p.36/1	(to) **apply for** sth. [ə'plaɪ]	sich um/für etwas bewerben; etwas beantragen	
	CV [siː 'viː]	Lebenslauf	**CV** *ist die Abkürzung für den lateinischen Begriff* **c***urriculum* **v***itae = „Lauf des Lebens".*
	birth [bɜːθ]	Geburt	Write down your address, **date of ~** (= Geburtsdatum) and **place of ~** (= Geburtsort).
	nationality [ˌnæʃə'næləti]	Nationalität, Staatsangehörigkeit	My husband and I are different **nationalities**. He's French, I'm Canadian.
	postcode ['pəʊstkəʊd]	Postleitzahl	the **postcode** 
	secondary school ['sekəndri]	weiterführende Schule	
	primary school ['praɪməri]	Grundschule	
	qualification [ˌkwɒlɪfɪ'keɪʃn]	Abschluss, Qualifikation	**!** Betonung: **qualifi<u>ca</u>tion** [ˌkwɒlɪfɪ'keɪʃn]
	first aid [ˌfɜːst‿'eɪd]	Erste Hilfe	
	certificate [sə'tɪfɪkət]	Bescheinigung, Zertifikat	
	reference ['refrəns]	Referenz, Empfehlung	**!** Betonung: **<u>re</u>ference** ['refrəns]
p.36/2	**advertisement** [əd'vɜːtɪsmənt] (*infml:* **ad** [æd], *BE auch:* **advert** ['ædvɜːt])	Anzeige, Inserat; *(im Fernsehen)* Werbespot	You find job **~s** in newspapers or on the internet. Lots of people change channels during the **~s**.
	Dear Sir or Madam [sɜː]; ['mædəm]	Sehr geehrte Damen und Herren *(Anrede in Briefen)*	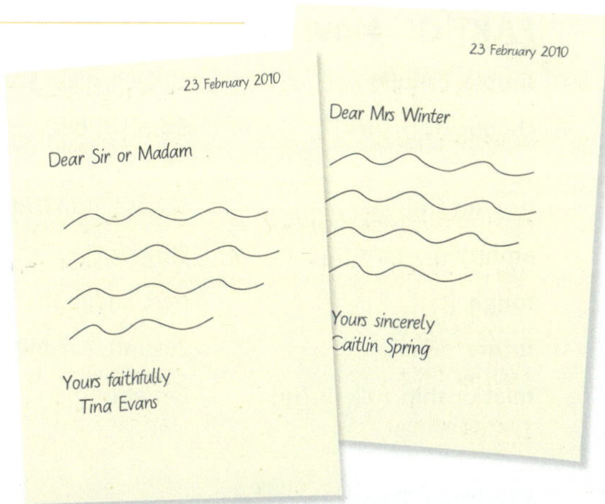
	Yours faithfully ['feɪθfəli]	Mit freundlichen Grüßen *(der Name des Empfängers / der Empfängerin ist unbekannt)*	
	Yours sincerely [sɪn'sɪəli]	Mit freundlichen Grüßen *(der Name des Empfängers / der Empfängerin ist bekannt)*	
	(to) **enclose** sth. [ɪn'kləʊz]	etwas *(einem Brief)* beilegen	I **enclose** my CV. *or* My CV **is enclosed**.
	reception [rɪ'sepʃn]	Rezeption, Empfang	
	(to) **look forward to** sth. ['fɔːwəd]	sich auf etwas freuen	I've always wanted to be a vet's assistant. So I'm really **looking ~ to** my apprenticeship.
p.37/P1	**similar (to)** ['sɪmələ]	ähnlich (wie)	A highway in the USA is **~ to** an *Autobahn* in Germany. The brothers look very **~**.

PART C A reality TV show

p.38/1	**candidate** ['kændɪdət]	Kandidat/in, Bewerber/in	! Betonung: **candidate** ['kændɪdət]
	(job) interview	Vorstellungsgespräch	
p.38/2	**carefully** ['keəfəli]	aufmerksam; vorsichtig; gründlich, sorgfältig	They listened ~. (= aufmerksam) Ride your bike ~. (= vorsichtig) He did his work ~. (= sorgfältig, gründlich)
	(to) **dress** [dres]	sich kleiden	Emily has very nice clothes and always **~es** well. ! „sich anziehen" im Sinne von „sich ankleiden, Kleidung anziehen" = (to) **get dressed**: After I got up, I **got dressed** and went to school.
	suitable ['su:təbl]	geeignet, passend	Jeans aren't ~ clothes for a job interview. Dress **suitably** when you go for a job interview.
	strength [streŋθ]	Stärke, Kraft	adjective: **strong** – noun: **strength**
p.38/3	**assessment** [ə'sesmənt]	Einschätzung, Beurteilung	
	sheet [ʃi:t]	Blatt, Bogen *(Papier)*	
p.40/P 3	**tie** [taɪ]	Krawatte, Schlips	
	(to) **tie** [taɪ]	binden	

He's **tying** his son's tie.

She's **tying** her hair back.

! -ing form: **tying**

p.41/P 5	**Hold the line.**	Bleiben Sie am Apparat.	
	exchange rate [ɪks'tʃeɪndʒ reɪt]	Wechselkurs	

PART D How to be a teenage millionaire

p.42	**simple** ['sɪmpl]	einfach, nicht kompliziert	
p.43	**cheque (for)** [tʃek]	Scheck (über)	Ashley's mum was surprised when they received a ~ **for** $ 2,700.
	(to) **run** sth.	etwas leiten *(Hotel, Firma usw.)*	My aunt is a mechanic and **~s** her own garage.
	ambition [æm'bɪʃn]	Ehrgeiz	
	tough [tʌf]	hart, knallhart	
p.44	**future** ['fju:tʃə]	Zukunft; Zukunfts-, zukünftige(r,s)	Have you got any plans for the ~?
	relationship [rɪ'leɪʃnʃɪp]	Beziehung	

Unit 3: Teen world

p.46	**only child** [ˌəʊnli 'tʃaɪld]	Einzelkind	Does she have any brothers or sisters? – No, she's an ~ **child**.
	(to) **get on well/badly (with** sb.**)**	sich gut/schlecht verstehen (mit jm.), gut/schlecht auskommen (mit jm.)	They ~ **on well with** each other. They're good friends.
	ideal [aɪ'di:əl]	ideal	
	(to) want to **be** sth.	etwas werden wollen *(beruflich)*	When I finish school I want to ~ a vet's assistant.

PART A Mobile teens

p.48/1	(to) **communicate** [kə'mju:nɪkeɪt]	kommunizieren	
	communication [kə,mju:nɪ'keɪʃn]	Kommunikation	

Verbs and their nouns

(to) **apply**	sich bewerben	(to) **present** [prɪ'zent]	präsentieren, vorstellen
application	Bewerbung	**presentation** [,prezn'teɪʃn]	Präsentation
(to) **communicate**	kommunizieren	(to) **produce**	produzieren
communication	Kommunikation	**production**	Produktion
(to) **discuss**	diskutieren	(to) **revise** [aɪ]	wiederholen; überarbeiten
discussion	Diskussion	**revision** [ɪ]	Wiederholung; Überarbeitung
(to) **organize** ['ɔ:gənaɪz]	organisieren	(to) **translate**	übersetzen
organization [,ɔ:gənaɪ'zeɪʃn]	Organisation	**translation**	Übersetzung

	(to) **get bored** [bɔ:d]	sich langweilen	I **got ~** at the party so I left early.
	(to) **be addicted (to** sth.**)** [ə'dɪktɪd]	abhängig (von etwas) sein, süchtig (nach etwas) sein	She**'s ~ to** chocolate – she eats it all the time.
	(to) **give** sth. **up**	auf etwas verzichten	Some people **~ up** sweets before Easter.
	alarm clock [ə'lɑ:m klɒk]	Wecker	 an **alarm clock**
	(to) **set the alarm clock (-tt-)** [set]**, set, set** [set]	den Wecker stellen	
	as usual ['ju:ʒuəl]	wie immer, wie üblich	We're waiting for Jo. He's late, **as ~**.
	annoying [ə'nɔɪɪŋ]	ärgerlich, lästig	I always lose my keys. It's so **~**. Sometimes my little brother is **~**. (... geht mir auf die Nerven.)
	not (...) at all [ət_'ɔ:l]	überhaupt nicht, ganz und gar nicht	Do you think my plan is crazy? – No, **not at ~**. I can't help you. I have**n't** got any money **at ~**.
p.49/1	**wedding** ['wedɪŋ]	Hochzeit, Trauung	
	funeral ['fju:nərəl]	Trauerfeier, Beerdigung	
	secretly ['si:krətli]	heimlich	• *(adv)* She **secretly** put some salt into his tea. • *(adj)* We had a **secret** meeting. (geheim) • *(n)* I can't tell you. It's a **secret**. (Geheimnis)
	(to) **ask** sb. **out**	sich mit jm. verabreden; jn. einladen, mit einem auszugehen	If you really like him, why don't you **~** him **out**?
	(to) **dump** sb. [dʌmp] *(infml)*	mit jm. Schluss machen	She **~ed** her boyfriend but now she'd like to have him back.
	perhaps [pə'hæps]	vielleicht	= maybe

p.50/P 1	(to) **get annoyed (with** sb./ **about** sth.**)** [ə'nɔɪd]	sich ärgern (über jn./etwas)	• I **got** really **annoyed with** him because he was late. = Ich habe mich über ihn geärgert ... • She was **annoyed**. = Sie war verärgert. • He's **annoying**. = Er geht mir auf die Nerven.
	(to) **ban (-nn-)** [bæn]	verbieten; ein (Aufenthalts-) Verbot erteilen	They've **~ned** smoking at our youth club. Sports stadiums should **~** people who use racist language.
	complete [kəm'pli:t]	vollständig, völlig	I'm sorry. I **~ly** forgot that it's your birthday today. verb: (to) **complete** – adjective: **complete** adverb: **completely**
p.51/P 3	(to) **save** sth. [seɪv]	etwas (ab)speichern *(Daten, Telefonnummern)*	
	(to) **miss** sth. [mɪs]	etwas verpassen	Jo has **~ed** his bus to school.
	contact ['kɒntækt]	Kontakt, Verbindung	**contacts** *(pl)* *(im Handy, im Mailprogramm)* = Liste von Bekannten/Kontakten
p.51/P 4	**phrase** [freɪz]	Ausdruck, (Rede-)Wendung	
	cash [kæʃ]	Bargeld	**!** (to) **pay cash** = bar bezahlen
	credit card ['kredɪt kɑ:d]	Kreditkarte	(to) **pay <u>by</u> credit card** = <u>mit</u> Kreditkarte bezahlen **!** Betonung: **<u>cre</u>dit card** ['kredɪt kɑ:d]
	receipt [rɪ'si:t]	Quittung; Kassenbon	
	(to) **enter** sth. ['entə]	etwas eingeben *(Geheimzahl)*	~ your PIN, please.
	headphones *(pl)* ['hedfəʊnz]	Kopfhörer	

PART B Teens in trouble

p.52/1	**troublemaker** ['trʌblmeɪkə]	Randalierer/in, Unruhestifter/in	
	(to) **vandalize** ['vændəlaɪz]	mutwillig beschädigen, mutwillig zerstören	A gang of kids has **~d** cars in the city centre.
	motorbike ['məʊtəbaɪk]	Motorrad	
	(to) **cause** [kɔ:z]	verursachen	They don't know what **~d** the fire.
	behaviour (towards sb.**)** [bɪ'heɪvjə]	Verhalten, Benehmen (gegenüber jm.)	His **~ towards** me has changed. He's very friendly now.
	order ['ɔ:də]	Befehl, Anweisung, Anordnung	
	court [kɔ:t]	Gericht(shof)	
	(to) **put** sth. **up**	etwas aufhängen	Let's **~** these posters **up** on the classroom wall.
p.53/2	(to) **hesitate** ['hezɪteɪt]	zögern	She **~d** for a moment before she answered the policeman's question.

	pressure ['preʃə]	Druck	
	shout [ʃaʊt]	Schrei, Ruf	noun: **shout** – verb: (to) **shout**
	(to) **shout at** sb.	jn. anschreien	Don't **shout** ~ me. It's not my fault.
p.54/P 1	(to) **decide (on** sth.**)** [dɪ'saɪd]	(etwas) beschließen; sich entscheiden (für etwas)	Have you **~d** what project you would like to do? We have **~d on** a project about jobs. (= We've **~d** to do a project about jobs.)
	decision [dɪ'sɪʒn]	Entscheidung	
p.55/P 3	**discipline** ['dɪsəplɪn]	Disziplin	
	easy-going [ˌiːzi'gəʊɪŋ]	gelassen, locker	Is your dad strict? – No, he's really ~.
	shocking ['ʃɒkɪŋ]	schockierend	! • It was **shocking** to see so many homeless people on the streets. (= schockierend) • Everybody was **shocked**. (= schockiert)

PART C Teens getting involved

p.56/1	**training** ['treɪnɪŋ]	*(berufliche)* Ausbildung	He had to do special ~ to become a paramedic.
	lazy ['leɪzi]	faul	
	(to) **make friends**	Freundschaften schließen, sich anfreunden	
p.57/P 1	(to) **sum** sth. **up (-mm-)** [ˌsʌm‿'ʌp]	etwas zusammenfassen	At the end of her speech, she **~med up** her main ideas.

PART D The caller

p.58	(to) **go red**	rot werden, erröten	She was so embarrassed that she **went** ~.
	unkind [ˌʌn'kaɪnd]	unfreundlich	**unkind ◄► kind**
	voice [vɔɪs]	Stimme	
	Nice try.	Netter Versuch. *(ironisch)*	**Nice try**. Maybe you'll be luckier next time.
p.59	**knock** [nɒk]	Klopfen	There was a ~ on the door. (= Es klopfte.)
	(to) **knock (at/on** sth.**)** [nɒk]	(an etwas) klopfen	He's **~ing at** the door.
	prayer ['preə]	Gebet	
	(to) **pray** [preɪ]	beten	
	(to) **hang up** [ˌhæŋ‿'ʌp], **hung, hung** [hʌŋ]	*(den Telefonhörer)* auflegen	After a one-hour telephone call I said goodbye and **hung** ~.
	(to) **dial** (*BE:* **-ll-**) ['daɪəl]	*(Telefonnummer)* wählen	
	(to) **leave** sb. **alone**	jn. in Ruhe lassen	Have you tidied your room, Phil? – Oh Mum, **leave** me ~.
	muddy ['mʌdi]	schlammig, matschig, schmutzig	
	mud [mʌd]	Schlamm, Matsch	**mud**

Unit 4: Exploring cities

p.70	**traffic jam** ['træfɪk dʒæm]	(Verkehrs-)Stau	a **traffic jam** 
	official [ə'fɪʃl]	offiziell, amtlich, Amts-	Canada has two ~ languages: French and English. ! Betonung: **official** [ə'fɪʃl]
	pollution [pə'lu:ʃn]	(Umwelt-)Verschmutzung	
	contrast ['kɒntrɑ:st]	Kontrast, Gegensatz	! Betonung: **contrast** ['kɒntrɑ:st]
	a third	ein Drittel	= ⅓
p.71	**unemployment** [,ʌnɪm'plɔɪmənt]	Arbeitslosigkeit	~ rose in the town after the factory closed.
	electricity [ɪ,lek'trɪsəti]	Strom, Elektrizität	
	suburb ['sʌbɜ:b]	Vorort	
p.71/2	**public transport** *(no pl)* [,pʌblɪk 'trænspɔ:t]	öffentlicher Personennahverkehr, öffentliche Verkehrsmittel	It's cheaper to use ~ **transport** than to go by car. ! Betonung: **transport** ['trænspɔ:t]

PART A Mumbai

p.72/1	**crazy** ['kreɪzi]	verrückt	You want to go out in this rain? You must be ~.
	positive ['pɒzətɪv]	positiv	**positive** ◄► **negative** ['negətɪv]
p.73/1	**typical (of)** ['tɪpɪkl]	typisch (für)	! Alan arrived ten minutes late. – That's ~ **of** him. (*not:* ... typical ~~for~~ him)
	(to) **live on** sth.	von etwas leben; sich von etwas ernähren	I don't know how they can **live** ~ £ 55 a week. Giraffes **live** ~ leaves and other plants.
	rush hour ['rʌʃ‿aʊə]	Hauptverkehrszeit	
	colourful ['kʌləfl]	farbenfroh, farbenprächtig, farbig	women in **colourful** saris 
	shock [ʃɒk]	Schock	
	sick [sɪk] *(besonders AE)*	krank	**ill** *(besonders BE)*
p.75/P 3	**flu** [flu:]	Grippe	I have a headache and a temperature. I think I have (the) ~.
	pain [peɪn]	Schmerz(en)	

	virus ['vaɪrəs], *pl* **viruses** ['vaɪrəsəz]	Virus	! Aussprache: **virus** ['vaɪrəs]
	cream [kriːm]	Salbe; Creme	
	medicine ['medsn, 'medɪsn]	Medizin	You'll feel better after you've taken your ~. She's studying ~ at university.
	pill [pɪl]	Pille, Tablette	
	prescription [prɪ'skrɪpʃn]	Rezept *(für Medikamente)*	The doctor gave me a ~ for some pills.

PART B Johannesburg

p.76/1	**honest** ['ɒnɪst]	ehrlich	Is my dress really OK? Be ~! ! Aussprache: **honest** ['ɒnɪst]
	how to do sth.	wie man etwas tut / tun kann / tun soll	

how to ... / what to ... / where to ... / ...

Nach **Fragewörtern** kannst du einen **Infinitiv mit *to*** verwenden.
Er entspricht einem Nebensatz mit „können", „sollen" usw.

Can you tell me **how to get** to the station?	Können Sie mir sagen, wie ich zum Bahnhof komme / kommen kann?
I don't know **what to do**.	Ich weiß nicht, was ich machen soll.
He had no idea **where to go** or **who to ask**.	Er hatte keine Ahnung, wohin er gehen sollte oder wen er fragen könnte.

p.77/2	**mainly** ['meɪnli]	hauptsächlich	The hotel was full of tourists, ~ from Germany.
	wood [wʊd]	Holz	a piece of **wood** 
	metal ['metl]	Metall	! Betonung: **metal** ['metl]
	way [weɪ]	Art und Weise	A good ~ to make friends is to join a club.
	hero ['hɪərəʊ], *pl* **heroes** ['hɪərəʊz]	Held/in; Idol, Vorbild	Nelson Mandela is a ~ to many people in South Africa. She was very brave. I think she's a ~.
	unforgettable [ˌʌnfə'getəbl]	unvergesslich	Working as a volunteer in Johannesburg was an ~ experience.
	especially [ɪ'speʃəli]	besonders, vor allem	I love chocolate, ~ chocolate from Belgium or Switzerland.

PART C Berlin: City survival kit

p.80	**survival** [sə'vaɪvl]	Überleben	**survival** of the fittest = das Überleben der Stärksten noun: **survival** – verb: (to) **survive**
	kit [kɪt]	Ausrüstung	**survival kit** = Überlebenspäckchen **first-aid kit** = Verbandskasten, Erste-Hilfe-Kasten **repair kit** = Flickzeug
	(to) **book** [bʊk]	buchen, reservieren	(to) ~ a room / a table / a flight / a holiday / a ticket

complicated [ˈkɒmplɪkeɪtɪd]	kompliziert	**complicated ◄► simple**
passport [ˈpɑːspɔːt]	(Reise-)Pass	
somewhere to stay	ein Platz zum Übernachten	
dormitory [ˈdɔːmətri] (*infml:* **dorm** [dɔːm])	Schlafsaal	
double room [ˌdʌbl ˈruːm]	Doppelzimmer	**single room** [ˌsɪŋgl ˈruːm] = Einzelzimmer
need to do sth.	etwas tun müssen; etwas zu tun brauchen	

need to do sth.

Everybody **needs <u>to</u>** sleep, eat and drink.	Jeder **muss** schlafen, essen und trinken.
You **don't need <u>to</u>** wait for me.	Du **brauchst nicht** auf mich zu warten.
I **didn't need <u>to</u>** tell her. She knew it already.	Ich **musste** es ihr **nicht** erzählen.
Do we **need <u>to</u>** book a table?	**Müssen** wir einen Tisch buchen?

basement [ˈbeɪsmənt]	Keller(geschoss)	
p. 81 **gate** [geɪt]	Tor; Pforte	
on top of sth. [ɒn ˈtɒp]	oben, oben drauf (auf etwas)	Can I have some cake with cream **on ~**, please?
Never mind. [ˌnevə ˈmaɪnd]	Macht nichts.	
(to) **queue** [kjuː]	sich anstellen; anstehen	verb: (to) **queue** – noun: **queue**
p. 83/P 2 (to) **check in** [ˌtʃek‿ˈɪn]	einchecken *(Hotel, Flughafen)*	(to) **check in ◄►** (to) **check out** (auschecken)
wake-up call	Weckanruf	
fully booked	ausgebucht	
pleasant [ˈpleznt]	angenehm	
stay [steɪ]	Aufenthalt	noun: **stay** – verb: (to) **stay**

gates

Have a ...

Have a pleasant stay.	Einen angenehmen Aufenthalt!
Have a good trip/journey.	Gute Reise!
Have a good holiday/weekend.	Schöne Ferien! / Schönes Wochenende!
Have a good time.	Viel Spaß!

	connection [kə'nekʃn]	Verbindung	
	(to) **connect (to/with)** [kə'nekt]	verbinden (mit)	verb: (to) **connect** – noun: **connection**
p.83/P 3	(to) **leave a message**	eine Nachricht hinterlassen	
	(to) **take a message**	eine Nachricht entgegen-nehmen	Can I **take a message** for her/him? (= Soll ich ihr/ihm etwas ausrichten?)
p.84/P 4	**talk** [tɔːk]	Vortrag, Rede	
	(to) **give a talk (on** sth.**)**	einen Vortrag / eine Rede halten (über etwas)	
	basic ['beɪsɪk]	grundlegend; Grund-, Haupt-	**basic** computer skills; the **basic** idea/problem/question
	(to) **divide** sth. **(into)** [dɪ'vaɪd]	etwas (auf)teilen (in)	The teacher **~d** the class **into** six groups.
	finally ['faɪnəli]	zuletzt, als letztes	We visited Mumbai, New Delhi and ~ Kolkata.
	slide [slaɪd]	Folie *(bei einer Computer-präsentation);* Dia	
	(to) **introduce** sth. [ˌɪntrə'djuːs]	etwas einführen *(Thema, Methode, Währung)*	In what year was the Euro **~d**?
	visual ['vɪʒuəl]	visuell; optisch	! Betonung: **<u>vi</u>sual** ['vɪʒuəl]
	material [mə'tɪəriəl]	Material	! Betonung: **ma<u>te</u>rial** [mə'tɪəriəl]

Das **Dictionary** enthält den Wortschatz der Bände 1 bis 5 von *English G 21.*
Wenn du wissen möchtest, was ein Wort bedeutet, wie man es ausspricht oder wie es geschrieben wird, kannst du hier nachschlagen.

Im **Dictionary** werden folgende **Abkürzungen und Symbole** verwendet:

jm. = jemandem	sb. = somebody	*pl = plural*	*AE = American English*
jn. = jemanden	sth. = something	*no pl = no plural*	*infml = informal*

- ° Mit diesem Kringel sind Wörter markiert, die nicht zum Lernwortschatz gehören.
- ► Der Pfeil verweist auf Kästchen im **Vocabulary** (S. 159–173), in denen du weitere Informationen zu diesem Wort findest.

Die **Fundstellenangaben** zeigen, wo ein Wort zum ersten Mal vorkommt.
Die Ziffern in Klammern bezeichnen Seitenzahlen:

I = Band 1 • II = Band 2 • III = Band 3 • IV = Band 4 • V = Band 5
V 1 (6) = Band 5, Unit 1, Seite 6
V 1 (6/160) = Band 5, Unit 1, Seite 160 (im Vocabulary, zu Seite 6)

Tipps zur Arbeit mit einem Wörterbuch findest du im Skills File auf Seite 130.

Tipp

Auf der **Audio-CD im Workbook** findest du sowohl dieses englisch-deutsche Wörterverzeichnis als auch ein deutsch-englisches Wörterverzeichnis mit dem Lernwortschatz der Bände 1–5.

A

a [ə]
1. ein, eine I
2. once/twice a week einmal/zweimal pro Woche III • **a bit** ein bisschen, etwas II • **a few** ein paar, einige II • **a little** ein wenig/ein bisschen IV • **a lot (of)** eine Menge, viel, viele II • **He likes her a lot.** Er mag sie sehr. I

able ['eɪbl]**: be able to do sth.** etwas tun können; fähig sein / in der Lage sein, etwas zu tun III

Aboriginal [ˌæbə'rɪdʒənl] *(bezüglich der Ureinwohner Australiens)* Aborigine- V 1 (9/160)

Aborigine [ˌæbə'rɪdʒəni] Ureinwohner/in Australiens V 1 (9)

about [ə'baʊt]
1. über I
2. ungefähr II
ask about sth. nach etwas fragen I • **How about ...?** Wie wär's mit ...? III • **This is about Mr Green.** Es geht um Mr Green. I
What about ...? 1. Was ist mit ...? / Und ...? I; **2.** Wie wär's mit ...? I
What are you talking about? Wovon redest du? I • **What was the best thing about ...?** Was war das Beste an ...? II

above [ə'bʌv] oben; über, oberhalb (von) IV

°academy [ə'kædəmi] Akademie

accent ['æksənt] Akzent II

accident ['æksɪdənt] Unfall II

across [ə'krɒs] (quer) über III

act [ækt] aufführen, spielen I
°Act out ... Spiele/Spielt ... vor.

action film ['ækʃn fɪlm] Actionfilm V 1 (18)

activity [æk'tɪvəti] Aktivität, Tätigkeit I

actor ['æktə] Schauspieler/in II

actually ['æktʃuəli] nebenbei bemerkt; übrigens IV

ad [æd] *(infml)* Anzeige, Inserat; *(im Fernsehen)* Werbespot V 2 (36/165)

°adapted [ə'dæptɪd] adaptiert, bearbeitet

add (to) [æd] hinzufügen, ergänzen, addieren (zu) I

addicted [ə'dɪktɪd]**: be addicted (to sth.)** abhängig (von etwas) sein, süchtig (nach etwas) sein V 3 (48)

address [ə'dres] Adresse, Anschrift II

adult ['ædʌlt] Erwachsene(r) III

advantage [əd'vɑːntɪdʒ] Vorteil IV

adventure [əd'ventʃə] Abenteuer IV

advert ['ædvɜːt] Anzeige, Inserat; *(im Fernsehen)* Werbespot V 2 (36)

advertisement [əd'vɜːtɪsmənt] Anzeige, Inserat; *(im Fernsehen)* Werbespot V 2 (36)

°advertising company ['ædvətaɪzɪŋ ˌkʌmpəni] Werbeagentur

advice *(no pl)* [əd'vaɪs] Rat, Ratschläge III

afraid [ə'freɪd]
1. be afraid (of) Angst haben (vor) I
2. I'm afraid leider II

African American [ˌæfrɪkən_ə'merɪkən] Afro-Amerikaner/in; afroamerikanisch IV

°Afrikaans [ˌæfrɪ'kɑːns] Afrikaans *(eine der elf Amtssprachen Südafrikas, aus dem Niederländischen entstanden)*

after ['ɑːftə] nach *(zeitlich)* I
after that danach I

after ['ɑːftə] nachdem II

afternoon [ˌɑːftə'nuːn] Nachmittag I • **in the afternoon** nachmittags, am Nachmittag I • **on Friday afternoon** freitagnachmittags, am Freitagnachmittag I

again [ə'gen] wieder; noch einmal I

against [ə'genst] gegen III

age [eɪdʒ] Alter III

ago [ə'gəʊ]**: a minute ago** vor einer Minute I

agree (on) [ə'griː] sich einigen (auf) I • **agree with sb./sth.** jm./etwas zustimmen; mit jm./etwas übereinstimmen II

aid: first aid [ˌfɜːst_'eɪd] Erste Hilfe V 2 (36)

air [eə] Luft V 1 (12) • **°School of the Air** *Fernunterricht über Kurzwellenfunk in den dünn besiedelten Gebieten Australiens, für die Primarstufe und die untere Sekundarstufe*

airport ['eəpɔːt] Flughafen III

alarm clock [ə'lɑːm klɒk] Wecker V 3 (48) • **set the alarm clock** den Wecker stellen V 3 (48/167)

alive [ə'laɪv] am Leben, lebendig IV

all [ɔːl] alle; alles I • **all day** den ganzen Tag (lang) I • **all over the world** auf der ganzen Welt III
all right gut, in Ordnung II • **all the time** die ganze Zeit I • **all**

the way den ganzen Weg IV • **from all over the UK/the world/England** aus dem gesamten Vereinigten Königreich/aus der ganzen Welt/aus ganz England III • **not (...) at all** überhaupt nicht, ganz und gar nicht V 3 (48) • **This is all wrong.** Das ist ganz falsch. I

allowed [ə'laʊd]**: be allowed to do sth.** etwas tun dürfen III

alone [ə'ləʊn] allein I • **leave sb. alone** jn. in Ruhe lassen V 3 (59)

along the street [ə'lɒŋ] entlang der Straße / die Straße entlang II

alphabet ['ælfəbet] Alphabet I

°**alphabetical** [,ælfə'betɪkl] alphabetisch

already [ɔ:l'redi] schon, bereits II

also ['ɔ:lsəʊ] auch II

always ['ɔ:lweɪz] immer I

am [,eɪ_'em]**: 7 am** 7 Uhr morgens/vormittags I

amazing [ə'meɪzɪŋ] erstaunlich, unglaublich II

ambition [æm'bɪʃn] Ehrgeiz V 2 (43)

ambulance ['æmbjələns] Krankenwagen III

American football [ə,merɪkən 'fʊtbɔ:l] Football I

amnesty ['æmnəsti] Amnestie, Straferlass, Begnadigung IV

an [ən] ein, eine I

ancestor ['ænsestə] Vorfahre/Vorfahrin V 1 (16)

and [ənd, ænd] und I

angel ['eɪndʒl] Engel II

angry (about sth./with sb.) ['æŋgri] wütend, böse (über etwas/auf jn.) II

animal ['ænɪml] Tier II • °**put down an animal** ein Tier einschläfern

announcement [ə'naʊnsmənt] Durchsage, Ansage; Ankündigung, Bekanntgabe III

annoyed [ə'nɔɪd]**: be annoyed** verärgert sein V 3 (50/168) • **get annoyed (with sb.; at/about sth.)** sich (über jn./über etwas) ärgern V 3 (50)

annoying [ə'nɔɪɪŋ] ärgerlich, lästig V 3 (48) • **sb. is annoying** jemand geht auf die Nerven V 3 (48/167)

anorak ['ænəræk] Anorak, Windjacke III

another [ə'nʌðə] ein(e) andere(r, s); noch ein(e) I • **another 45 p** weitere 45 Pence, noch 45 Pence II

answer ['ɑ:nsə] antworten; beantworten I

answer (to) ['ɑ:nsə] Antwort (auf) I

anti- ['ænti] anti- V 3 (52)

any ['eni] irgendein, irgendwelche; jede(r,s) IV • **any ...?** (irgend)welche ...? I • **not (...) any** kein, keine I • **not (...) any more** nicht mehr III

anybody ['enibɒdi] (irgend)jemand II; jede(r) IV • **not (...) anybody** niemand II

anyone ['eniwʌn] jede(r) IV

anything ['eniθɪŋ] (irgend)etwas II; alles IV • **anything else** [els] (irgend)etwas anderes IV • **not (...) anything** nichts II

anyway ['eniweɪ]
1. sowieso I
2. trotzdem II
3. aber egal; wie auch immer; wie dem auch sei IV

anywhere ['eniweə] irgendwo(hin) II • **not (...) anywhere** nirgendwo(hin) II

°**apartheid** [ə'pɑ:taɪt] Apartheid *(bis 1994 Trennung von Schwarzen und Weißen in Südafrika)*

apartment [ə'pɑ:tmənt] *(AE)* Wohnung IV

appetite ['æpɪtaɪt] Appetit III

apple ['æpl] Apfel I

application [,æplɪ'keɪʃn] Bewerbung V 2 (35) • **letter of application** Bewerbungsschreiben V 2 (35/164)

apply for sth. [ə'plaɪ] sich bewerben um/für etwas; etwas beantragen V 2 (36)

appointment [ə'pɔɪntmənt] Termin, Verabredung I

apprenticeship [ə'prentɪʃɪp] Lehre, Ausbildung V 2 (30)

April ['eɪprəl] April I

are [ɑ:] bist; sind; seid I • **How are you?** Wie geht es dir/Ihnen/euch? II • **The pencils are 35 p.** Die Bleistifte kosten 35 Pence. I • **You're joking, aren't you?** Du machst Witze, nicht wahr? / Das ist nicht dein Ernst, oder? II

area ['eəriə] Bereich; Gebiet, Gegend III

argue ['ɑ:gju:] sich streiten, sich zanken I

argument ['ɑ:gjumənt]
1. Argument IV
2. Streit IV

arm [ɑ:m] Arm I

armchair ['ɑ:mtʃeə] Sessel I

around [ə'raʊnd] um ... (herum); in ... umher, durch III • **around six** um sechs herum, gegen sechs III • **around the lake** um den See herum III • **around the town** in der Stadt umher, durch die Stadt III • **run/jump around** herumrennen, -springen III **walk around** herumgehen, umherspazieren III

arrival (arr) [ə'raɪvl] Ankunft III

arrive [ə'raɪv] ankommen, eintreffen II

art [ɑ:t] Kunst I

article ['ɑ:tɪkl] (Zeitungs-)Artikel III

artificial [,ɑ:tɪ'fɪʃl] künstlich, Kunst- III

artist ['ɑ:tɪst] Künstler/in; Grafiker/in III

artistic [ɑ:'tɪstɪk] künstlerisch V 2 (31)

as *(prep)* [əz, æz] als IV • **as a firefighter** als Feuerwehrmann, -frau IV

as *(conj)* [əz, æz] als, während II

as ... as [əz, æz] so ... wie II • **as old/big as** so alt/groß wie II

as usual [əz 'ju:ʒuəl] wie immer, wie üblich V 3 (48)

°**ASBO** ['æzbəʊ] **(anti-social behaviour order)** einstweilige Verfügung wegen antisozialen Verhaltens

ask [ɑ:sk] fragen I • **ask about sth.** nach etwas fragen I • **ask questions** Fragen stellen I • **ask sb. for directions** jn. nach dem Weg fragen; jn. um eine Wegbeschreibung bitten IV • **ask sb. out** sich mit jm. verabreden; jn. einladen mit einem auszugehen V 3 (49) **ask sb. the way** jn. nach dem Weg fragen II • **ask sb. to do sth.** jn. darum bitten etwas zu tun V 2 (32)

► S.164 ask/tell/expect/want sb. to do sth.

asleep [ə'sli:p]**: be asleep** schlafen I • °**fall asleep** einschlafen

°**aspect** ['æspekt] Aspekt

Assembly [ə'sembli] Versammlung *(morgendliche Schulversammlung, oft mit Andacht)* III

assessment [ə'sesmənt] Einschätzung, Beurteilung V 2 (38)

assistant: care assistant ['keər_ə,sɪstənt] Pfleger/in *(in einem Altenheim)* V 2 (30) • **vet's assistant** [,vets_ə'sɪstənt] Tierarzthelfer/in V 2 (30)

at [ət, æt]**: at 7 Hamilton Street** in der Hamiltonstraße 7 I • **at 8.45** um 8.45 I • **at break** in der Pause *(zwischen Schulstunden)* II • **at first** zuerst, am Anfang IV • **at home** daheim, zu Hause I • **at last** endlich, schließlich I • **at least** zumindest, wenigstens I **at night** nachts, in der Nacht I **at school** in der Schule I • **at that table** an dem Tisch (dort) / an den

Tisch (dort) I • **at the bottom (of)** unten, am unteren Ende (von) II
at the butcher's / at the chemist's beim Metzger/beim Apotheker III
at the end (of) am Ende (von) I
at the Shaws' house im Haus der Shaws / bei den Shaws zu Hause I
at the station am Bahnhof I • **at the top (of)** oben, am oberen Ende, an der Spitze (von) I • **at the weekend** am Wochenende I • **at work** bei der Arbeit / am Arbeitsplatz I • **not (...) at all** überhaupt nicht, ganz und gar nicht V 3 (48)
ate [et, eɪt] *siehe* **eat**
athletics [æθ'letɪks] Leichtathletik III
attack [ə'tæk] angreifen III
attack [ə'tæk] Angriff III
attitude (to/towards) ['ætɪtju:d] Haltung (gegenüber) Einstellung (zu) IV
audience ['ɔ:dɪəns] Publikum; Zuschauer/innen, Zuhörer/innen II
August ['ɔ:gəst] August I
aunt [ɑ:nt] Tante I • **auntie** ['ɑ:nti] Tante II
°**Aussie** ['ɒzi] *(infml)* Australier/in; australisch • °**Aussie Rules football** *Australischer Nationalsport*
°**auto-rickshaw** ['ɔ:təʊˌrɪkʃɔ:] Auto-Rikscha
autumn ['ɔ:təm] Herbst I
avenue ['ævənju:] Allee IV
average ['ævərɪdʒ] Durchschnitt, durchschnittlich, Durchschnitts- IV • **on average** im Durchschnitt
away [ə'weɪ] weg, fort I • **turn away** sich abwenden, sich wegdrehen IV
awesome ['ɔ:səm] *(AE, infml)* klasse, großartig IV
awful ['ɔ:fl] furchtbar, schrecklich II

B

baby ['beɪbi] Baby I • **have a baby** ein Baby/Kind bekommen II
back [bæk] Rücken V 1 (21)
back (to) [bæk] zurück (nach) I
back door [ˌbæk 'dɔ:] Hintertür II
background ['bækgraʊnd] Hintergrund II • **background file** *etwa:* Hintergrundinformation(en) II
backpack ['bækpæk] Rucksack IV
°**backwards** ['bækwədz] nach hinten
bacon ['beɪkən] Schinkenspeck II
bad [bæd] schlecht, schlimm I
be bad at sth. schlecht in etwas sein; etwas schlecht können IV
badly ['bædli]**: do badly (in)** schlecht abschneiden (in) III • **get on badly (with sb.)** sich schlecht verstehen (mit jm)., schlecht auskommen (mit jm.) V 3 (46)
badminton ['bædmɪntən] Badminton, Federball I • **badminton racket** Badmintonschläger III
bag [bæg] Tasche, Beutel, Tüte I
bagel ['beɪgl] Bagel *(ringförmiges Gebäck)* IV
baggy ['bægi] weit (geschnitten) III
°**bait** [beɪt] Köder
bakery ['beɪkəri] Bäckerei III
ball [bɔ:l]
1. Ball *(Sport)* I
2. Ball *(Tanzveranstaltung)* IV
ban (-nn-) [bæn] verbieten; ein (Aufenthalts-)Verbot erteilen V 3 (50)
banana [bə'nɑ:nə] Banane I
band [bænd] Band, (Musik-)Gruppe I
bank [bæŋk] Bank, Sparkasse I
bank robber Bankräuber/in I
bar [bɑ:] Bar II
barbecue ['bɑ:bɪkju:] Grillfest, Grillparty V 1 (6)
°**bark** [bɑ:k] Gebell, Bellen
baseball ['beɪsbɔ:l] Baseball I
baseball cap Baseballmütze II
basement ['beɪsmənt] Keller V 4 (80)
basic ['beɪsɪk] grundlegend; Grund-, Haupt- V 4 (84)
basket ['bɑ:skɪt] Korb I • **a basket of apples** ein Korb Äpfel I
basketball ['bɑ:skɪtbɔ:l] Basketball I
bat [bæt]**: table tennis bat** Tischtennisschläger III
bath [bɑ:θ] Bad, Badewanne II
have a bath baden, ein Bad nehmen II
bathroom ['bɑ:θru:m] Badezimmer I
be [bi:]**, was/were, been** sein I
be with sb. mit jemandem zusammen sein IV • **want to be sth.** etwas werden wollen *(beruflich)* V 3 (46)
beach [bi:tʃ] Strand II • **on the beach** am Strand II
bean [bi:n] Bohne IV
bear [beə] Bär II
beard [bɪəd] Bart IV
beat [bi:t]**, beat, beaten** schlagen; besiegen III
beaten ['bi:tn] *siehe* **beat**
beautiful ['bju:tɪfl] schön I
beauty ['bju:ti] Schönheit III
became [bɪ'keɪm] *siehe* **become**
because [bɪ'kɒz] weil I
become [bɪ'kʌm]**, became, become** werden II
bed [bed] Bett I • **Bed and Breakfast (B&B)** [ˌbed‿ən 'brekfəst] Frühstückspension *(wörtlich:* Bett und Frühstück) I • **go to bed** ins Bett gehen I
bedroom ['bedru:m] Schlafzimmer I
beef [bi:f] Rindfleisch III
been [bi:n] *siehe* **be**
before [bɪ'fɔ:] vor *(zeitlich)* I
before [bɪ'fɔ:] bevor II
beg (for) (-gg-) [beg] betteln (um); eindringlich bitten (um) IV
began [bɪ'gæn] *siehe* **begin**
begin (-nn-) [bɪ'gɪn]**, began, begun** beginnen, anfangen (mit) IV
beginning [bɪ'gɪnɪŋ] Beginn, Anfang; Einleitung II
begun [bɪ'gʌn] *siehe* **begin**
behaviour (towards sb.) [bɪ'heɪvjə] Verhalten, Benehmen (gegenüber jm.) V 3 (52)
behind [bɪ'haɪnd] hinter II
believe (in) [bɪ'li:v] glauben (an) IV
bell [bel] Klingel, Glocke III
The bell rang. Es klingelte. III
below [bɪ'ləʊ] unten; unter, unterhalb (von) IV
best [best] am besten II • **the best ...** der/die/das beste ...; die besten ... I • **like sth. best** etwas am meisten mögen III • **Best wishes** *etwa:* Alles Gute / Mit besten Grüßen *(als Briefschluss)* IV
What was the best thing about ...? Was war das Beste an ...? II
bet (-tt-) [bet]**, bet, bet** wetten III
better ['betə] besser I • **like sth. better** etwas lieber mögen II
between [bɪ'twi:n] zwischen II
°**beyond the story** [bɪ'jɒnd] über die Geschichte hinaus
big [bɪg] groß I • **big wheel** [ˌbɪg 'wi:l] Riesenrad III
bike [baɪk] Fahrrad I • **bike ride** (Rad-)Fahrt II • **ride a bike** Rad fahren I
bill [bɪl] Rechnung III
bin [bɪn] Mülltonne II
biology [baɪ'ɒlədʒi] Biologie I
bird [bɜ:d] Vogel I
birdcage ['bɜ:dkeɪdʒ] Vogelkäfig III
birth [bɜ:θ] Geburt V 2 (36) • **date of birth** Geburtsdatum V 2 (36)
place of birth Geburtsort V 2 (36/165)
birthday ['bɜ:θdeɪ] Geburtstag I
Happy birthday. Herzlichen Glückwunsch zum Geburtstag. I • **My birthday is in May.** Ich habe im

Mai Geburtstag. I • **My birthday is on 13th June.** Ich habe am 13. Juni Geburtstag. I • **When's your birthday?** Wann hast du Geburtstag? I
biscuit ['bɪskɪt] Keks, Plätzchen I
bit [bɪt]
1. a bit ein bisschen, etwas II
°**2.** kleines Teilchen, Stückchen
bit [bɪt] *siehe* **bite**
bite [baɪt]**, bit, bitten** beißen V 1 (9/160)
bite [baɪt] Biss V 1 (9)
bitten ['bɪtn] *siehe* **bite**
black [blæk] schwarz I
blame sb. (for) [bleɪm] jm. die Schuld geben (an); jm. Vorwürfe machen (wegen) III
blanket ['blæŋkɪt] Decke *(zum Zudecken)* V 1 (17)
bled [bled] *siehe* **bleed**
bleed [bli:d]**, bled, bled** bluten V 1 (22)
bleep [bli:p] piepsen II
bleep [bli:p] Piepton II
block [blɒk] (Häuser-, Wohn-)Block IV
blog [blɒg] Blog *(Internet-Tagebuch)* IV
blond [blɒnd] blond IV
blood [blʌd] Blut V 1 (21)
bloody ['blʌdi] blutig V 4 (78)
blue [blu:] blau I
board [bɔ:d] (Wand-)Tafel I
notice board Anschlagtafel, schwarzes Brett I
boat [bəʊt] Boot, Schiff I
body ['bɒdi] Körper I
°**Bollywood** ['bɒliwʊd] *indische Unterhaltungsfilmindustrie*
book [bʊk] Buch I • °**book review** [rɪ'vju:] Buchkritik, -besprechung
book [bʊk] buchen, reservieren V 4 (80)
booked [bʊkt]**: fully booked** ausgebucht V 4 (83)
boot [bu:t] Stiefel I
°**boot camp** ['bu:t kæmp] Erziehungslager *(für junge Straftäter/innen)*
border ['bɔ:də] Grenze IV
bored [bɔ:d]**: get bored** sich langweilen V 3 (48)
boring ['bɔ:rɪŋ] langweilig I
born [bɔ:n]**: be born** geboren sein/werden II
borough ['bʌrə, *AE:* 'bɜ:rəʊ] (Stadt-)Bezirk IV
boss [bɒs] Chef/in, Boss III
both [bəʊθ] beide I
bottle ['bɒtl] Flasche I • **a bottle of milk** eine Flasche Milch I
bottom ['bɒtəm] unteres Ende II
at the bottom (of) unten, am unteren Ende (von) II
bought [bɔ:t] *siehe* **buy**
bowl [bəʊl] Schüssel I • **a bowl of cornflakes** eine Schale Cornflakes I
box [bɒks] Kasten, Kästchen, Kiste I • **sandwich box** Brotdose I
boy [bɔɪ] Junge I
boyfriend ['bɔɪfrend] (fester) Freund IV
°**bracket** ['brækɪt] Klammer
brainstorm ['breɪnstɔ:m] brainstormen *(so viele Ideen wie möglich sammeln)* III
brave [breɪv] mutig IV
bread *(no pl)* [bred] Brot I
break [breɪk]**, broke, broken: break a journey** eine Reise unterbrechen III
break [breɪk] Pause I • **at break** in der Pause *(zwischen Schulstunden)* II • **take a break** eine Pause machen IV
breakfast ['brekfəst] Frühstück I
have breakfast frühstücken I
°**breath** [breθ] Atem
bridge [brɪdʒ] Brücke I
bright [braɪt] hell, leuchtend II
brilliant ['brɪliənt] toll, genial, großartig III
bring [brɪŋ]**, brought, brought** (mit-, her)bringen I
British ['brɪtɪʃ] britisch; Brite, Britin II
brochure ['brəʊʃə] Prospekt, Broschüre II
broke [brəʊk] *siehe* **break**
broken ['brəʊkən] *siehe* **break**
broken *(adj)* ['brəʊkən] gebrochen; zerbrochen, kaputt II
brother ['brʌðə] Bruder I
brought [brɔ:t] *siehe* **bring**
brown [braʊn] braun I
budgie ['bʌdʒi] Wellensittich I
build [bɪld]**, built, built** bauen II
builder ['bɪldə] Bauarbeiter/in V 2 (33)
building ['bɪldɪŋ] Gebäude II
°**building company** Bauunternehmen
built [bɪlt] *siehe* **build**
bulletin board ['bʊlətɪn bɔ:d] *(AE)* schwarzes Brett, Anschlagtafel IV
bully ['bʊli] einschüchtern, tyrannisieren II
bully ['bʊli] (Schul-)Tyrann III
bunk (bed) [bʌŋk] Etagenbett, Koje II
burger ['bɜ:gə] Burger IV
bus [bʌs] Bus I • **bus stop** Bushaltestelle III
bush [bʊʃ] Busch, Strauch V 1 (6/159)
the bush der Busch *(unkultiviertes, „wildes" Land in Australien, Afrika)* V 1 (6)
business ['bɪznəs] Geschäft; Handel IV • **Mind your own business.** Das geht dich nichts an! / Kümmere dich um deine eigenen Angelegenheiten! II • **start a business** eine Firma gründen V 2 (42)
businesswoman/businessman ['bɪznəswʊmən, -mən] Geschäftsfrau/Geschäftsmann V 3 (46)
busy ['bɪzi] belebt, verkehrsreich; hektisch III
but [bət, bʌt]
1. aber I
2. sondern IV
butcher ['bʊtʃə] Fleischer/in, Metzger/in III • **at the butcher's** beim Metzger III
butter ['bʌtə] Butter III
button ['bʌtn] Knopf III
buy [baɪ]**, bought, bought** kaufen I
by [baɪ]
1. von I
2. an; (nahe) bei II
3. by car/train/bike/... mit dem Auto/Zug/Rad/... II
4. bis spätestens, nicht später als III • **by ten o'clock** bis (spätestens) zehn Uhr III
5. by the way übrigens II
Bye. [baɪ] Tschüs! I

C

cab [kæb] Taxi • **get a cab** ein Taxi nehmen IV
cabin ['kæbɪn] Hütte III
cable ['keɪbl] Kabel; Kabel- IV
café ['kæfeɪ] *(kleines)* Restaurant, Imbissstube, Café II
cafeteria [ˌkæfə'tɪəriə] Cafeteria; *(USA)* Schulmensa IV
cage [keɪdʒ] Käfig I
cake [keɪk] Kuchen, Torte I
calendar ['kælɪndə] Kalender I
call [kɔ:l] rufen; anrufen; nennen I
call sb. names jn. mit Schimpfwörtern hänseln, jm. Schimpfwörter nachrufen III
call [kɔ:l] Anruf, Telefongespräch I
wake-up call Weckanruf V 4 (83)
called [kɔ:ld]**: be called** genannt werden, heißen IV
caller ['kɔ:lə] Anrufer/Anruferin V 3 (58)
calm [kɑ:m] ruhig, still V 2 (31)
calm down [ˌkɑ:m 'daʊn] sich beruhigen II

came [keɪm] *siehe* **come**
camel ['kæml] Kamel II
camera ['kæmərə] Kamera, Fotoapparat I
camp [kæmp] zelten III
camp [kæmp] Camp, (Ferien-)Lager IV • °**boot camp** Erziehungslager *(für junge Straftäter/innen)*
camping ['kæmpɪŋ] Camping, Campen V 1 (6)
can [kən, kæn]
1. können I
2. dürfen I
Can I help you? Kann ich Ihnen helfen?/ Was kann ich für Sie tun? *(im Geschäft)* I
canal [kə'næl] Kanal III
candidate ['kændɪdət] Kandidat/in, Bewerber/in V 2 (38)
°**cane toad** ['keɪn təʊd] Agakröte
canoe [kə'nu:] Kanu III
canoe [kə'nu:] Kanu fahren III
canteen [kæn'ti:n] Kantine, Schulmensa II
canyon ['kænjən] Schlucht, Canyon IV
cap [kæp] Mütze, Kappe II
capital ['kæpɪtl] Hauptstadt III
captain ['kæptɪn] Kapitän/in III
°**caption** ['kæpʃn] Bildunterschrift
car [kɑ:] Auto I • **car park** Parkplatz III
caravan ['kærəvæn] Wohnwagen II
card [kɑ:d] (Spiel-, Post-)Karte I
care [keə]**: I don't care.** Es ist mir egal. IV
care assistant ['keər_ə,sɪstənt] Pfleger/in *(in Altenheim)* V 2 (30)
career [kə'rɪə] Karriere III
careful ['keəfl]
1. vorsichtig II
2. sorgfältig II
3. aufmerksam V 2 (38)
caretaker ['keəteɪkə] Hausmeister/in II
carrot ['kærət] Möhre, Karotte I
carry ['kæri] tragen V 2 (31)
cartoon [kɑ:'tu:n] Cartoon (Zeichentrickfilm; Bilderwitz) II
case [keɪs] Fall II
cash [kæʃ] Bargeld V 3 (51) • **pay cash** [kæʃ] bar bezahlen V 3 (51)
castle ['kɑ:sl] Burg, Schloss II
cat [kæt] Katze I
catch [kætʃ]**, caught, caught** fangen; erwischen II
cathedral [kə'θi:drəl] Kathedrale, Dom III
°**cattle station** ['kætl steɪʃn] Rinderfarm
caught [kɔ:t] *siehe* **catch**

cause sth. [kɔ:z] etwas verursachen V 3 (52)
CD [,si:'di:] CD I • **CD player** CD-Spieler I
ceilidh ['keɪli] *Musik- und Tanzveranstaltung, vor allem in Schottland und Irland* III
cellphone ['selfəʊn] *(AE)* Handy, Mobiltelefon IV
Celsius (C) ['selsiəs] Celsius IV
cent (c) [sent] Cent I
centimetre (cm) ['sentɪmi:tə] Zentimeter III
central ['sentrəl] Zentral-, Mittel- III
centre ['sentə] Zentrum, Mitte I
city centre Stadtzentrum, Innenstadt I • **community centre** Gemeindezentrum V 3 (56) • **sports centre** Sportzentrum I
century ['sentʃəri] Jahrhundert II
cereal ['sɪəriəl] Getreideflocken, Frühstücksflocken IV
certificate [sə'tɪfɪkət] Zertifikat, Urkunde, Bescheinigung V 2 (36)
chair [tʃeə] Stuhl I
champion ['tʃæmpiən] Meister/in, Champion I
championship ['tʃæmpiənʃɪp] Meisterschaft III
change [tʃeɪndʒ]
1. (sich) ändern, (sich) verändern IV
2. wechseln IV
3. umsteigen III
4. sich umziehen IV
change channels umschalten *(Fernsehprogramm)* IV
change [tʃeɪndʒ]
1. (Ver-)Änderung; Wechsel IV
2. Wechselgeld I; Kleingeld IV
channel ['tʃænl] (Radio-, Fernseh-) Kanal, (Radio-, Fernseh-)Programm IV • **change channels** umschalten *(Fernsehprogramm)* IV
character ['kærəktə]
1. Charakter, Wesen IV
°**2.** Person, Figur *(in Roman, Film, Theaterstück)*
chart [tʃɑ:t] Diagramm V 1 (10)
chat (-tt-) [tʃæt] plaudern; chatten II
chat room ['tʃæt ru:m] Chatroom III
cheap [tʃi:p] billig I
check [tʃek]
1. (über)prüfen, kontrollieren I
2. check in einchecken *(Hotel, Flughafen)* V 4 (83) • **check out** auschecken *(Hotel)* V 4 (83/172)
checkpoint ['tʃekpɔɪnt] Kontrollpunkt *(hier auch: zur Selbstüberprüfung)* I
cheer [tʃɪə] jubeln, Beifall klatschen II

cheese [tʃi:z] Käse I
chemist ['kemɪst] Drogerie, Apotheke II • **at the chemist's** beim Apotheker III
cheque (for) [tʃek] Scheck (über) V 2 (43)
cherry ['tʃeri] Kirsche II
chicken ['tʃɪkɪn] Huhn; (Brat-)Hähnchen I • °**Don't be a chicken.** Sei kein Frosch/Feigling.
child [tʃaɪld], *pl* **children** ['tʃɪldrən] Kind I • **only child** Einzelkind V 3 (46)
°**children's home** [,tʃɪldrənz 'həʊm] Kinderheim
chips *(pl)* [tʃɪps]
1. *(BE)* Pommes frites I
2. *(AE)* Chips IV • **potato chips** *(AE)* Kartoffelchips IV
chocolate ['tʃɒklət] Schokolade I
choir ['kwaɪə] Chor I
choose [tʃu:z]**, chose, chosen** (sich) aussuchen, (aus)wählen I
chorus ['kɔ:rəs] Refrain III
chose [tʃəʊz] *siehe* **choose**
chosen ['tʃəʊzn] *siehe* **choose**
°**chrissake: for chrissake** ['kraɪseɪk] **(= for Christ's sake)** *(infml) etwa:* verdammt noch mal *(wörtlich: um Christus willen)*
Christmas ['krɪsməs] Weihnachten I
church [tʃɜ:tʃ] Kirche I
cinema ['sɪnəmə] Kino I • **go to the cinema** ins Kino gehen II
°**circle** ['sɜ:kl]**:** °**double circle** Doppelkreis, „Kugellager" *(als Kommunikationsform)*
circus ['sɜ:kəs] (runder) Platz III
citizen ['sɪtɪzn] (Staats-)Bürger/in, Staatsangehörige(r) IV
city ['sɪti] (Groß-)Stadt I • **city centre** Stadtzentrum, Innenstadt I
clap (-pp-) [klæp] (Beifall) klatschen IV
class [klɑ:s]
1. (Schul-)Klasse I
2. Unterricht; Kurs IV
class teacher Klassenlehrer/in I
classical ['klæsɪkl] klassisch III
classmate ['klɑ:smeɪt] Klassenkamerad/in, Mitschüler/in I
classroom ['klɑ:sru:m] Klassenzimmer I
clean [kli:n] sauber II
clean [kli:n] sauber machen, putzen I • **I clean my teeth.** Ich putze mir die Zähne. I
cleaner ['kli:nə] Putzfrau, -mann II
clear [klɪə] klar, deutlich I
clever ['klevə] schlau, klug I

click on sth. [klɪk] etwas anklicken II
climate ['klaɪmət] Klima V 1 (12)
climb [klaɪm] klettern; hinaufklettern (auf) I • **Climb a tree.** Klettere auf einen Baum. I
°**climb** [klaɪm] Anstieg
clinic ['klɪnɪk] Klinik II
clock [klɒk] (Wand-, Stand-, Turm-) Uhr I • **alarm clock** [ə'lɑːm klɒk] Wecker V 3 (48)
clone [kləʊn] Klon III
close (to) [kləʊs] nahe (bei, an) IV **That was close.** Das war knapp. II
close [kləʊz] schließen, zumachen I
closed [kləʊzd] geschlossen II
°**closing phrase** ['kləʊzɪŋ freɪz] Grußformel *(am Briefende)*
clothes *(pl)* [kləʊðz, kləʊz] Kleider, Kleidung(sstücke) II
cloud [klaʊd] Wolke II
cloudless ['klaʊdləs] wolkenlos IV
cloudy ['klaʊdi] bewölkt II
clown [klaʊn] Clown/in II
club [klʌb] Klub; Verein I
clumsy ['klʌmzi] ungeschickt, tollpatschig IV
coach [kəʊtʃ] Trainer/in III; Coach V 2 (38)
coast [kəʊst] Küste III • **on the coast** an der Küste III
coffee ['kɒfi] Kaffee IV • **coffee to go** Kaffee zum Mitnehmen IV
cola ['kəʊlə] Cola I
cold [kəʊld] kalt I • **be cold** frieren I
cold [kəʊld]
1. Kälte IV
2. Erkältung II • **have a cold** erkältet sein, eine Erkältung haben II
collect [kə'lekt] sammeln I
collector [kə'lektə] Sammler/in II
colour ['kʌlə] färben III
colour ['kʌlə] Farbe I • **What colour is ...?** Welche Farbe hat ...? I
colourful ['kʌləfl] farbenfroh, farbenprächtig, farbig V 4 (73)
colourless ['kʌlələs] farblos IV
°**combine** [kəm'baɪn] kombinieren, verbinden
come [kʌm], **came, come** kommen I • °**come for sb./sth.** kommen, um etwas/jn. zu holen • **come home** nach Hause kommen I
come in hereinkommen I
Come on. 1. Na los, komm. II; **2.** Ach komm! / Na hör mal! II • **come true** wahr werden; in Erfüllung gehen IV • **the lights came on** das Licht ging an V 3 (59)
comedy ['kɒmədi] Komödie; Comedy IV
comfortable ['kʌmftəbl] bequem, behaglich, angenehm IV • **Make yourself comfortable.** Machen Sie es sich bequem. / Mach es dir bequem. IV
comic ['kɒmɪk] Comic-Heft I
comment (on, about) ['kɒment] Kommentar (zu, über) IV
Commonwealth ['kɒmənwelθ]**: the Commonwealth** *Gemeinschaft der Länder des ehemaligen Britischen Weltreichs* III
communicate [kə'mjuːnɪkeɪt] kommunizieren V 3 (48)
communication [kə,mjuːnɪ'keɪʃn] Kommunikation V 3 (48/167)
community [kə'mjuːnəti]**: community centre** Gemeindezentrum V 3 (56) • **community hall** Gemeinschaftshalle, -saal, Gemeindehalle, -saal III
company ['kʌmpəni] Firma, Gesellschaft IV • °**advertising company** ['ædvətaɪzɪŋ ,kʌmpəni] Werbeagentur • °**building company** ['bɪldɪŋ ,kʌmpəni] Bauunternehmen
compare [kəm'peə] vergleichen V 1 (10)
comparison [kəm'pærɪsn] Steigerung; Vergleich II
competition [,kɒmpə'tɪʃn] Wettbewerb, Wettkampf III
complete [kəm'pliːt] völlig, vollständig V 3 (50)
complete [kəm'pliːt] ergänzen, vervollständigen V 3 (50/168)
complicated ['kɒmplɪkeɪtɪd] kompliziert V 4 (80)
computer [kəm'pjuːtə] Computer I
concert ['kɒnsət] Konzert III
conclusion [kən'kluːʒn] Schluss(folgerung) IV • **draw conclusions** Schlüsse ziehen, schlussfolgern IV
confident ['kɒnfɪdənt] selbstbewusst, (selbst)sicher V 2 (33)
connect (to/with) [kə'nekt] verbinden (mit) V 4 (83/173)
connection [kə'nekʃn] Verbindung V 4 (83)
contact ['kɒntækt] Kontakt, Verbindung V 3 (51) • **contacts** *(pl) Liste von Bekannten/Kontakten (im Handy, im Mailprogramm)* V 3 (51)
°**context** ['kɒntekst]**: from the context** aus dem Zusammenhang, aus dem Kontext
continent ['kɒntɪnənt] Kontinent V 4 (70)
contrast ['kɒntrɑːst] Kontrast, Gegensatz V 4 (70)
control: remote control [rɪ,məʊt kən'trəʊl] Fernbedienung IV
conversation [,kɒnvə'seɪʃn] Unterhaltung, Gespräch V 1 (15) • **have a conversation** ein Gespräch, eine Unterhaltung führen V 1 (15/161)
cook [kʊk] kochen, zubereiten II
cook [kʊk] Koch/Köchin III
cooker ['kʊkə] Herd I
cookie ['kʊki] Keks IV
cool [kuːl]
1. kühl II
2. cool I
copy ['kɒpi] kopieren; abschreiben II
copy ['kɒpi] Kopie II
corner ['kɔːnə] Ecke I • **on the corner of Green Street and London Road** Green Street, Ecke London Road II
cornflakes ['kɔːnfleɪks] Cornflakes I
correct [kə'rekt] berichtigen, korrigieren II
°**correct** [kə'rekt] richtig, korrekt
cost [kɒst]**, cost, cost** kosten IV
couch [kaʊtʃ] Couch, Sofa V 1 (13)
couch potato *(infml)* Stubenhocker/in *(jd., der immer nur vor dem Fernseher sitzt)* V 1 (13)
could [kəd, kʊd]
1. he could ... er konnte ... II
2. he could ... er könnte ... IV
count [kaʊnt] zählen II
countable ['kaʊntəbl] zählbar IV
country ['kʌntri] Land *(auch als Gegensatz zur Stadt)* II • **in the country** auf dem Land II
countryside ['kʌntrisaɪd] Land(schaft), Natur IV
course [kɔːs] Kurs, Lehrgang III
course: of course [əv 'kɔːs] natürlich, selbstverständlich I
court [kɔːt] Gericht(shof) V 3 (52)
cousin ['kʌzn] Cousin, Cousine I
cover ['kʌvə]
1. (CD-)Hülle I
°**2. front inside cover** [,frʌnt‿,ɪnsaɪd 'kʌvə] Umschlaginnenseite
cow [kaʊ] Kuh II
crazy ['kreɪzi] verrückt V 4 (72)
cream [kriːm] Sahne; Creme IV; Salbe V 4 (75) • **cream cheese** Frischkäse IV
credit card ['kredɪt kɑːd] Kreditkarte V 3 (51) • **pay by credit card** mit Kreditkarte bezahlen V 3 (51)
cricket ['krɪkɪt] Kricket *(Schlagballspiel)* V 1 (13)
crime [kraɪm] Kriminalität; Verbrechen IV • **crime film** Krimi IV
crime series Krimiserie IV • **crime story** Krimi IV

crisps *(pl)* [krɪsps] Kartoffelchips I
crocodile ['krɒkədaɪl] Krokodil II
cross [krɒs] überqueren II
cross [krɒs]**: be cross (with)** böse, sauer sein (auf) I
cross [krɒs] Kreuz V 1 (8)
crowd [kraʊd] (Menschen-)Menge, Masse; *(infml auch:)* Clique, Gruppe IV
crowded ['kraʊdɪd] überfüllt, voll V 1 (10)
cry [kraɪ] weinen IV
cultural ['kʌltʃərəl] kulturell V 1 (16)
culture ['kʌltʃə] Kultur IV • **culture shock** Kulturschock V 4 (73)
cup [kʌp]
1. Tasse III • **a cup of tea** eine Tasse Tee III
2. Pokal III
cupboard ['kʌbəd] Schrank I
curriculum vitae [kəˌrɪkjələm 'viːtaɪ] **(CV)** Lebenslauf V 2 (36)
curry ['kʌri] Curry(gericht) III
customer ['kʌstəmə] Kunde, Kundin II
cut (-tt-) [kʌt]**, cut, cut** schneiden III • **cut sth. off** etwas abtrennen, abschneiden III • **cut the grass** Rasen mähen IV
°**cuz** [kʊz] *(infml)* Freund/Freundin
CV [siː 'viː] **(curriculum vitae** [kəˌrɪkjələm 'viːtaɪ]**)** Lebenslauf V 2 (36)
cycle ['saɪkl] (mit dem) Rad fahren II • **cycle path** Radweg II

D

dad [dæd] Papa, Vati; Vater I
°**damn** [dæm] *(infml)* verdammt
dance [dɑːns] tanzen I
dance [dɑːns] Tanz I • **dance floor** Dancefloor, Tanzfläche IV
dancer ['dɑːnsə] Tänzer/in II
dancing ['dɑːnsɪŋ] Tanzen I **dancing lessons** Tanzstunden, Tanzunterricht I
danger ['deɪndʒə] Gefahr III
dangerous ['deɪndʒərəs] gefährlich II
dark [dɑːk] dunkel I
darling ['dɑːlɪŋ] Liebling V 3 (58)
date [deɪt] Datum I • **date of birth** Geburtsdatum V 2 (36) • **to date** bis heute V 2 (35)
daughter ['dɔːtə] Tochter I
day [deɪ] Tag I • **one day** eines Tages I • **days of the week** Wochentage I • **day trip** Tagesausflug IV • **one-day ticket** Tageskarte III • °**the old days** frühere Zeiten
dead [ded] tot I
dear [dɪə] Schatz, Liebling I • **Oh dear!** Oje! II
dear [dɪə]**: Dear Jay ...** Lieber Jay, ... I **Dear Sir or Madam** Sehr geehrte Damen und Herren *(Anrede in Briefen)* V 2 (36)
death [deθ] Tod IV
December [dɪ'sembə] Dezember I
decide (on sth.) [dɪ'saɪd] (etwas) beschließen; sich entscheiden (für etwas) V 3 (54)
decision [dɪ'sɪʒn] Entscheidung V 3 (54/169)
deep [diːp] tief V 1 (22)
deer, *pl* **deer** [dɪə] Reh, Hirsch II
degree [dɪ'griː] Grad II
deli ['deli] *Kombination aus Lebensmittelgeschäft und Fastfoodrestaurant* IV
delicious [dɪ'lɪʃəs] köstlich, lecker II
dentist ['dentɪst] Zahnarzt, -ärztin IV
department store [dɪ'pɑːtmənt stɔː] Kaufhaus II
departure (dep) [dɪ'pɑːtʃə] Abfahrt, Abflug; Abreise III
describe sth. (to sb.) [dɪ'skraɪb] (jm.) etwas beschreiben II
description [dɪ'skrɪpʃn] Beschreibung II
desert ['dezət] Wüste V 1 (20)
design [dɪ'zaɪn] entwerfen, gestalten II
design [dɪ'zaɪn] Design; Gestaltung; Entwurf V 2 (35)
desk [desk] Schreibtisch I
detail ['diːteɪl] Detail, Einzelheit II
detective [dɪ'tektɪv] Detektiv/in I
dial *(BE* **-ll-)** ['daɪəl] *(Telefonnummer)* wählen V 3 (59)
dialogue ['daɪəlɒg] Dialog III
°**diamond** ['daɪəmənd] Diamant
diary ['daɪəri] Tagebuch; Terminkalender I
dice, *pl* **dice** [daɪs] Würfel II
dictionary ['dɪkʃənri] Wörterbuch, *(alphabetisches)* Wörterverzeichnis I
did [dɪd] *siehe* **do** • **Did you go ...?** Bist du ... gegangen? / Seid ihr ... gegangen? I • **we didn't sing** ['dɪdnt] wir sangen nicht / wir haben nicht gesungen I
°**didgeridoo** [ˌdɪdʒəri'duː] Didgeridoo
die (of) *(-ing form:* **dying***)* [daɪ]
1. sterben (an) II
°2. ausgehen, ersterben
difference ['dɪfrəns] Unterschied IV
different (from) ['dɪfrənt] verschieden, unterschiedlich; anders (als) I
difficult ['dɪfɪkəlt] schwierig, schwer I
dining room ['daɪnɪŋ ruːm] Esszimmer I
°**dingo** ['dɪŋgəʊ], *pl* **dingoes** ['dɪŋgəʊz] Dingo *(australischer Wildhund)*
dinner ['dɪnə] Abendessen, Abendbrot I • **have dinner** Abendbrot essen I
directions *(pl)* [də'rekʃnz] Wegbeschreibung IV • **ask sb. for directions** jn. nach dem Weg fragen; jd. um eine Wegbeschreibung bitten IV
°**director** [də'rektə] Regisseur/in
dirty ['dɜːti] schmutzig II
disabled [dɪs'eɪbld] (körper)behindert III
disadvantage [ˌdɪsəd'vɑːntɪdʒ] Nachteil IV
disappear [ˌdɪsə'pɪə] verschwinden II
disappointed (about/in) [ˌdɪsə'pɔɪntɪd] enttäuscht (von/über) IV
discipline ['dɪsəplɪn] Disziplin V 3 (55)
disc jockey (DJ) ['dɪsk dʒɒki] Diskjockey III
disco ['dɪskəʊ] Disko I
discover [dɪ'skʌvə] entdecken IV
discuss [dɪ'skʌs] diskutieren, besprechen V 3 (48/167)
discussion [dɪ'skʌʃn] Diskussion II
dish [dɪʃ] Gericht *(Speise)* III
dishwasher ['dɪʃwɒʃə] Geschirrspülmaschine I
°**distance** ['dɪstəns] Entfernung, Distanz
divide sth. (into) [dɪ'vaɪd] etwas (auf)teilen (in) V 4 (84)
°**diving: scuba diving** ['skuːbə ˌdaɪvɪŋ] Sporttauchen
divorced [dɪ'vɔːst] geschieden I
DJ ['diː dʒeɪ] (Musik/CDs/Platten) auflegen *(in der Disko)* III
DJ ['diː dʒeɪ] Diskjockey III
do [duː]**, did, done** tun, machen I **Do you like ...?** Magst du ...? I **do a gig** einen Auftritt haben, ein Konzert geben III • **do a good job** gute Arbeit leisten II • **do a project** ein Projekt machen, durchführen II • **do an exercise** eine Übung machen II • **do badly/well (in)** schlecht/gut abschneiden (in) III • **do sport** Sport treiben I • **do work experience** ein Praktikum machen V 2 (35/165) • **How are you doing?** Wie geht's? V 1 (15)

doctor ['dɒktə] Doktor; Arzt/Ärztin II • **to the doctor's** zum Arzt III
documentary [ˌdɒkju'mentri] Dokumentation, Dokumentarfilm IV
dog [dɒg] Hund I
dollar ($) ['dɒlə] Dollar IV
done [dʌn] *siehe* **do** • **°Well done!** [ˌwel 'dʌn] Gut gemacht!
don't [dəʊnt]**: Don't listen to Dan.** Hör/Hört nicht auf Dan. I • **I don't know.** Ich weiß es nicht. I • **I don't like ...** Ich mag ... nicht. / Ich mag kein(e) ... I
door [dɔː] Tür I
doorbell ['dɔːbel] Türklingel I
dorm [dɔːm] *(infml)* Schlafsaal V 4 (80)
dormitory ['dɔːmətri] Schlafsaal V 4 (80)
dossier ['dɒsieɪ] Mappe, Dossier *(des Sprachenportfolios)* I
double ['dʌbl] zweimal, doppelt, Doppel- I • **°double circle** ['sɜːkl] Doppelkreis, „Kugellager" *(als Gesprächskreis)* • **double room** Doppelzimmer V 4 (80)
down [daʊn] hinunter, herunter, nach unten I • **down there** dort unten II • **fall down** hinfallen II
download [ˌdaʊn'ləʊd] runterladen, downloaden III
downloadable [ˌdaʊn'ləʊdəbl] herunterladbar, zum Herunterladen IV
downstairs [ˌdaʊn'steəz] unten; nach unten I
downtown [ˌdaʊn'taʊn] (im/in das) Stadtzentrum IV
°Down Under [ˌdaʊn‿'ʌndə] *umgangssprachliche Bezeichnung für Australien*
drama ['drɑːmə]
1. Schauspiel, darstellende Kunst I
2. Spielfilm *(im Fernsehen)* IV
drank [dræŋk] *siehe* **drink**
draw [drɔː]**, drew, drawn**
1. zeichnen III
2. draw conclusions Schlüsse ziehen, schlussfolgern IV
drawing ['drɔːɪŋ] Zeichnung III
drawn [drɔːn] *siehe* **draw**
dream [driːm] Traum I • **dream house** Traumhaus I
dream (of, about) [driːm] träumen (von) IV
dreamer ['driːmə] Träumer/in V 2 (32)
dress [dres] Kleid I
dress [dres] sich kleiden V 2 (38)
dress code ['dres kəʊd] Kleiderordnung, Bekleidungsvorschrift III
dressed [drest]**: get dressed** sich anziehen *(sich ankleiden, Kleidung anziehen)* I
drew [druː] *siehe* **draw**
drink [drɪŋk] Getränk I
drink [drɪŋk]**, drank, drunk** trinken I
drive [draɪv] Fahrt III
drive [draɪv]**, drove, driven** *(ein Auto / mit dem Auto)* fahren II
driven ['drɪvn] *siehe* **drive**
driver ['draɪvə] Fahrer/in II
drop (-pp-) [drɒp] fallen lassen I
drove [drəʊv] *siehe* **drive**
drug [drʌg] Droge, Rauschgift; Medikament • **be on drugs** Drogen, Rauschgift / Medikamente nehmen IV
drum [drʌm] Trommel III
drums *(pl)* [drʌmz] Schlagzeug III **play the drums** Schlagzeug spielen III
drunk [drʌŋk] *siehe* **drink**
drunk [drʌŋk] betrunken IV
dry [draɪ] trocken V 1 (12) • **°the dry season** [ˌdraɪ 'siːzn] die Trockenzeit
dump sb. [dʌmp] *(infml)* mit jm. Schluss machen V 3 (49)
°dumper: monster dumper truck [ˌmɒnstə 'dʌmpə trʌk] *Kipplaster mit gewaltigen Rädern*
°duration [dju'reɪʃn] Dauer
during ['djuːrɪŋ] während IV
dustbin ['dʌstbɪn] Mülltonne II
DVD [ˌdiː viː' diː] DVD I

E

each [iːtʃ] jeder, jede, jedes (einzelne) I
each other [iːtʃ‿'ʌðə] einander, sich (gegenseitig) III
°eagle ['iːgl] Adler
ear [ɪə] Ohr I
earache ['ɪəreɪk] Ohrenschmerzen II
early ['ɜːli] früh I
earn [ɜːn] verdienen IV
earring ['ɪərɪŋ] Ohrring I
earth [ɜːθ] Erde IV
earthquake ['ɜːθkweɪk] Erdbeben IV
east [iːst] Osten; nach Osten; östlich III
Easter ['iːstə] Ostern IV
easy ['iːzi] leicht, einfach I
easy-going [ˌiːzi'gəʊɪŋ] gelassen, locker V 3 (55)
eat [iːt]**, ate, eaten** essen I
eaten ['iːtn] *siehe* **eat**
editor ['edɪtə] Redakteur/in III **°letter to the editor** Leserbrief
education [ˌedʒʊ'keɪʃn] (Aus-)Bildung V 1 (12) • **outdoor education** Unterricht im Freien V 1 (12)
effect: special effect [ˌspeʃl‿ɪ'fekt] Spezialeffekt V 1 (18)
egg [eg] Ei II
elect sb. sth. [ɪ'lekt] jn. zu etwas wählen IV
election [ɪ'lekʃn] Wahl *(von Kandidaten bei einer Abstimmung)* IV
electric [ɪ'lektrɪk] elektrisch, Elektro- III
electricity [ɪˌlek'trɪsəti] Strom, Elektrizität V 4 (71)
electronic [ɪˌlek'trɒnɪk] elektronisch III
elementary school [ˌelɪ'mentri skuːl] *(USA) Grundschule für 6- bis 11-Jährige* IV
elephant ['elɪfənt] Elefant I
elevator ['elɪveɪtə] *(AE)* Fahrstuhl, Aufzug II
else [els]**: anything else** (irgend-) etwas anderes IV • **somebody else** jemand anders IV • **What else?** Was (sonst) noch? IV
e-mail, email ['iːmeɪl] E-Mail I
embarrassed [ɪm'bærəst]**: I'm embarrassed.** Das ist mir peinlich. IV
embarrassing [ɪm'bærəsɪŋ] peinlich IV
empty ['empti] leer I
°emu ['iːmjuː] Emu
enclose sth. [ɪn'kləʊz] etwas *(einem Brief)* beilegen V 2 (36)
end [end] Ende, Schluss I • **at the end (of)** am Ende (von) I • **in the end** schließlich, zum Schluss III **°the top end** [ˌtɒp‿'end] das obere Ende
end [end] (be)enden, zu Ende gehen IV
ending ['endɪŋ] Ende, (Ab-)Schluss *(einer Geschichte, eines Films usw.)* III
endless ['endləs] endlos IV
enemy ['enəmi] Feind/in II
energetic [ˌenə'dʒetɪk] aktiv, tatkräftig V 2 (33)
energy ['enədʒi] Energie V 2 (33/164)
engine ['endʒɪn] Motor IV
engineer [ˌendʒɪ'nɪə] Ingenieur/in II
English ['ɪŋglɪʃ] Englisch; englisch I
enjoy [ɪn'dʒɔɪ] genießen II • **Enjoy yourself.** Viel Spaß! / Amüsier dich gut! III
enough [ɪ'nʌf] genug I

enter ['entə]
1. betreten; eintreten (in) III
2. eingeben *(Geheimzahl)* V 3 (51)
equipment *(no pl)* [ɪ'kwɪpmənt] Ausrüstung, Geräte V 2 (34)
eraser [ɪ'reɪsər] *(AE)* Radiergummi IV
escape (from sb./sth.) [ɪ'skeɪp] fliehen (vor jm./aus etwas); entkommen III
especially [ɪ'speʃəli] besonders, vor allem V 4 (77)
essay (about, on) ['eseɪ] Aufsatz (über) I
°**ethnic** ['eθnɪk] ethnisch, Volks-
°**eucalyptus** [ˌjuːkə'lɪptəs] Eukalyptus
euro (€) ['jʊərəʊ] Euro I
even ['iːvn] sogar II
evening ['iːvnɪŋ] Abend I • **in the evening** abends, am Abend I
on Friday evening freitagabends, am Freitagabend I
event [ɪ'vent] Ereignis; Veranstaltung IV
ever? ['evə] je? / jemals? / schon mal? II
every ['evri] jeder, jede, jedes I
everybody ['evribɒdi] jeder, alle II
everyday *(adj)* ['evrideɪ] Alltags-; alltägliche(r, s) III
everyone ['evrɪwʌn] jeder, alle IV
everything ['evriθɪŋ] alles I
exact [ɪg'zækt] genau, exakt V 1 (16)
exactly [ɪg'zæktli] genau III
example [ɪg'zɑːmpl] Beispiel IV
for example zum Beispiel IV
excellent ['eksələnt] ausgezeichnet, hervorragend IV
exchange: exchange rate [ɪks'tʃeɪndʒ reɪt] Wechselkurs V 2 (41) • **exchange student** [ɪks'tʃeɪndʒ ˌstjuːdnt] Austauschschüler/in III
excited [ɪk'saɪtɪd] begeistert, aufgeregt III
exciting [ɪk'saɪtɪŋ] aufregend, spannend I
Excuse me, ... [ɪk'skjuːz miː] Entschuldigung, ... / Entschuldigen Sie, ... I
exercise ['eksəsaɪz]
1. Übung, Aufgabe I
2. *(no pl)* (körperliche) Bewegung, Training IV
exercise book ['eksəsaɪz bʊk] Schulheft, Übungsheft I
expect [ɪk'spekt] erwarten III
expensive [ɪk'spensɪv] teuer I
experience [ɪk'spɪəriəns] Erfahrung, Erlebnis V 2 (30) • **work experience** Praktikum; Arbeits-, Praxiserfahrungen V 2 (35) • **do work experience** ein Praktikum machen V 2 (35/165)
explain sth. to sb. [ɪk'spleɪn] jm. etwas erklären, erläutern II
explanation [ˌeksplə'neɪʃn] Erklärung II
explore [ɪk'splɔː] erkunden, erforschen I
explorer [ɪk'splɔːrə] Entdecker/in, Forscher/in II
explosion [ɪk'spləʊʒn] Explosion IV
extra ['ekstrə] zusätzlich I
extracurricular activities *(kurz:* **extracurriculars***)* [ˌekstrəkə'rɪkjələz] *schulische Angebote außerhalb des regulären Unterrichts, oft als Arbeitsgemeinschaften* IV
eye [aɪ] Auge I

F

face [feɪs] Gesicht I
fact [fækt] Tatsache, Fakt III
factory ['fæktri] Fabrik II
failure *(n)* ['feɪljə] ungenügend *(USA, Schulnote)* IV
fair [feə] fair, gerecht II
faithfully ['feɪθfəli]**: Yours faithfully** mit freundlichen Grüßen *(Briefschluss bei namentlich unbekanntem Empfänger)* V 2 (36)
fall [fɔːl]**, fell, fallen** fallen, stürzen II • °**fall asleep** einschlafen • **fall down** hinfallen II • **fall in love (with sb.)** sich verlieben (in jn.) IV
fall off herunterfallen (von) II
°**fall of the Wall** [fɔːl] der Fall der Mauer *(in Berlin 1989)*
fallen ['fɔːlən] *siehe* **fall**
false [fɔːls] falsch IV
family ['fæməli] Familie I • **family name** Nachname, Familienname V 2 (35/164) • **family tree** (Familien-)Stammbaum I
famous (for) ['feɪməs] berühmt (für, wegen) II
fan [fæn] Fan I
fantastic [fæn'tæstɪk] fantastisch, toll I
fantasy ['fæntəsi] Fantasy V 1 (18)
far [fɑː] weit (entfernt) II
farm [fɑːm] Bauernhof, Farm II
farmer ['fɑːmə] Landwirt/in, Bauer/Bäuerin IV
farmhouse ['fɑːmhaʊs] Farmhaus, Bauernhaus IV
farming ['fɑːmɪŋ] Landwirtschaft IV
fashion ['fæʃn] Mode II • **fashion show** ['fæʃn ʃəʊ] Modenschau V 3 (56)
fast [fɑːst] schnell II • **fast food** [ˌfɑːst 'fuːd] Fastfood III
fat [fæt] fett IV
father ['fɑːðə] Vater I
fault [fɔːlt]**: It's not my fault.** Es ist nicht meine Schuld. III
favourite ['feɪvərɪt] Lieblings- I
my favourite colour meine Lieblingsfarbe I
February ['februəri] Februar I
fed [fed] *siehe* **feed** • **be fed up (with sth.)** [ˌfed_'ʌp] die Nase voll haben (von etwas) II
feed [fiːd]**, fed, fed** füttern I
feel [fiːl]**, felt, felt** sich fühlen; fühlen; sich anfühlen II • **I feel sick.** Mir ist schlecht. IV
feet [fiːt] *Plural von „foot"* I
fell [fel] *siehe* **fall**
felt [felt] *siehe* **feel**
felt tip ['felt tɪp] Filzstift I
female ['fiːmeɪl] weiblich III
fence [fens] Zaun V 1 (18)
ferry ['feri] Fähre III
festival ['festɪvl] Fest, Festival, Festspiele III
few [fjuː]**: a few** ein paar, einige II
fiction: science fiction [ˌsaɪəns 'fɪkʃn] Sciencefiction V 1 (18)
fiddle ['fɪdl] *(infml)* Fiedel, Geige III
play the fiddle Geige, Fiedel spielen III
field [fiːld] Feld, Acker, Weide II
in the field auf dem Feld II
fight [faɪt]**, fought, fought** kämpfen III • **fight for** kämpfen (für, um) III
fight [faɪt] Kampf; Schlägerei IV
figure ['fɪgə] Zahl, Ziffer V 1 (10)
file [faɪl]**: background file** *etwa:* Hintergrundinformation(en) II
grammar file *Grammatikanhang* I • **skills file** *Anhang mit Lern- und Arbeitstechniken* I • **sound file** Tondatei, Soundfile III
fill in [ˌfɪl_'ɪn]
1. ausfüllen
°**2.** einsetzen
film [fɪlm] Film I • **action film** ['ækʃn fɪlm] Actionfilm V 1 (18)
°**film review** ['fɪlm rɪˌvjuː] Filmkritik, Filmbesprechung • **film star** Filmstar I
film [fɪlm] filmen V 3 (49)
final ['faɪnl] Finale, Endspiel III
final ['faɪnl] letzte(r, s); End- III
final score Endstand *(beim Sport)* III
finally ['faɪnəli] zuletzt, als letztes V 4 (84)
find [faɪnd]**, found, found** finden I
find out (about) herausfinden (über) I

finder ['faɪndə] Finder I
fine [faɪn]
1. gut, schön; in Ordnung II
2. *(gesundheitlich)* gut II
I'm/He's fine. Es geht mir/ihm gut. II
finger ['fɪŋgə] Finger I
finish ['fɪnɪʃ] beenden, zu Ende machen; enden I
fire ['faɪə] Feuer, Brand II • **fire safety** Verhalten im Brandfall IV **fire station** Feuerwache IV • **put out a fire** ein Feuer löschen IV
firefighter ['faɪəfaɪtə] Feuerwehrfrau, -mann IV
fireman ['faɪəmən] Feuerwehrmann II
firewoman ['faɪə,wʊmən] Feuerwehrfrau II
first [fɜːst]
1. erste(r, s) I
2. zuerst, als Erstes I
be first der/die Erste sein I • **first aid** Erste Hilfe V 2 (36) • **first-aid kit** Erste-Hilfe-Kasten, Verbandskasten V 4 (80/171) • **first name** Vorname V 2 (35) • **the first half** die erste Halbzeit III
fish [fɪʃ] fischen, angeln III
fish, *pl* **fish** [fɪʃ] Fisch I
fit (-tt-) [fɪt] passen I
fit [fɪt]: **be fit** fit sein III
fitness ['fɪtnəs] Fitness IV • **fitness centre** Fitnesscenter IV
flag [flæg] Flagge, Fahne V 1 (8)
flash [flæʃ] Lichtblitz III
flat [flæt] Wohnung I
flat screen ['flæt skriːn] Flachbildschirm IV
flew [fluː] *siehe* **fly**
flight [flaɪt] Flug II • **a 14-hour flight** ein 14-stündiger Flug, ein 14-Stunden-Flug III
floor [flɔː]
1. Fußboden I
2. Stockwerk IV
°**flow chart** ['fləʊ tʃɑːt] Flussdiagramm
flown [fləʊn] *siehe* **fly**
flu [fluː] Grippe V 4 (75)
flute [fluːt] Querflöte III
fly [flaɪ], **flew, flown** fliegen II
°**fly** [flaɪ] Fliege
fog [fɒg] Nebel II
foggy ['fɒgi] neblig II
folk music ['fəʊk ˌmjuːzɪk] Folk *(englische, schottische, irische oder nordamerikanische Volksmusik des 20. Jahrhunderts)* III
follow ['fɒləʊ] folgen; verfolgen I; befolgen V 3 (55) • °**the following ...** die folgenden ...

food [fuːd]
1. Essen; Lebensmittel I
2. Futter I
foot [fʊt], *pl* **feet** [fiːt]
1. Fuß I
2. Fuß *(Längenmaß: 30,48 cm)* IV
football ['fʊtbɔːl] Fußball I
football boots Fußballschuhe I
for [fə, fɔː] für I • **for breakfast/lunch/dinner** zum Frühstück/Mittagessen/Abendbrot I • **for example** zum Beispiel IV • **for lots of reasons** aus vielen Gründen I • **for miles** meilenweit II **for three days** drei Tage (lang) I **for 20 minutes** seit 20 Minuten; 20 Minuten lang IV • **just for fun** nur zum Spaß I • **What for?** Wofür? II • **What's for homework?** Was haben wir als Hausaufgabe auf? I
foreground ['fɔːgraʊnd] Vordergrund II
forest ['fɒrɪst] Wald II
forgave [fə'geɪv] *siehe* **forgive**
forget (-tt-) [fə'get], **forgot, forgotten** vergessen I
forgive [fə'gɪv], **forgave, forgiven** vergeben, verzeihen IV
forgiven [fə'gɪvn] *siehe* **forgive**
forgot [fə'gɒt] *siehe* **forget**
forgotten [fə'gɒtn] *siehe* **forget**
fork [fɔːk] Gabel III
forklift ['fɔːklɪft] Gabelstapler V 2 (30)
form [fɔːm]
1. (Schul-)Klasse I • **form teacher** Klassenlehrer/in I
2. Formular V 2 (35)
°**3.** Form
°**form** [fɔːm] bilden
°**formal letter** [ˌfɔːml 'letə] formeller Brief, förmlicher Brief
forward ['fɔːwəd]
1. look forward to sth. sich auf etwas freuen V 2 (36)
°**2.** vorwärts
fought [fɔːt] *siehe* **fight**
found [faʊnd] *siehe* **find**
found [faʊnd] gründen IV
fox [fɒks] Fuchs II
free [friː]
1. frei I • **free time** Freizeit, freie Zeit I
2. kostenlos I
French [frentʃ] Französisch I
French fries *(AE)* Pommes Frites IV
Friday ['fraɪdeɪ, 'fraɪdi] Freitag I
fridge [frɪdʒ] Kühlschrank I
friend [frend] Freund/in I • **make friends** Freundschaften schließen, sich anfreunden V 3 (56)

friendly ['frendli] freundlich III
fries [fraɪz]: **French fries** *(AE)* Pommes Frites IV
frog [frɒg] Frosch II
from [frəm, frɒm]
1. aus I
2. von I
from all over the UK/the world/England aus dem gesamten Vereinigten Königreich / aus der ganzen Welt / aus ganz England III
from Monday to Friday von Montag bis Freitag III • **I'm from ...** Ich komme aus ... / Ich bin aus ... I
Where are you from? Wo kommst du her? I
front [frʌnt]: **in front of** vor *(räumlich)* I • **front door** [ˌfrʌnt 'dɔː] Wohnungstür, Haustür I • °**front page** [ˌfrʌnt 'peɪdʒ] Titelseite
°**front inside cover** [ˌfrʌnt‿ˌɪnsaɪd 'kʌvə] vordere Umschlaginnenseite
fruit [fruːt] Obst, Früchte; Frucht I
fruit salad ['fruːt ˌsæləd] Obstsalat I
full [fʊl] voll I
fully [fʊli]: **fully booked** ausgebucht V 4 (83)
fun [fʌn] Spaß I • **have fun** Spaß haben, sich amüsieren I • **Have fun!** Viel Spaß! I • **just for fun** nur zum Spaß I • **Riding is fun.** Reiten macht Spaß. I
funeral ['fjuːnərəl] Trauerfeier, Beerdigung V 3 (49)
°**funnel web spider** ['fʌnl web 'spaɪdə] Trichternetzspinne
funny ['fʌni] witzig, komisch I
future ['fjuːtʃə] Zukunft; Zukunfts-, zukünftige(r, s) V 2 (44)

G

°**gallery walk** ['gæləri wɔːk] Galerierundgang
game [geɪm] Spiel I
°**gap** [gæp] Lücke
garage ['gærɑːʒ]
1. Garage II
2. Autowerkstatt V 2 (30)
garbage ['gɑːrbɪdʒ] *(AE)* Müll, Abfall IV
garden ['gɑːdn] Garten I
gardener ['gɑːdnə] Gärtner/in V 2 (33)
gate [geɪt]
1. Flugsteig III
2. Tor V 4 (81)
°**gateway** ['geɪtweɪ] Tor (zu)
gave [geɪv] *siehe* **give**
°**Gazette** [gə'zet] Blatt, Anzeiger

°GCSE (General Certificate of Secondary Education) [sə'tɪfɪkət] *Schulabschlussprüfungen für 16-Jährige in England, Wales und Nordirland, vergleichbar der mittleren Reife oder der Fachoberschulreife*
general ['dʒenrəl] allgemeine(r, s) III • **in general** im allgemeinen IV
generation [,dʒenə'reɪʃn] Generation V 1 (17)
geography [dʒi'ɒgrəfi] Geografie, Erdkunde I
German ['dʒɜ:mən] Deutsch; deutsch; Deutsche(r) I
Germany ['dʒɜ:məni] Deutschland I
get (-tt-) [get], **got, got**
1. bekommen, kriegen II
2. holen, besorgen II
3. gelangen, (hin)kommen I
4. **get angry/hot/...** wütend/heiß/... werden II
5. **get off (the train/bus)** (aus dem Zug/Bus) aussteigen I • **get on (the train/bus)** (in den Zug/Bus) einsteigen I
6. **get up** aufstehen I
get a cab ein Taxi nehmen IV
get bored sich langweilen V 3 (48)
get dressed sich anziehen I • **get married (to sb.)** (jn.) heiraten IV
get on well/badly (with sb.) sich gut/schlecht verstehen (mit jm.), gut/schlecht auskommen (mit jm.) V 3 (46) • **get ready (for)** sich fertig machen (für), sich vorbereiten (auf) I • **get things ready** Dinge fertig machen, vorbereiten I • **get to know sb.** jn. kennenlernen IV
getting by in English [,getɪŋ 'baɪ] *etwa:* auf Englisch zurechtkommen I
ghost [gəʊst] Geist, Gespenst II
gig [gɪg] *(infml)* Gig, Auftritt III
do a gig einen Auftritt haben, ein Konzert geben III
giraffe [dʒə'rɑ:f] Giraffe II
girl [gɜ:l] Mädchen I
girlfriend ['gɜ:lfrend] (feste) Freundin IV
give [gɪv], **gave, given** geben I
give a talk (on sth.) einen Vortrag/eine Rede halten (über etwas) V 4 (84) • **give sth. up** auf etwas verzichten V 3 (48) • **give up** aufgeben, resignieren IV
given ['gɪvn] *siehe* **give**
glad [glæd] froh, dankbar III
glass [glɑ:s] Glas I • **a glass of water** ein Glas Wasser I
glasses *(pl)* ['glɑ:sɪz] (eine) Brille I
glue [glu:] (auf-, ein)kleben II
glue [glu:] Klebstoff I • **glue stick** ['glu: stɪk] Klebestift I
go [gəʊ], **went, gone** gehen I; fahren II • **go by car/train/bike/...** mit dem Auto/Zug/Rad/... fahren II • **go for a walk** spazieren gehen, einen Spaziergang machen II • **go home** nach Hause gehen I • **go on** weitermachen I • **°How does the story go on?** Wie geht die Geschichte weiter? • **go on a trip** einen Ausflug machen II • **go on holiday** in Urlaub fahren II • **go red** rot werden, erröten V 3 (58)
go riding reiten gehen I • **go shopping** einkaufen gehen I • **go surfing** wellenreiten gehen, surfen gehen II • **go swimming** schwimmen gehen I • **go to bed** ins Bett gehen I • **go to the cinema** ins Kino gehen II • **go together** zusammenpassen, -gehören II • **go well** gut (ver)laufen, gutgehen III
°go through with sth. etwas durchziehen • **go with** gehören zu, passen zu III • **coffee to go** Kaffee zum Mitnehmen IV • **Let's go.** Auf geht's! (*wörtlich:* Lass uns gehen.) I
goal [gəʊl] Tor *(im Sport)* III
goalkeeper ['gəʊlki:pə] Torwart, Torfrau III
God [gɒd] Gott IV
go-kart ['gəʊkɑ:t] Gokart III
gold [gəʊld] Gold IV
golden ['gəʊldən] goldene(r, s) IV
gone [gɒn] *siehe* **go**
good [gʊd]
1. gut I
2. brav II
Good afternoon. Guten Tag. *(nachmittags)* I • **Good luck (with ...)!** Viel Glück (bei/mit ...)! I • **Good morning.** Guten Morgen. I
Good to have you back. Schön, dass du wieder da bist. IV • **be good at sth.** gut in etwas sein; etwas gut können IV
Goodbye. [,gʊd'baɪ] Auf Wiedersehen. I • **say goodbye** sich verabschieden I
got [gɒt] *siehe* **get**
got [gɒt]: **I've got ...** Ich habe ... I
I haven't got a chair. Ich habe keinen Stuhl. I
government ['gʌvənmənt] Regierung V 1 (17)
grab sth. (-bb-) [græb] sich etwas schnappen IV
grade [greɪd]
1. Klasse, Jahrgangsstufe IV
2. (Schul-)Note, Zensur IV
grammar ['græmə] Grammatik I
grammar file *Grammatikanhang* I
°gran [græn] *(infml)* Oma
grand [grænd] eindrucksvoll, beeindruckend IV
grandchild ['græntʃaɪld], *pl* **grandchildren** Enkel/in I
grandfather ['grænfɑ:ðə] Großvater I
grandma ['grænmɑ:] Oma I
grandmother ['grænmʌðə] Großmutter I
grandpa ['grænpɑ:] Opa I
grandparents ['grænpeərənts] Großeltern I
granny ['græni] Oma II
grape [greɪp] Weintraube IV
grass [grɑ:s] Gras, Rasen IV • **cut the grass** Rasen mähen IV
great [greɪt] großartig, toll I
green [gri:n] grün I
grew [gru:] *siehe* **grow**
grey [greɪ] grau II
°groan [grəʊn] stöhnen
ground [graʊnd] (Erd-)Boden III
grounded ['graʊndɪd]: **be grounded** Ausgehverbot/Hausarrest haben III
group [gru:p] Gruppe I • **group word** Oberbegriff II
grow [grəʊ], **grew, grown**
1. *(Getreide usw.)* anbauen, anpflanzen II
2. **grow up** erwachsen werden; aufwachsen III
grown [grəʊn] *siehe* **grow**
grumble ['grʌmbl] murren, nörgeln I
°guard [gɑ:d] Wächter/in
guess [ges] raten, erraten, schätzen III
guest [gest] Gast I
guide [gaɪd] (Fremden-)Führer/in, Reiseleiter/in IV
guidebook ['gaɪdbʊk] Reiseführer IV
guilty ['gɪlti] schuldig IV
guinea pig ['gɪni pɪg] Meerschweinchen I
guitar [gɪ'tɑ:] Gitarre I
°Gujarati [,gu:dʒə'rɑ:ti] Gujarati *(in Gujarat, Indien, gesprochene Sprache)*
gun [gʌn] Gewehr, Schusswaffe IV
guy [gaɪ] *(infml)* Typ, Kerl IV
guys *(pl)* [gaɪz] *(AE, infml)* Leute III
gym [dʒɪm] Sport-, Turnhalle; Fitnessstudio IV

H

had [hæd] *siehe* **have** *und* **have got**
hair *(no pl)* [heə] Haar, Haare I
hairdresser ['heədresə] Friseur/Friseurin IV
hairless ['heələs] haarlos, kahl, unbehaart IV
half [hɑːf], *pl* **halves** [hɑːvz]
1. Hälfte III
2. Halbzeit III
half [hɑːf]: **half an hour** eine halbe Stunde III • **half past 11** halb zwölf (11.30/23.30) I • **three and a half days** dreieinhalb Tage IV
half-time [ˌhɑːf 'taɪm] Halbzeit(pause) III
hall [hɔːl] Flur, Diele I • **study hall** *(AE) Zeit zum selbstständigen Arbeiten/Lernen in der Schule* IV
halves [hɑːvz] *Plural von „half"*
hamburger ['hæmbɜːgə] Hamburger I
hamster ['hæmstə] Hamster I
hand [hænd] Hand I
handball ['hændbɔːl] Handball III
hang [hæŋ], **hung, hung:**
1. hang out (with friends) *(infml)* rumhängen, abhängen (mit Freunden/Freundinnen) III
2. hang up *(den Telefonhörer)* auflegen V 3 (59)
happen (to) ['hæpən] geschehen, passieren (mit) I
happiness ['hæpinəs] Glück IV
happy ['hæpi] glücklich, froh I
Happy birthday. Herzlichen Glückwunsch zum Geburtstag. I
happy ending Happyend II
harbour ['hɑːbə] Hafen II
hard [hɑːd] hart; schwer, schwierig II • **work hard** hart arbeiten II
hard-working [ˌhɑːd 'wɜːkɪn] fleißig, tüchtig V 2 (31)
hat [hæt] Hut II
hate [heɪt] hassen, gar nicht mögen I
have [həv, hæv], **had, had** haben, besitzen II • **have a baby** ein Baby/Kind bekommen II • **have a bath** baden, ein Bad nehmen II **have a cold** erkältet sein, eine Erkältung haben II • **have a conversation** ein Gespräch, eine Unterhaltung führen V 1 (15/161) • **Have a good holiday.** Schöne Ferien! V 4 (83/173) • **Have a good time.** Viel Spaß! V 4 (83/173) • **Have a good trip/journey.** Gute Reise! V 4 (83/173) • **Have a good weekend.** Schönes Wochenende! V 4 (83/173) **have a look** ansehen, einen Blick werfen auf IV • **have a picnic** ein Picknick machen I • **Have a pleasant stay.** Einen angenehmen Aufenthalt. V 4 (83) • **have a sauna** in die Sauna gehen II • **have a shower** (sich) duschen I • **have a sore throat** Halsschmerzen haben II • **have a temperature** Fieber haben II • **have breakfast/dinner** frühstücken/Abendbrot essen I • **have ... for breakfast** ... zum Frühstück essen/trinken I **have fun** Spaß haben, sich amüsieren I • **have sleepovers** Schlafpartys veranstalten III • **have to do** tun müssen I • **Good to have you back.** Schön, dass du wieder da bist. IV • **I'll have** *(bei einer Bestellung)* Ich nehme ... IV
► S.173 Have ...
have got: I've got ... [aɪv 'gɒt] Ich habe ... I • **I haven't got a chair.** Ich habe keinen Stuhl. I
he [hiː] er I
head [hed] Kopf I • **head teacher** Schulleiter/in III
headache ['hedeɪk] Kopfschmerzen II
°**heading** ['hedɪŋ] Überschrift, Titel
headline ['hedlaɪn] Schlagzeile IV
headphones *(pl)* ['hedfəʊnz] Kopfhörer V 3 (51)
health [helθ] Gesundheit; Gesundheitslehre IV
healthy ['helθi] gesund II
hear [hɪə], **heard, heard** hören I
heard [hɜːd] *siehe* **hear**
heart [hɑːt] Herz II
heaven ['hevn] Himmel IV
heavy ['hevi] schwer *(Gewicht)* V 2 (31)
hedgehog ['hedʒhɒg] Igel II
held [held] *siehe* **hold**
helicopter ['helɪkɒptə] Hubschrauber, Helikopter II
hell [hel] Hölle IV
Hello. [hə'ləʊ] Hallo. / Guten Tag. I
helmet ['helmɪt] Helm III
help [help] helfen I • **Help yourself!** Bedien dich! / Greif zu! III **Can I help you?** Kann ich Ihnen helfen? / Was kann ich für Sie tun? *(im Geschäft)* I
help [help] Hilfe I
helpful ['helpfl] hilfsbereit; hilfreich V 2 (33)
helpless ['helpləs] hilflos V 1 (18)
her [hə, hɜː]
1. ihr, ihre I
2. sie; ihr I
here [hɪə]
1. hier I
2. hierher I
Here you are. Bitte sehr. / Hier bitte. I
hero ['hɪərəʊ], *pl* **heroes** ['hɪərəʊz] Held/in; Idol, Vorbild V 4 (77)
hers [hɜːz] ihrer, ihre, ihrs II
herself [hə'self, hɜː'self] sich (selbst) III
hesitate ['hezɪteɪt] zögern V 3 (53)
Hey. [heɪ] Hallo! III
Hi! [haɪ] Hallo! I • **Say hi to Dilip for me.** Grüß Dilip von mir. I
hid [hɪd] *siehe* **hide**
hidden ['hɪdn] *siehe* **hide**
hide [haɪd], **hid, hidden** sich verstecken; *(etwas)* verstecken I
high [haɪ] hoch III • **high school** *(USA) Schule für 14-18-Jährige* IV
°**highlighted** ['haɪlaɪtɪd] hervorgehoben
hike [haɪk] wandern IV
hike [haɪk] Wanderung IV • **go on a hike** wandern gehen IV
hill [hɪl] Hügel II
hilly ['hɪli] hügelig III
him [hɪm] ihn; ihm I
himself [hɪm'self] sich (selbst) III
°**Hindi** ['hɪndi] Hindi
hip hop ['hɪp hɒp] Hip Hop III
hippo ['hɪpəʊ] Flusspferd II
his [hɪz]
1. sein, seine I
2. seiner, seine, seins II
history ['hɪstri] Geschichte I
hit (-tt-) [hɪt], **hit, hit** schlagen II
hobby ['hɒbi] Hobby I
hockey ['hɒki] Hockey I • **hockey shoes** Hockeyschuhe I
hold [həʊld], **held, held** halten II
Hold the line, please. Bitte bleiben Sie am Apparat. V 2 (41)
hole [həʊl] Loch V 1 (20)
holiday ['hɒlədeɪ]
1. Ferien I
2. Feiertag IV
holiday flat Ferienwohnung II
go on holiday in Urlaub fahren II
a two-week holiday ein zweiwöchiger Urlaub III • **Have a good holiday.** Schöne Ferien! V 4 (83/173)
► S.173 Have ...
home [həʊm] Heim, Zuhause I
at home daheim, zu Hause I
°**children's home** Kinderheim
come home nach Hause kommen I • **get home** nach Hause kommen I • **go home** nach Hause gehen I • **old people's home** Alten-, Seniorenheim V 2 (30)
homeless ['həʊmləs] obdachlos IV

homesick ['həʊmsɪk]**: be homesick** Heimweh haben IV
hometown ['həʊmtaʊn] Heimatstadt IV
homework *(no pl)* ['həʊmwɜːk] Hausaufgabe(n) I • **do homework** die Hausaufgabe(n) machen I **What's for homework?** Was haben wir als Hausaufgabe auf? I
honest ['ɒnɪst] ehrlich V 4 (76)
Hooray! [hu'reɪ] Hurra! II
hope [həʊp] hoffen II
hope [həʊp] Hoffnung III
horrible ['hɒrəbl] scheußlich, grauenhaft II
horse [hɔːs] Pferd I
hospital ['hɒspɪtl] Krankenhaus II
hostel ['hɒstl] Herberge, Wohnheim III • **youth hostel** Jugendherberge III
hot [hɒt] heiß I • **hot chocolate** heiße Schokolade I
hotel [həʊ'tel] Hotel II
hotline ['hɒtlaɪn] Hotline II
hour ['aʊə] Stunde II • **half an hour** [ˌhɑːf‿ən‿'aʊə] eine halbe Stunde III • **a 14-hour flight** ein 14-stündiger Flug, ein 14-Stunden-Flug III • **a 24-hour supermarket** ein Supermarkt, der 24 Stunden geöffnet ist III • **°hours of work** Arbeitszeiten • **rush hour** Hauptverkehrszeit V 4 (73)
house [haʊs] Haus I • **at the Shaws' house** im Haus der Shaws / bei den Shaws zu Hause I
how [haʊ] wie I • **How about ...?** Wie wär's mit ...? III • **How am I doing?** Wie komme ich voran? *(Wie sind meine Fortschritte?)* III **How are you?** Wie geht es dir/ Ihnen/euch? II • **How are you doing?** Wie geht's? V 1 (15) • **How do you know ...?** Woher weißt/ kennst du ...? I • **how long?** seit wann? IV • **how many?** wie viele? I • **how much?** wie viel? I **How much is/are ...?** Was kostet/ kosten ...? / Wie viel kostet/kosten ...? I • **How old are you?** Wie alt bist du? I • **how to do sth**. wie man etwas tut / tun kann/ tun soll V 4 (76) • **How was ...?** Wie war ...? I
► S.171 how to .../ what to ... / where to ...
huge [hjuːdʒ] riesig, sehr groß III
hundred ['hʌndrəd] hundert I
hung [hʌŋ] *siehe* **hang**
hungry ['hʌŋgri] hungrig III • **be hungry** Hunger haben, hungrig sein III
hunt [hʌnt] jagen III
hunt [hʌnt] Jagd III
hurry ['hʌri] eilen; sich beeilen II **hurry up** sich beeilen I
hurry ['hʌri]**: be in a hurry** in Eile sein, es eilig haben I
hurt [hɜːt]**, hurt, hurt** wehtun; verletzen I
hurt [hɜːt] verletzt II
husband ['hʌzbənd] Ehemann II
hutch [hʌtʃ] (Kaninchen-)Stall I

I

I [aɪ] ich I • **I'm** [aɪm] ich bin I **I'm from ...** Ich komme aus ... / Ich bin aus ... I • **I'm ... years old.** Ich bin ... Jahre alt. I • **I'm sorry.** Entschuldigung. / Tut mir leid. I
ice [aɪs]**: ice cream** (Speise-)Eis I **ice hockey** Eishockey • **ice rink** Schlittschuhbahn II
idea [aɪ'dɪə] Idee, Einfall I
ideal [aɪ'diːəl] ideal V 3 (46)
if [ɪf]
1. falls, wenn II
2. ob II
ill [ɪl] krank II
illegal [ɪ'liːgl] illegal, ungesetzlich IV
illness ['ɪlnəs] Krankheit IV
imagine sth. [ɪ'mædʒɪn] sich etwas vorstellen IV
immigrant ['ɪmɪgrənt] Einwanderer/Einwanderin IV
impolite [ˌɪmpə'laɪt] unhöflich V 2 (31/163)
important (to) [ɪm'pɔːtnt] wichtig (für) II
impossible [ɪm'pɒsəbl] unmöglich II
impressed [ɪm'prest] beeindruckt IV
°improve [ɪm'pruːv] verbessern
in [ɪn] in I • **in ... Street** in der ...straße I • **in English** auf Englisch I • **in front of** vor *(räumlich)* I • **in here** hier drinnen I • **in my opinion** meiner Meinung nach IV • **in the afternoon** nachmittags, am Nachmittag I • **in the country** auf dem Land II • **in the end** schließlich, zum Schluss III **in the evening** abends, am Abend I • **in the field** auf dem Feld II **in the morning** am Morgen, morgens I • **in the photo** auf dem Foto I • **in the picture** auf dem Bild I • **in time** rechtzeitig II **in 1837** 1837, im Jahre 1837 IV
include [ɪn'kluːd] (mit) einschließen, enthalten *(beinhalten)* V 1 (16)
independent [ˌɪndɪ'pendənt] unabhängig V 1 (9)
indoor ['ɪndɔː] *(nur vor Nomen)* Hallen-; im Gebäude V 1 (12/160) • **indoor market** Markthalle V 1 (12/160) **indoor swimming pool** Hallenbad V 1 (12/160) • **indoor toilet** Innentoilette V 1 (12/160)
► S.160 indoor – outdoor
industrial [ɪn'dʌstriəl] industriell, Industrie IV
industry ['ɪndəstri] Industrie IV
infinitive [ɪn'fɪnətɪv] Infinitiv *(Grundform des Verbs)* I
information (about/on) *(no pl)* [ˌɪnfə'meɪʃn] Information(en) (über) II
inline skating ['ɪnlaɪn ˌskeɪtɪŋ] Inlineskaten III
inside [ˌɪn'saɪd]
1. innen (drin), drinnen I
2. nach drinnen II
3. **inside the car** ins Auto (hinein), ins Innere des Autos II
°front inside cover [ˌfrʌnt‿ˌɪnsaɪd 'kʌvə] Umschlaginnenseite
install [ɪn'stɔːl] installieren, einrichten II
instant messages *(pl)* [ˌɪnstənt 'mesɪdʒɪz] *Nachrichten, die man im Internet austauscht (in Echtzeit)* III
instructions *(pl)* [ɪn'strʌkʃnz] (Gebrauchs-)Anweisung(en), Anleitung(en) II
instrument ['ɪnstrəmənt] Instrument III
interest ['ɪntrəst] Interesse III
interested ['ɪntrəstɪd]**: be interested (in)** interessiert sein (an), sich interessieren (für) III
interesting ['ɪntrəstɪŋ] interessant I
international [ˌɪntə'næʃnəl] international III
internet ['ɪntənet] Internet III **surf the internet** im Internet surfen III
interview ['ɪntəvjuː] Interview I **(job) interview** Vorstellungsgespräch, Bewerbungsgespräch V 2 (38)
interview ['ɪntəvjuː] interviewen, befragen II
interviewer ['ɪntəvjuːə] Interviewer/in, Befrager/in V 2 (39)
into ['ɪntə, 'ɪntʊ] in ... (hinein) I
introduce sth. [ˌɪntrə'djuːs] etwas einführen *(Thema, Methode, Währung)* V 4 (84)
introduction (to) [ˌɪntrə'dʌkʃn] Einführung (in) III

invitation (to) [ˌɪnvɪ'teɪʃn] Einladung (zu) I
invite (to) [ɪn'vaɪt] einladen (zu) I
°**irregular** [ɪ'regjələ] unregelmäßig
is [ɪz] ist I
island ['aɪlənd] Insel II
it [ɪt] er/sie/es I • **It's £1.** Er/Sie/Es kostet 1 Pfund. I • **It says here: ...** Hier steht: ... / Es heißt hier: ... II
its [ɪts] sein/seine; ihr/ihre I
itself [ɪt'self] sich (selbst) III

J

jacket ['dʒækɪt] Jacke, Jackett II
jail [dʒeɪl] Gefängnis IV
jam: traffic jam ['træfɪk dʒæm] (Verkehrs-)Stau V 4 (70)
January ['dʒænjuəri] Januar I
jazz [dʒæz] Jazz III
jealous (of) ['dʒeləs] neidisch (auf); eifersüchtig (auf) III
jealousy ['dʒeləsi] Eifersucht IV
jeans *(pl)* [dʒi:nz] Jeans I
jewellery ['dʒu:əlri] Schmuck III
job [dʒɒb] Aufgabe, Job I • **job interview** Vorstellungsgespräch, Bewerbungsgespräch V 2 (38) • °**job profile** Anforderungsprofil
jobless ['dʒɒbləs] ohne Job, arbeitslos V 4 (78)
join sb. [dʒɔɪn] sich jm. anschließen; bei jm. mitmachen II
joke [dʒəʊk] Witz I
joke [dʒəʊk] scherzen, Witze machen II
journey ['dʒɜ:ni] Fahrt, Reise III
Have a good journey. Gute Reise! V 4 (83)
► S.173 Have ...
judge sb. (by) [dʒʌdʒ] jn. beurteilen (nach) IV
judo ['dʒu:dəʊ] Judo I • **do judo** Judo machen I
jug [dʒʌg] Krug I • **a jug of milk** ein Krug Milch I
juice [dʒu:s] Saft I
juicy ['dʒu:si] saftig V 4 (78)
July [dʒu'laɪ] Juli I
jumble sale ['dʒʌmbl seɪl] Wohltätigkeitsbasar I
jump [dʒʌmp] springen II • **jump around** herumspringen III
June [dʒu:n] Juni I
junior ['dʒu:niə] Junioren-, Jugend- I
just [dʒʌst]
1. (einfach) nur, bloß I
2. gerade (eben), soeben II

K

kangaroo [ˌkæŋgə'ru:] Känguru II
keep [ki:p], **kept, kept:**
keep fit fit bleiben • **keep in touch** in Verbindung bleiben, Kontakt halten III • **keep sth. warm/cool/open/...** etwas warm/kühl/offen/... halten II
kept [kept] *siehe* **keep**
key [ki:] Schlüssel • **key ring** Schlüsselring II • **key word** Stichwort, Schlüsselwort I
keyboard ['ki:bɔ:d] Keyboard *(elektronisches Tasteninstrument)* III
kick [kɪk] treten IV
kid [kɪd] Kind, Jugendliche(r) I
kidney ['kɪdni] Niere III
kill [kɪl] töten I
kilogram (kg) ['kɪləgræm], **kilo** ['ki:ləʊ] Kilogramm, Kilo (kg) III
two kilos of oranges zwei Kilo Orangen III • **a 150-kilogram bear** ein 150 Kilogramm schwerer Bär III
kilometre (km) ['kɪləmi:tə] Kilometer III • **a ten-kilometre walk** eine Zehn-Kilometer-Wanderung III
kind [kaɪnd] freundlich, nett V 3 (58/169)
kind (of) [kaɪnd] Art III • **What kind of car...?** Was für ein Auto III
kindergarten ['kɪndəgɑ:tn] Kindergarten; *(USA)* Vorschule *(für 5- bis 6-jährige)* IV
king [kɪŋ] König I
kiss [kɪs] küssen IV
kiss [kɪs] Kuss IV
kit [kɪt] Ausrüstung V 4 (80)
first-aid kit Erste-Hilfe-Kasten, Verbandskasten V 4 (80/171)
repair kit Flickzeug V 4 (80/171)
survival kit Überlebenspäckchen V 4 (80)
kitchen ['kɪtʃɪn] Küche I
kite [kaɪt] Drachen I
kiwi ['ki:wi:] Kiwi II
knee [ni:] Knie I
knew [nju:] *siehe* **know**
knife [naɪf], *pl* **knives** [naɪvz] Messer III
knock [nɒk] Klopfen V 3 (59)
knock (at/on sth.) [nɒk] (an etwas) klopfen V 3 (59/169)
know [nəʊ], **knew, known**
1. wissen I
2. kennen I
know about sth. von etwas wissen; über etwas Bescheid wissen II
get to know sb. jn. kennenlernen IV • **How do you know ...?** Woher weißt du ...? / Woher kennst du ...? I • **I don't know.** Ich weiß es nicht. I • **..., you know.** ..., wissen Sie. / ..., weißt du. I • **You know what, Sophie?** Weißt du was, Sophie? I
known [nəʊn] *siehe* **know**
koala [kəʊ'ɑ:lə] Koala V 1 (9)

L

°**label** ['leɪbl] beschriften, etikettieren
laid [leɪd] *siehe* **lay**
lake [leɪk] (Binnen-)See II
lamb [læm] Lamm(fleisch) III
lamp [læmp] Lampe I
land [lænd] landen II
land [lænd] Land, Grund und Boden II
lane [leɪn] Gasse, Weg III
language ['læŋgwɪdʒ] Sprache I
large [lɑ:dʒ] groß II
lasagne [lə'zænjə] Lasagne I
last [lɑ:st] letzte(r, s) I • **the last day** der letzte Tag I • **at last** endlich, schließlich I
late [leɪt] spät; zu spät I • **be late** zu spät sein/kommen I • **Sorry, I'm late.** Entschuldigung, dass ich zu spät bin/komme. I
later ['leɪtə] später I
latest ['leɪtɪst] neueste(r, s) III
laugh [lɑ:f] lachen I • **laugh at sb.** jn. auslachen IV
laughter ['lɑ:ftə] Gelächter II
°**lavatory** ['lævətri] *(veraltet oder gehoben)* Toilette
law [lɔ:] Gesetz IV
lay [leɪ], **laid, laid:**
lay the table den Tisch decken I
°**layout** ['leɪaʊt] Layout *(Text- und Bildgestaltung eines Buches, einer Zeitschrift)*
lazy ['leɪzi] faul V 3 (56)
leader ['li:də] (An-)Führer/in, Leiter/in, III
leaf [li:f], *pl* **leaves** [li:vz] Blatt *(an Pflanzen)* V 1 (11)
learn [lɜ:n] lernen I • **learn sth. about sth.** etwas über etwas erfahren/herausfinden II
least [li:st] am wenigsten IV • **like sth. least** etwas am wenigsten mögen III • **at least** zumindest, wenigstens I
leave [li:v], **left, left**
1. (weg)gehen; abfahren II
2. verlassen II
3. zurücklassen II
leave a message eine Nachricht hinterlassen V 4 (83) • **leave sb. alone** jn. in Ruhe lassen V 3 (59)

leaves [liːvz] *Plural von „leaf“* V 1 (11)
left [left] *siehe* **leave**
left [left] linke(r, s) II • **look left** nach links schauen II • **on the left** links, auf der linken Seite II • **turn left** (nach) links abbiegen II
leg [leg] Bein I
legal ['liːgl] legal, gesetzlich IV
leisure centre ['leʒə sentə] Freizeitzentrum, -park II
lemonade [ˌlemə'neɪd] Limonade I
less [les] weniger IV
lesson ['lesn] (Unterrichts-)Stunde I • **lessons** *(pl)* Unterricht I
let [let], **let, let** lassen II • **Let's go.** Auf geht's! (*wörtlich:* Lass uns gehen.) I
letter ['letə]
1. Buchstabe I
2. **letter (to)** Brief (an) II
letter of application [ˌæplɪ'keɪʃn] Bewerbungsschreiben V 2 (35/164)
°**letter to the editor** ['edɪtə] Leserbrief • °**formal letter** ['fɔːml] formeller Brief, förmlicher Brief
lettuce ['letɪs] (Kopf-)Salat II
library ['laɪbrəri] Bibliothek, Bücherei I
license plate ['laɪsns pleɪt] *(AE)* Nummernschild IV
life [laɪf], *pl* **lives** [laɪvz] Leben I
lifeguard ['laɪfgɑːd] Rettungsschwimmer/in V 1 (14) • **lifeguard station** Station der Rettungsschwimmer/innen V 1 (14)
lift [lɪft] Fahrstuhl, Aufzug II
light [laɪt] Licht III
like [laɪk] wie I • **What was the weather like?** Wie war das Wetter? II
like [laɪk] mögen, gernhaben I
like sth. best/least etwas am meisten/wenigsten mögen III
like sth. better etwas lieber mögen II • **I like swimming/dancing.** Ich schwimme/tanze gern. I • **I'd like ... (= I would like ...)** Ich hätte gern ... / Ich möchte gern ... I • **I'd like to talk about ... (= I would like to talk about ...)** Ich möchte/würde gern über ... reden I • **Would you like ...?** Möchtest du ...? / Möchten Sie ...? I • **Would you like some?** Möchtest du etwas/ein paar? / Möchten Sie etwas/ein paar? I
likeable ['laɪkəbl] liebenswert, nett, sympathisch IV
line [laɪn]
1. Zeile II
2. (U-Bahn-)Linie III
3. *(AE)* Schlange, Reihe *(wartender Menschen)* IV
4. **Hold the line, please.** Bitte bleiben Sie am Apparat. V 2 (41)
link [lɪŋk] verbinden, verknüpfen I
link [lɪŋk] Verbindung, Verknüpfung III
linking word ['lɪŋkɪŋ wɜːd] Bindewort II
lion ['laɪən] Löwe II
list [lɪst] Liste I
list [lɪst] auflisten, aufzählen II
listen (to) ['lɪsn] zuhören; sich etwas anhören I
listener ['lɪsnə] Zuhörer/in II
listing ['lɪstɪŋ]: **TV listings** *(pl)* Fernsehprogramm IV
little ['lɪtl]
1. klein I
2. wenig IV • **a little** ein wenig/ein bisschen
live [lɪv] leben, wohnen I • **live on sth.** von etwas leben; sich von etwas ernähren V 4 (73)
live music [laɪv] Livemusik II
liver ['lɪvə] Leber III
lives [laɪvz] *Plural von „life“* I
living room ['lɪvɪŋ ruːm] Wohnzimmer I
local ['ləʊkl] Orts-, örtlich II; einheimisch V 1 (16)
location [ləʊ'keɪʃn] Wohn-/Standort, Lage III
lock [lɒk] abschließen; sperren III
long [lɒŋ] lang I
look [lʊk]
1. schauen, gucken I
2. **look different/great/old** anders/toll/alt aussehen I
look after sth./sb. auf etwas/jn. aufpassen; sich um etwas/jn. kümmern II • **look at** ansehen, anschauen I • **look for** suchen II
look forward to sth. sich auf etwas freuen V 2 (36) • **look left/right** nach links/rechts schauen II • **look round** sich umsehen I
look sth. up etwas nachschlagen III • **look up (from)** hochsehen, aufschauen (von) II
look [lʊk] Blick • **have a look at sth.** sich etwas ansehen, einen Blick werfen auf etwas IV
lorry ['lɒri] Lastwagen III
lose [luːz], **lost, lost** verlieren II
lost [lɒst] *siehe* **lose**
lot [lɒt]: **a lot (of)** eine Menge, viel, viele II • **Thanks a lot!** Vielen Dank! I • **He likes her a lot.** Er mag sie sehr. I • **lots more** viel mehr I • **lots of** eine Menge, viele, viel I
°**lot** [lɒt] *(infml)* Bande
loud [laʊd] laut I
love [lʌv] lieben, sehr mögen II
love [lʌv] Liebe II • **Love ...** Liebe Grüße, ... *(Briefschluss)* I • **love story** Liebesgeschichte IV • **fall in love (with sb.)** sich verlieben (in jn.) IV
°**lozenges** ['lɒzɪndʒɪz]: **throat lozenges** Halspastillen, Lutschtabletten für den Hals
luck [lʌk]: **Good luck (with ...)!** Viel Glück (bei/mit ...)! I
luckily ['lʌkɪli] zum Glück, glücklicherweise II
lucky ['lʌki]: **be lucky (with)** Glück haben (mit) IV
lunch [lʌntʃ] Mittagessen I
lunch break Mittagspause I

M

°**Ma'am** [mæm] *kurz für* **Madam**
machine [mə'ʃiːn]
1. Automat IV
2. Maschine I
mad [mæd] verrückt I • **be mad about sth.** verrückt nach/auf etwas sein III
madam
°1. *Anrede für eine Kundin/eine Vorgesetzte*
2. **Dear Sir or Madam** Sehr geehrte Damen und Herren *(Anrede in Briefen)* V 2 (36)
made [meɪd] *siehe* **make**
madness ['mædnəs] Verrücktheit IV
magazine [ˌmægə'ziːn] Zeitschrift, Magazin I
maid [meɪd] Dienstmädchen IV
mail [meɪl] schicken, senden *(per Post oder E-Mail)* III • **mail sb.** jn. anmailen II
mail [meɪl] Mail III
mailbox ['meɪlbɒks] Mailbox V 3 (51)
main [meɪn] Haupt-; wichtigste(r, s) IV
mainly ['meɪnli] hauptsächlich V 4 (77)
majority [mə'dʒɒrəti] Mehrheit IV
make [meɪk], **made, made** machen; bauen I • **make a mess** alles durcheinanderbringen, alles in Unordnung bringen I • **make a speech** eine Rede halten IV
make friends Freundschaften schließen, sich anfreunden V 3 (56)
°**make it** (es) überleben • °**make sb. do sth.** jn. dazu bringen etwas zu tun • **Make yourself comfortable.** Machen Sie es sich bequem. / Mach es dir bequem. IV
make-up ['meɪkʌp] Make-up II

male [meɪl] männlich III
mall [mɔːl]: **(shopping) mall** Einkaufspassage, überdachtes Einkaufszentrum IV
man [mæn], *pl* **men** [men] Mann I
°**manager** ['mænɪdʒə] Geschäftsführer/in, Leiter/in
many ['meni] viele I • **how many?** wie viele? I
map [mæp] Landkarte, Stadtplan II
°**Marathi** [mə'rɑːti] Marathi *(in West- und Zentralindien gesprochene Sprache)*
March [mɑːtʃ] März I
mark [mɑːk] (Schul-)Note, Zensur IV
mark sth. up [ˌmɑːk‿'ʌp] etwas markieren, kennzeichnen II
market ['mɑːkɪt] Markt II
marmalade ['mɑːməleɪd] (Orangen-)Marmelade I
married (to) ['mærɪd] verheiratet (mit) I • **get married (to sb.)** (jn.) heiraten IV
mashed potatoes [ˌmæʃt pə'teɪtəʊz] Kartoffelbrei, Kartoffelpüree III
match [mætʃ] Spiel, Wettkampf I
°**match** [mætʃ]
1. passen zu
2. zuordnen
°**Match the letters and numbers.** Ordne die Buchstaben den Zahlen zu.
mate [meɪt] *(infml)* Freund/in, Kumpel III
material [mə'tɪəriəl] Material V 4 (84)
maths [mæθs] Mathematik I
matter ['mætə]: **What's the matter?** Was ist los? / Was ist denn? II
May [meɪ] Mai I
may [meɪ] dürfen III
maybe ['meɪbi] vielleicht I
me [miː] mir; mich I • **Me too.** Ich auch. I • **more than me** mehr als ich II • **That's me.** Das bin ich. I **Why me?** Warum ich? I
meal [miːl] Mahlzeit, Essen III
mean [miːn], **meant, meant**
1. bedeuten III • **What does 'forest' mean?** Was bedeutet „forest“? III
2. meinen *(sagen wollen)* II
meaning ['miːnɪŋ] Bedeutung III
meant [ment] *siehe* **mean**
meat [miːt] Fleisch I
mechanic [mə'kænɪk] Mechaniker/in V 2 (30)
medal ['medl] Medaille III
media *(pl)* ['miːdiə] Medien III
mediation [ˌmiːdi'eɪʃn] Vermittlung, Sprachmittlung, Mediation II
medicine ['medsn, 'medɪsn] Medizin V 4 (75)
medium ['miːdiəm] mittel(groß) II
meet [miːt], **met, met**
1. treffen; kennenlernen I
2. sich treffen I
Nice to meet you. Nett, dich kennenzulernen. III
meeting ['miːtɪŋ] Versammlung, Besprechung IV
member ['membə] Mitglied IV
men [men] *Plural von „man“* I
menu ['menjuː] Speisekarte II
mess [mes]: **be a mess** sehr unordentlich sein; fürchterlich aussehen II • **make a mess** alles durcheinanderbringen, alles in Unordnung bringen I
message ['mesɪdʒ] Nachricht III
leave a message eine Nachricht hinterlassen V 4 (83) • **take a message** eine Nachricht entgegennehmen V 4 (83/173) • **Can I take a message for him/her?** Kann ich ihm/ihr etwas ausrichten? V 4 (83/173) • **text message** SMS III
met [met] *siehe* **meet**
metal ['metl] Metall V 4 (77)
metre ['miːtə] Meter II
mice [maɪs] *Plural von „mouse“* I
microphone ['maɪkrəfəʊn] Mikrofon III
middle (of) ['mɪdl] Mitte I; Mittelteil II • **middle school** *(USA) Schule für 11- bis 14-Jährige* IV
might [maɪt]: **She might be too busy.** Sie könnte zu beschäftigt sein. / Vielleicht ist sie zu beschäftigt. IV
mild [maɪld] mild III
mile [maɪl] Meile *(= ca. 1,6 km)* II
for miles meilenweit II
milk [mɪlk] Milch I
million ['mɪljən] Million III
°**millionaire** [ˌmɪljə'neə] Millionär/Millionärin
mime [maɪm] pantomimisch darstellen, vorspielen II
mind [maɪnd]: **Mind your own business.** Das geht dich nichts an! / Kümmere dich um deine eigenen Angelegenheiten! II • **Never mind.** Macht nichts. V 4 (81)
mind map ['maɪnd mæp] Mindmap („Gedankenkarte“, „Wissensnetz“) I
mine [maɪn] meiner, meine, meins II
minority [maɪ'nɒrəti] Minderheit IV
mints *(pl)* [mɪnts] Pfefferminzbonbons I
minus ['maɪnəs] minus IV
minute ['mɪnɪt] Minute I • **Wait a minute.** Warte mal! / Moment mal! II
mirror ['mɪrə] Spiegel II
miss [mɪs]
1. vermissen II
2. verpassen V 3 (51)
3. **Miss a turn.** Einmal aussetzen. II
Miss White [mɪs] Frau White *(unverheiratet)* I
missing ['mɪsɪŋ]: **be missing** fehlen II • °**the missing information/words** die fehlenden Informationen/Wörter
mistake [mɪ'steɪk] Fehler I
mix [mɪks] mischen, mixen III
mix [mɪks] Mix, Mischung III
°**mixed-race** [ˌmɪkst'reɪs] gemischtrassische(r, s)
mixture ['mɪkstʃə] Mischung III
mobile (phone) ['məʊbaɪl] Mobiltelefon, Handy I
model ['mɒdl] Modell*(-flugzeug, -schiff usw.)* I; (Foto-)Modell II
modern ['mɒdən] modern III
mole [məʊl] Maulwurf II
mom [mɒm, *AE* mɑːm] *(AE)* Mama, Mutti; Mutter III
moment ['məʊmənt] Moment III
Monday ['mʌndeɪ, 'mʌndi] Montag I • **Monday morning** Montagmorgen I
money ['mʌni] Geld I • **raise money (for)** Geld sammeln (für) IV
monitor ['mɒnɪtə] Monitor, Bildschirm III
monkey ['mʌŋki] Affe II
monster ['mɒnstə] Ungeheuer, Monster II • °**monster dumper truck** [ˌmɒnstə 'dʌmpə trʌk] *Kipplaster mit gewaltigen Rädern*
month [mʌnθ] Monat I
moon [muːn] Mond II
moped ['məʊped] Moped V 2 (36)
more [mɔː] mehr I • **lots more** viel mehr I • **more than** mehr als II • **more than me** mehr als ich II **more boring (than)** langweiliger (als) II • **no more music** keine Musik mehr I • **not (...) any more** nicht mehr III
morning ['mɔːnɪŋ] Morgen, Vormittag I • **in the morning** morgens, am Morgen I • **Monday morning** Montagmorgen I • **on Friday morning** freitagmorgens, am Freitagmorgen I
most [məʊst] (der/die/das) meiste ...; am meisten II • **most people** die meisten Leute I • **(the) most**

boring der/die/das langweiligste ...; am langweiligsten II
mostly ['məʊstli] hauptsächlich, überwiegend V 2 (33)
motel [məʊ'tel] Motel IV
mother ['mʌðə] Mutter I
motorbike ['məʊtəbaɪk] Motorrad V 3 (52)
mountain ['maʊntən] Berg II
mouse [maʊs], *pl* **mice** [maɪs] Maus I
mouth [maʊθ] Mund I
move [mu:v]
1. bewegen; sich bewegen II **Move back one space.** Geh ein Feld zurück. II • **Move on one space.** Geh ein Feld vor. II
2. move (to) umziehen (nach, in) II • **move in** einziehen II • **move out** ausziehen II
movement ['mu:vmənt] Bewegung II
movie ['mu:vi] Film III
MP3 player [ˌempi:'θri: ˌpleɪə] MP3-Spieler I
Mr ... ['mɪstə] Herr ... I
Mrs ... ['mɪsɪz] Frau ... I
Ms ... [mɪz, məz] Frau ... II
much [mʌtʃ] viel I • **how much?** wie viel? I • **How much is/are ...?** Was kostet/kosten ...? / Wie viel kostet/kosten ...? I • **like/love sth. very much** etwas sehr mögen/ sehr lieben II
mud [mʌd] Schlamm, Matsch V 3 (59/169)
muddy ['mʌdi] schlammig, matschig, schmutzig V 3 (59)
muesli ['mju:zli] Müsli IV
multiple choice [ˌmʌltɪpl 'tʃɔɪs] Multiple-Choice II
mum [mʌm] Mama, Mutti; Mutter I
museum [mju'zi:əm] Museum I
mushroom ['mʌʃrʊm] Pilz III
music ['mju:zɪk] Musik I
musical ['mju:zɪkl] Musical I
must [mʌst] müssen I • °**must-see sights** Sehenswürdigkeiten, die man sehen muss
must [mʌst]**: a must** ein Muss IV
mustn't do ['mʌsnt] nicht tun dürfen II
my [maɪ] mein/e I
myself [maɪ'self] mir/mich (selbst) III

N

name [neɪm] Name I • **My name is ...** Ich heiße ... / Mein Name ist ... I • **What's your name?** Wie heißt du? I • **family name** Nachname, Familienname V 2 (35/164)
name [neɪm] nennen; benennen II
nation ['neɪʃn] Nation IV
national ['næʃnəl] national III **national park** Nationalpark IV
nationality [ˌnæʃə'næləti] Staatsangehörigkeit, Nationalität V 2 (36)
Native American [ˌneɪtɪv_ə'merɪkən] amerikanische(r) Ureinwohner/in, Indianer/in IV
near [nɪə] in der Nähe von, nahe (bei) I
nearly ['nɪəli] fast, beinahe V 1 (10)
neat [ni:t] gepflegt II • **neat and tidy** schön ordentlich II
neck [nek] Hals, Genick V 1 (20)
need [ni:d] brauchen, benötigen I **need to do sth.** etwas tun müssen; etwas zu tun brauchen V 4 (80)
► S.172 need to do sth.
needn't do ['ni:dnt] nicht tun müssen, nicht zu tun brauchen II
negative ['negətɪv] negativ V 4 (72/170)
neighbour ['neɪbə] Nachbar/in I
nephew ['nefju:] Neffe IV
nervous ['nɜ:vəs] nervös, aufgeregt I
nervousness ['nɜ:vəsnəs] Nervosität IV
°**network** ['netwɜ:k] (Wörter-)Netz
never ['nevə] nie, niemals I **Never mind.** Macht nichts. V 4 (81)
new [nju:] neu I
news *(no pl)* [nju:z] Nachrichten, Neuigkeiten III • **That's good news.** Das sind gute Nachrichten. III
newspaper ['nju:speɪpə] Zeitung I
next [nekst]**: be next** der/die Nächste sein I • **the next morning/day** am nächsten Morgen/Tag I • **What have we got next?** Was haben wir als Nächstes? I
next to [nekst] neben II
nice [naɪs] schön, nett I • **Nice to meet you.** Nett, dich kennenzulernen. III • **Nice try.** Netter Versuch. V 3 (58)
niece [ni:s] Nichte IV
night [naɪt] Nacht, später Abend I **at night** nachts, in der Nacht I **on Friday night** freitagnachts, Freitagnacht I
nightlife ['naɪtlaɪf] Nachtleben V 4 (76)
nil [nɪl] null III
no [nəʊ] nein I
no [nəʊ] kein, keine I • **no more music** keine Musik mehr I • **no one** ['nəʊ wʌn] niemand IV **No smoking.** Rauchen verboten. III • **No way!** Auf keinen Fall! / Kommt nicht in Frage! II
nobody ['nəʊbədi] niemand II
nod (-dd-) [nɒd] nicken (mit) II
noise [nɔɪz] Geräusch; Lärm I
noisy ['nɔɪzi] laut, lärmend II
normal ['nɔ:ml] normal, üblich V 2 (32)
north [nɔ:θ] Norden; nach Norden; nördlich III
north-east [ˌnɔ:θ'i:st] Nordosten; nach Nordosten; nordöstlich III
north-west [ˌnɔ:θ'west] Nordwesten; nach Nordwesten; nordwestlich III
nose [nəʊz] Nase I
not [nɒt] nicht I • **not (...) any** kein, keine I • **not (...) any more** nicht mehr III • **not (...) anybody** niemand II • **not (...) anything** nichts II • **not (...) anywhere** nirgendwo(hin) II • **not (...) at all** überhaupt nicht, ganz und gar nicht V 3 (48) • **not (...) yet** noch nicht II
note [nəʊt] Mitteilung, Notiz I °**make notes** sich Notizen machen **take notes** sich Notizen machen I
nothing ['nʌθɪŋ] nichts II
notice board ['nəʊtɪs bɔ:d] Anschlagtafel, schwarzes Brett I
°**novel** ['nɒvl] Roman
November [nəʊ'vembə] November I
now [naʊ] nun, jetzt I • °**now and then** gelegentlich, hier und da
number ['nʌmbə] Zahl, Ziffer, Nummer I • **number plate** Nummernschild IV
nut [nʌt] Nuss IV

O

o [əʊ] null I
o'clock [ə'klɒk]**: eleven o'clock** elf Uhr I
October [ɒk'təʊbə] Oktober I
°**odd** [ɒd] seltsam, komisch
of [əv, ɒv] von I • **two kilos of oranges** zwei Kilo Orangen III
of course [əv 'kɔ:s] natürlich, selbstverständlich I
off [ɒf]**: a week/day/month ... off** eine Woche / einen Tag / einen Monat ... frei IV • **cut sth. off** etwas abtrennen, abschneiden III **fall off** herunterfallen (von) II **get off (the train/bus)** (aus dem Zug/Bus) aussteigen I • **take sth.**

off etwas ausziehen *(Kleidung)* II
take 10 c off 10 Cent abziehen I
turn on/off ein-/ausschalten III
offer ['ɒfə] anbieten IV
offer ['ɒfə] Angebot IV
office ['ɒfɪs] Büro V 2 (30) • **office worker** Büroangestellte(r) V 2 (30)
°**officer** ['ɒfɪsə] *hier: Anrede für einen Polizisten, wenn man seinen Rang nicht weiß*
official [ə'fɪʃl] offiziell, amtlich, Amts- V 4 (70)
often ['ɒfn] oft, häufig I
Oh dear! [əʊ 'dɪə] Oje! II
Oh well ... [əʊ 'wel] Na ja ... / Na gut ... I
°**Oi!** [ɔɪ] *(infml)* He!
oil [ɔɪl] Öl III • **oil rig** ['ɔɪl rɪg] (Öl-)Bohrinsel III
OK [əʊ'keɪ] okay, gut, in Ordnung I
I'll/You'll/She'll/ ... be OK. Mir/Dir/Ihr/...wird nichts passieren. IV
okay [əʊ'keɪ] okay IV
old [əʊld] alt I • **old people's home** Alten-, Seniorenheim V 2 (30) • **a sixteen-year-old** ein/e Sechzehnjährige/r III • **a sixteen-year-old girl** ein sechzehnjähriges Mädchen III • °**the old days** frühere Zeiten
old-fashioned [ˌəʊld'fæʃnd] altmodisch III
on [ɒn]
1. auf I
2. eingeschaltet sein, an sein *(Radio, Licht usw.)* II
on 13th June am 13. Juni I • **on Friday** am Freitag I • **on Friday afternoon** freitagnachmittags, am Freitagnachmittag I • **on Friday evening** freitagabends, am Freitagabend I • **on Friday morning** freitagmorgens, am Freitagmorgen I • **on Friday night** freitagnachts, Freitagnacht I • **on my shift** in meiner Schicht IV • **on the beach** am Strand II • **on the board** an die Tafel I • **on the bus** im Bus III **on the coast** an der Küste III • **on the corner of Green Street and London Road** Green Street, Ecke London Road II • **on the left** links, auf der linken Seite II • **on the phone** am Telefon I • **on the plane** im Flugzeug II • **on the radio** im Radio I • **on the right** rechts, auf der rechten Seite II **on the train** im Zug I • **on TV** im Fernsehen I • **be on** gezeigt werden, laufen *(im Fernsehen/Kino)* IV • **the lights came on** das Licht ging an V 3 (59) • **What page are we on?** Auf welcher Seite sind wir? I • **go on holiday** in Urlaub fahren II • **straight on** geradeaus weiter II
once [wʌns] einmal III • **once a week** einmal pro Woche III
one [wʌn] eins, ein, eine I • **one day** eines Tages I • **one-day ticket** Tageskarte III • **a new one** ein neuer / eine neue / ein neues II • **my old ones** meine alten II • **no one** niemand IV
onion ['ʌnjən] Zwiebel III
online [ˌɒn'laɪn] online, Online- III
only ['əʊnli]
1. nur, bloß I
2. **the only guest** der einzige Gast I • **only child** Einzelkind V 3 (46)
onto ['ɒntə, 'ɒntu] auf (... hinauf) III
open ['əʊpən] öffnen, aufmachen I
open ['əʊpən] offen, geöffnet II
°**opening sentence** [ˌəʊpənɪŋ 'sentəns] Einleitungssatz
opera: soap opera ['səʊp‿ɒprə] Seifenoper IV
operation (on) [ˌɒpə'reɪʃn] Operation (an) III
opinion [ə'pɪnjən] Meinung IV
opposite ['ɒpəzɪt] Gegenteil I
or [ɔ:] oder I
orange ['ɒrɪndʒ] orange(farben) I
orange ['ɒrɪndʒ] Orange, Apfelsine I • **orange juice** ['ɒrɪndʒ dʒu:s] Orangensaft I
order ['ɔ:də] bestellen IV
order ['ɔ:də]
1. Befehl, Anweisung, Anordnung V 3 (52)
°2. Reihenfolge • **in the right order** in der richtigen Reihenfolge **word order** Wortstellung
organization [ˌɔ:gənaɪ'zeɪʃn] Organisation V 3 (48/167)
organize ['ɔ:gənaɪz] ordnen, organisieren III
organized ['ɔ:gənaɪzd] (gut) organisiert V 2 (31)
orphan ['ɔ:fn] Waise, Waisenkind V 1 (17)
other ['ʌðə] andere(r, s) I • **the others** die anderen I • **the other way round** anders herum II
Ouch! [aʊtʃ] Autsch! I
our ['aʊə] unser, unsere I
ours ['aʊəz] unserer, unsere, unseres II
ourselves [aʊə'selvz] uns (selbst) III
out [aʊt] heraus, hinaus; draußen II **out of ...** aus ... (heraus/hinaus) I
outback: the outback ['aʊtbæk] *(Australien)* das Hinterland V 1 (6)
outdoor ['aʊtdɔ:] *(nur vor Nomen)* Außen-; im Freien, Freiluft- V 1 (12) • **outdoor education** Unterricht im Freien V 1 (12) • **outdoor swimming pool** Freibad V 1 (12/160) **outdoor temperature** Außentemperatur V 1 (12/160)
► S.160 outdoor – indoor
outfit ['aʊtfɪt] Outfit *(Kleidung; Ausrüstung)* II
°**outline** ['aʊtlaɪn] Gliederung
outside [ˌaʊt'saɪd]
1. draußen I
2. nach draußen II
3. **outside his room** vor seinem Zimmer; außerhalb seines Zimmers I
over ['əʊvə]
1. über, oberhalb von I
2. **be over** vorbei/zu Ende sein I **all over the world** auf der ganzen Welt III • **from all over the UK/the world/England** aus dem gesamten Vereinigten Königreich / aus der ganzen Welt / aus ganz England III • **over there** da drüben, dort drüben I • **over to ...** hinüber zu/nach ... II
own [əʊn]: **our own pool** unser eigenes Schwimmbad II

P

pack [pæk] packen, einpacken II
packet ['pækɪt] Päckchen, Packung, Schachtel I • **a packet of mints** ein Päckchen/eine Packung Pfefferminzbonbons I
pads *(pl)* [pædz] *(Knie- usw.)*Schützer *(für Inlineskater)*; Schulterpolster *(beim American Football)* III
page [peɪdʒ] (Buch-, Heft-)Seite I **What page are we on?** Auf welcher Seite sind wir? I
paid [peɪd] *siehe* **pay**
pain [peɪn] Schmerz(en) V 4 (75)
paint [peɪnt] (an)malen I
painter ['peɪntə] Maler/in II
pair [peə]: **a pair (of)** ein Paar II
palace ['pæləs] Palast, Schloss III
panic ['pænɪk] Panik V 1 (18)
pants *(pl)* [pænts] *(AE)* Hose IV
paper ['peɪpə]
1. Papier I
2. Zeitung II
paragraph ['pærəgrɑ:f] Absatz *(in einem Text)* II
Paralympics [ˌpærə'lɪmpɪks] Paralympische Spiele *(Olympische Spiele für Sportler/innen mit körperlicher Behinderung)* III

paramedic [ˌpærəˈmedɪk] Sanitäter/in II
paraphrase [ˈpærəfreɪz] umschreiben, anders ausdrücken III
parcel [ˈpɑːsl] Paket I
parents [ˈpeərənts] Eltern I
park [pɑːk] Park I • **(park) ranger** *Ranger sind eine Art Aufseher/in in Nationalparks, die auch Führungen machen und als Wald- und Wildhüter/innen arbeiten* IV
parliament [ˈpɑːləmənt] Parlament III
parrot [ˈpærət] Papagei I
part [pɑːt] Teil I • **be part of sth.** Teil von etwas sein V 3 (56)
partner [ˈpɑːtnə] Partner/in I
party [ˈpɑːti] Party I
°**party** [ˈpɑːti] feiern
pass [pɑːs]
1. (herüber)reichen, weitergeben I
pass round herumgeben I
°**2. pass out** ohnmächtig werden
passport [ˈpɑːspɔːt] (Reise-)Pass V 4 (80)
past [pɑːst] Vergangenheit I
past [pɑːst] vorbei (an), vorüber (an) II • **half past 11** halb zwölf (11.30/23.30) I • **quarter past 11** Viertel nach elf (11.15/23.15) I
pasta *(no pl)* [ˈpæstə] Pasta, Nudeln, Teigwaren IV
path [pɑːθ] Pfad, Weg II
pavement [ˈpeɪvmənt] Gehweg, Bürgersteig IV
pay (for) [peɪ], **paid, paid** bezahlen II • **pay by credit card** mit Kreditkarte bezahlen V 3 (51) • **pay cash** bar bezahlen V 3 (51)
pay [peɪ] Bezahlung, Lohn V 2 (31)
PE [ˌpiː‿ˈiː], **Physical Education** [ˌfɪzɪkəl‿edʒuˈkeɪʃn] Turnen, Sportunterricht I
pea [piː] Erbse III
pen [pen] Kugelschreiber, Füller I
pence (p) *(pl)* [pens] Pence *(Plural von „penny")* I
pencil [ˈpensl] Bleistift I • **pencil case** Federmäppchen I • **pencil sharpener** Bleistiftanspitzer I
penny [ˈpeni] *kleinste britische Münze* I
people [ˈpiːpl] Menschen, Leute I
old people's home Alten-, Seniorenheim V 2 (30)
pepper [ˈpepə] Pfeffer V 1 (21/162)
per [pɜː, pə] pro III
per cent (%) [pəˈ sent] Prozent III
perfect [ˈpɜːfɪkt] perfekt; ideal; vollkommen IV
perhaps [pəˈhæps] vielleicht V 3 (49)

period [ˈpɪəriəd] (Unterrichts-/Schul-)Stunde IV
person [ˈpɜːsn] Person II
personal [ˈpɜːsənl] persönliche(r, s) III
°**personality** [ˌpɜːsəˈnæləti] Persönlichkeit
pet [pet] Haustier I • **pet shop** Tierhandlung I
petrol [ˈpetrəl] Benzin V 1 (22)
phone [fəʊn] Telefon I • **on the phone** am Telefon I • **phone call** Anruf, Telefongespräch I • **phone number** Telefonnummer I
phone [fəʊn] telefonieren, anrufen I
photo [ˈfəʊtəʊ] Foto I • **in the photo** auf dem Foto I • **take photos** Fotos machen, fotografieren I
photographer [fəˈtɒgrəfə] Fotograf/in III
phrase [freɪz] Ausdruck, (Rede-)Wendung V 3 (51)
piano [piˈænəʊ] Klavier, Piano I
play the piano Klavier spielen I
°**pick of the day** [pɪk] das Beste von heute
pick up [ˌpɪk‿ˈʌp]: **pick sb. up** jn. abholen III • **pick sth. up** etwas hochheben, aufheben II
picnic [ˈpɪknɪk] Picknick I • **have a picnic** ein Picknick machen I
picture [ˈpɪktʃə] Bild I • **in the picture** auf dem Bild I • **picture story** Bildergeschichte IV
pie [paɪ] Obstkuchen; Pastete II
piece [piːs]: **a piece of** ein Stück I
a piece of paper ein Stück Papier I
piercing [ˈpɪəsɪŋ] Piercing III
pig [pɪg] Schwein III
pill [pɪl] Pille, Tablette V 4 (75)
pink [pɪŋk] pink(farben), rosa I
pirate [ˈpaɪrət] Pirat, Piratin I
pitch [pɪtʃ] Fußball-/Hockeyplatz III
pizza [ˈpiːtsə] Pizza I
place [pleɪs] Ort, Platz I • **place of birth** Geburtsort V 2 (36/165)
°**placemat** [ˈpleɪsmæt] Set, Platzdeckchen
plan [plæn] Plan I
plan (-nn-) [plæn] planen I
plane [pleɪn] Flugzeug II • **on the plane** im Flugzeug II
planet [ˈplænɪt] Planet II
plant [plɑːnt] Pflanze V 1 (16)
plant [plɑːnt] pflanzen, einpflanzen V 1 (16/161)
plate [pleɪt]
1. Teller I • **a plate of chips** ein Teller Pommes frites I

2. license plate *(AE)* Nummernschild IV • **number plate** *(BE)* Nummernschild IV
platform [ˈplætfɔːm] Bahnsteig, Gleis IV
°**platypus** [ˈplætɪpəs] Schnabeltier
play [pleɪ] spielen I • **play football** Fußball spielen I • **play the drums** *(pl)* Schlagzeug spielen III
play the fiddle Geige, Fiedel spielen III • **play the guitar** Gitarre spielen I • **play the piano** Klavier spielen I
play [pleɪ] Theaterstück I
player [ˈpleɪə] Spieler/in I
pleasant [ˈpleznt] angenehm V 4 (83)
please [pliːz] bitte *(in Fragen und Aufforderungen)* I
plug [plʌg] Stecker III
plus [plʌs] plus IV
pm [ˌpiː‿ˈem]: **7 pm** 7 Uhr abends/19 Uhr I
pocket [ˈpɒkɪt] Tasche *(an Kleidungsstück)* II • **pocket money** Taschengeld II
poem [ˈpəʊɪm] Gedicht I
point [pɔɪnt] Punkt II • **10.4 (ten point four)** 10,4 (zehn Komma vier) III
point (at/to sth.) [pɔɪnt] zeigen, deuten (auf etwas) II
poison [ˈpɔɪzn] Gift V 1 (9/160)
poisonous [ˈpɔɪzənəs] giftig V 1 (9)
police *(pl)* [pəˈliːs] Polizei I • **police station** Polizeiwache, Polizeirevier II
policeman [pəˈliːsmən] Polizist II
policewoman [pəˈliːswʊmən] Polizistin II
°**policy** [ˈpɒləsi] Politik, Vorgehensweise
polite [pəˈlaɪt] höflich V 2 (31)
pollution [pəˈluːʃn] (Umwelt-)Verschmutzung V 4 (70)
poltergeist [ˈpəʊltəgaɪst] Poltergeist I
poor [pɔː, pʊə]
1. arm I • **poor Sophie** (die) arme Sophie I
°**2.** schlecht, armselig
pop [pɒp] Pop(musik) III
popcorn [ˈpɒpkɔːn] Popcorn II
popular [ˈpɒpjələ] beliebt, populär III
population [ˌpɒpjuˈleɪʃn] Bevölkerung, Einwohner(zahl) IV
pork [pɔːk] Schweinefleisch III
positive [ˈpɒzətɪv] positiv V 4 (72)
possible [ˈpɒsəbl] möglich II
postcard [ˈpəʊstkɑːd] Postkarte II
postcode [ˈpəʊstkəʊd] Postleitzahl V 2 (36)

poster ['pəʊstə] Poster I
post office ['pəʊst_ɒfɪs] Postamt II
postscript (PS) ['pəʊstskrɪpt] Postskript (PS) *(Nachschrift unter Briefen)* III
potato [pə'teɪtəʊ], *pl* **potatoes** Kartoffel I • **potato chips** *(AE)* Kartoffelchips IV
°**pouch** [paʊtʃ] Beutel
poultry ['pəʊltri] Geflügel IV
pound (£) [paʊnd] Pfund *(britische Währung)* I
practice ['præktɪs] *hier:* Übungsteil I
practise ['præktɪs] üben; trainieren I
pray [preɪ] beten V 3 (59/169)
prayer ['preə] Gebet V 3 (59)
prejudice (against) ['predʒudɪs] Voreingenommenheit (gegen), Vorurteil (gegenüber) IV
prepare (for) [prɪ'peə] vorbereiten; sich vorbereiten (auf) II
prescription [prɪ'skrɪpʃn] Rezept *(für Medikamente)* V 4 (75)
present ['preznt]
1. Gegenwart I
2. Geschenk I
present sth. (to sb.) [prɪ'zent] (jm.) etwas präsentieren, vorstellen V 3 (48/167)
presentation [ˌprezn'teɪʃn] Präsentation, Vorstellung I
presenter [prɪ'zentə] Moderator/in II
president ['prezɪdənt] Präsident/in IV
press [pres] drücken III
pressure ['preʃə] Druck V 3 (53)
pretty ['prɪti] hübsch I
pretty healthy/good/useful ... ['prɪti] ziemlich gesund/gut/nützlich ... II
price [praɪs] (Kauf-)Preis I
primary school ['praɪməri skuːl] Grundschule V 2 (36)
print [prɪnt] drucken V 2 (32)
printer ['prɪntə] Drucker V 2 (32/164)
prison ['prɪzn] Gefängnis V 1 (9/160)
prisoner ['prɪznə] Gefangene(r) V 1 (9)
°**private detective** [ˌpraɪvət dɪ'tektɪv] Privatdetektiv/in
prize [praɪz] Preis, Gewinn I
probably ['prɒbəbli] wahrscheinlich II
problem ['prɒbləm] Problem II
produce [prə'djuːs] produzieren, herstellen III
product ['prɒdʌkt] Produkt IV
production [prə'dʌkʃn] Produktion V 3 (48/167)
profile ['prəʊfaɪl] Porträt, Steckbrief III; Profil V 2 (34) • °**job profile** Anforderungsprofil
programme ['prəʊgræm]
1. Programm I
2. (Fernseh-)Sendung IV
project (about, on) ['prɒdʒekt] Projekt (über, zu) I • **do a project** ein Projekt machen, durchführen II
promise ['prɒmɪs] versprechen II
°**pronounce** [prə'naʊns] aussprechen
pronunciation [prəˌnʌnsi'eɪʃn] Aussprache I
proof *(no pl)* [pruːf] Beweis(e) II
protect [prə'tekt] schützen IV
proud (of sb./sth.) [praʊd] stolz (auf jn./etwas) II
PS [ˌpiː_'es] **(postscript** ['pəʊstskrɪpt]**)** PS (Postskript; *Nachschrift unter Briefen*) III
pub [pʌb] Kneipe, Lokal II
public ['pʌblɪk] öffentlich; Öffentlichkeit IV • **public transport** *(no pl)* [ˌpʌblɪk 'trænspɔːt] öffentliche Verkehrsmittel, öffentlicher Personennahverkehr V 4 (71)
publish ['pʌblɪʃ] veröffentlichen III
pull [pʊl] ziehen I
pullover ['pʊləʊvə] Pullover II
purple ['pɜːpl] violett; lila I
purse [pɜːs] Geldbörse II
push [pʊʃ] drücken, schieben, stoßen I
put (-tt-) [pʊt], **put, put** legen, stellen, *(etwas wohin)* tun I • °**put down an animal** ein Tier einschläfern • **put out a fire** ein Feuer löschen IV • **put sth. on** etwas anziehen *(Kleidung)* II • **put sth. up** etwas aufhängen V 3 (52) • °**Put up your hand.** Heb deine Hand. / Hebt eure Hand.
puzzled ['pʌzld] verwirrt II
pyjamas *(pl)* [pə'dʒɑːməz] Schlafanzug II

Q

qualification [ˌkwɒlɪfɪ'keɪʃn] Abschluss, Qualifikation V 2 (36)
quality ['kwɒləti] Qualität; Eigenschaft V 2 (33)
quarter ['kwɔːtə]: **quarter past 11** Viertel nach 11 (11.15/23.15) I
quarter to 12 Viertel vor 12 (11.45/ 23.45) I
quay [kiː] Kai, Kaimauer III
queen [kwiːn] Königin III
question ['kwestʃn] Frage I • **ask questions** Fragen stellen I
°**question word** Fragewort
°**questionnaire** [ˌkwestʃə'neə] Fragebogen
queue [kjuː] sich anstellen; anstehen V 4 (81)
queue [kjuː] Schlange, Reihe *(wartender Menschen)* IV
quick [kwɪk] schnell I
quiet ['kwaɪət] leise, still, ruhig I
quite bad/quick/good ... [kwaɪt] ziemlich schlimm/schnell/gut/... II
quiz [kwɪz], *pl* **quizzes** ['kwɪzɪz] Quiz, Ratespiel I

R

rabbit ['ræbɪt] Kaninchen I
rabbit-proof ['ræbɪtpruːf] kaninchen-sicher, kaninchen-fest V 1 (18)
race [reɪs] Rasse V 1 (17)
racist ['reɪsɪst] rassistisch; Rassist/ Rassistin V 1 (17)
racket ['rækɪt]: **badminton racket** Badmintonschläger III
radio ['reɪdiəʊ] Radio I • **on the radio** im Radio I
rafting ['rɑːftɪŋ] Rafting IV
railway ['reɪlweɪ] Eisenbahn II
rain [reɪn] Regen II
rain [reɪn] regnen II
rainproof ['reɪnpruːf] regendicht *(Kleidung)* V 1 (18/162)
rainy ['reɪni] regnerisch II
raise money (for) [reɪz] Geld sammeln (für) IV
ran [ræn] *siehe* **run**
rang [ræŋ] *siehe* **ring**
ranger ['reɪndʒə]: **(park) ranger** *Ranger sind eine Art Aufseher/in in Nationalparks, die auch Führungen machen und als Wald- und Wildhüter/innen arbeiten* IV
rap [ræp] Rap *(rhythmischer Sprechgesang)* I
rapper ['ræpə] Rapper/in IV
rate: **exchange rate** [ɪks'tʃeɪndʒ reɪt] Wechselkurs V 2 (41)
RE [ˌɑːr_'iː], **Religious Education** [rɪˌlɪdʒəs_edʒu'keɪʃn] Religion, Religionsunterricht I
read [riːd], **read, read** lesen I
°**read out** vorlesen • °**Read out loud.** Lies laut vor. • °**Read the poem to a partner.** Lies das Gedicht einem Partner/einer Partnerin vor.
read [red] *siehe* **read**
reader ['riːdə] Leser/in II
ready ['redi] bereit, fertig I • **get ready (for)** sich fertig machen (für), sich vorbereiten (auf) I • **get**

things ready Dinge fertig machen, vorbereiten I
real [rɪəl] echt, wirklich I
realistic [ˌriːəˈlɪstɪk] realistisch, wirklichkeitsnah III
reality [riˈæləti] Realität, Wirklichkeit IV
really [ˈrɪəli] wirklich I
reason [ˈriːzn] Grund, Begründung I • **for lots of reasons** aus vielen Gründen I
receipt [rɪˈsiːt] Quittung, Kassenbon V 3 (51)
receive [rɪˈsiːv] empfangen IV
°**recently** [ˈriːsntli] in letzter Zeit; neulich, vor kurzem
reception [rɪˈsepʃn] Rezeption, Empfang V 2 (36)
°**receptionist** [rɪˈsepʃənɪst] Rezeptionist/in; Empfangsdame
record [rɪˈkɔːd] (*Musik / einen Film*) aufnehmen III
recorder [rɪˈkɔːdə] Blockflöte III
recording [rɪˈkɔːdɪŋ] Aufnahme, Aufzeichnung III
recycled [ˌriːˈsaɪkld] wiederverwertet, wiederverwendet, recycelt II
recycling [ˌriːˈsaɪklɪŋ] Wiederverwertung, Recycling II
red [red] rot I • **go red** rot werden, erröten V 3 (58)
reef [riːf] Riff V 1 (11)
reference [ˈrefrəns] Referenz, Empfehlung V 2 (36)
reggae [ˈregeɪ] Reggae III
regular [ˈregjələ] normal (*Größenangabe bei Getränken/Fastfood*) IV
rehearsal [rɪˈhɜːsl] Probe (*am Theater*) I
rehearse [rɪˈhɜːs] proben (*am Theater*) I
relations *(pl)* [rɪˈleɪʃnz] Beziehungen IV
relationship [rɪˈleɪʃnʃɪp] Beziehung V 2 (44)
relax [rɪˈlæks] (sich) entspannen, sich ausruhen II
relaxed [rɪˈlækst] entspannt, gelassen V 1 (18)
reliable [rɪˈlaɪəbl] zuverlässig, verlässlich V 2 (32)
remember sth. [rɪˈmembə]
1. sich erinnern (an etwas) I
2. sich etwas merken I
remote control [rɪˌməʊt kənˈtrəʊl] Fernbedienung IV
rent sth. [rent] etwas mieten, etwas leihen V 1 (15)
repair sth. [rɪˈpeə] etwas reparieren V 1 (20) • **repair kit** Flickzeug V 4 (80/171)
°**repeat** [rɪˈpiːt] wiederholen
°**replace** [rɪˈpleɪs] ersetzen
report (on) [rɪˈpɔːt] Bericht, Reportage (über) I
report (to sb.) [rɪˈpɔːt] (jm.) berichten II
reporter [rɪˈpɔːtə] Reporter/in IV
represent [ˌreprɪˈzent] repräsentieren, vertreten III
rescue helicopter [ˈreskjuː ˌhelɪkɒptə] Rettungshubschrauber II
research (on) *(no pl)* [rɪˈsɜːtʃ, ˈriːsɜːtʃ] Recherche (zu, über); Nachforschungen (zu, über) IV • **do research** recherchieren IV
respect [rɪˈspekt] achten, respektieren V 1 (16)
respect [rɪˈspekt] Achtung, Respekt V 1 (16/161)
rest [rest] Rest II
restaurant [ˈrestrɒnt] Restaurant II
result [rɪˈzʌlt] Ergebnis, Resultat I
return [rɪˈtɜːn] zurückkehren IV **return ticket** Rückfahrkarte II
return [rɪˈtɜːn] Rückkehr IV
°**reunification** [ˌriːˌjuːnɪfɪˈkeɪʃn] Wiedervereinigung
°**review** [rɪˈvjuː]: **film/book review** Film-/Buchkritik, Film-/Buchbesprechung
revise [rɪˈvaɪz]
1. überarbeiten III
2. wiederholen III
revision [rɪˈvɪʒn] Wiederholung (*des Lernstoffs*) I
°**rewrite** [ˌriːˈraɪt] neu schreiben
rhino [ˈraɪnəʊ] Nashorn II
rice [raɪs] Reis IV
rich [rɪtʃ] reich II
ridden [ˈrɪdn] *siehe* **ride**
ride [raɪd], **rode, ridden** reiten I **go riding** [ˈraɪdɪŋ] reiten gehen I **ride a bike** Rad fahren I
ride [raɪd]: **(bike) ride** (Rad-)Fahrt II
right [raɪt] Recht IV
right [raɪt] richtig I • **all right** [ɔːl ˈraɪt] gut, in Ordnung II • **be right** Recht haben I • **That's right.** Das ist richtig. / Das stimmt. I • **You need a school bag, right?** Du brauchst eine Schultasche, stimmt's? / nicht wahr? I
right [raɪt] rechte(r, s) II • **look right** nach rechts schauen II • **on the right** rechts, auf der rechten Seite II • **turn right** (nach) rechts abbiegen II
right [raɪt]: **right now** jetzt sofort; jetzt gerade I
ring [rɪŋ] Ring II
ring [rɪŋ], **rang, rung** klingeln, läuten II • **The bell rang.** Es klingelte. III
ringtone [ˈrɪŋtəʊn] Klingelton III
river [ˈrɪvə] Fluss II
RnB [ˌɑːr‿ənˈbiː] RnB (*Rhythm and Blues; Form des Blues, in der Rhythmus eine große Rolle spielt*) III
road [rəʊd] Straße I • °**go on a road trip** auf große Fahrt gehen **Park Road** [ˌpɑːk ˈrəʊd] Parkstraße I • °**road train** [ˈrəʊd treɪn] Lkw-Zug (*LKW mit mehreren Anhängern; in Australien*)
°**roadhouse** [ˈrəʊdhaʊs] Raststätte
rock [rɒk] Fels, Felsen III
rock (music) [rɒk] Rock(musik) III
rode [rəʊd] *siehe* **ride**
role [rəʊl] Rolle III • **role play** Rollenspiel II
roll [rəʊl] Brötchen I
rollerblades [ˈrəʊləbleɪdz] Rollerblades IV
rollerskating [ˈrəʊləskeɪtɪŋ] Rollerskaten IV
Roman [ˈrəʊmən] römisch; Römer, Römerin II
roof [ruːf] Dach V 2 (30/163)
roofer [ˈruːfə] Dachdecker/in V 2 (30)
room [ruːm] Raum, Zimmer I **double room** Doppelzimmer V 4 (80) • **single room** Einzelzimmer V 4 (80/172)
round [raʊnd] rund II
round [raʊnd] um ... (herum); in ... umher II • **the other way round** anders herum II
route [ruːt] Strecke, Route IV
rubber [ˈrʌbə] Radiergummi I
rubbish [ˈrʌbɪʃ] (Haus-)Müll, Abfall II
rucksack [ˈrʌksæk] Rucksack III
rude [ruːd] unhöflich, unverschämt II
rule [ruːl] Regel, Vorschrift III
ruler [ˈruːlə] Lineal I
run [rʌn] (Wett-)Lauf II
run (-nn-) [rʌn], **ran, run**
1. laufen, rennen I • **run around** herumrennen III
2. **run sth.** etwas leiten, führen V 2 (43)
rung [rʌŋ] *siehe* **ring**
runner [ˈrʌnə] Läufer/in II
running shoes [ˈrʌnɪŋ ʃuːz] Laufschuhe III
rush hour [ˈrʌʃ‿aʊə] Hauptverkehrszeit V 4 (73)

S

sad [sæd] traurig II
saddle [ˈsædl] Sattel III

safe (from) [seɪf] sicher, in Sicherheit (vor) II
safety ['seɪfti] Sicherheit IV • **fire safety** Verhalten im Brandfall IV
said [sed] *siehe* **say**
sailor ['seɪlə] Seemann, Matrose II
salad ['sæləd] Salat *(als Gericht oder Beilage)* I
sale [seɪl] (Aus-, Schluss-)Verkauf IV • **for sale** *(auf Schild)* zu verkaufen IV
salt [sɔ:lt] Salz V 1 (21)
same [seɪm]**: the same ...** der-/die-/dasselbe ...; dieselben ... I • **be/look the same** gleich sein/aussehen I
°**sanctuary** ['sæŋktʃʊəri] *hier:* Tierpark
sandwich ['sænwɪtʃ] Sandwich, *(zusammengeklapptes)* belegtes Brot I • **sandwich box** Brotdose I
sang [sæŋ] *siehe* **sing**
°**sank** [sæŋk] *siehe* **sink**
sat [sæt] *siehe* **sit**
satellite ['sætəlaɪt] Satellit IV
Saturday ['sætədeɪ, 'sætədi] Samstag, Sonnabend I
sauna ['sɔ:nə] Sauna II • **have a sauna** in die Sauna gehen II
sausage ['sɒsɪdʒ] (Brat-, Bock-)Würstchen, Wurst I
save [seɪv]
1. retten II
2. sparen II
3. (ab)speichern *(Daten, Telefonnummern)* V 3 (51)
saw [sɔ:] *siehe* **see**
saxophone ['sæksəfəʊn] Saxophon III
say [seɪ]**, said, said** sagen I • **It says here: ...** Hier steht: ... / Es heißt hier: ... II • **say goodbye** sich verabschieden I • **Say hi to Dilip for me.** Grüß Dilip von mir. I **say sorry** sich entschuldigen II
scan a text (-nn-) [skæn] einen Text schnell nach bestimmten Wörtern/Informationen absuchen II
scared [skeəd] verängstigt II • **be scared (of)** Angst haben (vor) I
scarf [skɑ:f]**,** *pl* **scarves** [skɑ:vz] Schal III
scary ['skeəri] unheimlich; gruselig I
scene [si:n] Szene I
schedule ['skedʒu:l] *(AE)*
1. Fahrplan IV
2. Stundenplan IV
school [sku:l] Schule I • **at school** in der Schule I • **school bag** Schultasche I • °**School of the Air** *Fernunterricht über Kurzwellenfunk in den dünn besiedelten Gebieten Australiens, für die Primarstufe und die untere Sekundarstufe* • **school subject** Schulfach I
science ['saɪəns] Naturwissenschaft I • **science fiction** [ˌsaɪəns 'fɪkʃn] Sciencefiction V 1 (18)
score [skɔ:] Spielstand; Punktestand III • **final score** Endstand *(beim Sport)* III • **What's the score? – 2–0 (two nil)** Wie steht es? *(beim Sport)* – 2:0. III
score (a goal) [skɔ:] ein Tor schießen, einen Treffer erzielen III
scoreless ['skɔ:ləs] torlos IV
°**scrabble** ['skræbl] Scrabble
°**scrapbook** ['skræpbʊk] Sammelalbum
scream [skri:m] schreien, kreischen IV
screen [skri:n] Bildschirm IV • **flat screen** Flachbildschirm IV
°**scuba diving** ['sku:bə ˌdaɪvɪŋ] Sporttauchen
sea [si:] Meer, *(die)* See I
season ['si:zn] Jahreszeit V 1 (8)
second ['sekənd] zweite(r, s) I
second-hand [ˌsekənd 'hænd] gebraucht; aus zweiter Hand III
secondary school ['sekəndri sku:l] weiterführende Schule V 2 (36)
secret ['si:krət] Geheimnis V 3 (49/167)
secret ['si:krət] geheim V 3 (49/167)
secretly ['si:krətli] heimlich V 3 (49)
section ['sekʃn] Abschnitt, Teil, (Themen-)Bereich III
see [si:]**, saw, seen**
1. sehen I
2. see sb. jn. besuchen, jn. aufsuchen II
I see. Ich verstehe. / Aha. / Ach so. V 1 (14) • **See?** Siehst du? I • **See you.** Tschüs. / Bis bald. I • **Wait and see!** Wart's ab! III
seem (to be/do) [si:m] (zu sein / zu tun) scheinen IV
seen [si:n] *siehe* **see**
sell [sel]**, sold, sold** verkaufen II
semester [sɪ'mestə] Semester *(Schulhalbjahr in den USA)* IV
semi-final [ˌsemi'faɪnl] Halbfinale III
send (to) [send]**, sent, sent** schicken, senden (an) II
sent [sent] *siehe* **send**
sentence ['sentəns] Satz I
September [sep'tembə] September I
series, *pl* **series** ['sɪəri:z] (Sende-)Reihe, Serie II
serious ['sɪəriəs] ernst, ernsthaft IV
be serious about sth. etwas ernst nehmen V 2 (33)
serve [sɜ:v] bedienen *(Kunden)* V 2 (31)
°**Sesotho** [ses'u:tu:] *Sprache in Südafrika*
set (-tt-) [set]**, set, set:**
set the alarm clock den Wecker stellen V 3 (48/167)
setup ['setʌp] Setup II
sex [seks] Geschlecht III
shake [ʃeɪk]**, shook, shaken** schütteln; zittern V 1 (21)
shaken ['ʃeɪkn] *siehe* **shake**
share sth. (with sb.) [ʃeə] sich etwas teilen (mit jm.) I
she [ʃi:] sie I
sheep, *pl* **sheep** [ʃi:p] Schaf II
sheet [ʃi:t] Blatt, Bogen *(Papier)* V 2 (38)
shelf [ʃelf]**,** *pl* **shelves** [ʃelvz] Regal(brett) I
shift [ʃɪft] Schicht IV
shine [ʃaɪn]**, shone, shone** scheinen *(Sonne)* II
ship [ʃɪp] Schiff I
shirt [ʃɜ:t] Hemd I
shock [ʃɒk] Schock V 4 (73)
shocked [ʃɒkt] schockiert III
shocking ['ʃɒkɪŋ] schockierend V 3 (55)
shoe [ʃu:] Schuh I
shone [ʃɒn] *siehe* **shine**
shook [ʃʊk] *siehe* **shake**
shoot [ʃu:t]**, shot, shot** schießen, erschießen III
shop [ʃɒp] Laden, Geschäft I
shop assistant ['ʃɒp‿əˌsɪstənt] Verkäufer/in I • **shop window** Schaufenster II
shop (-pp-) [ʃɒp] einkaufen (gehen) I
shopping ['ʃɒpɪŋ] (das) Einkaufen I
go shopping einkaufen gehen I
shopping mall Einkaufspassage, überdachtes Einkaufszentrum IV
shopping list Einkaufsliste I
short [ʃɔ:t]
1. kurz I
2. klein *(Person)* IV
shorts *(pl)* [ʃɔ:ts] Shorts, kurze Hose I
shot [ʃɒt] *siehe* **shoot**
should [ʃəd, ʃʊd]**: we should ...** wir sollten ... IV
shoulder ['ʃəʊldə] Schulter I
shout [ʃaʊt] schreien, rufen I
shout at sb. jn. anschreien V 3 (53/169)
shout [ʃaʊt] Schrei, Ruf V 3 (53)
show [ʃəʊ] Show, Vorstellung I

show [ʃəʊ], **showed, shown** zeigen I
shower ['ʃaʊə] Dusche I • **have a shower** (sich) duschen I
shown [ʃəʊn] *siehe* **show**
shut up [ˌʃʌt_'ʌp], **shut, shut** den Mund halten II
shy [ʃaɪ] schüchtern, scheu II
sick [sɪk]
1. I feel sick. Mir ist schlecht. IV
2. *(besonders AE)* krank V 4 (73)
side [saɪd] Seite II
sidewalk ['saɪdwɔːk] *(AE)* Gehweg, Bürgersteig IV
sights *(pl)* [saɪts] Sehenswürdigkeiten II
sightseeing trip ['saɪtsiːɪŋ trɪp] Besichtigungstour IV
sign [saɪn] Schild; Zeichen III
silent letter [ˌsaɪlənt 'letə] „stummer" Buchstabe *(nicht gesprochener Buchstabe)* II
silly ['sɪli] albern, dumm I
SIM card [sɪm] SIM-Karte V 3 (51)
similar (to) ['sɪmələ] ähnlich (wie) V 2 (37)
simple ['sɪmpl] einfach, nicht kompliziert V 2 (42)
since [sɪns]**: since April 4th** seit dem 4. April IV
sincerely [sɪn'sɪəli]**: Yours sincerely** mit freundlichen Grüßen *(Briefschluss bei namentlich bekanntem Empfänger)* V 2 (36)
sing [sɪŋ], **sang, sung** singen I
singer ['sɪŋə] Sänger/in II
single ['sɪŋgl]
1. ledig, alleinstehend I
2. single room Einzelzimmer V 4 (80/172)
single (ticket) ['sɪŋgl] einfache Fahrkarte *(nur Hinfahrt)* III
°**sink** [sɪŋk], **sank, sunk** sinken; versenken
sink [sɪŋk] Spüle, Spülbecken I
sir [sɜː, sə]
°**1.** *Anrede für einen Kunden/Vorgesetzten*
2. Dear Sir or Madam Sehr geehrte Damen und Herren *(Anrede in Briefen)* V 2 (36)
°**sis** [sɪs] *(infml) kurz für* **sister**
sister ['sɪstə] Schwester I
sit (-tt-) [sɪt], **sat, sat** sitzen; sich setzen I • **sit down** sich hinsetzen II • **Sit with me.** Setz dich zu mir. / Setzt euch zu mir. I
size [saɪz] Größe I
skate ['skeɪt] Inliner fahren I
skateboard ['skeɪtbɔːd] Skateboard I
skates *(pl)* [skeɪts] Inliner I

sketch [sketʃ] Sketch I
ski [skiː] Ski fahren/laufen III
ski [skiː] Ski III
skill [skɪl] Fähigkeit, Fertigkeit V 2 (30)
skills file ['skɪlz faɪl] *Anhang mit Lern- und Arbeitstechniken* I
skim a text (-mm-) [skɪm] einen Text überfliegen *(um den Inhalt grob zu erfassen)* III
skin [skɪn] Haut IV
skinny ['skɪni] mager IV
skirt [skɜːt] Rock II
sky [skaɪ] Himmel II
skyscraper ['skaɪskreɪpə] Wolkenkratzer IV
slave [sleɪv] Sklave, Sklavin II
sledge [sledʒ] Schlitten III
sleep [sliːp], **slept, slept** schlafen I
sleep [sliːp] Schlaf III
sleepless ['sliːpləs] schlaflos IV
sleepover ['sliːpəʊvə] Schlafparty III
slept [slept] *siehe* **sleep**
slide [slaɪd] Folie *(bei einer Computerpräsentation);* Dia V 4 (84)
slow [sləʊ] langsam II
slum [slʌm] Slum, Elendsviertel V 4 (70)
small [smɔːl] klein I
smart [smɑːt] clever, schlau II
smell [smel] riechen II
smell [smel] Geruch II
smile [smaɪl] lächeln I • **smile at sb.** jn. anlächeln II
smile [smaɪl] Lächeln II
smoke [sməʊk] rauchen III • **No smoking.** Rauchen verboten. III
smoke [sməʊk] Rauch III
snack [snæk] Snack, Imbiss II
°**Swati Snack** ['swɒtɪ snæk] *Fastfoodrestaurants, die traditionelle indische Küche anbieten*
snake [sneɪk] Schlange I
snow [snəʊ] Schnee II
snowball ['snəʊbɔːl] Schneeball IV
snowshoe ['snəʊʃuː] Schneeschuh III
snowshoeing ['snəʊʃuːɪŋ] Schneeschuhwandern III
so [səʊ]
1. also; deshalb, daher I • **So?** Und? / Na und? II
2. so sweet so süß I
3. Do you really think so? Meinst du wirklich? / Glaubst du das wirklich? II
soap [səʊp] Seife I • **soap opera** ['səʊp_ɒprə] *(kurz:* **soap***)* Seifenoper IV
soccer ['sɒkə] Fußball IV
social ['səʊʃl] sozial, Sozial- IV

sock [sɒk] Socke, Strumpf I
soda ['səʊdə] *(AE)* Limonade IV
soda machine *(AE)* Getränkeautomat IV
sofa ['səʊfə] Sofa I
soft [sɒft] weich IV • **soft drink** alkoholfreies Getränk IV
software ['sɒftweə] Software II
sold [səʊld] *siehe* **sell**
soldier ['səʊldʒə] Soldat/in IV
solve [sɒlv] lösen V 2 (32)
some [səm, sʌm] einige, ein paar I
some cheese/juice etwas Käse/Saft I
somebody ['sʌmbədi] jemand I
Find/Ask somebody who ... Finde/Frage jemanden, der ... II
somebody else jemand anders IV
someone ['sʌmwʌn] jemand IV
something ['sʌmθɪŋ] etwas II
sometimes ['sʌmtaɪmz] manchmal I
somewhere ['sʌmweə] irgendwo(hin) II • **somewhere to stay** ein Platz zum Übernachten V 4 (80)
son [sʌn] Sohn I
song [sɒŋ] Lied, Song I
soon [suːn] bald I
sore [sɔː]**: have a sore throat** Halsschmerzen haben II
sorry ['sɒri]**: (I'm) sorry.** Entschuldigung. / Tut mir leid. I • **Sorry, I'm late.** Entschuldigung, dass ich zu spät bin/komme. I • **Sorry?** Wie bitte? I • **say sorry** sich entschuldigen II
sort [sɔːt] Art, Sorte II
sound [saʊnd] klingen, sich *(gut usw.)* anhören I
sound [saʊnd] Laut; Klang I
sound file ['saʊnd faɪl] Tondatei, Soundfile III
soundtrack ['saʊndtræk] Soundtrack, Filmmusik V 1 (18)
soup [suːp] Suppe II
south [saʊθ] Süden; nach Süden; südlich III
south-east [ˌsaʊθ'iːst] Südosten; nach Südosten, südöstlich III
south-west [ˌsaʊθ'west] Südwesten; nach Südwesten; südwestlich III
souvenir [ˌsuːvə'nɪə] Souvenir, Mitbringsel IV
°**Soweto** [sə'wetəʊ] **(South Western Townships)** *südwestliche Wohngebiete in Johannesburg*
space [speɪs]**: Move back one space.** Geh ein Feld zurück. II • **Move on one space.** Geh ein Feld vor. II
spaghetti [spə'geti] Spaghetti II
speak (to) [spiːk], **spoke, spoken** sprechen (mit), reden (mit) II

special ['speʃl] besondere(r,s) I • **a special day** ein besonderer Tag I **special effect** Spezialeffekt V 1 (18)
speech [spi:tʃ] Rede IV • **make a speech** eine Rede halten IV °**speech bubble** Sprechblase
spell [spel] buchstabieren I
spelling ['spelɪŋ] (Recht-)Schreibung, Schreibweise III
spend [spend]**, spent, spent: spend money (on)** Geld ausgeben (für) II • **spend time (on)** Zeit verbringen (mit) II
spent [spent] *siehe* **spend**
°**spice** [spaɪs] Gewürz
spicy ['spaɪsi] würzig, scharf gewürzt III
spider ['spaɪdə] Spinne V 1 (6)
spoke [spəʊk] *siehe* **speak**
spoken ['spəʊkən] *siehe* **speak**
spoon [spu:n] Löffel III
sport [spɔ:t] Sport; Sportart I **do sport** *(BE)* Sport treiben I **sports centre** Sportzentrum I
sportsman ['spɔ:tsmən] Sportler IV
sportswoman ['spɔ:tswʊmən] Sportlerin IV
sporty ['spɔ:ti] sportlich III
spotlight ['spɒtlaɪt] Spotlight IV
spring [sprɪŋ] Frühling I
spy [spaɪ] Spion/in I
square [skweə] Platz III
squirrel ['skwɪrəl] Eichhörnchen II
stadium ['steɪdiəm] Stadion III
stage [steɪdʒ] Bühne III
stairs *(pl)* [steəz] Treppe; Treppenstufen I
stamp [stæmp] Briefmarke I
stand [stænd]**, stood, stood** stehen; sich (hin)stellen II
star [stɑ:]
1. Stern II
2. (Film-, Pop-)Star I
start [stɑ:t] starten, anfangen, beginnen (mit) I • **start a business** eine Firma gründen V 2 (42)
state [steɪt] Staat III
statement ['steɪtmənt] Aussage, Feststellung III
station ['steɪʃn]
1. Bahnhof I • **at the station** am Bahnhof I
°**2. cattle station** ['kætl steɪʃn] Rinderfarm
statue ['stætʃu:] Statue II
stay [steɪ]
1. bleiben I
2. wohnen, übernachten II
somewhere to stay ein Platz zum Übernachten V 4 (80)
stay [steɪ] Aufenthalt V 4 (83)
Have a pleasant stay. Einen angenehmen Aufenthalt. V 4 (83)
► S.173 Have ...
steak [steɪk] Steak III
steal [sti:l]**, stole, stolen** stehlen II
steel [sti:l] Stahl III • **steel drum** [ˌsti:l 'drʌm] Steeldrum III
°**steer** [stɪə] junger Ochse
step [step] Schritt I
stereo ['steriəʊ] Stereoanlage I
°**stick** [stɪk] Stock
still [stɪl] (immer) noch I
stole [stəʊl] *siehe* **steal**
stolen ['stəʊlən] *siehe* **steal**
stomach ['stʌmək]
1. Magen II
2. Bauch III
stomach ache Magenschmerzen, Bauchweh II
stone [stəʊn] Stein II
stood [stʊd] *siehe* **stand**
stop [stɒp] Halt IV
stop (-pp-) [stɒp]
1. aufhören I
2. anhalten I
Stop that! Hör auf damit! / Lass das! I
storm [stɔ:m] Sturm; Gewitter II
stormy ['stɔ:mi] stürmisch II
story ['stɔ:ri] Geschichte, Erzählung I
straight on [streɪt‿'ɒn] geradeaus weiter II
strange [streɪndʒ] seltsam, sonderbar; fremd IV
strawberry ['strɔ:bəri] Erdbeere II
street [stri:t] Straße I • **at 7 Hamilton Street** in der Hamiltonstraße 7 I
strength [streŋθ] Stärke, Kraft V 2 (38)
stress [stres] Betonung III
strict [strɪkt] streng III
strike [straɪk] Streik III • **be on strike** streiken, sich im Streik befinden III • **go on strike** streiken, in den Streik treten III
strong [strɒŋ] stark II
structure ['strʌktʃə] strukturieren, aufbauen II
student ['stju:dənt] Schüler/in; Student/in I
study ['stʌdɪ] studieren; sorgfältig durchlesen; lernen IV • **study hall** *Zeit zum selbstständigen Arbeiten/ Lernen in der Schule* IV • **study skills** *(pl)* Lern- und Arbeitstechniken I
stuff [stʌf] Zeug, Kram II
stupid ['stju:pɪd] blöd, dämlich II
subject ['sʌbdʒɪkt]
1. Schulfach I
°**2.** *Betreff in einer E-Mail*
suburb ['sʌbɜ:b] Vorort V 4 (71)
subway ['sʌbweɪ]**: the subway** *(AE)* die U-Bahn II
successful [sək'sesfl] erfolgreich IV
suddenly ['sʌdnli] plötzlich, auf einmal I
sugar ['ʃʊgə] Zucker II
suitable ['su:təbl] geeignet, passend V 2 (38)
suitcase ['su:tkeɪs] Koffer II
sum sth. up (-mm-) [ˌsʌm‿'ʌp] etwas zusammenfassen V 3 (57)
summarize sth. ['sʌməraɪz] etwas zusammenfassen IV
summary ['sʌməri] Zusammenfassung IV
summer ['sʌmə] Sommer I
sun [sʌn] Sonne II
Sunday ['sʌndeɪ, 'sʌndi] Sonntag I
sung [sʌŋ] *siehe* **sing**
sunglasses *(pl)* ['sʌnglɑ:sɪz] (eine) Sonnenbrille I
°**sunk** [sʌnk] *siehe* **sink**
sunny ['sʌni] sonnig II
sunrise ['sʌnraɪz] Sonnenaufgang V 1 (16)
sunscreen ['sʌnskri:n] Sonnenschutzmittel V 1 (12)
sunset ['sʌnset] Sonnenuntergang V 1 (16/161)
super ['su:pə] super IV
supermarket ['su:pəmɑ:kɪt] Supermarkt II • **a 24-hour supermarket** ein Supermarkt, der 24 Stunden geöffnet ist III
sure [ʃʊə, ʃɔ:] sicher, klar • **be sure** sicher sein II
surf the internet [sɜ:f] im Internet surfen III
surfboard ['sɜ:fbɔ:d] Surfbrett II
surfing ['sɜ:fɪŋ]**: go surfing** wellenreiten gehen, surfen gehen II
surname ['sɜ:neɪm] Nachname V 2 (35)
surprise [sə'praɪz] Überraschung III
surprised (at sth.) [sə'praɪzd] überrascht (über etwas) IV
surprising [sə'praɪzɪŋ] überraschend, erstaunlich IV
survey (on) ['sɜ:veɪ] Umfrage, Untersuchung (über) II
survival [sə'vaɪvl] Überleben V 4 (80) • **survival kit** Überlebenspäckchen V 4 (80)
survive [sə'vaɪv] überleben II
swam [swæm] *siehe* **swim**
swap sth. (for sth.) (-pp-) [swɒp] etwas (ein)tauschen (für etwas/ gegen etwas) IV

°**Swati Snacks** ['swɒtɪ snæks] *Fastfoodrestaurant in Mumbai, das traditionelle indische Küche anbietet*
sweatshirt ['swetʃɜːt] Sweatshirt I
sweet [swiːt] süß I
sweetheart ['swiːthɑːt] Liebling, Schatz II
sweets *(pl)* [swiːts] Süßigkeiten I
swim (-mm-) [swɪm]**, swam, swum** schwimmen I • **go swimming** schwimmen gehen I
swimmer ['swɪmə] Schwimmer/in II
swimming ['swɪmɪŋ]**: swimming pool** Schwimmbad, Schwimmbecken I • **swimming trunks** *(pl)* ['swɪmɪŋ trʌŋks] Badehose III
swimsuit ['swɪmsuːt] Badeanzug III
swum [swʌm] *siehe* **swim**
syllable ['sɪləbl] Silbe I
system ['sɪstəm] System IV

T

table ['teɪbl] Tisch I
table tennis ['teɪbl tenɪs] Tischtennis I • **table tennis bat** Tischtennisschläger III
take [teɪk]**, took, taken**
1. nehmen I
2. (weg-, hin)bringen I
3. dauern, *(Zeit)* brauchen III
°4. einnehmen, annektieren
take a break eine Pause machen IV • **take a message** eine Nachricht entgegennehmen V 4 (83/173)
Can I take a message for him/her? Kann ich ihm/ihr etwas ausrichten? V 4 (83/173) • **take notes** sich Notizen machen I • **take off** *(infml)* sich davonmachen, sich aus dem Staub machen IV • **take out** herausnehmen I • °**take over a plane** die Kontrolle über ein Flugzeug übernehmen • **take photos** Fotos machen, fotografieren I • **take place** stattfinden IV • **take sth. off** etwas ausziehen *(Kleidung)* II • **take 10 c off** 10 Cent abziehen I • °**Take turns.** Wechselt euch ab. • **We'll take them.** *(beim Einkaufen)* Wir nehmen sie. I
taken ['teɪkən] *siehe* **take**
talk (to sb. about sth.) [tɔːk] (mit jm. über etwas) reden, sich (mit jm. über etwas) unterhalten I
talk [tɔːk] Vortrag, Rede V 4 (84)
give a talk (on sth.) einen Vortrag/eine Rede halten (über etwas) V 4 (84/173)
tall [tɔːl] hoch *(Bäume, Türme usw.)*; groß *(Person)* IV
°**task** [tɑːsk] Aufgabe
taught [tɔːt] *siehe* **teach**
taxi ['tæksi] Taxi III
tea [tiː] Tee; *(auch:) leichte Nachmittags- oder Abendmahlzeit* I
teach [tiːtʃ]**, taught, taught** unterrichten, lehren I
teacher ['tiːtʃə] Lehrer/in I • **head teacher** Schulleiter/in III
team [tiːm] Team, Mannschaft I
teaspoon ['tiːspuːn] Teelöffel III
°**techie** ['teki] Technikfreak, -narr/närrin
technology [tek'nɒlədʒi] Technologie V 2 (33)
teddy ['tedi] Teddy III
teen [tiːn] Teenager-, Jugend- III
teenager ['tiːneɪdʒə] Teenager, Jugendliche(r) II
teeth [tiːθ] *Plural von „tooth"* I
telephone ['telɪfəʊn] Telefon I
telephone number Telefonnummer I • **What's your telephone number?** Was ist deine Telefonnummer? I
television (TV) ['telɪvɪʒn] Fernsehen I
tell (about) [tel]**, told, told** erzählen (von), berichten (über) I • **Tell me your names.** Sagt mir eure Namen. I • **tell sb. the way** jm. den Weg beschreiben II • **tell sb. to do sth.** jm. sagen, dass er/sie etwas tun soll V 2 (32/164)
► S.164 ask/tell/expect/want sb. to do sth.
temperature ['temprətʃə] Temperatur II • **have a temperature** Fieber haben II
tennis ['tenɪs] Tennis I
tent [tent] Zelt IV
term [tɜːm] Trimester II
terrible ['terəbl] schrecklich, furchtbar I
°**territory** ['terətri] Territorium
test [test] Test, Prüfung II
text [tekst] Text I
text sb. [tekst] jm. eine SMS schicken III
text message ['tekst ˌmesɪdʒ] SMS III
than [ðæn, ðən] als II • **more than** mehr als II • **more than me** mehr als ich II
thank [θæŋk]**: Thank you.** Danke (schön). I • **Thanks.** Danke. I
Thanks a lot! Vielen Dank! I
Thanks very much! Danke sehr! / Vielen Dank! II
that [ðət, ðæt]
1. das (dort) I
2. jene(r, s) I
That's me. Das bin ich. I • **That's right.** Das ist richtig. / Das stimmt. I • **That's up to you.** Das liegt bei dir. / Das kannst/musst du (selbst) entscheiden. III • **that's why** deshalb, darum V 1 (8) • **That was close.** Das war knapp. II
that [ðət, ðæt] der, die, das; die *(Relativpronomen)* III
that [ðət, ðæt] dass I
that far/good/bad/... [ðæt] so weit/gut/schlecht/... III
the [ðə, ði] der, die, das; die I
theatre ['θɪətə] Theater II
°**theft** [θeft] Diebstahl
their [ðeə] ihr, ihre *(Plural)* I
theirs [ðeəz] ihrer, ihre, ihrs II
them [ðəm, ðem] sie; ihnen I
themselves [ðəm'selvz] sich (selbst) III
then [ðen] dann, danach I • °**now and then** gelegentlich, hier und da
there [ðeə]
1. da, dort I
2. dahin, dorthin I
down there dort unten II • **over there** da drüben, dort drüben I
there are es sind (vorhanden); es gibt I • **there's** es ist (vorhanden); es gibt I • **there isn't a ...** es ist kein/e ...; es gibt kein/e ... I
thermometer [θə'mɒmɪtə] Thermometer II
these [ðiːz] diese, die (hier) I
they [ðeɪ] sie *(Plural)* I
thief [θiːf], *pl* **thieves** [θiːvz] Dieb/in II
thing [θɪŋ] Ding, Sache I • **What was the best thing about ...?** Was war das Beste an ...? II
think [θɪŋk]**, thought, thought** glauben, meinen, denken I
think about 1. nachdenken über II; **2.** denken über, halten von II
think of 1. denken über, halten von II; **2.** denken an; sich ausdenken II
third [θɜːd] dritte(r, s) I
third [θɜːd]**: a third** ein Drittel V 4 (70)
this [ðɪs]
1. dies (hier) I
2. diese(r, s) I
This is Isabel. Hier spricht Isabel. / Hier ist Isabel. *(am Telefon)* II
this morning/afternoon/evening heute Morgen/Nachmittag/Abend I • **this way** hier entlang, in diese Richtung II
those [ðəʊz] die (da), jene (dort) I
thought [θɔːt] *siehe* **think**
thought [θɔːt] Gedanke III

thousand ['θaʊznd] tausend I
threw [θruː] *siehe* **throw**
throat [θrəʊt] Hals, Kehle II
°**throat lozenges** ['lɒzɪndʒɪz] Halspastillen, Lutschtabletten für den Hals
through [θruː] durch II
throw [θrəʊ], **threw, thrown**
1. werfen I
°2. **throw up** sich übergeben
thrown [θrəʊn] *siehe* **throw**
°**thump** [θʌmp] pochen
Thursday ['θɜːzdeɪ, 'θɜːzdi] Donnerstag I
°**tick** [tɪk] Häkchen
°**tick** [tɪk] ankreuzen, ein Häkchen machen
ticket ['tɪkɪt]
1. Eintrittskarte I
2. Fahrkarte II • **return ticket** Rückfahrkarte II • **single ticket** einfache Fahrkarte *(nur Hinfahrt)* III
tidy ['taɪdi] aufräumen I
tidy ['taɪdi] ordentlich, aufgeräumt II
tie [taɪ] Krawatte V 2 (40)
tie *(-ing form:* **tying***)* [taɪ] binden V 2 (40/166)
tiger ['taɪgə] Tiger II
tight [taɪt] eng III
till [tɪl] bis *(zeitlich)* I
time [taɪm]
1. Zeit; Uhrzeit I
2. **time(s)** Mal(e); -mal II
Have a good time. Viel Spaß! V 4 (83/173) • **in time** rechtzeitig III **three times** dreimal III • **What's the time?** Wie spät ist es? I
► S.173 Have ...
°**timeline** ['taɪmlaɪn] Zeitleiste
timetable ['taɪmteɪbl]
1. Stundenplan I
2. Fahrplan II
timing ['taɪmɪŋ] Timing IV
°**tinned** [tɪnd] Dosen-
tip [tɪp] Tipp II
tired ['taɪəd] müde I • **be tired of sth.** genug von etwas haben, etwas satt haben IV
title ['taɪtl] Titel, Überschrift I
to [tə, tu]
1. zu, nach I • **to Jenny's** zu Jenny I • **to the doctor's** zum Arzt III °**to the front** nach vorn
2. **an e-mail to** eine E-Mail an I **write to** schreiben an I
3. **quarter to 12** Viertel vor 12 (11.45/23.45) I • **from Monday to Friday** von Montag bis Freitag III
4. **try to help/to play/...** versuchen, zu helfen/zu spielen/... I
5. um zu II
°**toad: cane toad** ['keɪn təʊd] Agakröte
toast [təʊst] Toast(brot) I
tobacco [tə'bækəʊ] Tabak II
today [tə'deɪ] heute I
toe [təʊ] Zeh I
together [tə'geðə] zusammen I
toilet ['tɔɪlət] Toilette I
told [təʊld] *siehe* **tell**
tomato [tə'mɑːtəʊ], *pl* **tomatoes** Tomate II
tomorrow [tə'mɒrəʊ] morgen I
tomorrow's weather das Wetter von morgen II
tonight [tə'naɪt] heute Nacht, heute Abend I • **tonight's programme** das Programm von heute Abend; das heutige Abendprogramm II
too [tuː]: **from Bristol too** auch aus Bristol I • **Me too.** Ich auch. I
too much/big/... [tuː] zu viel/ groß/... I
took [tʊk] *siehe* **take**
tooth [tuːθ], *pl* **teeth** [tiːθ] Zahn I
toothache ['tuːθeɪk] Zahnschmerzen II
top [tɒp]
1. Spitze, oberes Ende I • **at the top (of)** oben, am oberen Ende, an der Spitze (von) I • **on top of sth.** oben, oben drauf (auf etwas) V 4 (81) • °**top end** [ˌtɒp‿'end] oberes Ende
2. Top, Oberteil I
topic ['tɒpɪk] Thema, Themenbereich I • **topic sentence** *Satz, der in das Thema eines Absatzes einführt* II
tornado [tɔː'neɪdəʊ] Tornado, Wirbelsturm II
tortoise ['tɔːtəs] Schildkröte I
touch [tʌtʃ] berühren, anfassen II
keep in touch in Verbindung bleiben, Kontakt halten III
tough [tʌf] knallhart, streng V 2 (43)
tour (of the house) [tʊə] Rundgang, Tour (durch das Haus) I
°**tourism** ['tʊərɪzəm] Tourismus
tourist ['tʊərɪst] Tourist/in II
tourist information Fremdenverkehrsamt II
towards sb./sth. [tə'wɔːdz] auf jn./ etwas zu II
tower ['taʊə] Turm I
town [taʊn] (Klein-)Stadt I
°**township** ['taʊnʃɪp] *Bezeichnung für die während der Apartheid in Südafrika eingerichteten Wohngegenden für die nicht weiße Bevölkerung*
tradition [trə'dɪʃn] Tradition IV
traditional [trə'dɪʃənl] traditionell V 1 (16)
traffic ['træfɪk] Verkehr II • **traffic jam** ['træfɪk dʒæm] (Verkehrs-) Stau V 4 (70)
train [treɪn] Zug I • **on the train** im Zug I
train [treɪn] trainieren III
trainers *(pl)* ['treɪnəz] Turnschuhe II
training ['treɪnɪŋ]
1. (berufliche) Ausbildung V 3 (56)
2. **training session** ['seʃn] Trainingsstunde, -einheit III
tram [træm] Straßenbahn III
translate (from ... into) [træns'leɪt] übersetzen (aus ... ins) III
translation [træns'leɪʃn] Übersetzung III
°**transparency** [træns'pærənsi] Folie *(für Overheadprojektoren)*
transport ['trænspɔːt] Beförderung, Transport III • **public transport** *(no pl)* [ˌpʌblɪk 'trænspɔːt] öffentliche Verkehrsmittel, öffentlicher Personennahverkehr V 4 (71)
travel (-ll-) ['trævl] reisen II
Travelcard ['trævlkɑːd] Tagesfahrkarte *(der Londoner Verkehrsbetriebe)* III
tree [triː] Baum I
trendy ['trendi] modisch, schick III
trick [trɪk]
1. (Zauber-)Kunststück, Trick I
do tricks (Zauber-)Kunststücke machen I
2. Streich II
trip [trɪp] Reise; Ausflug I • **day trip** Tagesausflug IV • **go on a trip** einen Ausflug machen II °**go on a road trip** auf große Fahrt gehen • **Have a good trip.** Gute Reise! V 4 (83/173)
► S.173 Have ...
tropical ['trɒpɪkl] tropisch, Tropen- V 1 (12)
trouble ['trʌbl] Schwierigkeiten, Ärger II • **be in trouble** in Schwierigkeiten sein; Ärger kriegen II
troublemaker ['trʌblmeɪkə] Randalierer/in, Unruhestifter/in V 3 (52)
trousers *(pl)* ['traʊzəz] Hose II
truck [trʌk] LKW, Lastkraftwagen V 1 (6) • **monster dumper truck** [ˌmɒnstə 'dʌmpə trʌk] *Kipplaster mit gewaltigen Rädern*
true [truː] wahr II • **come true** wahr werden; in Erfüllung gehen IV
trumpet ['trʌmpɪt] Trompete III
try [traɪ]
1. versuchen I

2. probieren, kosten I
try and do sth. / try to do sth. versuchen, etwas zu tun I • **try on** anprobieren *(Kleidung)* I
try [traɪ] Versuch V 3 (58) • **Nice try.** Netter Versuch. V 3 (58)
T-shirt ['tiːʃɜːt] T-Shirt I
tsunami [tsuː'nɑːmi] Tsunami IV
tube [tjuːb]**: the Tube** *(no pl)* die Londoner U-Bahn III
Tuesday ['tjuːzdeɪ, 'tjuːzdi] Dienstag I
tunnel ['tʌnl] Tunnel II
turkey ['tɜːki] Truthahn III
turn [tɜːn]
1. sich umdrehen II • **turn away** sich abwenden, sich wegdrehen IV
turn left/right (nach) links/rechts abbiegen II • **turn to sb.** sich jm. zuwenden; sich an jn. wenden II
2. turn on/off ein-/ausschalten III
3. turn sth. down/up etwas leiser/lauter stellen IV
turn [tɜːn]**: It's your turn.** Du bist dran / an der Reihe. I • **Miss a turn.** Einmal aussetzen. II • **°Take turns.** Wechselt euch ab. • **Whose turn is it?** Wer ist dran / an der Reihe? II
°tusk [tʌsk] Hauer *(Eckzahn eines Wildschweines)*
TV [tiː'viː] Fernsehen I; Fernsehgerät IV • **on TV** im Fernsehen I • **watch TV** fernsehen I • **TV listings** *(pl)* Fernsehprogramm IV
twice [twaɪs] zweimal III • **twice a week** zweimal pro Woche III
twin [twɪn]**: twin brother** Zwillingsbruder I • **twins** *(pl)* Zwillinge I
type [taɪp] *(infml)* Typ III
typical (of) ['tɪpɪkl] typisch (für) V 4 (73)

U

unbelievable [ˌʌnbɪ'liːvəbl] unglaublich IV
unbreakable [ʌn'breɪkəbl] unzerbrechlich IV
uncle ['ʌŋkl] Onkel I
uncomfortable [ʌn'kʌmftəbl] unbequem, unbehaglich, unangenehm IV
uncool [ˌʌn'kuːl] *(infml)* uncool III
uncountable [ʌn'kaʊntəbl] unzählbar IV
under ['ʌndə] unter I
underground ['ʌndəgraʊnd]**: the underground** die U-Bahn II
°underline [ˌʌndə'laɪn] unterstreichen
understand [ˌʌndə'stænd]**, understood, understood** verstehen, begreifen I
understood [ˌʌndə'stʊd] *siehe* **understand**
underwear ['ʌndəweə] Unterwäsche III
unemployment [ˌʌnɪm'plɔɪmənt] Arbeitslosigkeit V 4 (71)
unfair [ˌʌn'feə] unfair III
unforgettable [ˌʌnfə'getəbl] unvergesslich V 4 (77)
unforgivable [ˌʌnfə'gɪvəbl] unverzeihlich V 4 (78)
unfriendly [ʌn'frendli] unfreundlich III
unhappy [ʌn'hæpi] unglücklich III
unhealthy [ʌn'helθi] ungesund III
uniform ['juːnɪfɔːm] Uniform I
unit ['juːnɪt] Lektion, Kapitel I
united: the United Kingdom (UK) [juˌnaɪtɪd 'kɪŋdəm], [ˌjuː 'keɪ] das Vereinigte Königreich *(Großbritannien und Nordirland)* III • **United States (US)** [juˌnaɪtɪd 'steɪts], [ˌjuː‿'es] die Vereinigten Staaten *(von Amerika)* III
unkind [ˌʌn'kaɪnd] unfreundlich V 3 (58)
unlock [ˌʌn'lɒk] aufschließen; entsperren III
unreadable [ʌn'riːdəbl] unleserlich IV
unrealistic [ˌʌnrɪə'lɪstɪk] unrealistisch IV
unsafe [ʌn'seɪf] nicht sicher, gefährlich III
untidy [ʌn'taɪdi] unordentlich III
until [ən'tɪl] bis III
up [ʌp] hinauf, herauf, nach oben I
up the hill den Hügel hinauf II
°be up to sth. etwas vorhaben, etwas im Schilde führen • **That's up to you.** Das liegt bei dir. / Das kannst/musst du (selbst) entscheiden. III
upset [ˌʌp'set] aufgebracht, gekränkt, mitgenommen III
upset sb. (-tt-) [ʌp'set]**, upset, upset** jn. ärgern, kränken, aus der Fassung bringen III
upstairs [ˌʌp'steəz] oben; nach oben I
us [əs, ʌs] uns I
use [juːz] benutzen, verwenden I
useful ['juːsfəl] nützlich IV
useless ['juːsləs] nutzlos IV
usual ['juːʒuəl]**: as usual** wie immer, wie üblich V 3 (48)
usually ['juːʒuəli] meistens, gewöhnlich, normalerweise I

V

vacation [və'keɪʃn, *AE:* veɪ'keɪʃn] *(AE)* Urlaub, Ferien III
valley ['væli] Tal II
vandalize ['vændəlaɪz] mutwillig beschädigen, mutwillig zerstören V 3 (52)
vegetable ['vedʒtəbl] *(ein)* Gemüse III
vegetarian [ˌvedʒə'teəriən] vegetarisch IV; Vegetarier/in IV
very ['veri] sehr I • **like/love sth. very much** etwas sehr mögen/sehr lieben II • **Thanks very much!** Danke sehr! / Vielen Dank! II
vet [vet] Tierarzt/-ärztin V 2 (30)
vet's assistant [ˌvets‿ə'sɪstənt] Tierarzthelfer/in V 2 (30)
victim ['vɪktɪm] Opfer III
video ['vɪdiəʊ] Video III
view [vjuː] Aussicht, Blick II
°view [vjuː] ansehen, betrachten
viewer ['vjuːə] Zuschauer/in IV
village ['vɪlɪdʒ] Dorf I
violin [ˌvaɪə'lɪn] Violine, Geige III
virus ['vaɪrəs]**,** *pl* **viruses** ['vaɪrəsəs] Virus V 4 (75)
visit ['vɪzɪt] besuchen II
visit ['vɪzɪt] Besuch II
visitor ['vɪzɪtə] Besucher/in, Gast I
visual ['vɪʒuəl] visuell; optisch V 4 (84)
vitae: curriculum vitae [kəˌrɪkjələm 'viːtaɪ] **(CV)** Lebenslauf V 2 (36)
vocabulary [və'kæbjələri] Vokabelverzeichnis, Wörterverzeichnis I
voice [vɔɪs] Stimme V 3 (58)
voicemail ['vɔɪsmeɪl] Voicemail III
volleyball ['vɒlibɔːl] Volleyball I
volume ['vɒljuːm] Lautstärke IV
volunteer [ˌvɒlən'tɪə] Freiwillige(r) IV • **volunteer work** Arbeit als Freiwillige(r) IV
°volunteer [ˌvɒlən'tɪə] sich freiwillig melden, sich bereit erklären

W

wait (for) [weɪt] warten (auf) I
Wait a minute. Warte mal! / Moment mal! II • **Wait and see!** Wart's ab! III • **I can't wait to see ...** ich kann es kaum erwarten, ... zu sehen I
waiter ['weɪtə] Kellner II
waiting room ['weɪtɪŋ ruːm] Wartezimmer IV
waitress ['weɪtrəs] Kellnerin II

wake [weɪk], **woke, woken:**
1. wake sb. (up) jn. (auf)wecken IV
2. wake up aufwachen IV
wake-up call ['weɪk‿ʌp ˌkɔ:l] Weckanruf V 4 (83)
walk [wɔ:k] (zu Fuß) gehen I
walk around herumlaufen, umherspazieren III • **walk around the town** in der Stadt umhergehen, durch die Stadt gehen III
walk [wɔ:k] Spaziergang II • **go for a walk** spazieren gehen, einen Spaziergang machen II • **a ten-kilometre walk** eine Zehn-Kilometer-Wanderung III
wall [wɔ:l] Wand; Mauer II
want [wɒnt] (haben) wollen I
want to do sth. etwas tun wollen I • **want sb. to do sth.** möchten/wollen, dass jd. etwas tut V 2 (32)
want to be sth. etwas werden wollen *(beruflich)* V 3 (46)
► S.164 ask/tell/expect/want sb. to do sth.
wardrobe ['wɔ:drəʊb] Kleiderschrank I
warm [wɔ:m] warm II
was [wəz, wɒz]**: (I/he/she/it) was** *siehe* **be**
wash [wɒʃ] waschen I • **I wash my face.** Ich wasche mir das Gesicht. I
washing machine ['wɒʃɪŋ məˌʃi:n] Waschmaschine I
watch [wɒtʃ] beobachten, sich etwas ansehen; zusehen I
watch TV fernsehen I
watch [wɒtʃ] Armbanduhr I
water ['wɔ:tə] Wasser I; Mineralwasser IV
°**waterfall** ['wɔ:təfɔ:l] Wasserfall
waterproof ['wɔ:təpru:f] wasserdicht *(Uhr, Kleidung)* V 1 (18/162)
wave [weɪv] winken II
way [weɪ]
1. Weg II • **all the way** den ganzen Weg IV • **ask sb. the way** jn. nach dem Weg fragen II • **on the way (to)** auf dem Weg (zu/nach) II • **tell sb. the way** jm. den Weg beschreiben II
2. Richtung II • **the other way round** anders herum II • **the wrong way** in die falsche Richtung II • **this way** hier entlang, in diese Richtung II • **which way?** in welche Richtung? / wohin? II
3. Art und Weise V 4 (77) • °**in one way** auf eine Art
4. **by the way** übrigens II
5. **No way!** Auf keinen Fall! / Kommt nicht in Frage! II
we [wi:] wir I
weak [wi:k] schwach II
weakness ['wi:knəs] Schwäche IV
wear [weə], **wore, worn** tragen, anhaben *(Kleidung)* I
weather ['weðə] Wetter II
weatherproof ['weðəpru:f] wetterfest *(Kleidung)* V 1 (18/162)
webcam ['webkæm] Webcam, Internetkamera III
website ['websaɪt] Website II
wedding ['wedɪŋ] Hochzeit, Trauung V 3 (49)
Wednesday ['wenzdeɪ, 'wenzdi] Mittwoch I
week [wi:k] Woche I • **days of the week** Wochentage I • **a two-week holiday** ein zweiwöchiger Urlaub III
weekend [ˌwi:k'end] Wochenende I
at the weekend am Wochenende I • **Have a good weekend.** Schönes Wochenende! V 4 (83/173)
► S.173 Have ...
welcome ['welkəm]
1. Welcome (to Bristol). Willkommen (in Bristol). I
2. You're welcome. Gern geschehen. / Nichts zu danken. I
welcome sb. (to) ['welkəm] jn. begrüßen, willkommen heißen (in) I
They welcome you to ... Sie heißen dich in ... willkommen I
well [wel]
1. gut II • **get on well (with sb.)** sich gut verstehen (mit jm.), gut auskommen (mit jm.) V 3 (46) • **go well** gut (ver)laufen, gutgehen III
do well (in) gut abschneiden (in) III • **You did well.** Das hast du gut gemacht. II • **Oh well ...** Na ja ... / Na gut ... I • **Well, ...** Nun, ... / Also, ... I • °**Well done!** [ˌwel 'dʌn] Gut gemacht!
2. *(gesundheitlich)* gut; gesund, wohlauf II
Welsh [welʃ] walisisch; Walisisch II
went [went] *siehe* **go**
were [wə, wɜ:]**: (we/you/they) were** *siehe* **be**
west [west] Westen; nach Westen; westlich III
western ['westən] westlich, West- III
wet [wet] feucht, nass III • °**the wet season** [ˌwet 'si:zn] Regenzeit
what [wɒt]
1. was I
2. welche(r, s) I
What about ...? 1. Was ist mit ...? / Und ...? I; **2.** Wie wär's mit ...? I
What are you talking about? Wovon redest du? I • **What colour is ...?** Welche Farbe hat ...? I
What for? Wofür? II • **What have we got next?** Was haben wir als Nächstes? I • **What kind of car ...?** Was für ein Auto...? III • **What page are we on?** Auf welcher Seite sind wir? I • **What's for homework?** Was haben wir als Hausaufgabe auf? I • **What's the matter?** Was ist los? / Was ist denn? II • **What's the time?** Wie spät ist es? I • **What's your name?** Wie heißt du? I • **What's your telephone number?** Was ist deine Telefonnummer? I • **What was the weather like?** Wie war das Wetter? II • **I don't know what to do** Ich weiß nicht, was ich machen soll. V 4 (76/171)
► S.171 how to .../ what to ... / where to ...
°**whatever** [wɒt'evə] was (auch) immer
wheel [wi:l] Rad III • **big wheel** Riesenrad III
wheelchair ['wi:ltʃeə] Rollstuhl I
when [wen] wann I • **When's your birthday?** Wann hast du Geburtstag? I
when [wen]
1. wenn I
2. als I
where [weə]
1. wo I
2. wohin I
Where are you from? Wo kommst du her? I • **He had no idea where to go.** Er hatte keine Ahnung, wohin er gehen sollte. V 4 (76/171)
► S.171 how to .../ what to ... / where to ...
which [wɪtʃ]**: Which picture ...?** Welches Bild ...? I • **which way?** in welche Richtung? / wohin? II
which [wɪtʃ] der, die, das; die *(Relativpronomen)* III
while [waɪl] während III
whisky ['wɪski] Whisky II
whisper ['wɪspə] flüstern I
whistle ['wɪsl] pfeifen II
white [waɪt] weiß I
who [hu:]
1. wer I
2. wen / wem II
Who else? Wen (sonst) noch? IV
He had no idea who to ask. Er hatte keine Ahnung, wen er fragen könnte. V 4 (76/171)
► S.171 how to .../ what to ... / where to ...
who [hu:] der, die, das; die *(Relativpronomen)* III • **Find/Ask somebody who ...** Finde/Frage jemanden, der ... II

whole [həʊl] ganze(r,s), gesamte(r,s) IV
whole-grain ['həʊlgreɪn] Vollkorn- IV
whose? [huːz] wessen? II • **Whose are these?** Wem gehören diese? II **Whose turn is it?** Wer ist dran / an der Reihe? II
why [waɪ] warum I • **Why me?** Warum ich? I • **that's why** deshalb, darum V 1 (8)
wife [waɪf], *pl* **wives** [waɪvz] Ehefrau II
wild [waɪld] wild II
will [wɪl]: **you'll be cold (= you will be cold)** du wirst frieren II • **you won't be cold** [wəʊnt] **(= you will not be cold)** du wirst nicht frieren II
win (-nn-) [wɪn], **won, won** gewinnen I
wind [wɪnd] Wind I
window ['wɪndəʊ] Fenster I
windproof ['wɪndpruːf] winddicht V 1 (18/162)
windsurfing ['wɪndsɜːfɪŋ] Windsurfen III
windy ['wɪndi] windig I
wine [waɪn] Wein IV
wing [wɪŋ] Flügel IV
winner ['wɪnə] Gewinner/in, Sieger/in II
winter ['wɪntə] Winter I
wishes ['wɪʃɪz]: **Best wishes** *etwa:* Alles Gute / Mit besten Grüßen *(als Briefschluss)* IV
with [wɪð]
1. mit I
2. bei I
be with sb. mit jemandem zusammen sein IV • **go with** gehören zu, passen zu III • **Sit with me.** Setz dich zu mir. / Setzt euch zu mir. I
without [wɪ'ðaʊt] ohne I
witness ['wɪtnəs] Zeuge/Zeugin V 1 (14)
wives [waɪvz] *Plural von „wife"* II
woke [wəʊk] *siehe* **wake**
woken [wəʊkən] *siehe* **wake**
wolf [wʊlf], *pl* **wolves** [wʊlvz] Wolf II
woman ['wʊmən], *pl* **women** ['wɪmɪn] Frau I
won [wʌn] *siehe* **win**
wonder ['wʌndə] sich fragen, gern wissen wollen II
won't [wəʊnt]: **you won't be cold (= you will not be cold)** du wirst nicht frieren; ihr werdet nicht frieren II
wood [wʊd] Holz V 4 (77)
woodpecker ['wʊdpekə] Specht II
word [wɜːd] Wort I • **word building** Wortbildung II
°**word order** Wortstellung
wore [wɔː] *siehe* **wear**
work [wɜːk]
1. arbeiten I
2. funktionieren V 2 (32)
work hard hart arbeiten II
work on sth. an etwas arbeiten I
work sth. out etwas herausarbeiten, herausfinden IV
work [wɜːk] Arbeit I • **at work** bei der Arbeit/am Arbeitsplatz I
work experience Praktikum; Arbeits-, Praxiserfahrungen V 2 (35)
do work experience ein Praktikum machen V 2 (35/165)
worker ['wɜːkə] Arbeiter/in II
office worker ['ɒfɪs wɜːkə] Büroangestellte(r) V 2 (30)
worksheet ['wɜːkʃiːt] Arbeitsblatt I
workshop ['wɜːkʃɒp] Workshop, Lehrgang III
world [wɜːld] Welt I • **all over the world** auf der ganzen Welt III • **from all over the UK/the world/England** aus dem gesamten Vereinigten Königreich / aus der ganzen Welt / aus ganz England II
worn [wɔːn] *siehe* **wear**
worried ['wʌrid] besorgt, beunruhigt (wegen, um) IV
worry ['wʌri] Sorge, Kummer II
worry (about) ['wʌri] sich Sorgen machen (wegen, um) I • **Don't worry.** Mach dir keine Sorgen. I
worse [wɜːs] schlechter, schlimmer II
worst [wɜːst]: **(the) worst** am schlechtesten, schlimmsten; der/die/das schlechteste, schlimmste ... II
would [wəd, wʊd]: **I/you/... would ...** ich würde/du würdest ... III • **I'd like ... (= I would like ...)** Ich hätte/möchte gern ... I • **Would you like ...?** Möchtest du ...? /Möchten Sie ...? I • **Would you like some?** Möchtest du etwas/ein paar? / Möchten Sie etwas/ein paar? I
I'd like to talk about ... (= I would like to talk about ...) Ich möchte über ... reden / Ich würde gern über ... reden I
write [raɪt], **wrote, written** schreiben I • **write down** aufschreiben I • **write to** schreiben an I
writer ['raɪtə] Schreiber/in; Schriftsteller/in II
written ['rɪtn] *siehe* **write**
wrong [rɒŋ] falsch, verkehrt I
be wrong 1. falsch sein I; 2. sich irren, Unrecht haben II • **the wrong way** in die falsche Richtung II
wrote [rəʊt] *siehe* **write**

Y

yard [jɑːd] Hof II • **in the yard** auf dem Hof II
yawn [jɔːn] gähnen II
year [jɪə]
1. Jahr I
2. Jahrgangsstufe I
a sixteen-year-old ein/e Sechzehnjährige/r III • **a sixteen-year-old girl** ein sechzehnjähriges Mädchen III
yellow ['jeləʊ] gelb I
°**yelp** [jelp] aufjaulen
yes [jes] ja I
yesterday ['jestədeɪ, 'jestədi] gestern I • **yesterday morning/afternoon/evening** gestern Morgen/Nachmittag/Abend I • **yesterday's homework** die Hausaufgaben von gestern II
yet [jet]: **not (...) yet** noch nicht II
yet? schon? II
yoga ['jəʊgə] Yoga I
you [juː]
1. du; Sie I
2. ihr I • **you two** ihr zwei I
3. dir; dich; euch I
young [jʌŋ] jung I
your [jɔː]
1. dein/e I
2. Ihr I
3. euer/eure I
yours [jɔːz]
1. deiner, deine, deins II
2. Ihrer, Ihre, Ihrs II
3. eurer, eure, eures II
yourself [jɔː'self] dir/dich (selbst) III
yourselves [jɔː'selvz] euch (selbst) III
youth [juːθ] Jugend, Jugend- III
youth club Jugendclub III • **youth group** Jugendgruppe IV • **youth hostel** Jugendherberge III
yuck [jʌk] igitt III

Z

zebra ['zebrə] Zebra II
zone [zəʊn] Zone, Gebiet IV
zoo [zuː] Zoo IV • °**zoo worker** Tierpfleger
°**Zulu** ['zuːluː] Zulu *(Sprache der Zulu, südafrikanisches Volk)*

English sounds (Englische Laute)

Die Lautschrift in den eckigen Klammern zeigt dir, wie ein Wort ausgesprochen wird.
In der folgenden Übersicht findest du alle Lautzeichen.

Vokale (Selbstlaute)

[iː]	green	[ʊ]	book	[ɪə]	here
[i]	happy	[ʌ]	mum	[eə]	where
[ɪ]	in	[ɜː]	T-shirt	[ʊə]	tour
[e]	yes	[ə]	a partner		
[æ]	black	[eɪ]	skate		
[ɑː]	park	[aɪ]	time		
[ɒ]	song	[ɔɪ]	boy		
[ɔː]	morning	[əʊ]	old		
[uː]	blue	[aʊ]	now		

Konsonanten (Mitlaute)

[b]	box	[l]	hello	[ʒ]	television
[p]	play	[r]	red	[tʃ]	teacher
[d]	dad	[w]	we	[dʒ]	Germany
[t]	ten	[j]	you	[θ]	thanks
[g]	good	[f]	full	[ð]	this
[k]	cat	[v]	very	[h]	he
[m]	mum	[s]	sister	[x]	loch
[n]	no	[z]	please		
[ŋ]	sing	[ʃ]	shop		

Betonung

['] und [ˌ] sind **Betonungszeichen**
Sie stehen immer vor der betonten Silbe

['] zeigt die Hauptbetonung
[ˌ] zeigt die Nebenbetonung

Beispiel
mobile phone [ˌməʊbaɪl 'fəʊn]
Hauptbetonung auf **phone**
Nebenbetonung auf der ersten Silbe **mobile**

Der „Bindebogen"

Der **Bindebogen** [‿] zeigt an, dass zwei Wörter beim Sprechen aneinandergebunden und wie ein Wort ausgesprochen werden.

Beispiel
What colour is ...? [ˌwɒt 'kʌlər‿ɪz]
Mum and Dad [ˌmʌm‿ən 'dæd]
This is ... ['ðɪs‿ɪz]

The English alphabet (Das englische Alphabet)

a	[eɪ]	**h**	[eɪtʃ]	**o**	[əʊ]	**v**	[viː]
b	[biː]	**i**	[aɪ]	**p**	[piː]	**w**	['dʌbljuː]
c	[siː]	**j**	[dʒeɪ]	**q**	[kjuː]	**x**	[eks]
d	[diː]	**k**	[keɪ]	**r**	[ɑː]	**y**	[waɪ]
e	[iː]	**l**	[el]	**s**	[es]	**z**	[zed]
f	[ef]	**m**	[em]	**t**	[tiː]		
g	[dʒiː]	**n**	[en]	**u**	[juː]		

Key to 'How am I doing?'

Unit 1 ▸ p. 23

1 Brisbane, Canberra, Melbourne, Sydney, Perth, Darwin 3 of these, 1 point each
2 kangaroo, koala, spider, crocodile, emu, wombat, platypus, cane toad
3 of these, 1 point each
3 Australian protect themselves from the sun with: clothes, sunglasses, hats, sunscreen 2 of these, 1 point each
4 surfing, Aussie Rules football, cricket, hiking, swimming, rugby
3 of these, 1 point each

One point for each correct answer to questions 5 – 13.

5 B summer
6 C outback
7 D the Whites.
8 B were taken away by Whites.
9 a) Kim said that she would have / she'd have a great time Down Under.
b) Jess said that she just loved kangaroos.
c) Tom said that Frank wanted to visit Uluru.
d) Lara said that she could come back.
10 C compare
11 B crowded
12 D rent
13 C sunrise

The chart on the right shows where the Australian population lives: in cities, near or far from cities. The biggest group (69%) lives in cities. The second biggest group lives near cities and the smallest group lives far from cities. So 31% of the population don't live in cities.
1 point for each answer – 6 points

Getting ready for a test 1 ▸ pp. 24–29

1 LISTENING Travelling to Australia ▸ p. 26

1 B Gate 17
2 C (chicken salad or pasta)
3 A just over there
4 B AU$ 52.50
5 C 07:00–10:30

2 LISTENING Shark attack ▸ p. 27

a) (Part 1 of recording)
1 B surfing
2 C leg
3 A swam off
4 B scared
5 A friends

b) (Part 2 of recording)
1 False
2 True
3 True
4 False
5 True

3 LISTENING What are they talking about? ▸ p. 28

Conversation 1: C (homework)
Conversation 2: E (magazine)
Conversation 3: A (mobile phone)
Conversation 4: D (boy and girl in love)
Conversation 5: G (holidays on the beach)

4 WRITING A scary moment ▸ p. 28

(individuelle Lösung)

Key to 'How am I doing?'

Unit 2 ▸ p. 45

One point for each correct answer.

1 a) similar
   b) reliable
   c) polite
   d) artistic
   e) energetic

2 You get one point for each correct pair.
   a) calm, helpful
   b) hard-working, reliable
   c) organized, confident

3 a) B Education
   b) A Personal statement
   c) B Work experience

4 B you don't know the name of the person you're writing to.

5 A at the beginning of the letter.

6 B long verb forms.

7 A your CV.

8 B Yours sincerely ...

9 a) mechanic
   b) care assistant
   c) builder
   d) vet's assistant
   e) gardener

10 a) first name
   b) surname
   c) date of birth
   d) place of birth

Key to 'How am I doing?'

Unit 3 ▸ p. 61

One point for each correct answer to questions 1–10.

1 C can't live a day without it.
2 D antisocial behaviour.
3 B can be banned from some areas of your town.
4 D help other people.
5 C cash
6 B contacts
7 a) dial 911
b) dump someone
c) communicate with someone
d) enter your PIN
8 a) Don't forget to set your alarm clock.
b) If you really like her, you should ask her out.
c) Listen carefully, that is really important.
d) Knock on the door before you enter the room.
9 a) Well, he's my friend, but yesterday I didn't like his behaviour at all.
b) He was late for school as usual.
c) You're right, I agree with you completely.
d) Sorry, but I can only listen to one at a time.
10 a) I have no sisters or brothers. I'm an only child.
b) My sister got married yesterday. It really was a very nice wedding.
c) Don't tell Tim what I just told you. It's a secret.
d) I can't decide what to do. Should I go to the cinema with Pia or should I stay at home?
11 One point for one correct answer to each part.
a) You agree with an opinion:
I agree (with you) (completely). / That's true. / You're right. / ...
b) You disagree with an opinion:
I don't agree (with you) (at all). / No, that's not right. / I don't think you can say that. / Sorry, but I think ... / I see what you mean. But I still think ... / Yes, but ... / ...
c) You want to ask for his/her opinion:
What do you think? / What's your opinion? / I want to hear what you have to say. / ...
d) You haven't finished and you want to say something more about this topic:
Wait a minute. / Let me finish. / Sorry, I want to say ...

Key to 'How am I doing?'

Getting ready for a test 2

► pp. 62–69

1 READING Magazines ► p. 64

1 Student A: Magazine 5
2 Student B: Magazine 2
3 Student C: Magazine 4
4 Student D: Magazine 6
5 Student E: Magazine 1

2 MEDIATION A visit to London ► p. 65

(individuelle Lösung)

3 READING Dev Patel ► pp. 66–67

a) 1 True
2 False
3 True
4 True
5 False
6 False

b) 1 C Being in a play.
2 D Dev answered an advertisement in a newspaper.
3 A a famous British film director's daughter saw him in the TV series *Skins*.
4 B *Slumdog Millionaire* was filmed there.

4 SPEAKING Describing a picture ► p. 68

(individuelle Lösung)

5 SPEAKING Hi! ► p. 68

(individuelle Lösung)

Unit 4

► p. 85

One point for eacht correct answer for question 1–8 and 10–11; three points for question 9.

1 a) India
b) South Africa
2 C Bollywood
3 B earthquakes
4 C townships
5 B – D – A – C
6 a) sum up
b) finally
c) contrast
d) basic
7 a) double room
b) suburb
c) check out
d) leave a message
8 a) Pia and Linn can't have a room in the hotel because it is fully booked.
b) Not far away is a hostel where they can stay but only in a dormitory.
c) There are lots of people waiting outside the museum so Pia and Linn have to queue.
9 the flue, a pain in my arm (or leg), a virus, a headache, a temperature, a stomach ache, an earache, sore throat, a cold, ...
Three points for three correct words or phrases.
10 a) Buses and trains are always full in the rush hour.
b) Today there was a big traffic jam because of an accident on one of the main streets.
c) 'That's typical,' my friend said. 'Something always happens when I'm in a hurry.'
d) I said, 'Never mind. – Look, there's our teacher. He's late for school too.'
11 a) cloudless
b) unforgettable
c) creamy

First names (Vornamen)

Aaron ['eərən]
Adnan ['ɑ:dˌnɑ:n, ˌɑ:d'nɑ:n]
Aggie ['ægi]
Alex ['ælɪks]
Amy ['eɪmi]
Anna ['ænə]
Ashley ['æʃli]
Balu ['bɑlu:]
Barbara ['bɑ:brə]
Bill [bɪl]
Billy ['bɪli]
Brad [bræd]
Brian ['braɪən]
Carla ['kɑ:lə]
Charlie ['tʃɑ:li]
Chloe ['kləʊi]
Colm [kɒlm, 'kɒləm]
Daisy ['deɪzi]
Dan [dæn]
Darren ['dærən]
David ['deɪvɪd]
Deepa ['di:pə]
Delaney [dɪ'leɪni]
Dolly ['dɒli]
Dougie ['dʌgi]
Drew [dru:]
Ella ['elə]
Emma ['emə]
Everlyn ['evəlɪn]
Fabio ['feɪbiəʊ, 'fɑ:biəʊ]
Framji ['fræmdʒi]
Gracie ['greɪsi]
Greg [greg]
Gwen [gwen]
Hannah ['hænə]
Ian ['i:ən]
Jade [dʒeɪd]
Jake [dʒeɪk]
James [dʒeɪmz]
Jemma ['dʒemə]
Jeremy ['dʒerəmi]
Jess [dʒes]
Jordan ['dʒɔ:dn]
Karen ['kærən]
Keira ['kɪərə]
Keisha ['ki:ʃə]
Kirsty ['kɜ:sti]
Kitty ['kɪti]
Kofi ['kəʊfi]
Laura ['lɔ:rə]
Leena ['leənə]
Lily ['lɪli]
Lina ['li:nə]
Lindsay ['lɪndzi]
Louise [lu'i:z]
Lucy ['lu:si]
Luke [lu:k]
Lulla ['lʌlə]
Mahatma [mə'hɑ:tmə]
Mani ['mæni]
Margaret ['mɑ:grət]
Mark [mɑ:k]
Martin ['mɑ:tɪn]
Mia ['mi:ə]
Michael ['maɪkl]
Michelle [mɪ'ʃel]
Missy ['mɪsi]
Molly ['mɒli]
Nelson ['nelsən]
Pearl [pɜ:l]
Phil [fɪl]
Phillip ['fɪlɪp]
Rachel ['reɪtʃəl]
Reece [ri:s]
Rita ['ri:tə]
Rob [rɒb]
Robert ['rɒbət]
Rochelle [rɒ'ʃel]
Rohan ['rəʊən]
Roshan ['rɒʃʌn]
Sandra ['sɑ:ndra]
Sarah ['seərə]
Shane [ʃeɪn]
Sinita [sɪ'ni:tə]
Steve [sti:v]
Sunny ['sʌni]
Tara ['tɑ:rə]
Tianna [ti'ænə]
Todd [tɒd]
Tyson ['taɪsn]
Victor ['vɪktə]
Zahid ['zæhɪd]
Zoe ['zəʊi]
Zita [zɪ:tə]

Family names / Surnames (Familiennamen)

Armstrong ['ɑ:mstrɒŋ]
Bains [beɪnz]
Bluebell ['blu:bel]
Brown [braʊn]
Cook [kʊk]
Denham ['denəm]
Gandhi ['gændi]
Gubbins ['gʌbɪnz]
Hunter ['hʌntə]
Kishore [ˌkɪ'ʃɔ:r]
Luther ['lu:θə]
Mandela [mæn'delə]
McMahon [mək'mɑ:n]
McQueen [mək'kwi:n]
Monaghan ['mɒnəhən]
Murray ['mʌri]
Noyce [nɔɪs]
Parton ['pɑ:tn]
Pitt [pɪt]
Preston ['prestn]
Qualls [kwɒlz, kwɔ:lz]
Ravenhill ['reɪvənhɪl]
Sampi ['sæmpi]
San Souci [ˌsæn su:'si]
Sansbury ['sænzbri]
Saunders ['sɔ:ndəz]
Smith [smɪθ]
Wallace ['wɒlɪs]
Williams ['wɪljəmz]
Wilson ['wɪlsn]
Yates [jeɪts]

Place names (Ortsnamen)

Alice Springs [ˌælɪs 'sprɪŋz]
Atlanta [ət'læntə]
Ayers Rock [ˌeəz 'rɒk]
Bangkok [ˌbæŋ'kɒk]
Berlin [bɜ:'lɪn]
Bloemfontein ['blu:mfənˌteɪn]
Bombay [ˌbɒm'beɪ]
Bondi Beach [ˌbɒndaɪ 'bi:tʃ]
Brisbane ['brɪzbən]
Bristol ['brɪstl]
Cambridge ['keɪmbrɪdʒ]
Canberra ['kænbərə]
Cape Town ['keɪp taʊn]
Cardiff ['kɑ:dɪf]
The **Chauncy School** ['tʃɔ:nsi sku:l]
Checkpoint Charlie [ˌtʃekpɔɪnt 'tʃɑ:li]
Darlington ['dɑ:lɪŋtən]
Darwin ['dɑ:wɪn]
Detroit [də'trɔɪt, dɪ'trɔɪt]
Dublin ['dʌblɪn]
Eugene [ju:'dʒi:n]
Great Barrier Reef [ˌgreɪt 'bæriə ri:f]
Healesville ['hi:lzvɪl]
Hertford ['hɑ:tfəd]
Hertfordshire ['hɑ:tfədʃə]
Hollywood ['hɒliwʊd]
Hong Kong [ˌhɒŋ 'kɒŋ]
Ife ['i:feɪ]
Joburg ['dʒəʊbɜ:g]
Johannesburg [dʒəʊ'hænɪsbɜ:g]
Jozi ['dʒəʊzi]
Juhu Beach ['dʒu:hʊ]
Kakadu NP (National Park) [ˌkækə'du:]
Kent [kent]
London ['lʌndən]
Los Angeles [lɒs 'ændʒəli:z]
Melbourne ['melbən]
Mumbai [ˌmʊm'baɪ]
New York [ˌnju: 'jɔ:k]
New Mexico [ˌnjʊ: 'meksɪkəʊ]
Oregon ['ɒrɪgən]
Perth [pɜ:θ]
Pretoria [pri'tɔ:rɪə]
Queensland ['kwi:nzlənd]
Sandtown ['sændtən]
San Francisco [ˌsæn frən'sɪskəʊ]
Swindon ['swɪndən]
Sydney ['sɪdni]
Tasmania [tæz'meɪnɪə]
Toronto [tə'rɒntəʊ]
Uluru [u:'lu:ru:, ʊlə'ru:]
Uluru-Kata Tjuta [ˌu:ləru: ˌkætə 'tju:tə]
Wiltshire ['wɪltʃə]
Yulara [ju'lɑ:rə]

Other names (Andere Namen)

Bay View [ˌbeɪ 'vju:]
Brandenburg Gate [ˌbrændənbɜ:g 'geɪt]
Brookfield ['brʊkfi:ld]
Daintree ['deɪntri]
Flipper ['flɪpə]
Hadham ['hædəm]
Kruger ['kru:gə]
Oakwood ['əʊkwʊd]
Parkville ['pɑ:kvɪl]
Rusty ['rʌsti]
Simpson Desert ['sɪmpsn]
Tin Annie [ˌtɪn 'æni]
Torres Strait Islander [ˌtɒrəs ˌstreɪt_'aɪləndə]
Victoria [vɪk'tɔriə]

Country/Continent	Adjective	Person	People
Africa ['æfrɪkə] *Afrika*	African ['æfrɪkən]	an African	the Africans
America [ə'merɪkə] *Amerika*	American [ə'merɪkən]	an American	the Americans
Asia ['eɪʃə, 'eɪʒə] *Asien*	Asian ['eɪʃn, 'eɪʒn]	an Asian	the Asians
Australia [ɒ'streɪliə] *Australien*	Australian [ɒ'streɪliən]	an Australian	the Australians
Austria ['ɒstriə] *Österreich*	Austrian ['ɒstriən]	an Austrian	the Austrians
Belgium ['beldʒəm] *Belgien*	Belgian ['beldʒən]	a Belgian	the Belgians
Bosnia-Herzegovina [ˌbɒzniə ˌhɜtsəgə'vi:nə] *Bosnien-Herzegowina*	Bosnian ['bɒzniən]	a Bosnian	the Bosnians
Canada ['kænədə] *Kanada*	Canadian [kə'neɪdiən]	a Canadian	the Canadians
China ['tʃaɪnə] *China*	Chinese [ˌtʃaɪ'ni:z]	a Chinese	the Chinese
Croatia [krəʊ'eɪʃə] *Kroatien*	Croatian [krəʊ'eɪʃn]	a Croatian	the Croatians
the Czech Republic [ˌtʃek rɪ'pʌblɪk] *Tschechien, die Tschechische Republik*	Czech [tʃek]	a Czech	the Czechs
Denmark ['denmɑ:k] *Dänemark*	Danish ['deɪnɪʃ]	a Dane [deɪn]	the Danes
England ['ɪŋglənd] *England*	English ['ɪŋglɪʃ]	an Englishman/-woman	the English
Europe ['jʊərəp] *Europa*	European [ˌjʊərə'pi:ən]	a European	the Europeans
Finland ['fɪnlənd] *Finnland*	Finnish ['fɪnɪʃ]	a Finn [fɪn]	the Finns
France [frɑ:ns] *Frankreich*	French [frentʃ]	a Frenchman/-woman	the French
Georgia ['dʒɔ:dʒə] *Georgien*	Georgian ['dʒɔ:dʒən]	a Georgian	the Georgians
Germany ['dʒɜ:məni] *Deutschland*	German ['dʒɜ:mən]	a German	the Germans
(Great) Britain ['brɪtn] *Großbritannien*	British ['brɪtɪʃ]	a Briton ['brɪtn]	the British
Greece [gri:s] *Griechenland*	Greek [gri:k]	a Greek	the Greeks
Holland ['hɒlənd] *Holland, die Niederlande*	Dutch [dʌtʃ]	a Dutchman/-woman	the Dutch
Hungary ['hʌŋgəri] *Ungarn*	Hungarian [hʌŋ'geəriən]	a Hungarian	the Hungarians
India ['ɪndiə] *Indien*	Indian ['ɪndiən]	an Indian	the Indians
Ireland ['aɪələnd] *Irland*	Irish ['aɪrɪʃ]	an Irishman/-woman	the Irish
Italy ['ɪtəli] *Italien*	Italian [ɪ'tæliən]	an Italian	the Italians
Japan [dʒə'pæn] *Japan*	Japanese [ˌdʒæpə'ni:z]	a Japanese	the Japanese
Korea [kə'riə] *Korea*	Korean [kə'riən]	a Korean	the Koreans
the Netherlands ['neðələndz] *die Niederlande, Holland*	Dutch [dʌtʃ]	a Dutchman/-woman	the Dutch
New Zealand [ˌnju: 'zi:lənd] *Neuseeland*	New Zealand [ˌnju: 'zi:lənd]	a New Zealander	the New Zealanders
Nigeria [naɪ'dʒɪəriə] *Nigeria*	Nigerian [naɪ'dʒɪəriən]	a Nigerian	the Nigerians
Norway ['nɔ:weɪ] *Norwegen*	Norwegian [nɔ:'wi:dʒən]	a Norwegian	the Norwegians
Pakistan [ˌpækɪ'stæn, ˌpɑ:kɪ'stɑ:n] *Pakistan*	Pakistani [ˌpækɪ'stæni, ˌpɑ:kɪ'stɑ:ni]	a Pakistani	the Pakistanis
Poland ['pəʊlənd] *Polen*	Polish ['pəʊlɪʃ]	a Pole [pəʊl]	the Poles
Portugal ['pɔ:tʃʊgl] *Portugal*	Portuguese [ˌpɔ:tʃʊ'gi:z]	a Portuguese	the Portuguese
Puerto Rico [ˌpwɜ:təʊ 'ri:kəʊ] *Puerto Rico*	Puerto Rican [ˌpwɜ:təʊ 'ri:kən]	a Puerto Rican	the Puerto Ricans
Russia ['rʌʃə] *Russland*	Russian ['rʌʃn]	a Russian	the Russians
Scotland ['skɒtlənd] *Schottland*	Scottish ['skɒtɪʃ]	a Scotsman/-woman, a Scot [skɒt]	the Scots, the Scottish
Slovakia [sləʊ'vɑ:kiə, sləʊ'vækiə] *die Slowakei*	Slovak ['sləʊvæk]	a Slovak	the Slovaks
Slovenia [sləʊ'vi:niə] *Slowenien*	Slovenian [sləʊ'vi:niən], Slovene ['sləʊvi:n]	a Slovene, a Slovenian	the Slovenes, the Slovenians
Spain [speɪn] *Spanien*	Spanish ['spænɪʃ]	a Spaniard ['spænɪəd]	the Spaniards
Sweden ['swi:dn] *Schweden*	Swedish ['swi:dɪʃ]	a Swede [swi:d]	the Swedes
Switzerland ['swɪtsələnd] *die Schweiz*	Swiss [swɪs]	a Swiss	the Swiss
Turkey ['tɜ:ki] *die Türkei*	Turkish ['tɜ:kɪʃ]	a Turk [tɜ:k]	the Turks
the United Kingdom (the UK) [juˌnaɪtɪd 'kɪŋdəm, ju:'keɪ] *das Vereinigte Königreich (Großbritannien und Nordirland)*	British ['brɪtɪʃ]	a Briton ['brɪtn]	the British
the United States of America (the USA) [juˌnaɪtɪd ˌsteɪts‿əv‿ə'merɪkə, ju:‿es‿'eɪ] *die Vereinigten Staaten von Amerika*	American [ə'merɪkən]	an American	the Americans
Wales [weɪlz] *Wales*	Welsh [welʃ]	a Welshman/-woman	the Welsh

Illustrationen

Silke Bachmann, Hamburg (S. 15; 22 (u. 92); 51; 54; 103 5. v. unten (u. 115); 114 unten-115); **Roland Beier**, Berlin (S. 14; 19 (u. 91); 47; 50; 127-132; 134-173); **Carlos Borrell**, Berlin (vordere und hintere Umschlaginnenseite; S. 7 map; 10 (u. 90); 23; 70 map (M); 108/109 Hintergrund); **Graham-Cameron Illustration**, UK (S. 58-60: **Eoin Coveney**); **Dylan Gibson**, Pitlochry (S. 32; 103 4. v. oben (u. 110-112)); **Christian Görke**, Berlin (S. 107; 114 oben; 133 oben u. unten); **Jeongsook Lee**, Köln (S. 129 unten); **Alfred Schüssler**, Frankfurt/Main (S. 106)

Bildquellen

Alamy, Abingdon (Inhaltsverz. oben 3. v. li. (u. 47 oben): Steve Skjold, Inhaltsverz. unten (u. 30 oben li.): JUPITERIMAGES/BananaStock (RF), Inhaltsverz. unten re. (u. 70 Bild C): frans lemmens, Inhaltsverz. oben 4. v. li. (u. 71 Bild E): Thomas Cockrem; S. 6 li. (M): JUPITERIMAGES/ Comstock Images (RF), Bild G: Nic van Oudtshoorn; S. 7 Bild A: Blend Images (RF), Bild E: Bruce Miller; S. 9 oben li.: The London Art Archive; S. 11 (u. 89) oben: imagebroker; S. 12 Bild C: Bill Bachman, Bild D: Robert Harding Picture Library Ltd., Bild E: Ern Mainka, Bild F: Sylvia Cordaiy Photo Library Ltd; S. 13 Bild 1: Steffan Hill, Bild 5: Robert Harding Picture Library Ltd.; S. 15: imagebroker; S. 16 2. v. unten: LOOK Die Bildagentur der Fotografen GmbH, Mitte li. u. unten: Susanna Bennett; S. 20 Mitte li.: David Noble Photography; S. 24 oben re.: CulturalEyes-AusGS2; S. 28 unten re.: Brownstock Inc. (RF), Bild E: John Powell Photographer, Bild G: Johan Furusjö; S. 30 Mitte li. (M): Gabe Palmer (RF), Mitte re.: Jim West, unten li.: Tetra Images (RF); S. 31 unten: Digital Vision (RF); S. 33: Helene Rogers; S. 34 Bild 1: PHOTOTAKE/Yoav Levy, Bild 3: Image Source White; S. 39 football Mitte (M) (u. 86 und 88): artpartner-images.com, unten: Corbis Super RF (RF); S. 41 Bild B (u. 95 oben): Photodisc (RF), Bild D (u. 95 unten): Digital Vision (RF), Bild C (u. 95 2. v. unten): image100 (RF); S. 52 oben: Janine Wiedel Photolibrary; S. 56 scrabble pieces: face to face Bildagentur GmbH (RF), unten li.: MTC Media; S. 57: image100 (RF); S. 62 oben li.: Christian Darkin (RF), unten li. (M): Lebrecht Music and Arts Photo Library; S. 65 2. v. unten: JTB Photo Communications, Inc., unten (M): peter jordan; S. 70 Bild B: Tibor Bognar; S. 71 Bild D: Eric Nathan, Bild F: Peter Horree; S. 72 Deepa: Idealink Photography, unten re.: Dinodia Images, Mitte re.: Julio Etchart, Mitte li.: Ladi Kirn, unten li.: Ron Boon; S. 73 oben: PhotosIndia.com LLC (RF); S. 74: Radius Images (RF); S. 75 oben: PhotosIndia.com RM 16; S. 76 oben re.: AfriPics.com, Mitte: Alan Gignoux, Mitte li.: MBI (RF), unten re.: Bart Nedobre, oben li.: Gallo Images (RF), unten li.: Gerard Velthuizen; S. 77 oben: Tom Whipps, unten: West Africa Photography; S. 78: AfriPics.com; S. 82: Adrian Sherrat; S. 83: Geoff Williamson SuperPrime; S. 92 Mitte oben: imagebroker; S. 103 2. v. unten (u. 123 2. v. unten): Greatstock Photographic Library (RF); S. 105 oben: Alex Maddox, Bild 4: David Page; S. 108 unten re.: Horizon International Images Limited; S. 113 re.: G P Bowater; S. 122 unten re.: Dinodia Images (RF), 2. v. oben: Imagestate Media Partners Limited - Impact Photos / Christopher Cormack; S. 123 oben li.: Blend Images (RF), 2. v. oben li.: imagebroker, 2. v. oben re.: Imagestate Media Partners Limited - Impact Photos, 3. v. oben: Gallo Images (RF), 4. v. oben li.: Gallo Images (RF); **BE-ME Foundation**, Wolverhampton (S. 52 unten - 53: BE-ME Foundation, Wolverhampton / www.be-me.org); **Chuck Braverman. Art and Design ©2004 New Video Group, Inc.** (S. 55); **CartoonStock**, Bath (S. 49: Dave Carpenter); **Cinetext**, Frankfurt/Main (S. 122 Mitte: Cinetext Bildarchiv); **Corbis**, Düsseldorf (Inhaltsverz. oben 2. v. li. (u. 30 unten re.): moodboard (RF), Inhaltsverz. oben re. (u. 46 li.): Peter M. Fisher; S. 6 Bild I: Otto Rogge, Bild J: Charles Bowman/Robert Harding World Imagery; S. 7 Bild F: Frans Lanting; S. 9 cane toad: Oliver Strewe, Cook: PoodlesRock; S. 11 (u. 89) jumping kangaroo: Frans Lanting; S. 12 oben: David Ashley (RF), Bild B: Theo Allofs; S. 13 Bild 2: Theo Alloffs; S. 16 2. v. oben: Catherine Karnow, 3. v. oben: Hannah Mason; S. 30 oben re.: moodboard (RF); S. 40 oben (u. 94): Simon Jarratt (RF); S. 46 re.: James Marshall; S. 56 unten re.: Ralf-Finn Hestoft; S. 68 Mitte: Image Source (RF); S. 70 Bild A: Frédéric Soltan; S. 92 Mitte re.: Frans Lanting; S. 123 re.: Sygma/Yves Forestier); **Cornelsen Verlag**, Berlin (S. 38 oben (u. 40 Bild 4); S. 40 Bild 1 u. 5: Michael Weihrauch); **Rob Cousins**, Bristol (S. 48); **Fotosearch**, Waukesha (S. 103 5. v. oben (u. 113 li.) (RF)); **GeoBeats, Inc.**, Rockville (S. 73 unten); **Getty Images**, München (S. 6 Bild K (u. 128): Ghislain & Marie David de Lossy; S. 9 Mitte re.; S. 11 unten (u. 91 oben): Jeff Hunter (RF); S. 13 oben li.: Anthony Ong (RF), Bild 3, Bild 4: Tony Lewis; S. 16 oben li. (u. Hintergrund): Doug Armand; S. 27 oben: Annie Griffiths Belt; S. 30 Mitte li. (M): Peter Teller; S. 68 oben: Image Source (RF); S. 103 2. v. oben (u. 107 oben): Getty Images News/Handout; S. 109 unten re.: Getty Images Sport/Quinn Rooney; S. 126 unten Mitte: AFP); **Bonnie Glänzer**, Berlin (S. 42 unten); **Guardian News & Media Ltd 2008** (S. 17: Barbara McMahon); **iStockphoto**, Calgary (S. 6 li. (M): gocosmonaut; S. 8 oben: David Iliff; S. 9 emu: Nicola Stratford; S. 19 unten re.: blue_iq, unten li.: Duncan Walker, oben re.: Jacob Wackerhausen, oben li.: ranplett, Mitte: paul kline; S. 20 oben: Timothy Ball; S. 24 Mitte li.: Gene Chutka, Mitte re.: Jeffrey Smith; S. 26 oben: Carlos Santa Maria, Mitte li.: Elnur Amikishiyev; S. 27 unten: Chuck Babbitt; S. 32 Bild A: wrangel, Bild B: btrenkel; S. 38 unten (u. 40 3. v. oben): dawn liljenquist; S. 64 Mitte: Chris Schmidt, 2. v. li.: Rich Legg, 2. v. re.: ronen, li.: Søren Sielemann, re.: Suzanne Tucker; S. 70 pink pattern: Niels Laan; S. 73 2. v. oben: Silvia Jansen, 3. v. oben: VikramRaghuvanshi; S. 75 unten: ChrisHepburn; S. 77 Mitte: stevenallan; S. 103 oben (u. 105 Bild 5: James Bowyer, 3. v. unten (u. 121, 122 oben): RENE DROUYER; S. 104 /105 (Bild 1): Linda & Colin McKie; S. 105 Bild 2 u. Bild 3: david franklin; S. 106 background (M): Paul Morton; S. 109 Mitte re.: susan flashman; S. 123 oben re. u. 4. v. oben re.: Henrique NDR Martins, unten re.: Cliff Parnell; S. 126 2. v. re.: snowkoala, unten li.: suhhui kuk, unten re.: Westbury); **Mary Evans Picture Library**, London (S. 9 oben re.); **Masterfile**, Düsseldorf (S. 33); **Newspix**, Surry Hills NSW (S. 7 Bild C: News Ltd./3rd Party Managed Reproduction & Supply Rights); **Okapia**,

Frankfurt/Main (S. 11 Mitte re. (u. 89 unten re.): Klein Hubert/BIOS; S. 21: Hans Reinhard); **Photolibrary**, London (S. 108 oben re.: Jörg Reuther); **Picture Alliance**, Frankfurt/Main (S. 6 Bild H: dpa; S. 9 spider: NHPA/photoshot, platypus (u. 109 oben re.): NHPA/photoshot/Dave Watts; S. 16 oben re.: dpa Bilderdienste; S. 32 Bild D: dpa – Report; S. 34 Bild 2: OKAPIA /Christine Steimer; S. 54: Sander; S. 66: empics; S. 107 unten: NHPA/photoshot; S. 121 unten dpa); **Picture Desk**, London (S. 67: Film 4/Celador Films/Pathe International/The Kobal Collection; S. 122 unten li.: Pathe Pictures LTC/The Kobal Collection); **Daniel Raven-Ellison**, Thatcham (S. 79 oben Bild A u. B); **Rumbalara Films**, Moore Park, Australia (S. 18): **Marion Schönenberger**, Berlin (S. 80-81); **Jakob Schröck**, Berlin (S. 84); **Shooting Jozi**, a project of Global Studio 2007 and the individuals who participated (S. 79 unten Bild A, B, C); **Shutterstock**, New York (Inhaltsverz. Uluru: Ronald Sumners, Inhaltsverz. kangaroo: Tap10; S. 7 Bild B: Chee-Onn Leong, Bild D: Ben Jeayes; S. 8 Mitte: Andrei Marincas, unten: Dimitrios Kaisaris; S. 9 cave painting: Kaspars Grinvalds, koala: Merryl McNaughton; S. 11 kangaroo with baby (u. 89): Kitch Bain; S. 12 Bild A: Tom Cummins; S. 20 Mitte re.: aliciahh, unten li.: Ashley Whitworth; S. 24 unten: Kim Pin Tan, oben li.: Rob Wilson; S. 25 re.: Anton Harder, li. u. Mitte: Neale Cousland; S. 26 unten li. u. re.: Joe Gough, unten Mitte: Nayashkova Olga, Mitte u. re.: Robyn Mackenzie; S. 28 Bild A: nart, Bild B: 26kot, Bild C: Irina Tischenko, Bild D: Kurhan, Bild F: jocialek, Bild H: Roxana Gonzalez; S. 31 oben: Marcin Balcerzak, Mitte: Nicholas Sutcliffe; S. 32 Bild C: Ilja Mašik; S. 39 oben: Yuri Arcurs; S. 41 Bild A (u. 95 2. v. oben): Vling; S. 44 oben re.: Alexia Khruscheva, oben Mitte: AXL, oben li.: zeber, unten re.: hfng, unten li. (M): vectorstock; S. 47 unten li.: Andresr; S. 56 oben li.: Slavko Sereda, oben re.: Yuri Arcurs; S. 62 unten re. (M): Christophe Schmid; S. 63 oben: Alan Freed, unten man reading (M): dragon_fang, bottle (M): Gino Santa Maria; S. 65 2. v. oben: AND Inc., unten (M): emin kuliyev, oben: kmiragaya; S. 68 unten: Monkey Business Images; S. 70 South African flag u. Indian flag (M): Andrew Chin, German flag (M): ARTEKI, S. 71 orange pattern (u. 123): Ferin; S. 72 Balu: Mandy Godbehear; S. 73 heart: adsheyn; S. 76 Mitte re.: senai aksoy; S. 103 unten (u. 126 oben li.): Jenna Layne Voigt, 3. v. oben (u. 109 oben li.): Patsy A. Jacks, 4. v. unten: Laurent Renault; S. 108 li.: tororo reaction; S. 109 unten li.: hocus-focus; S. 121 Mitte: Map Resources; S. 123 unten li.: 1171, 3. v. unten li.: Johan Gerber, 3. v. unten re.: michaeljung; S. 126 oben re.: Alexey Goosev, 2. v. li.: Mike Liu; S. 135: Holger Mette; **Martynka Wawrzyniak**, New York (S. 42 oben; S. 43)

Titelbild

Corbis, Düsseldorf: Corbis Edge/Theo Allofs (M); **Corel Library** (flag Hintergrund (M)); **Plainpicture**, Hamburg (jeans with map (M): Sina Preikschat)

Textquellen

S. 17 *Children were stolen - Now a nation says sorry*. Adapted from "Snatched from home for a racist ideal. Now a nation says sorry" by Barbara McMahon, 11.2.2008. http://www.guardian.co.uk/world/2008/feb/11/australia. Copyright Guardian News & Media Ltd 2008; **S. 20–23** *In the outback*. Abridged and adapted from „Children of the Wind - A Prayer for Blue Delaney" by Kirsty Murray. Allen & Unwin, Crows Nest, Australia, 2005 (www.allenandunwin.com); **S. 52** *Bad boy?* Abridged and adapted from „ASBO made me give up life as a yob". From http://www.mirror.co.uk/news/top-stories/2007/11/13/asbo-made-me-give-up-life-as-a-yob-115875-20099323/ by Jeremy Armstrong, 13.11.2007. Mirror Syndication International, London; **S. 58–59** *The caller*. Abridged and adapted. Reprinted by permission of Carus Publishing Company, from DARE TO BE SCARED: THIRTEEN STORIES TO CHILL AND THRILL by Daniel D. San Souci, text © 2003 by Robert D. San Souci; **S. 114–116** *Bus attack Part 1, Bus attack Part 2.* Abridged and adapted from case study 4, taken from http://www.restorativejustice.org.uk/Media/pdf/Case%20Study%20-%20Bus%20Co.pdf (30.06.2009). Used by permission of Restorative Justice Consortium, London; **S. 117–120** *Famous*. Abridged and adapted from "TOTALLY OVER YOU" Copyright © Mark Ravenhill, 2003. All rights whatsoever in this play are strictly reserved and application for performance etc., must be made before rehearsal to Casarotto Ramsey & Associates Ltd., 7-12 Noel Street, London W1F 8GQ. No performance may be given unless a license has been obtained; **S. 124–125** *Nelson Mandela: A South African Hero*. Abridged from "The Black Pimpernel". Text: Magnus Bergmar & Marlene Winberg. Pictures: Jan-Ake Winqvist. http://childrensworld.org/downloads/mandela_en.pdf. © World's Children's Prize for the Rights of the Child, Mariefred. The World's Children's Prize for the Rights of the Child (WCPRC) is based on the UN Child Convention. The WCPRC strengthens the voices of children and young people, promotes their 'humanitarian growth' into global citizens, and helps them to demand respect for the rights of the child. Millions of children have awarded Mandela and his wife Graça Machel as child rights heroes; **S. 130** Auszug v. S. 516 aus „English G 2000 Wörterbuch – Das Wörterbuch zum Lehrwerk". Herausgegeben von der Langenscheidt-Redaktion Wörterbücher und der Cornelsen-Redaktion Englisch. © 2002 Cornelsen Verlag GmbH & Co. OHG, Berlin und Langenscheidt KG, Berlin und München.; **S. 131**: Screenshot Google: http://www.google.de/search?hl=de&q=%22flying+doctor%22+Australia&meta=&aq=f&oq= (Stand: 13.04.2010)

Liedquellen

S. 113 *Nine to five*. Text, OT: Dolly Parton. Copyright: Velvet Apple Music. Neue Welt Musikverlag GmbH, Hamburg, *Car Wash*. Text, OT: Norman Whitfield. Copyright: Universal Duchess Music Corporation. Universal/MCA Music Publishing GmbH, Berlin

Infinitive	Simple past form	Past participle	
(to) **be**	**was/were**	**been**	sein
(to) **beat**	**beat**	**beaten**	schlagen; besiegen
(to) **become**	**became**	**become**	werden
(to) **begin**	**began**	**begun**	beginnen, anfangen (mit)
(to) **bet**	**bet**	**bet**	wetten
(to) **bite** [aɪ]	**bit** [ɪ]	**bitten** [ɪ]	beißen
(to) **bleed** [iː]	**bled** [e]	**bled** [e]	bluten
(to) **break** a journey	**broke**	**broken**	eine Reise unterbrechen
(to) **bring**	**brought**	**brought**	(mit-, her)bringen
(to) **build**	**built**	**built**	bauen
(to) **buy**	**bought**	**bought**	kaufen
(to) **catch**	**caught**	**caught**	fangen; erwischen
(to) **choose** [uː]	**chose** [əʊ]	**chosen** [əʊ]	(aus)wählen; (sich) aussuchen
(to) **come**	**came**	**come**	kommen
(to) **cost**	**cost**	**cost**	kosten
(to) **cut**	**cut**	**cut**	schneiden
(to) **do**	**did**	**done** [ʌ]	tun, machen
(to) **draw**	**drew**	**drawn**	zeichnen
(to) **drink**	**drank**	**drunk**	trinken
(to) **drive** [aɪ]	**drove**	**driven** [ɪ]	*(ein Auto)* fahren
(to) **eat**	**ate** [et, eɪt]	**eaten**	essen
(to) **fall**	**fell**	**fallen**	(hin)fallen, stürzen
(to) **feed**	**fed**	**fed**	füttern
(to) **feel**	**felt**	**felt**	(sich) fühlen; sich anfühlen
(to) **fight**	**fought**	**fought**	kämpfen
(to) **find**	**found**	**found**	finden
(to) **fly**	**flew**	**flown**	fliegen
(to) **forget**	**forgot**	**forgotten**	vergessen
(to) **forgive**	**forgave**	**forgiven**	vergeben, verzeihen
(to) **get**	**got**	**got**	bekommen; holen; werden; (hin)kommen
(to) **give**	**gave**	**given**	geben
(to) **go**	**went**	**gone** [ɒ]	gehen, fahren
(to) **grow**	**grew**	**grown**	wachsen; anbauen, anpflanzen
(to) **hang**	**hung**	**hung**	hängen
(to) **have (have got)**	**had**	**had**	haben, besitzen
(to) **hear** [ɪə]	**heard** [ɜː]	**heard** [ɜː]	hören
(to) **hide** [aɪ]	**hid** [ɪ]	**hidden** [ɪ]	(sich) verstecken
(to) **hit**	**hit**	**hit**	schlagen
(to) **hold**	**held**	**held**	halten
(to) **hurt**	**hurt**	**hurt**	wehtun; verletzen
(to) **keep**	**kept**	**kept**	(be)halten
(to) **know** [nəʊ]	**knew** [njuː]	**known** [nəʊn]	wissen; kennen
(to) **lay** the table	**laid**	**laid**	den Tisch decken

Infinitive	Simple past form	Past participle	
(to) **leave**	**left**	**left**	(weg)gehen; abfahren; verlassen; zurücklassen
(to) **let**	**let**	**let**	lassen
(to) **lose** [uː]	**lost** [ɒ]	**lost** [ɒ]	verlieren
(to) **make**	**made**	**made**	machen; bauen; bilden
(to) **mean** [iː]	**meant** [e]	**meant** [e]	bedeuten; meinen
(to) **meet**	**met**	**met**	(sich) treffen
(to) **pay**	**paid**	**paid**	bezahlen
(to) **put**	**put**	**put**	legen, stellen, *(wohin)* tun
(to) **read** [iː]	**read** [e]	**read** [e]	lesen
(to) **ride** [aɪ]	**rode**	**ridden** [ɪ]	reiten; *(Rad)* fahren
(to) **ring**	**rang**	**rung**	klingeln, läuten
(to) **run**	**ran**	**run**	rennen, laufen
(to) **say** [eɪ]	**said** [e]	**said** [e]	sagen
(to) **see**	**saw**	**seen**	sehen; besuchen, aufsuchen
(to) **sell**	**sold**	**sold**	verkaufen
(to) **send**	**sent**	**sent**	schicken, senden
(to) **set** the alarm clock	**set**	**set**	den Wecker stellen
(to) **shake**	**shook**	**shaken**	schütteln; zittern
(to) **shine**	**shone** [ɒ]	**shone** [ɒ]	scheinen *(Sonne)*
(to) **shoot** [uː]	**shot** [ɒ]	**shot** [ɒ]	schießen, erschießen
(to) **show**	**showed**	**shown**	zeigen
(to) **shut up**	**shut**	**shut**	den Mund halten
(to) **sing**	**sang**	**sung**	singen
(to) **sit**	**sat**	**sat**	sitzen; sich setzen
(to) **sleep**	**slept**	**slept**	schlafen
(to) **speak**	**spoke**	**spoken**	sprechen
(to) **spend**	**spent**	**spent**	*(Zeit)* verbringen; *(Geld)* ausgeben
(to) **stand**	**stood**	**stood**	stehen; sich (hin)stellen
(to) **steal**	**stole**	**stolen**	stehlen
(to) **swim**	**swam**	**swum**	schwimmen
(to) **take**	**took**	**taken**	nehmen; (weg-, hin)bringen; dauern, *(Zeit)* brauchen
(to) **teach**	**taught**	**taught**	unterrichten, lehren
(to) **tell**	**told**	**told**	erzählen, berichten
(to) **think**	**thought**	**thought**	denken, glauben, meinen
(to) **throw**	**threw**	**thrown**	werfen
(to) **understand**	**understood**	**understood**	verstehen
(to) **upset**	**upset**	**upset**	ärgern, kränken, aus der Fassung bringen
(to) **wake** up	**woke**	**woken**	aufwachen; wecken
(to) **wear** [eə]	**wore** [ɔː]	**worn** [ɔː]	tragen *(Kleidung)*
(to) **win**	**won** [ʌ]	**won** [ʌ]	gewinnen
(to) **write**	**wrote**	**written**	schreiben

Was DU im Klassenzimmer sagen kannst	What YOU can say in the classroom
Du brauchst Hilfe	**You need help**
Tut mir leid, ich habe das nicht verstanden.	**Sorry, I don't understand.**
Können Sie/Kannst du das bitte noch einmal sagen?	**Can you say that again, please?**
Können Sie/Kannst du bitte lauter sprechen.	**Can you speak louder, please?**
Kann ich eine Frage stellen?	**Can I ask a question, please?**
Können Sie/Kannst du mir bitte helfen?	**Can you help me, please?**
Was bedeutet ...?	**What does ... mean?**
Ist ... das richtige Wort für ...?	**Is ... the right word for ...?**
Ich habe ... – ist das auch richtig?	**I've got ... – is that right too?**
Können Sie ... bitte buchstabieren?	**Can you spell ..., please?**
Wie spricht man das erste Wort in Zeile 2 aus?	**How do you say the first word in line 2?**
Können Sie es bitte an die Tafel schreiben?	**Can you write that on the board, please?**
Können wir das bitte noch einmal hören?	**Can we listen to that again, please?**
Tut mir leid, ich finde es nicht. Auf welcher Seite sind wir?	**Sorry, I can't find it. What page are we on?**
Was haben wir (als Hausaufgabe) auf?	**What's for homework?**
Du hast ein Problem	**You're in trouble**
Entschuldigung, dass ich zu spät komme / meine Hausaufgaben nicht gemacht habe, Herr ... / Frau ...	**Sorry, I'm late / I haven't done my homework, Mr/Mrs/Ms/Miss ...**
Tut mir leid, dass ich mein Schulheft vergessen habe.	**Sorry, I've forgotten my exercise book.**
Ich bin noch nicht fertig.	**I haven't finished yet.**
Entschuldigung, ich habe nicht zugehört / das weiß ich nicht.	**Sorry, I wasn't listening / I don't know.**
Ich kann Nummer 3 nicht lösen.	**I can't do number 3.**
Über Texte reden	**Talking about texts**
Die Geschichte/Das Theaterstück/Das Gedicht/Das Lied/Der Film handelt von ...	**The story/play/poem/song/film is about ...**
Die Handlung spielt während/in ...	**The action takes place during/in ...**
In Zeile 15–20 steht, dass ...	**In lines 15–20 it says that ...**
Die Hauptfigur ist ...	**The main character is ...**
Der Mann/Die Frau/... scheint sehr einsam/zornig/traurig/... zu sein.	**The man/woman/... seems to be very lonely/angry/sad/...**
Die Beziehung zwischen ... und ... ist sonderbar/...	**The relationship between ... and ... is strange/...**
Es war lustig/unheimlich/langweilig/... als ...	**It was funny/scary/boring/... when ...**
Ich fand es gut/nicht gut als ...	**I liked it/didn't like it when ...**
Ich fand den Schluss überraschend/enttäuschend/blöd/ ..., weil ...	**I found the ending surprising/disappointing/stupid/... because ...**
Ich finde die Geschichte ist lustig/aufregend/...,weil ...	**I think the story is funny/exciting/... because ...**
Die Geschichte hat mich glücklich/wütend/... gemacht.	**The story made me (feel) happy/angry/...**
In einer Diskussion	**In a discussion**
Meiner Meinung nach ...	**In my opinion ...**
Ich will dir ein Beispiel geben: ...	**Let me give you an example: ...**
Erstens ... / Zweitens ... / Und schließlich ...	**First ... / Second ... / And finally ...**
Ich stimme (...) zu/nicht zu, weil ...	**I agree/disagree (with ...) because ...**
Ja, du hast Recht. / Genau!	**Yes, you're right. / Exactly!**
Was Tim sagt, ist richtig/falsch.	**What Tim says is right/wrong.**
Du sagst ..., aber ...	**You say ..., but ...**
Was genau meinst du?	**What do you mean exactly?**
Du könntest Recht haben, aber ...	**You may be right, but ...**
Ich bin mir nicht sicher. Vielleicht ...	**I'm not so sure. Maybe/Perhaps ...**
Was meinst du (zu ...)?	**What do you think (about ...)?**

Bei der Partner- oder Gruppenarbeit	Working with a partner or in a group
Kann ich mit ... arbeiten?	**Can I work with ...?**
Was machen wir als Erstes?	**What are we going to do first?**
Lass/Lasst uns die Aufgabe noch einmal lesen.	**Let's read the task again.**
Wer ist dran? – Ich bin/Du bist dran, das zu schreiben/ die Fragen zu stellen.	**Whose turn is it? – It's my/your turn to write/ ask questions.**
Ich finde, wir sollten/könnten	**I think we should/could ...**
Hast du eine Idee/einen Vorschlag?	**Have you got any ideas?**
Mir gefällt deine Idee sehr gut. / Das klingt gut.	**I really like your idea. / That sounds good.**
Wo können wir etwas finden zu ...?	**Where can we find out about ...?**
Was hast du im Internet gefunden?	**What did you find on the internet?**
Was hältst du von meinem Text/Bild/...?	**What do you think of my text/picture/...?**
Ich verstehe nicht, was du meinst. / Ich bin mir nicht sicher.	**I don't understand what you mean. / I'm not sure about that.**
Lass/Lasst uns ... auf unser Poster schreiben.	**Let's write ... on our poster.**
Lass/Lasst uns das Bild hier hinsetzen/-kleben.	**Let's put the picture here.**
Wie viel Zeit haben wir (noch)?	**How much (more) time do we have?**
Wir haben nur noch ... Minuten Zeit.	**We've only got ... minutes left.**
Lass/Lasst uns ... schnell machen und dann mit ... fortfahren.	**Let's do ... quickly and then go on to ...**
Vielleicht sollten wir ... weglassen / etwas zu ... sagen.	**Maybe we should leave out / say something about ...**
Wir sind fast fertig. / Ich denke, wir sollten ... weglassen.	**We've nearly finished. / I think we should leave out ...**

Bei einer Präsentation	Giving a talk / presentation
Das Thema meines Vortrags ist ...	**The topic of my talk/presentation is ...**
Ich werde meinen Vortrag in ... Teile gliedern.	**I'm going to divide my talk into ... parts.**
Erstens/Als nächstes/ ... würde ich gern ...	**First/Next/... I would like to ...**
Zum Schluss werde ich etwas über ... erzählen.	**Finally, I'll tell you something about ...**
Auf dem ersten Bild links/rechts könnt ihr sehen ...	**On the first slide on the left/right you can see ...**
Zusammenfassend (möchte ich sagen) ...	**To sum things up (I'd like to say) ...**
Gibt es/Habt ihr Fragen oder Kommentare dazu?	**Are there any questions or comments?**

What YOUR TEACHER says / Was DEIN/E LEHRER/IN sagt

What YOUR TEACHER says	Was DEIN/E LEHRER/IN sagt
Copy/Fill in the chart/form.	Kopiert/Füllt die Tabelle/das Formular aus.
Correct the mistakes.	Verbessert die Fehler.
Don't forget to check your spelling.	Vergesst nicht die Rechtschreibung zu überprüfen.
Be careful with the word order.	Achtet auf die Satzstellung.
Write it on the board, please.	Schreibe es bitte an die Tafel.
Compare your sentences/answers/... with your partner.	Vergleiche deine Sätze/Antworten/... mit deinem Partner/deiner Partnerin.
Discuss ... with your partner.	Diskutier mit deinem Partner/deiner Partnerin.
Discuss in your group.	Diskutiert in eurer Gruppe.
Practise/Act out the dialogues with a partner, please.	Bitte übe/spiele den Dialog mit deinem Partner/deiner Partnerin.
Listen to the song/CD.	Hört euch das Lied/die CD an.
Take/Make notes.	Macht euch Notizen.
Imagine you are ...	Stellt euch vor, ihr seid ...
What do you think of ...?	Was haltet ihr von ...?
Have you got any other ideas?	Habt ihr andere/sonstige Ideen?
Give three reasons.	Nenne drei Gründe.
Have you finished?	Seid ihr/Bist du fertig?
Present your talk/poster/... to the class.	Präsentiere dein Referat/Poster/... vor der Klasse.
Do exercise 3 for homework, please.	Macht bitte Übung 3 als Hausaufgabe.